Multicultural Literature for Latino Bilingual Children

Multicultural Literature for Latino Bilingual Children

Their Words, Their Worlds

Ellen Riojas Clark, Belinda Bustos Flores,
Howard L. Smith, and
Daniel Alejandro González

ROWMAN & LITTLEFIELD
Lanham • Boulder • New York • London

Published by Rowman & Littlefield
A wholly owned subsidiary of The Rowman & Littlefield Publishing Group, Inc.
4501 Forbes Boulevard, Suite 200, Lanham, Maryland 20706
www.rowman.com

Unit A, Whitacre Mews, 26-34 Stannary Street, London SE11 4AB

British Library Cataloguing in Publication Information Available

Library of Congress Cataloging-in-Publication Data

Names: Clark, Ellen Riojas, editor of compilation.
Title: Multicultural literature for Latino bilingual children / edited by Ellen Riojas Clark,
    Howard L. Smith, Belinda Bustos Flores, and Daniel Alejandro González.
Description: Lanham, Maryland : Rowman & Littlefield, 2016. | Includes bibliographical
    references and index.
Identifiers: LCCN 2015030326| ISBN 9781475814910 (hardcover) | ISBN
    9781475814927 (pbk.) | ISBN 9781475814934 (e-book)
Subjects: LCSH: Hispanic American children—Education—Language arts. | Hispanic
    American children—Language. | Hispanic American children—Ethnic identity. |
    English language—Study and teaching—Spanish speakers. | Education, Bilingual—
    United States. | Language and education—United States.
Classification: LCC LC2672.4 .M85 2016 | DDC 371.829/68073—dc23 LC record
    available at http://lccn.loc.gov/2015030326

Printed in the United States of America

Contents

Foreword: Literature in the Lives of Latino Children

Alma Flor Ada, PhD, Professor Emerita,
University of San Francisco

Books let me fly,
they let me soar.
Books open windows
and magic doors.
Sometimes they whisper,
sometimes they roar.

Sometimes I find
someone who looks like me,
feels like me,
thinks like me,
dreams like me.

Sometimes I find
more of who I want to be.

Books let me fly,
they let me soar.
They open windows
and magic doors.

Sometimes they whisper,
sometimes they roar.

—Alma Flor Ada, 2015

It was midafternoon by the time the two other college students and I had finished giving the children in the run-down orphanage their weekly bath. As usual, I offered to tell them a story, and the children quickly gathered around. Although they were all Mexican, only a few of the older children could speak Spanish. So I began to tell a story in English, with the youngest girl sitting on my lap. I had only spoken the first few words of the story when she whispered in my ear, "Please, talk 'the other way.'" "But why do you want me to speak in Spanish if you don't understand it?" I asked her. "I don't understand it," she said, "but that's the way my mother used to sound."

That's the way my mother used to sound. The words of that young girl in Colorado in 1956 have resonated in my ears ever since, and have continued to inspire my work.

THE RIGHT TO HAVE ONE'S IDENTITY VALIDATED

Children's identification with their mother tongue begins before birth, as they listen to the cadence of their mother's voice through the amniotic fluid that surrounds them. They are able to recognize her voice minutes after birth: a voice that speaks in a particular language, with sounds and rhythms of its own.

Yet while language is the most important marker of a culture, it is not the only one.

The care and nurturing required by each human being to grow and develop is provided within a particular cultural milieu. When children, as they grow up, encounter recognition and support for their families and communities, appreciation and celebration of their worldviews, they can more easily continue to honor their parents or caretakers as their first teachers.

Society places a great deal of value on books. Yet when the books that are available to children do *not* recognize their families and communities, when children do not have the opportunity to see themselves portrayed in those pages, those books may remain alien to them. What's worse, children may encounter difficulties in validating their own identities. Reducing children's opportunities to learn about and to appreciate their own cultural heritage runs contrary to their basic educational rights.

In the United States, as the multiple groups that compose our society have struggled to achieve equal rights and recognition, the case has been made that all children deserve access to books that mirror their own experiences and reflect their own realities, the realities of their parents, families, and communities. These books need to be written by authors who can portray those realities authentically, from their own lived experience, their own intimate association with a particular culture, and their own continued learning.

Authoring texts that represent and honor particular groups is a first step toward guaranteeing the right of all children to access books that reflect their own context. Yet other steps must follow, including publication, dissemination, and awareness by those who can help these books reach the hands of children.

In the classroom, teachers' cultural efficacy and their commitment to an authentic pedagogy of transformation help catalyze the power of authentic Latino children's literature as a resource for learning. The goal is to support all children in developing their full potential, including a strong sense of identity, the courage to transform their own personal reality, and the commitment to creating a just society.

This book is an excellent contribution toward creating awareness of existing quality Latino literature. It illustrates various approaches for utilizing this literature to support the linguistic, academic, and psychological development of Latino children and young adults. It also points to the need to offer these books to children of *all* backgrounds, so that they may gain a better understanding of Latino people and cultures, who are a significant and growing part of the social makeup of this country.

THE POWER OF TWO LANGUAGES

Living in the twenty-first century, we find ourselves surprised on a daily basis by new technological achievements and scientific discoveries. Nonetheless, language remains the most significant of all human creations. All of the advances of science and technology are possible only due to this prior achievement: human beings' creation of language.

Language allows us to communicate experiences and add to the growing heritage that each new generation receives. Language offers us the means to explore our feelings and emotions, to create meaningful relationships with others, and thus, to better understand our own selves. Through language, we learn and teach and engage in social projects.

Going further, we can affirm that *language frees us from the prison of reality* because language allows us to transcend what is and imagine what could be. Through language we can conceive of what has never existed before, share dreams and visions with others, and work together to make them come true.

Latino children have the possibility of enjoying the benefits derived from mastering two languages, including the creative potential of combining these languages as a reflection of their two worlds. Yet the misguided language policies that currently prevail tend to rob our children of the potential educational and economic benefits of having two languages and deprive them of their human right to a strong foundation in their heritage language. Despite the multiple benefits of speaking more than one language, our social policies have created a situation where the majority of those who seek the benefits of "dual language" programs tend to be middle-class non-Latino families. As these families well know, language is power, and the more languages that our children are able to master, the better.

After presenting the multiple linguistic realities of Latinos, this book offers suggestions for inviting students to critically reflect on their own interactions with language, that they may discover its potentials for their own personal development.

FROM LANGUAGE TO LITERATURE

From ancient times, people of all cultures have felt a thirst for beauty and aesthetic enjoyment. Even practical items—canoes or spears, baskets or clay pots—have been created in artful ways. Just as people around the world have surrounded themselves with beauty through their material creations, they have also enjoyed language as a form of creative expression, not just as a means for communication, learning, or planning. Thus, every civilization has developed a body of literature.

We must not become confused by the connection between the word "literature" and the word "letter"; throughout the world, literature originates in an oral form. All cultures have created poetry, songs, chants, and ballads in which words are chosen and language is formed not only for meaning but also for aesthetic value. Stories are not a mere recounting of facts, but facts connected and presented in such a way as to arouse expectations or intrigue, surprise or delight, and thus to leave us with a lasting impression.

In literature, language is taken to its highest and deepest dimensions. Whether reflecting on something already existing or creating a more imaginary realm, literature offers us the possibility of seeing in new ways, and entering new realities.

For many centuries, most literature was shared orally. Myths, legends, fairy tales, and stories were enjoyed by all, adults and children alike. Eventually in Western cultures, the desire to offer guidance led to the creation of fables, cautionary tales, rhymes, and poems with a moral content that were intended specifically for children. In contrast, contemporary literature for children and young adults has a much greater aesthetic and social focus.

The twentieth century saw an extraordinary outpouring of literature for young people, including a remarkable expansion of themes to include broader social issues. We have also seen a movement to explore what lies beyond, including the far-away worlds of fantasy and science fiction. Yet no matter what form they take, the worlds that authors create are always shaped by their own worldviews. Thus, *who* is published has continued to determine *what* is available for children and youth to read.

THE VALUE OF *TESTIMONIOS*

One of the practices recommended in this book is the use of *testimonios*. In keeping with this spirit, I would like to offer a few *testimonios* of my own. Many adult Latinos have told me of their experience of never seeing themselves in books while growing up. I was particularly struck by an encounter that took place about twenty years ago, when books by Latino authors were still rare. I was signing books at a booth during one of the conferences of the National Association for Bilingual Education. A teacher stood in front of the books in silence, but with tears rolling down her cheeks. I kept company with her silence until she turned to me, and began to speak: "These are tears of sadness," she said, "because I never, ever, in my childhood saw so many books that I could relate to. But they are also tears of joy, thinking of the children of today, who have these treasures to enjoy."

The lack of knowledge about our heritage that results from this invisibility has become painfully evident to me during school visits. To introduce my book *The Lizard and the Sun*, I show students the magnificent art of Felipe Dávalos, depicting the city of Tenochtitlán in all its glory. I tell them that this legend took place in a beautiful city by a lake, next to majestic pyramids, and I ask whether they can guess where that city is located. It breaks my heart whenever I hear the whole class answer, "Egypt!"

Similarly, it breaks my heart when I ask students if they know who César Chávez was, and they answer, "A boxer." Yet I have also witnessed the power of books to strengthen students' sense of cultural pride. It's not uncommon, when I visit schools in farm-working communities in California, for students to be reluctant to raise their hands when I ask who has relatives who are farm workers. But when I tell them that I have written a book in celebration of the valuable work that farm workers do, and begin sharing Simón Silva's powerful illustrations of *Gathering the Sun*, there is hardly a student whose hand does not go up, as they proudly begin to share their experiences in the fields.

TRACING THE BIRTH OF AN
AUTHENTIC LATINO LITERATURE

The road toward a children's literature that reflects the richness of Latino culture and promotes social transformation has been a long and arduous one.

In 1889, the visionary leader José Martí was living in New York, writing for numerous newspapers in Spanish and English, and working to develop the unity that would secure Cuba and Puerto Rico's independence from Spain. That year, he wrote four issues of a magazine for children, *La edad de oro*, widely regarded as the beginning of Latin American children's literature.

Martí was born in Cuba, but early on he was exiled to Spain as a result of his political activism. He later lived in Mexico, Guatemala, Venezuela, and Costa Rica, still in exile during most of this time. During Martí's residence in New York, he served as consul for Argentina, Chile, and Uruguay. This recognition reflected the widespread respect garnered by his work toward "la Patria Grande," a broad collaboration among all of the Spanish-speaking countries in the Americas. Martí saw this transnational unity as including a shared responsibility for honoring Latin America's indigenous roots and defending the equal rights of all its peoples.

Martí was only able to publish four issues of his ground-breaking magazine, as he refused to comply with his publisher's directive to include explicit references to the fear of God in his articles, which instead sought to teach about compassion and service by example. In spite of the magazine's brief life, it had a significant impact as it was published widely as a book after Martí's death. The four issues included a variety of genres: biographical portraits, historical narratives, poetry, and original stories as well as retellings of traditional tales. In one informative text, Martí describes with admiration the accomplishments of the ancient civilizations of the Americas, in particular those of Mexico, a country he dearly loved. Throughout the magazine, each word and concept was carefully chosen to communicate his respect for his young readers and his determination to speak to them truthfully.

Martí lived the complexity that being Latino implies. While he dedicated his life to Cuba's and Puerto Rico's fight for independence from Spain, he also knew that his fight was against the Spanish government, not the Spanish people. He celebrated those Spaniards who, throughout history, had also struggled against their country's tyranny. This awareness that all cultures contain both noble and unjust people is reflected in an article devoted to Bartolomé de las Casas. He extols the courage and humanity of this Spanish priest, author of *Destrucción de las Indias*, one of the strongest denunciations of the cruelty of the Spanish conquest.

Martí also takes a sobering look at social disparity in the poem "Los zapaticos de rosa" [The rose-colored shoes] and touches on the blindness of prejudice in the story "La muñeca negra" [The black doll]. His poem "Los dos príncipes" [The two princes] emphasizes how all people, regardless of their social position, share in death a common human condition. With what now seems like visionary foresight, Martí devotes a long piece to Vietnam and the struggles of the Vietnamese people to liberate themselves, first from the Chinese conquerors and then later from the French colonial empire. "Un paseo por la tierra de los anamitas" [Traveling through the land of the anamitas] is an example of his strong advocacy for freedom and self-determination.

GROWING EFFORTS

It would take a long time for the seeds contained in *La edad de oro* to germinate and grow into the Latino literature of today. Great pioneers like Ernesto Galarza, with his *mini-libros* in California, and Pura Belpré, whose storytelling brought joy to three generations of children at the New York Public Library, helped develop the awareness that Latino children deserved the best of contemporary literature, as Martí had dreamt for them.

Slowly other voices began to emerge. George Ancona and his camera portrayed diverse aspects of Latino life. Piri Thomas wrote about the "mean streets" of New York. Nicholasa Mohr depicted the struggle for identity of a Puerto Rican girl in *Felita* and shared her own journey in the memoir *In My Own Words: Growing Up Inside the Sanctuary of My Imagination.* In 1972 *Bless Me, Ultima* was published, and Rudolfo Anaya became an inspiration for generations of Chicano writers.

In spite of Latino activists' struggle for equality and the enactment in 1968 of Title VII of the Elementary and Secondary Education Act in support of bilingual education, quality books in Spanish published in the U.S. were scarce. There was clearly a need for us to write our own stories. Inspired by Paulo Freire's work, I began spending evenings and weekends with children and parents, engaging them in telling their own stories and creating their own self-published books. This work grew over the decades, as described in *Authors in the Classroom: A Transformative Education Process*, coauthored with F. Isabel Campoy. You can see some samples of these books written by parents, children, and teachers at www.authorsintheclassroom.com.

At the same time, as part of the dialogical process of learning to "read the world," Latino children also needed access to formally published books. Mariucca Iacconi had embraced the task of identifying which books published abroad would be valuable to Latino children in bilingual programs. Working together, we discovered how few connections existed among people who were dedicated to children's literature within the different Spanish-speaking countries. In 1978, a small group of us conceived the quixotic idea of creating an Asociación Internacional de Literatura Infantil en Español y Portugués. With support from Susan Benson from the Organization of American States, we organized a first congress in San Francisco. This was followed by a second congress in Mexico City (preceded by a symposium in Coyoacán) and a third congress in Tucson, Arizona. The response was unexpected and extraordinary. These gatherings of authors, illustrators, librarians, scholars, and educators from all over the Spanish-speaking world led to the development and the strengthening of sections of the International Board of Books for Young People (IBBY) in several different countries. It also spread the awareness that Latinos in the U.S. represent a significant and unique group.

The Asociación created a literary award, given in 1978 to Pura Belpré, who honored the congress with her presence and was introduced by Anne Pellowski. At the second congress in Mexico the award was bestowed on both Ernesto Galarza and Gabilondo Soler "Cri-Crí." The third year in Tucson, the award was given to the Puerto Rican poet Esther Feliciano Mendoza. More of the history of this period is described in further detail in *A Magical Encounter: Latino Children's Literature in the Classroom.*

Here in the United States, the publication of original children's literature in Spanish was limited to a few publishers, of which the most prolific was Santillana. Later on, Arte Público Press and Children's Book Press helped to launch many of today's recognized Latino authors. The work of these small presses was a significant contribution, as many larger publishers preferred to publish Spanish translations of well-known children's books written originally in English by mainstream authors. That trend unfortunately persists to a large degree to this day.

After moving to the U.S. in 1970, I was offered contracts to translate books into Spanish thanks to the recommendation of Anne Pellowski, who knew the children's books I had published in Perú as a result of her work with UNESCO. I enjoy translating work, since I hold it as an art form and believe that Spanish-speaking children deserve to read good literature from around the world, regardless of the language in which it was first written. Yet it saddens me that publishers have not shown an equal interest in translating children's books originally written in Spanish, into English. Furthermore, many Latino authors have encountered significant challenges to breaking into mainstream children's publishing in the United States. For me, this journey took twenty long years. When *The Gold Coin* was published by Atheneum in 1990 (after thirteen rejection letters) and went on to receive the Christopher Award, it was a major turning point in my own life, as well as a sign of the changing times.

WHERE WE ARE TODAY

Much has happened in the last twenty-five years. Latino authors who were already publishing in the 1990s, including Rudolfo Anaya, Pat Mora, and Gary

Soto, have continued to create significant works, while many new authors have begun to contribute to the growing body of Latino literature. Clearly it's time to celebrate the many titles mentioned in this book which now comprise a substantial body of Latino literature for children and young adults. While authentic Latino literature continues to be seriously underrepresented in proportion to the number of books published annually in the United States, we need to acknowledge what we have achieved thus far.

The evolving body of literature for Latino children reflects the language shifts that continue to take place within Latino families in the U.S. Due to a long history of social oppression and marginalization that continues into the present, a growing number of Latinos today do not speak Spanish. Others have varied levels of fluency in their heritage language. For many of us, Spanish will continue to be the language of our hearts, even after we have become fluent in English.

These diverse linguistic realities are also present in contemporary Latino children's literature. A few authors write in both English and Spanish; others write in one of the two languages, with the hope that their books will be translated and published in the other one. Some works are published in simultaneous editions, one in English and one in Spanish; others are published as bilingual editions with facing texts in both languages; still others exist in only one of the two languages.

Although the "trend" of celebrating ethnicity can sometimes result in lip service rather than authentic cultural creations, it is undeniable that Latino children's literature has come of age. As this book clearly recognizes, the Latino experience has been forged from an interaction between valued traditions and new developments; our literature reflects this range. Our authors write about Latino life in the U.S. and also embrace the larger Spanish-speaking world. Our authors enjoy the freedom to write about any topic, serious or humorous, real or imaginary, knowing that whether they write realistic fiction or fantasy, their work will reflect their own worldviews.

Thanks to Latino authors, all children, Latinos or not, can encounter the multiplicity of Latino experiences in the U.S.; in addition, they also encounter the gifts of Latin American experiences. Thanks to books by Pam Muñoz Ryan and Monica Brown, children can encounter Pablo Neruda; thanks to Carmen Bernier Grant, they can admire Alicia Alonso's tenacity in overcoming physical challenges to become prima ballerina; thanks to Yuyi Morales, they can delight in Frida's celebration of life; thanks to Margorie Agosín, they can begin to appreciate the culture of Chile.

Our authors are beginning to receive some of the mainstream acclaim they deserve, as David Díaz is awarded the Caldecott Medal and Yuyi Morales a Caldecott Honor and Margarita Engle receives a Newbery Honor. Every year, the Pura Belpré Award and the International Latino Book Awards recognize new books of extraordinary quality.

All of these rich and various aspects of our literature, from the oral tradition to contemporary themes, from Latinos in the U.S. to life in our various countries of origin, are represented and explored in this well-researched volume.

THE WORK CONTINUES

What you are now holding in your hands is a significant and comprehensive key for gaining knowledge about the many wonderful Latino children's books available in the U.S. today. It includes a wealth of helpful suggestions to guide educators in the selection and use of quality Latino literature. At the same time, we each need to do everything we can to continue spreading the word about the existence and the value of these resources.

In addition, we need to focus on developing the voice and agency of our young people, supporting them to realize that they each have valuable perspectives to offer, perspectives that are both personal and unique, that only they can share. We need to encourage our young people to tell their own stories, and to develop the skills they need to do so. We need to advocate for creative-writing courses and seminars specifically for those who want to write in Spanish or whose bilingual expression needs support.

Our children and youth, "*la esperanza del mundo*" in Martí's words, deserve to be reminded frequently of the power of language, the richness of their cultural heritage, and the value of their parents' and grandparents' efforts to provide them with greater opportunities, as well as the courage and resources that exist within each young person to overcome any challenges they may be facing. When these reminders are offered by means of engaging books, including exceptionally interesting nonfiction, powerful narratives, inventive plays, and evocative poetry, these messages are more likely to resonate in their hearts, to be internalized and remembered.

My heartfelt congratulations to all of the authors and contributors in this book for their scholarship and for the quality of their research, for the sincerity of their reflections, and for their efforts to identify exemplary books that can inspire and delight. I especially appreciate the tools designed to help teachers and librarians offer this powerful literature as a means of growth and transformation. May each person who reads and uses this book experience the joy of seeing their efforts bear fruit, for the benefit of all our children and youth.

Preface: *Derrumbando Fronteras/* Breaking Boundaries

Ellen Riojas Clark and Belinda Bustos Flores

I'm looking forward to a whole new world—and a new me. The times now seem to be evolving with voices of color. All voices are important, and yet it seems that people of color have a lot to say, particularly if you look through the poetry of the young—a lot of questions and a lot of concerns about immigration and security issues, you name it, big questions. All this is swirling in the air.

—Juan Felipe Herrera, first U.S. Mexican-American poet laureate
(*Washington Post*, 2015)

As editors of this volume, *Multicultural Literature for Latino Bilingual Children*, each of us recalls and reflects on our own experiences, as individuals and educators, with Latino literature and the need for Latino multicultural literature. While we learned how to negotiate our own cultural knowledge, history, and identity, as well as those of the broader society as educators and transworld citizens, we know that many others have not had these opportunities. This volume builds on the authors' experiences that reflect the realities of Latino communities. Our work is grounded in theories of transworld pedagogy and the need to work in the social cultural context of our worlds. We believe that our work in cultural literacy has been to present the values of friendship, a positive, culturally rich portrayal of Latino families, language, and cultures in whatever work we do. This is a focal point as we have prepared teachers and others to work in our schools and communities. Over our forty years of involvement in education, we focus on promoting the importance of a culturally diverse society, bilingualism, and ethnic identity.

We use the term "Latino" in this volume instead of "Hispanic" and/or "Chicano" for many reasons. Using the appropriate ethnic or cultural identity term is difficult because the underlying meaning and context needs to be considered before any term is used. We think our readers would enjoy the following thoughts by Sandra Cisneros and me (personal communication, 2015), in response to a question regarding ethnic and cultural identity labels. According to Cisneros,

> Chicano is not a blanket term grouping Latinos from the Southwest. It is a term that was born of the Chicano Movement of the 1960s, and it is used by those individuals in the U.S. who are aware of the political and social history of oppression of people of Mexican descent in the United States. To call yourself Chicano is akin to calling yourself a "feminist." It is a word you use to define and defend yourself as one allied with a cause. Just as being born female does not make you a feminist, being born in the United States of Mexican descent does not make you a Chicano. It is a word one voluntarily accepts when you have political consciousness regarding injustices of race and class.

I, on the other hand, synthesize by saying,

> I am most proud to say that I am a Chicana because I am politically active, I vote in every election, and I'm involved in all my communities.

The term "Latino" is clarified by Cisneros:

> Some Latinos prefer the term "Hispanic" utilized since the Reagan era, while some reject it as a colonizer's term since the community already had its own word of self-identity—"Latinos," whereas the term "Hispanic" was imposed on the community by an unpopular president (unpopular among most U.S. Latino groups, since it was only a minority upper class/white/exile Cuban community that had the President's ear).
>
> Then and now the term "Latino" is used to identify oneself as a citizen of the U.S., but with Latin-American roots. This is a more neutral and acceptable term, except among the more upwardly mobile, Euro-centric, or, to put it kindly, politically innocent.

When teaching, I explain to my classes,

I always verbalized the following: I can be identified as a Caucasian, if one uses race labels, but not White, which is a cultural label. I am a Latina based on your explanation and in no way a Hispanic because that's a government term developed by the Census bureau based on language use. Specifically, I am a Mexican American because of my family's ancestry but don't call me a Mexican because I am a U.S. citizen. Though I am a Mexicana because of my cultural heritage as that is where my family originated and therefore, that is the culture I live.

The lesson to our future educators is to understand the labels in their context from a knowledge base and choose the one that best defines them. We must know the meaning of all labels and we must select the term that best describes us. Do not take a label that is given to you, but choose one that you can affirm. Or as Sandra Cisneros says,

When in doubt, ask someone what term they prefer to be called. It's only polite, don't you think? If President Reagan had asked the majority what we called ourselves, we wouldn't be in this quagmire. But then again, U.S. history has never heeded Benito Juarez's famous dictum—"Among individuals, as among nations, respect for the rights of others is peace."

In this volume, we have decided to use "Latino" as a neutral, global term versus "Latino/a" or "Latin@" because the inherent historical, political, gender aspects of each of these terms merit an in-depth discussion. In some cases, we use terms interchangeably within the chapter depending on author usage. While no term is totally neutral, we do want to state that we know, understand, and accept the conceptual use of the various terms.

Our edited volume attempts to respectively capture this sense of Latino identity and provides authentic examples in the various chapters of the concrete application of our research on culture, language, and literacy. Duncan Tonatiuh has provided us with a visual gift. His *Reflection* artwork on the cover of this volume so vividly captures children reading multicultural literature in two languages. It is an honor to have the eminent children's literature scholar Alma Flor Ada write the foreword for this volume. We then asked noted Latino children's writers and illustrators such as Sandra Cisneros, Maya Christina González, Xavier Garza, Carolyn Flores, Joe Cepeda, Lindsey Olivares, Pat Mora, Duncan Tonatiuh, and Diane Gonzáles Bertrand to provide us with quotes and illustrations reflecting their perspective regarding literature for Latino children. We have sprinkled their thoughts and illustrations throughout the volume. This generation of writers and illustrators inspired by the legacy of our generation is continuing this valuable work for generations to come. Furthermore, we feel certain that the use of this text by future teachers, administrators, curriculum developers, librarians, and others in our communities will have a positive effect on the ethnic identity development and academic success of Latino students.

Though we are considered educators and not literary writers, our reasoning for developing this volume is rather simple: our experiences. Our personal stories, or *testimonios*, regarding our literary reading experience are presented in chapter 14 and the postscript. It was a long-time quest for me, Ellen Riojas Clark, when it became obvious that my friends, colleagues, and others were not as aware of Latino literature and that it was not considered part of the canon of U.S. or American literature. Because of my long-time interest, friendship, and experience with the pioneers in Chicano literature, my knowledge of the genre was established. I acted upon my deep interest through three National Endowment for the Humanities (NEH) grants, *Derrumbando Fronteras/Breaking Boundaries*: Summer Institutes for Integrating Mexican American and Latino Literatures and Culture into the Curriculum. During 1999, 2001, and 2003, English teachers from across the U.S. participated in a variety of *Derrumbando Fronteras* learning activities that included lectures and discussions with renowned Latino scholars such as Drs. María Herrera-Sobek, Arturo Madrid, Tomás Ybarra-Frausto, Tey Diane Rebolledo, and others. Writers like Sandra Cisneros, Pat Mora, Martín Espada, Helena María Viramontes, Julia Alvarez, Carmen Tafolla, Virgil Suárez, Cristina García, Denise Chavez, Ben Sáenz, and others came from all over the U.S. to read their works.

The underrepresentation of Latino literature in published book reviews in newspapers later provoked my interest, being that it is an accessible public avenue for learning about new books. I developed a dialogical style to conduct critical book reviews and discussion through our culturally diverse lens, me, a Chicana born in the U.S., and María Eugenía Cossio, a Mexican now living in the U.S. The writing of these literature book reviews featuring Latino and Latin American authors for the general public generated great interest, provoked intellectual challenge and discussion, were used by classroom teachers, and most importantly, increased interest in reading in San Antonio and beyond. These reviews range from novels to artistic, cultural, historical, political, literary, linguistic treaties written for the general public by many noted Latino authors. Now, on a national scale, I continue writing book reviews and author interviews with children on books by Latinos.

It was important to establish a basis for developing this volume. I conducted an informal survey of friends, colleagues, teachers, students, and people in general, asking two questions: (1) Name some Latino children's book titles, and (2) Name some Latino children's book authors. To my dismay, no one could name many authors or books. The most-named author was Sandra Cisneros, who has published one book for children, *Hairs/Pelitos* (1994), as her *The House on Mango Street* (2009) is not written specifically for children. So where does the blame lie with this underrepresentation? Is it the publishers, the marketing, the sales, or worse, is it just unawareness and lack of exposure? We decided it was important to address the issue of literature for Latino children with those who are pivotally involved in educating our youth.

Multicultural Literature for Latino Bilingual Children aims to stimulate the knowledge base of educators and our communities and to acknowledge the resources and power of being bicultural and bilingual for all children. We see educators as teachers, librarians, the parents, and also those interested in the broadening of minds and identity through the power of literature. The contributors to this volume understand that Latino children have valuable skills as well as unique experiences and perspectives that can be leveraged through multicultural children's literature.

An important quality many bicultural Latino children possess is their bilingualism and their dual frame of reference. One aspect of biculturalism is bilingualism, which is a skill-set with varying degrees of proficiency. Even at an early age, Latino children commonly engage in highly sophisticated communicative activities like translanguaging and language brokering, without the benefit of any formal training. They intuitively use English or Spanish, deciding which of their languages is more appropriate for a given situation. When Spanish monolingual parents need to communicate with an English monolingual adult (e.g., school principal, healthcare provider, postal clerk), the children often act as language brokers. They not only interpret the words of the adults, but also mediate the negotiations. For that reason, current research on the linguistic behaviors of Latino students (Bligh, 2014; Flores, Sheets, & Clark, 2010; García, 2009; Wallace, 2014) advocates for the term "bilingual learners" (BL) because it acknowledges the multiple linguistic proficiencies they possess. The term frames not only the process of English language learning, but also the home language as an asset that should be incorporated into the school curriculum for academic achievement. Thus, "bilingual learner" is the term employed in this volume.

Another asset is the bilingual learner's biculturalism, composed of the beliefs, customs, traditions, skills, and personal values of both U.S. and Latino cultures. Fielding and Harbon (2013) explain the power of biculturalism:

Students across the range of educational levels and settings bring to their formal schooling a multitude of life experiences, encounters with languages in addition to their first language, and connections to diverse cultures. Such experiences have an impact on classroom learning in that they help children determine who they are, where they belong in the world, and how they are related to others within and beyond their school and home communities. (p. 528)

The children's literature referenced in the following chapters capitalizes on this dual perspective gained through biculturalism, and in doing so, engage the reader on multiple planes.

We value the notion that we learn from others, thereby generating new knowledge in this dialogic act. As in previous work, we have established a principle of transformative pedagogy in which the expert guides the novice. Therefore, in developing this volume, we have encouraged senior scholars to collaborate with emerging scholars.

In our volume, you will note reference to either the national or common standards. Over twenty years ago, national standards for all content areas had been identified (Darling-Hammond, 1994), though not all states used these standards in their curriculum. The Common Core Curriculum Standards' focus is on English Language Arts and Mathematics (Porter, McMaken, Hwang, & Yang, 2011); however, these do not address the needs of bilingual learners.

We have divided the volume into five sections with specific chapters in each: Part I, "Framing the Discussions: Theory and Rationale," with two chapters; Part II, "Multicultural Children's Literature Representing Latino Realities," with four chapters; Part III, "Multicultural Children's Literature in the Content Areas: Language Arts, Social Studies, Science, and Mathematics," with four chapters; Part IV, "Multiple Modes of Multicultural Children's Literature," with four chapters; and finally, Part V, "*Una Fuente de Recursos*: Resources for Teachers and Children," with one chapter, as well as a postscript. All the chapters conclude with a series of discussion questions to be utilized after reading chapters, and suggestions for activities to guide educators in their selection of high quality, authentic Latino children's literature, and professional readings.

Part I: In the first chapter, titled "Multicultural Latino Children's Literature: A Tool to Enrich the Lives and the Learning of Latino Bilingual Learners," Clark and Flores emphasize that books for our Latino children should represent concrete reflections of culture and language experiences. They also discuss the positive effect that Latino literature has on Latino children's ethnic identity development and their academic success (Clark & Flores, 2001). More importantly, they affirm Latino literature is a genre that is part of the literary canon of U.S. literature. The coeditors, in this case Smith, Flores, and González, in chapter 2, trace the historical foundation of Latino children's literature, including important milestones and recognitions. Using a socioconstructive theoretical framework, they present Latino children's literature as a tool of cultural representation and a powerful resource to contest deficit beliefs about the languages and cultures found in the Americas.

In Part II, chapter 3, "Beyond *Calaveras* and *Quinceañeras*: Fostering Bilingual Latino Students' Identity Development with Culturally Relevant

Literature," discusses how children's and adolescent's books about diverse Latino cultures can be influential in assisting Latino bilingual learners as they develop their ethnic identities. This chapter explores common themes in Latino literature and the potential influences on the identity development of Latino bilingual youth. Patricia Sánchez and Maité Landa in chapter 4, "*Cruzando Fronteras:* Negotiating the Stories of Latino Immigrant and Transnational Children," discuss how Latino students in the U.S. are a population affected by immigration. Though the majority of Latino students are overwhelmingly second generation, meaning that either one or both of their parents were born outside of the U.S., many Latino students might have an undocumented family member. They make the point that educators need to ensure that classrooms and school libraries are full of stories that depict migration, border crossings, and transnational ties in a humanizing and authentic manner. It also examines texts that bravely address challenging topics such as deportation, the criminalization of undocumented migrants, and xenophobia.

Chapter 5, by Mari Riojas-Cortez and Raquel Cataldo, focuses on families and how educators need to think about how to best expand the concept of *familismo* within the context of their classrooms or libraries. In order to understand *familismo,* one must understand the important role that family members play in all aspects of child development, particularly the socioemotional facet. According to Riojas-Cortez and Cataldo, while official definitions of family may exist, individuals have distinct definitions of family. The authors present several examples of children's book depicting *la familia* and other cultural values important to the Latino community.

In chapter 6, "Using Culturally Relevant Literature for Latino Children in the Early Childhood Classroom," Axelrod and Gillanders comment that there are several authors, such as Alma Flor Ada, Monica Brown, Maya Christina González, Duncan Tonatiuh, who portray Latino children and families and who incorporate Spanish in their work. Nevertheless, it is still a challenge for teachers to find ways to select texts that are authentic for the children in their classrooms and to then incorporate these books into their curriculum. They offer a guide for selecting authentic Latino children's book for young children.

In chapter 7 of part III, "Embracing the Complexity of Language: Bringing All Forms of Knowledge into the Language Arts through Latino Children's Literature," DeNicolo highlights instructional methods that utilize children's literature by Latino authors to promote language learning. She also explains how the Common Core State Standards have led to shifts in language arts instruction. Literature that promotes cultural connections can support bilingual learners in accessing prior knowledge, building vocabulary, engaging comprehension strategies, and modeling a variety of language practices. She suggests that literature discussion, multimodal presentations, *testimonio*, and dual-language texts draw on students' cultural and linguistic knowledge while providing opportunities to develop and use language across domains and language(s).

In chapter 8, *"En Aquel Entonces y Hoy en Día*: Using Latino Children's Literature to Situate Social Studies Education," Mary Esther Soto Huerta and Carmen Tafolla, poet laureate for the state of Texas, point out that effective teaching of social studies requires a personal and emotional interaction and student identification with integrated historical concepts. One of the best methods to teach social studies to Latino students and to help them achieve a personal interaction with its concepts is through the utilization of relevant Latino literature. As the authors put it, a good book lends itself to critical dialogue, engaging students in a counternarrative through the presentation of conflicting viewpoints and a constructivist understanding of history, leading to the effective teaching of social studies to Latino students.

In chapter 9, *"Dichos y Adivinanzas*: Literary Resources That Enhance Science Learning and Teaching in the Bilingual Classroom" by Arreguín-Anderson and Ruiz-Escalante, the concept of linguistic and symbolic experiences with nature is presented. Children's natural inclination to connect with nature can be capitalized on by deliberately infusing their science activities with opportunities to explore culturally relevant literature and resources. In this chapter, the presentation of a model science inquiry lesson serves to illustrate practical applications and connections to students' experiential knowledge.

Carlos LópezLeiva and Yoo Kyung Sung in chapter 10, *"Tiempo y Cultura*: Exploring Latino Stories through Mathematics," describe an innovative approach to teaching mathematics, specifically, teaching concepts of time by using Latino children's literature. Through their *mestizo* framework, they argue that culture, storytelling, and time are intricately related. By using multiple Latino children's stories, and analyzing and representing them on an open timeline, they show how this approach supports children's learning about time and culture.

In chapter 11, "Cultural Multiliteracies: Integrating Technology with Latino Children's Literature," Ek, Sánchez, and Guerra stress the need to examine the various and diverse literacies that make up students' daily lives. This chapter uses a multiliteracies theoretical framework to focus on new digital literacies and on how teachers can incorporate these into their classroom practices.

In chapter 12, "Latino Children's Literature in Picture Book Format," Martinez, Roser, Zapata, and Greeter review research focused on children's responses to Latino picture books and explore the aesthetic appeal and culturally specific content of these books. They focus on the unique features of this culturally and linguistically diverse literature through discussions of favorite picture book titles.

In chapter 13, *"Técnica Con/Safos*: Visual Iconography in Latino Picture Books as a Tool for Cultural Affirmation," Lettycia Terrones uses a critical theory framework to examine how Latino art aesthetics are used in picture books to impart messages that affirm cultural wealth and transmit cultural knowledge among children. A content analysis of contemporary picture books examines how visual tropes work alongside narratives to mirror real-world experiences of Mexican American children as navigators and social brokers. She also analyzes how messages of inclusivity, social equity, and cultural self-worth are imparted by the conscious use of specific Latino cultural iconography.

In chapter 14, "Latino Children's Literature and Literacy Practices as Social Imagination: Becoming a Culturally Efficacious Educator," Flores, Clark, and Smith use *testimonios* to reflect on the authors' literacy experiences and the impact of these experiences on their lives and worldviews. They reflect on how Latino children's literature and literacy practices, as transworld pedagogy, can provoke the social imagination and ensure social justice. In this chapter, the authors also discuss the educators' role in creating spaces for social imagination and social justice.

Cerrando con un broche de oro [Closing with a gold broad stroke], Oralia Garza de Cortés, a noted librarian active with library Latino issues and the founder of REFORMA, challenges us in chapter 15, "Realizing and Capitalizing on Our Cultural Literary Heritage: The Big Brown Elephant in the Room." Following is "Cultural Dignity" by Daniel Alejandro González reflecting on his experience with this genre. We end with "*Una Fuente de Recursos:* A Literary Guide." This section provides an expansive list of children's book titles and professional resources for educators by González and Amanda A. Hernández, children's literature specialist. In addition, Garza de Cortés and Daniel Alejandro González have developed a listing of Spanish language book titles that are available for teachers and librarians.

In sum, this volume provides a multitude of resources for use in many learning settings. We hope our readers gain understanding and become more curious, excited, and eager to share this knowledge with others. We also hope that it will inspire others to write authentic, meaningful, and dignified Latino children's literature.

REFERENCES

Bligh, C. (2014). *The silent experiences of young bilingual learners: A sociocultural study into the silent period.* Rotterdam, Netherlands: Sense Publishers.

Cisneros, S. (1994) *Hairs/Pelitos.* New York, NY: Knopf.

———. (2009). *The house on Mango Street.* New York, NY: Vintage Books.

Clark, E. R., & Flores, B. B. (2001). Who am I? The social construction of ethnic identity and self-perceptions of Latino preservice teachers. *Urban Review, 33*(2), 69–86.

Darling-Hammond, L. (1994). Performance-based assessment and educational equity. *Harvard Educational Review, 64*(1), 5–31.

Fielding, R., & Harbon, L. (2013). Examining bilingual and bicultural identity in young students. *Foreign Language Annals, 46*(4), 527–44.

Flores, B. B., Sheets, R. S., & Clark, E. R. (2011). *Teacher preparation for bilingual student populations: Educar para transformar.* New York, NY: Routledge.

García, O. (2009). Emergent bilingual and TESOL. What's in a name? *TESOL Quarterly, 43*(2), 322–26.

Herrera, J. F. (2015). First U.S. Latino poet laureate. *Washington Post.* Retrieved June 14, 2015 from www.washingtonpost.com/entertainment/books/juan-felipe-herrera-becomes-first-hispanic-american-us-poet-laureate/2015/06/09/12de51b8-0eb0-11e5-adec-e82f8395c032_story.html.

Porter, A., McMaken, J., Hwang, J., & Yang, R. (2011). Common core standards: The new U.S. intended curriculum. *Educational Researcher, 40*(3), 103–16.

Wallace, C. (2014). *Literacy and the bilingual learner: Texts and practices in London schools.* Houndmills, UK: Palgrave Macmillan.

Acknowledgments

We thank all those who have stimulated our lives with literature that reflects us. And to those who continue to struggle to have their voices and our voices heard, we honor each and every one of you. *Nuestras gracias* to Alma Flor Ada for her passion about reading and writing *y su Sangre*. We thank the Academy for Teacher Excellence for continued support in writing this volume. A special thank you to Juan Diego Robledo for his critical eye during the editing process. And *gracia*s to Hector and *Starpatch*, our home that has provided the setting for the conception and compilation of this book. We give thanks to all in our communities.

I, Ellen Riojas Clark, thank my mother, who played such an integral part in developing our lifelong interest in reading, she who would read aloud to us and then provoke us with her questions, who continuously role-modeled the enjoyment and satisfaction she garnered with every poem, story, and book she read. We take after her, my sister and I, my children and grandchildren, reading late into the night and then into the morning. As she underwent a long and painful death, she would ask me to read to her daily. I treasure Octavio Paz's treatise on *Sor Juan* for as I would read to her, she would signal to me to reread a particular passage to her. And then, toward the end, I read children's stories to her.

I, Belinda Bustos Flores, thank all who have inspired me and exposed me to literature, beginning with Mamá Julia, my parents, Art and Frances Bustos, and especially my husband, Mario, who reads and discusses with me his favorite various Spanish literary greats beginning with Cervantes and Lope de Vega, as well as other acclaimed Latin American writers such as Fuentes,

Borges, Sor Juana de la Cruz, Vargas Llosa, Paz, and Gabriela Mistral, and his favorite Chicano celebrated writers: Tomás Rivera, Rudolfo Anaya, *y otros revolucionarios*. I also thank my daughter, Janelle, an avid reader, who as a child extended my knowledge of U.S. children's authors, and who to this date continues to discuss this literature with me.

Like my colleagues, I, Howard L. Smith, wish to thank my mother and the long line of teachers in my family who taught me the importance of reading and my duty to help others join the "literacy club." I want to acknowledge the hard work and dedication of Mary Ellen Saldutti, my first Spanish teacher, who gave me a love for the language. I must also thank Dr. William Simonson, Dr. William Calvano, and Dr. Antonio O. Boyd, my undergraduate professors, who demanded that I should only communicate with them in Spanish until I (finally) became a competent speaker. I am indebted to my doctoral mentors—Dr. Adela Allen and Dr. Arminda Fuentevilla. The former showed me how to select authentic children's literature; and the latter—when I was her research assistant—tasked me with the selection of multicultural books and the creation of a children's library for her classes. Finally, I want to acknowledge my wonderfully bilingual/biliterate daughter, Milagros, who still loves her daddy's stories in whatever language and laughs at his jokes—no matter how bad they are.

I, Daniel Alejandro González, send thanks to the classmates and teachers of my past, my present, and my future, beginning with my mother, Margie, my grandparents, *tías* Della, Yolanda, and Gloria, and the historian and amazing storyteller Uncle Butch—they all shared important things about who we are, where we've been, and what is important in life. *Gracias* to the whole of my extended family and community. Many *mil gracias* to my colleagues and coeditors for sharing their wisdom, training, and this space in which to work and learn alongside them. And thank you for engaging, criticizing, and expounding on this work in the future.

Gracias, a todos in this book for expanding *nuestros conocimientos.*

Part I

FRAMING THE DISCUSSIONS: THEORY AND RATIONALE

Figure 1.1.

When children don't see themselves reflected in their books, a common experience for most Latino children, they are being told in one of the most effective and powerful ways that their experience is not valuable, and by extension, neither are they. This does not make for a positive learning environment inside or outside the classroom or support the development of personal worth within the larger context of society.

We need children's literature that provides relevant reflection for our children, not just our visual image, but also our voice, our experience, the way we think, the way we digest the world. As Latinos in the U.S. we must straddle two realities, a Latino one and a Western one. Herein lies our power and our strength. Tapping into that as a resource instead of a deficit is the secret.

—Maya Christina González, April 4, 2015

Chapter One

Multicultural Latino Children's Literature: A Tool to Enrich the Lives and the Learning of Latino Bilingual Learners

Ellen Riojas Clark and Belinda Bustos Flores

It's important for all children to see themselves mirrored in books to confirm that their lives matter that their stories matter. This is especially true for Latino children and poor children whose histories are often forgotten, sidestepped, or maligned. Nourishment, guidance, medicine; stories are all these. Best of all, stories give children permission to dream.

—Sandra Cisneros, personal communication, January 26, 2015

INTRODUCTION

Our work emphasizes the realities of our communities and is based on the theory of transformative pedagogy, cultural literacy, and the need to work in a social cultural context. We focus on promoting the importance of a culturally diverse society, bilingualism, biculturalism, and ethnic identity development through the use of Latino literature that presents a positive, culturally rich portrayal of Latino families. Latino children's multicultural literature should be sprinkled throughout with the values of friendship, family, language, traditions, and cultures. Books for our Latino children should represent concrete reflections of culture and language experiences and weave them seamlessly into storylines and characters' creations and actions. The positive effect of literature that deals with Latino culture can have a strong bearing on Latino children's ethnic identity development, and their academic success can be predicted as a result (Clark & Flores, 2001; see chapters 2 and 3).

Understanding and drawing strength from one's past and cultural history, beliefs, and values is central to our culturally diverse approach. We take Maxine Greene's premise of social imagination, that is, to imagine beyond our realities as the conduit for our increasing diverse, contradictory, and complex world as a postulate to establishing our approach to Latino literature for children. In an interview, she points out "that works of art have to be achieved in terms of persons' authentic feelings, their own lived lives, that each has to be constructed as meaningful by living" in our communities (Ayers, 1995). Since we feel strongly that there is a symbiotic relationship that is dialogical and catalytic between theory and praxis, that is, one of a dynamic exchange of ideas, we choose to work in the social cultural context of our communities in the development of literature that children can understand, see as meaningful, and which provokes their social imagination.

We also aim to conceptualize the different forms of social knowledge that can serve as cultural resources for transforming self and identity. The intended outcome of this volume then is to create a heightened awareness of the cultural and linguistic capital held by the Latino community, to increase Latino students' social capital through the design of critical pedagogical practices for Latino students, and to promote the formulation of a new perspective, that of Latino multicultural literature for children.

While there are several volumes that fall into the category of children's literature, there appear to be relatively few that explore the needs of bilingual learners and the linguistic and sociocultural context of Latino bilingual children's literature. In its totality, this volume makes a needed contribution by addressing the social, cultural, academic, and linguistic needs of bilingual learners (BLs) who continue to be underserved through current school practices. It is our challenge, then, to make sure that we can speak to how to identify authentic multicultural Latino literature and to ensure its availability for all students and, in particular, for Latino children and bilingual learners.

We use theoretical, research-based, and critical pedagogical practices to explore the use of multicultural Latino children's literature as a means to support the linguistic, academic, and psychological development of Latino children in the process of becoming bilingual and acquiring English. This will ensure that Latino children have the opportunity to become successful in schools and in life. Our contributions in this volume cover a broad spectrum of issues related to the effective use of children's literature with BLs to include identity development, critical pedagogy, biliteracy development, and holistic literacy instruction (Flores, Sheets, & Clark, 2011; Flores, Vásquez, & Clark, 2014). We hope to guide teachers, librarians, and others as educators in their awareness and approaches to Latino children's multicultural literature.

THEORETICAL FRAMEWORK

Genre of U.S. Latino Literature

Latino literature is defined as the literary work of various Latino groups in the U.S. and is written in either Spanish and English, as well as bilingually, and it can be said that it represents a rich historical culture in the U.S. Though there is still significant underrepresentation in mainstream publishing, it is growing in popularity as evidenced by the production rate of independent presses and, more recently, inroads made into mainstream publishing houses. Significantly, Latino literature straddles a number of different national and cultural histories (see chapter 2). Some of its influences are Latin American, while others are an integral part of U.S. literary history; it is a bona-fide literature of the Americas. As Deleuze and Guattari (1989) note, "A minor literature doesn't come from a minor language; it is rather that which a minority constructs within a major language" (59). The syncretic, bicultural nature of Latino literature and culture, however, does not result in a simple "hybrid" form (Clark, 1999, 2001, 2003). Rather, Latino literature is moving beyond what was seen as an insignificant or "minor" literature to one with its own integrity, one that rises from Latino culture. As an emerging field, Latino literature and culture fills an important critical gap in literary studies maintaining and promoting the literary influences of many of our writers from the Americas, such as Gabriel García Márquez, Elena Poniatowska, Carlos Fuentes, and Isabel Allende. To quote Alistair Thomson (2007), stories allow us to explore "the relationships between the past and present, between memory and personal identity, and between individual and collective memory" (54). Therefore, to productively read the genre of Latino literature, it is important to understand its relationship to many cultural forms; in other words, we must appreciate the allusions to and depictions of culturally specific practices, traditions, customs, folk beliefs, and mythologies that often serve as the basis for themes in Latino literature.

We do not seek to make an argument of exceptionality for Latino literature; rather, we would like to situate it within the larger U.S. history of artistic expression by people of Mexican, Puerto Rican, Cuban, Haitian, Dominican, etc. descent. Our Latino literary production reflects the multiplicity of interests and influences of the many different forces of all Latinos in the U.S. and elsewhere. Our literature is formally influenced by the Mexican literary tradition as it is by all other Latin American groups, but it derives much of its force from the context of Latino culture and dynamics in the U.S. (see chapter 2). The development of Latino literature has been based on the thoughts and conflicts associated with the process of struggle, denial, acceptance, revitalization, and validation of self in the U.S. An understanding of these shifting sociocultural worlds and their complexity forms the premise for many Latino authors' literary works. Julia Alvarez's *How the García Girls Lost Their Accents* (1991), Oscar Zeta Acosta's *The Revolt of the Cockroach People* (1989), Sandra Cisneros's *Caramelo* (2002), and Reyna Grande's *Across a Hundred Mountains* (2007), among others, serve as examples for adult readers. Other Latino books for adults, such as Junot Diaz's *The Brief Wondrous Life of Oscar Wao* (2008), have become popularized and are often required reading in college courses, while Sandra Cisneros's *House on Mango Street* (1984) is being used at middle and high school levels, both books forming part of the genre of Latino literature. A whole community has undergone and continues to explore a cultural, linguistic, ethnic self-acceptance and an awakening of self to understand the subtleties of living in the U.S. As a result, it has propelled a vibrant production of what we accept as a genre and part of the literary canon of the Americas. We can forcefully say, as expressed by Rodríguez (2014) and González (2014), that our literature

- serves as a positive mechanism for ethnic dignity and strong sense of identity within a bicultural or multicultural society;
- includes a process of expression, reflection, and identity formation;
- explores how these narratives and cultures continue to inform our identities;
- brings to the forefront how the conflicts of negotiating two cultural communities problematize the development of individual and collective ethnic identity;
- speaks to the resilience of narratives among Mexicans, Caribbean Americans, Central Americans, and Latin Americans who live in the U.S.;
- examines how the Latino population in the U.S. continues to be maintained despite centuries of efforts to eradicate them;
- emphasizes the importance of ethnic community physical and cultural spaces; and
- demonstrates how new stories—based on ancient stories—continue to be created and adapted to modern society.

In this time of major demographic shifts within the U.S., cultural responses are of special significance because they are the vigorous nature with which cultural traditions help people adapt and negotiate their place in society. Latinos have found ways to retain culturally specific means of expression through literature. Latino literature is a genre and a form of creative cultural expression, and the exploration of its significance as a mode of cultural expression is a valid one. An extended examination of Latino writings reveals much about the cultural, social, and political change of our experiences.

The canon of U.S. literature, as well as that of Western literature, has now been impacted, and the inclusion of the Latino literature canon has been evidenced by the acceptance of the works by Latinos in the U.S. and other Spanish-speaking countries. Latino literature is part of the canon, *punto*.

Multicultural Latino Children's Literature

We consider multicultural Latino children's literature as representative of the various groups who comprise the Latino population in the U.S. As such, Mexican Americans, Puerto Ricans, Cubans, Dominicans, and others form a Latino ethnic group whose members are in many ways similar, yet whose different nationalities distinguish them due to variations in their language, history, culture, and experiences. We consider multicultural literature to be much more than just books "by and about people of color," but it is about books specific to the many Latino groups in the U.S. (Cooperative Children's Book Center, 2014).

Latino children's multicultural literature has its roots within the U.S. Authors like Pat Mora, Alma Flor Ada, and others speak to the experiences of Puerto Ricans, Cubans, Mexican Americans, and those from Central America. The prize-winning children's author and illustrator Duncan Tonatiuh, for example, has used his experiences to create books known for their unique and beautiful illustrations as well as for their serious subject matter: "desegregation in schools or the dangerous journeys of undocumented immigrants" (personal blog, 2014; see chapter 13).

As has been stated previously, just as adults need and deserve to see books that reflect them and the worlds in which they live, so do Latino children and youth. It is a right that needs to be respected. Again as Tonatiuh (2014) states in his blog, "Hopefully my books help Latino children realize that their stories and their voices are important." The recovery of this work broadens the breadth and scope of Latino literature and contributes to our ongoing reassessment of literatures of the Americas. Latino children's multicultural literature needs to be seen as reflective of a tradition that has survived and has undergone cultural adaptation within the scope of the social cultural context of the U.S. and all places where Latinos reside.

Nature of Latino Bilingual Learners in the U.S.

> There is a very limited amount of literature where Latino children can see themselves and their culture reflected. I think it is important for children to see themselves in books they read because it lets them know that their voices and stories are important.
>
> —Duncan Tonatiuh, personal communication, October 29, 2014

To understand the need for Latino multicultural children's literature, it is important to know Latino children's presence within the U.S. context. At present, it is estimated that nearly 21 percent of the U.S. populace is bilingual (Ryan, 2013) and that approximately 50 percent of the world is bilingual (Grosjean, 2010). In fact the U.S. population majority is comprised of distinct linguistic and culturally diverse groups with Latinos being the largest group (Passel & Cohn, 2008) and Spanish being the language most spoken within the home (Ryan, 2013).

Projections also indicate that the majority (52 percent) of Latinos are U.S. born whose parents were immigrants from Mexico, Central, or South America, while only 11 percent are foreign-born (Fry & Passel, 2009). According to a recent report, "The Condition of Latinos in Education 2015," the population of young Latino children, age 5 and under, is projected to increase to 39 percent by the year 2023 and they will represent the majority of all children in the U.S. Currently, Latinos represent 24 percent of students enrolled in U.S. public schools, and projections suggest an increase to 30 percent in 2023. In other southwestern states, like Texas and California, this number is likely to be five out of every ten children in public schools (Fry & Passel, 2009).

Most demographic analyses often report the increasing number of English learners without taking into account their generational status or the home context. First and second generation Latino children are likely to be in homes and communities in which Spanish is spoken the majority of the time (Fry & Passel, 2009). In the case of individuals age 5 and over, U.S. Census findings reveal that 62 percent of those reporting that another language was spoken in the home indicated Spanish as the home language. Of these, 58 percent reported "speaking English very well" (Ryan, 2013). Thus, even when Spanish is the home language, Latino children are likely becoming bilingual within the larger schooling and community context.

The Sociocultural Context of Latino Children Demographics

To further understand this population beyond numbers, it is also important to study the societal context in which Latinos have lived, starting with the Treaty of Guadalupe Hidalgo (Treaty of Peace, Friendship, Limits and Settlement between the United States of America and the Mexican Republic; Griswold del Castillo, 1990). This peace treaty signed in 1848 between the U.S. and Mexico set the Rio Grande River as a boundary and gave Texas, California, New Mexico, Arizona, Nevada, Utah, and parts of Colorado to the U.S. Mexicans living in those areas were to be compensated for their lands, given citizenship, and granted the right to their language, promises which are violated to this day. Thus, it is important to speak to the historical experiences faced by Latinos such as segregation, struggles for civil rights, and the violation of rights within the U.S. context as well as current experiences, such as deportation and the ongoing violation of human dignity. These stories are often not depicted in historically based books or in traditional children's literature. Deborah Caldwell-Stone, deputy director of the American Library Association, says,

> We have seen challenges to books where the content [probes] received wisdom on issues like poverty and class or offers an alternative political view point on a situation. Challenges to books that unmask societal fissures along economic and class lines are a symptom of wider woes and rising tensions around inequality, low wages, poverty and insecurity. Ensuring that literature addressing these issues remains freely available is a worthy cause in pursuit of social justice. (O'Hara, 2014)

A popular Spanish proverb, *Cada cabeza es un mundo*, is a critical perspective and a cultural principle that encapsulates our belief that our experiences shape our world perspective. Latino children's literature can help our students, teachers, librarians, and others have a sense of equality based on equity rights and can support group affinity. Positive group affinity or solidarity enhances social esteem and ethnic identity (Clark & Flores, 2014).

Authentic Literature for Latino Bilingual Learners

> My decisions to write for children were inspired by my own two children who moved within a multicultural family without any books to celebrate this fact and that nagging question of my own childhood that had haunted me: Where were the children like me in books?
>
> —Diane Gonzáles Bertrand, personal communication, October, 2014

Over the years, we have seen the number of multicultural books grow, but literature by Latinos still represents a small percentage of the overall number of books published for children and teenagers. Diversity in children's books has been tracked by the Cooperative Children's Book Center in Wisconsin (2014) for the past twenty-five years as indicated by figure 1.2.

African or African American–content publications increased significantly from 93 titles in 2013 to 179 in 2014, a sizeable growth though not reflective of African American demographics. An increase in books with Asian/Pacific-American content was not as significant, with 69 titles in 2013 increasing to 112 in 2014. The most dismal numbers are those regarding American Indians (thirty-four titles in 2013 and thirty-six titles in 2014) and Latinos, which do not reflect an increase. Latinos, which constitute a large presence in the U.S.,

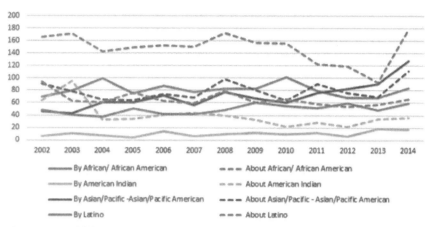

Figure 1.2.   Children's Books By and About People of Color

were only represented by fifty-seven titles in 2013 and sixty-six in 2014, a sad state of affairs for Latino children, libraries, schools, and all communities. It is not acceptable to see that the number of books for and by Latinos has not increased over the years when there should be a strong presence of Latino multicultural literature in the lives of our children.

Publishers are just not producing the number of books needed for the numbers of Latinos reflected in the U.S. During the 2015 American Library Association's Midwinter Conference, the Association of Library Services and the Children's Book Council organized "A Day of Diversity for Children." It brought together a group of more than one hundred ethnically diverse people including publishers, editors, librarians, booksellers, and authors with the goal of asking the hard questions dealing with the issue of lack of representation in books, published authors, marketing, etc. and of how to deal with the issue of privilege and inequality. In 2015, former REFORMA president Oralia Garza de Cortés said,

> Until publishers lacking in multicultural literature—and that's very different from diversity, set up goals for themselves and hold themselves publicly accountable for publishing more books that reflect the colorline, this conversation will be just that—a conversation: civil and tepid, with not much real hope for change so long as we are muzzled into niceness with silly rules designed to deflate the much-need tension required for that change to take place. . . . My take, particularly when 22% of all children in the U.S. are Latino-and growing. Basta! Enough with the talk. Show me the marketing plans and financial investment for publishing great multicultural books; show me the goals for producing more books. Time to walk the walk! (Lee & Low Books blog commentary, 2015)

Her comments reinforce a major complaint that marketing of Latino's children literature is not at the same level as for other books; therefore, advertising needs to be at the same level as for other books. According to the Cooperative Children's Book Center (2014), what the low numbers for multicultural literature mean is that publishing for children and teenagers has a long way to go before reflecting the rich diversity of perspectives and experiences within and across race, ethnicity, and culture in the U.S. According to Milliot (2014), Latinos in the U.S. publishing industry constitute a mere 3 percent. It stands to reason then that the publication of Latino material is at such a low level. We consider it a remarkable premise that a national publishing company, Lee & Low Books, has as its primary mission the discovery of new writers of color as they work to publish multicultural fiction for young readers.

Whether you are preparing to become a teacher, librarian, or administrator, our U.S. diversity and the growing number of Latino children requires that you recognize the importance and the rationale for the use of Latino literature in our various communities. In recognizing the sociocultural, historical, and political context of the lived lives of Latino children, we can support their cultural, linguistic, and cognitive development through appropriate literature. We must acknowledge their ways of thinking and being. In an interview, Tonatiuh states, "I try to make books about themes that interest me and that I care about like social justice, art and history. I hope that readers first of all find the books interesting and entertaining. Hopefully they will also learn something about their culture or the culture of their classmates" (Davis & Clark, 2015).

The many different ways language, culture, and ethnicity play into the social construction of Latino/bilingual children's identity and learning are factors that must be taken into consideration and should form themes for children's literature. As Tonatiuh (2014) says in his blog, "Hopefully in my books they see themselves and some of their reality reflected. I hope they see familiar objects, learn about their history and traditions, and feel proud." Migrant student stories formed the core for his book that received the 2014 Tomás Rivera Mexican American Children's Book Award, *Pancho Rabbit and the Coyote* (2013), which recounts the dangerous journeys of many undocumented immigrants coming to the United States (see chapters 4 and 13). This story was also documented in the recent opera *Cruzar la cara de la luna* (Martínez, 2011) featuring the Mariachi Vargas de Tecalitlán, commissioned by the Houston Grand Opera, and premiered in 2010. This opera, that chronicles the immigrant experience of being divided by countries and cultures, depicts the emotional and spiritual connection of immigrants to their home country, and shows the challenges of being in a strange country, played to sold-out audiences in its travel throughout the U.S. and in Europe.

As a Spanish *dicho* coined by Vásquez, Flores, and Clark (2013, 114) tells us, *Celebra quién eres* [Celebrate who you are], for most of our schooling experiences do not celebrate the groups represented in our communities. Schools tend to model and socialize us into a mold that is not reflective of us. Latino literature can help us to "reclaim our cultural identity and restore our self-respect through a critical understanding of the socio-cultural, historical, and political contexts that have mediated the development of our identities" (Vásquez, Flores, & Clark, 2013, 114). Strong cultural and ethnic identities can lead to equity, ethnic solidarity, and power; build empathy; and promote social justice in our schools. We must take pride and celebrate our rich culture in our literature so others can learn from our deeds; we must open our minds to new thoughts, new points of view, and expand our world through our literature.

Ethnic Identity Development

> We live in a diverse country with cultural riches. Latino children, and all our children, deserve to see their lives in the pages of the books they read. Books convey powerful messages about what—and who—matters.
>
> —Pat Mora, personal communication, January, 2015

We, along with teachers and our students, must explore and comprehend our own identity in order to appreciate the impact it will have on our learning and teaching. The use of Latino children's literature can help teachers and librarians understand not only the social construction of identity but also the role of culture in order to motivate learning. Ethnic identity development according to Clark and Flores (2001, 78) "starts with understanding others and their identity and to looking within to formulate our own identity." As educators who work with Latino children, it is important for us to clearly understand ethnic identity in order to promote children's ethnic development and recognize them as ethnic beings (Clark & Flores, 2014). Ethnic identity is socially constructed, complex, and multidimensional consisting of: ethnic identity formation, ethnic identification, language, bilingualism, self-esteem, immigration status, and degrees of ethnic consciousness and ethnic unconsciousness (Bernal, Knight, Garza, Ocampo, & Cota, 1990; Clark & Flores, 2001, 2014; Phinney, 1991; Phinney, Chavira, & Tate, 1993; Quintana & Vera, 1999). In the case of BLs, their identity is intimately tied to their bilingualism and biculturalism (Clark & Flores, 2001).

It is also important to consider the parents' socialization toward ethnicity in understanding Latino children's ethnic identity (Quintana & Vera, 1999). Personal ethnic identity formation tells us that for children and adults to develop a positive sense of identity, there must be an affinity and connectedness to the ethnic group, in our case as a Latino or more specifically, a specific national group such as Mexican American, Puerto Rican, Guatemalan, etc. (Honneth, 2004; Heidegren, 2002). We, as educators, as well as our BLs, can identity and have affinity with our country of origin, country of immigration, or our heritage country. Essentially, ethnicity is central to the child's image; affiliation or a sense of belonging can provide a child with emotional support.

Flores and Clark (2004) have expressed the need for educators to understand the sociocultural, historical, and political context as a mediator of their students' identity. Tying together the strands of culture and language and language learning for children is important for educators who see its impact on learning and cognition. Consistent with other work, our research confirms two postulates: (1) a positive ethnic identity is associated with positive self-conceptualization, and (2) a well-defined ethnic identity can have an impact on academic success (Clark & Flores, 2014). So how we look at language and culture affects how we look at Latino children's literature as a pedagogical tool to promote a positive ethnic identity in our students and the personal and professional efficacy of our teachers and our librarians, as well.

Bilingualism, Biliteracy, and Biculturalism Development

In the case of children acquiring two or more languages, throughout this text we use the term "bilingual learner," as we used in prior works (Flores, Sheets, & Clark, 2011; Flores, Vásquez, & Clark, 2014). The term "bilingual learner" reflects the notion that within a bilingual context, learners are acquiring two or more languages along a continuum within varying contexts (Hornberger & Skilton-Sylvester, 2000; Hornberger, 2003, 2004). Latino bilingual learners may be acquiring and exposed to two or more distinct languages and cultures within the home, school, and the community. The term "bilingual learner" stands in contrast to the terms "English learner," "English as a second language learner," or "emergent bilingual." "Bilingual learner" acknowledges that children are continuously acquiring literacy in both formal and informal settings rather than simply considering learning as only occurring within the school setting.

Latino children have valuable skills as well as unique experiences and perspectives that can be leveraged through multicultural children's literature. In this text, our focus is on the Latino population given their presence throughout the U.S. While not all Latino children are bilingual, they may be exposed to their heritage language in extended family settings or the community. Latino children, who are English dominant, may in fact have remnants of some Spanish words in their repertoire, such as words of endearment, *mijo/*

mija, abuelita, and *mamá,* or words for Latino cuisine such as *pan dulce, en-chiladas, mofongo, tacos, tostones, tortilla,* etc. These linguistic and cultural experiences should be captured in Latino children's multicultural literature.

Latino children's bilingualism is clearly a benefit in many ways and has many implications for learning and teaching. In reality, bilingualism is a multiple skill-set with varying degrees of proficiency. Even at an early age, Latino children commonly engage in highly sophisticated communicative activities like code-switching (Zentella, 1997), translanguaging (García, 2009), and language brokering (Morales & Hanson, 2005), without the benefit of any formal training. In the case of code-switching, bilingual children intuitively alternate between English and Spanish with other bilinguals either within a sentence (*intrasentential*) or between sentences (*intersentential*). Code-switching is a unique phenomena that occurs among bilinguals, and García (2009) extends this by introducing the notion of translanguaging to acknowledge the cognitive functions and processes that occur when bilinguals alternate languages. She suggests that language alternation, which occurs naturally, requires the child to decide which of their languages is more appropriate for a given situation or audience. Language brokering is yet another positive benefit of bilingualism. When Spanish monolingual parents need to communicate with an English monolingual adult (e.g., a librarian, school principal, health care provider, or postal clerk), children act as language brokers. They not only interpret the words of the adults, they must also mediate the negotiations. For that reason, current research on the linguistic behaviors of Latino students (Bligh 2014; Flores, Sheets, & Clark, 2011; Wallace, 2013) advocate the term "bilingual learner" because it acknowledges the multiple linguistic proficiencies these students possess. The term frames not only the process of English language learning but also their home language as an asset that should be incorporated into the school curriculum or any learning context to ensure academic and cognitive development.

Many Latino children are also biliterate making them *bilingual/biliterate learners.* This term reflects the notion that within a bilingual context, learners are acquiring two distinct literacies skills along a continuum (Hornberger & Skilton-Sylvester, 2000; Hornberger, 2003, 2004). In the case of Latino bilingual learners, they are exposed to two or more distinct literacies in the home, the school, or the community. Unlike "limited English proficiency students" (LEPs) or "English language learners" (ELLs), the terms "bilingual learner" and "bilingual/biliterate learner" respect the contributions of English and Spanish to the linguistic, literate, and cognitive development of the learner.

Latino children are also often bicultural. Biculturalism is not based on bilingualism but rather on cultural competence; therefore, children might not be bilingual but they can be bicultural. Their biculturalism is composed of the beliefs, customs, traditions, skills, and personal values of both U.S. and Latino cultures. Fielding and Harbon (2013) explain the power of biculturalism:

> Students across the range of educational levels and settings bring to their formal schooling a multitude of life experiences, encounters with languages in addition to their first language, and connections to diverse cultures. Such experiences have an impact on classroom learning in that they help children determine who they are, where they belong in the world, and how they are related to others within and beyond their school and home communities. (p. 528)

Literature can have an impact on children's acquisition of bilingualism, biliteracy, and biculturalism if books are present in schools, classrooms, homes, and libraries. The children's literature referenced in the following chapters capitalizes on this dual perspective gained through bilingualism and/or biculturalism, and in so doing, engages the reader on multiple planes. Unfortunately, the benefits of bilingualism, biliteracy, and biculturalism are not recognized in past or recent national academic standards.

Academic Development (Standards)

In our volume, you will note reference to either the national or common standards. While national standards for all content areas had been identified nearly twenty years ago (Darling-Hammond, 1994), not all states used these standards in developing or delivering their curriculum. The intent behind the Common Core was for all states to implement a common curriculum in English Language Arts and Mathematics in order to ensure career and college readiness (Porter, McMaken, Hwang, & Yang, 2011). A major concern to us is that the Common Core State Standards (CCSS) do not recognize bilingual learners; rather they only refer to English language learners (ELLs). The CCSS are proving to be very a controversial issue as these get implemented throughout the country. With the goal of preparing students for academic success, the CCSS are a set of "clear, consistent guidelines for what every student should know and be able to do in math and English language arts from kindergarten through 12th grade" (García, 2015). The standards integrate the literacy skills of speaking, writing, reading, and listening across the academic content areas for all students (García, 2015). The concern voiced by many is that by raising academic standards, it presents challenges for ELLs, though others see it as an opportunity to improve performance. According to Carol Scheffner Hammer, ELL students need far more language instruction than what they are receiving as it seems that teachers need to target students' vocabulary and oral language for CCSS (García, 2015). Nevertheless, others have indicated that the Common Core, like state standards, can provide appropriate academic opportunities for ELLs. For example, Californians Together identifies the 4Cs—communication, collaboration, critical thinking, and creativity—for ELLs that should be integrated into the curriculum. Using these 4Cs, we elaborate on the benefit of Latino multicultural literature to the bilingual learner's academic development.

- Communication: Supports the bilingual learners' language development through meaningful stories that connect to their lives and experiences.
- Collaboration: Engages bilingual learners' in learning about themselves and other Latinos, while sharing their cultural resources with others who are not Latino.
- Critical thinking: Engages bilingual learners in critical reflection about issues such as immigration, segregation, and violation of human rights.
- Creativity: Provokes bilingual learners' social imagination by connecting them to the protagonists in the literature.

Though the useful guideline of CCSS for how English-speaking educators can better support all students' linguistic development is stated, several needs stand out. We must better prepare teachers and librarians to work with bilingual learners, develop high-quality textbooks and other literary works better aligned with the new standards, provide specific professional development on the common core, and provide better information to parents and community. Reading Latino children's literature in schools, libraries, and in the home can have an impact on our students, schools, and communities.

PRAXIS: APPLICATION OF THEORY

We have intentionally chosen to use the term "praxis." Freire (1971) uses the notion of praxis to signal the iterative act of critical reflection, transformation, and action that occurs as a result of dialogue. Actualizing praxis requires the educator to be culturally efficacious with positive identity, critical consciousness, and positive teaching efficacy. Culturally efficacious educators believe that their critical/cultural practices will have a positive impact on learners, thereby increasing their opportunities.

Hence, through their praxis, culturally efficacious educators are able to act upon the world to transform it (Flores, Clark, Claeys, & Villarreal, 2007; Flores, Vasquez, & Clark, 2014). Throughout this volume, you will read about various pedagogical approaches (e.g., culturally responsive and transformative pedagogy). While each of these has distinct origins, an underlying commonality is that these pedagogies aim to respond to the needs of the learner by anchoring the construction of knowledge on the cultural capital of the learner.

Flores, Vásquez, and Clark (2014) extend this aforementioned pedagogy by recognizing that bilingual learners live in a complex world. They further acknowledge that the privileging of Western knowledge and the quest for modernity has obliterated the multiple ways of knowing of our *antepasados*, has negated our present knowledge, and will continue to refute our knowledge claims. As a counternarrative, they propose the notion of a transworld pedagogy/*pedagogía transmundial* that

> aim[s] to prepare learners to live in a world that demands the ability to move in and out of multiple perspectives and identities, while participating in the multiple imagined worlds that constitute life in the twenty-first century. (18)

Pedagogía transmundial is grounded in four theoretical constructs: the dialogical method, Vygotskian's notion of culture, critical bilingual/bicultural pedagogy, and the sacred sciences. Each of these constructs is evident when employing Latino children's multicultural literature as a pedagogical tool and integrates the aforementioned 4Cs for bilinguals as elaborated in the following paragraphs.

Vásquez, Clark, and Flores (2014) posit that the dialogical method occurs when individuals participate in discourse that is mutual and respectful. Educators can engage children in conversations with knowledgeable others or peers about their understanding of a selected book from their point of view. In allowing children to freely express their thoughts, we learn about the children's world and how they make sense of the world.

Vygotskian's notion of culture accounts for "the child's intellectual history as foundational for learning and development" (Flores et al., 2014, 9). In considering this notion of culture, they suggest that *pedagogía transmundial* builds on children's knowledge base at present, while extending their intellectual boundaries by connecting to the cultural group's history of accomplishments. Latino children's multicultural literature is a tool for connecting and extending the bilingual learner's knowledge base and intellectual capital.

Critical bilingual/bicultural pedagogy requires that the educator use pedagogical tools that promote the linguistic and cultural development of the child. Using Latino children's multicultural literature affirms children's linguistic and cultural practices as situated in their daily lives in their home and community.

The notion of sacred sciences recognizes our *antepasados* knowledge and contributions to our modern world. Vásquez et al. (2014) embraces an indigenous perspective in which all living and nonliving entities exist in harmony and balance, and all are honored as sacred. When we read or have bilingual learners read Latino children's multicultural literature, we are creating a learning setting with harmony and balance in which children feel that their knowledge is sacred.

As culturally efficacious educators, we must take into account the multiple, embedded cultural worlds that Latino children encounter (see chapter 14). The use of Latino children's multicultural literature in which language and knowledge acquisition occurs, while acknowledging learners' culture, identity, and potential and honoring the sacred is transworld pedagogy. When we enact these tenets collectively, we are generating transworld pedagogy that is the praxis that can transform the world for educator and learner alike.

CONCLUSION

As our goal is to ensure student success, we emphatically state that children's Latino literature must be included in our schools, homes, and libraries. Our belief is that a solid understanding of self, a strong cultural foundation, and a developed, positive ethnic identity form the framework for academic achievement and public success and strong citizens. Our Latino children need to see themselves as cultural beings reflected in the literature represented in our schools, our homes, our libraries, and our communities and as solid voices in our books and popular media. That is how equity, ethnic solidarity, and power can build empathy and promote social justice in our schools and communities, thereby impacting all of our society in a most positive and just manner. For us, the path toward accomplishment of our premise of honoring culture, identity, and the potential of all learners is through the framework of transworld pedagogy. *Abriendo nuestros mundos* is to open ourselves in all totality to new thoughts and new points of view, and to expand our worlds beyond ourselves. Our minds, all our minds can be expanded through the voices of our cultures and through our literature, specifically Latino literature.

REFERENCES

Acosta, O. Z. (1989). *The revolt of the cockroach people.* New York, NY: Vintage Books.

Alvarez, J. (2005). *How the García girls lost their accents.* New York, NY: Plume.

Ayers, W. (1995). Social imagination: A conversation with Maxine Green. *International Journal of Qualitative Studies in Education, 8*(4), 319–28.

Bernal, M. E., Knight, G. P., Garza, C. A., Ocampo, K. A., & Cota, M. K. (1990). The development of ethnic identity in Mexican-American children. *Hispanic Journal of Behavioral Sciences, 12*(1), 3–24.

Bligh, Caroline. 2014. *The silent experiences of young bilingual learners: A sociocultural study into the silent period.* Rotterdam, The Netherlands: Sense Publishers.

Cisneros, S. (1984). *The house on Mango Street.* New York, NY: Vintage Books.

———. (2002) *Caramelo.* New York, NY: Knopf.

Clark, E. R. (1999, 2001, 2003). Derrumbando fronteras/Breaking boundaries: Institute for the inclusion of Mexican American and Latino literature and culture in the classroom. National Endowment for the Humanities Summer Institute Grants.

Clark, E. R., & Flores, B. B. (2001). Who am I? The social construction of ethnic identity and self-perceptions of bilingual preservice teachers. *Urban Review, 33*(2), 69–86.

———. (2014). The metamorphosis of teacher identity: An intersection of ethnic consciousness, self-conceptualization, and belief systems. In P. Jenlink, *Teacher identity and struggle for recognition: Meeting the challenges of a diverse society* (pp. 3–14). Lanham, MD: Rowman & Littlefield.

Cooperative Children's Book Center in Wisconsin (2014). Retrieved December 15, 2014, from https://ccbc.education.wisc.edu/.

Darling-Hammond, L. (1994). National standards and assessments: Will they improve education? *American Journal of Education, 102*(4), 478–510.

Davis, M., & Clark, E. R. (2015). Interview with prize-winning author Duncan Tonatiuh. *NABE Perspectives* (January–March 2015), 15–16.

de Cortes, Oralia Garza (2015). Commentary. Lee & Low Books, the Open Book. Retrieved from http://blog.leeandlow.com/2015/02/06/ala-midwinter-day-of-diversity-recap-and-reflections/.

Deleuze, G., & Guattari, F. (1986). *Kafka: Toward a minor literature.* Minneapolis, MN: University of Minnesota Press.

Díaz, J. (2008). *The brief wondrous life of Oscar Wao.* New York, NY: Riverhead Books.

Fielding, R., & Harbon, L. (2013). Examining bilingual and bicultural identity in young students. *Foreign Language Annals, 46*(4), 527–44.

Flores, B. B., & Clark, E. R. (2004). *Normalistas*: A critical examination of *normalistas* self-conceptualization and teacher efficacy. *Hispanic Journal of Behavioral Sciences, 26*(2), 230–57.

Flores, B. B., Clark, E. R., Claeys, L., & Villarreal, A. (2007). Academy for teacher excellence: Recruiting, preparing, and retaining Latino teachers though learning communities. *Teacher Education Quarterly, 34*(4), 53–69.

Flores, B. B., Sheets, R. S., & Clark, E. R. (2011). *Teacher preparation for bilingual student populations: Educar para transformar.* New York, NY: Routledge.

Flores, B. B., Vásquez, O. A., & Clark, E. R. (2014). *Generating transworld pedagogy: Reimagining La Clase Mágica.* Lanham, MD: Lexington Books.

Freire, P. (1971). *Pedagogy of the oppressed.* New York, NY: Continuum Press.

Fry, R., & Passel, J. E. (2009). Latino children: A majority are U.S.-born offspring of immigrants. Washington, D.C.: Pew Hispanic Center. Retrieved June 15, 2014, from www.pewhispanic.org/2009/05/28/latino-children-a-majority-are-us-born -offspring-of-immigrants/.

García, A. (2015). The common core just might be the greatest (or worst) thing to happen to DLLs. Retrieved May 30, 2014, from www.edcentral.org/dllsandccss/.

García, O. (2009). Emergent bilingual and TESOL. What's in a Name? *TESOL Quarterly, 43*(2), 322–26.

González, D. A. (2014). Identity, space, and visual art: Reflexivity in visual ethnography and positionality. Unpublished manuscript.

Grande, R. (2007). *Across a hundred mountains: A novel.* New York, NY: Washington Square Press.

Griswold del Castillo, R. (1990). *The treaty of Guadalupe Hidalgo: A legacy of conflict.* Norman, OK: University of Oklahoma Press.

Grosjean, F. (2010). Bilingualism, biculturalism, and deafness. *International Journal of Bilingual Education and Bilingualism, 13*(2), 133–45.

Heidegren, C. (2002). Anthropology, social theory, and politics: Axel Honneth's theory of recognition. *Inquiry, 45*, 433–46.

Honneth, A. (2004). Recognition and justice: Outline of a plural theory of justice. *Acta Sociologica, 47*(4), 351–64.

Hornberger, N. H. (2003). *Continua of biliteracy: An ecological framework for educational policy, research, and practice in multilingual settings.* Buffalo, NY: Multilingual Matters.

———. (2004). The continua of biliteracy and the bilingual educator: Educational linguistics in practice. Multilingual Matters. Reprinted from *International Journal of Bilingual Education and Bilingualism, 7*(2 & 3), 155–71.

Hornberger, N. H., & Skilton-Sylvester, E. (2000) Revisiting the continua of biliteracy: International and critical perspectives. *Language and Education: An International Journal, 14*(2), 96–122.

Martínez, J. (2011). *Cruzar la cara de la luna* [opera]. Albany, NY.

Milliot, J. (2014). Publishing's holding pattern: 2014 salary survey. Publishers Weekly. http://publishersweekly.com/pw/by-topic/industry-news/publisher-news/ article/64083-publishing-s-holding-pattern-2013-salary-survey.html.

Morales, A., & Hanson, W. E. (2005). Language brokering: An integrative review of the literature. *Hispanic Journal of Behavioral Sciences, 27*(4), 471–503.

O'Hara, M. (2014). Poverty and class: The latest themes to enter the US banned books debate. Retrieved May 5, 2014, from www.theguardian.com/society/2014/ oct/21/us-adds-poverty-to-dangerous reading-lists.

Passel, J. S., & Cohn, D. (2008). U.S. population projections: 2005–2050. Washington, D.C.: Pew Hispanic Center.

Phinney, J. S. (1991). Ethnic identity and self-esteem: A review and integration. *Hispanic Journal of Behavioral Sciences, 13*(2), 193–208.

Phinney, J. S., Chavira, V., & Tate, J. D. (1993). The effect of ethnic threat on ethnic self-concept and own-group rating. *Journal of Social Psychology, 133*(4), 469–79.

Porter, A., McMaken, J., Hwang, J., & Yang, R. (2011). Common core standards: The new U.S. intended curriculum. *Educational Researcher, 40*(3), 103–16.

Quintana, S. M., & Vera, E. M. (1999). Mexican American children's ethnic identity, understanding of ethnic prejudice, and parental ethnic socialization. *Hispanic Journal of Behavioral Sciences, 21*(4), 387–404.

Rodríguez, R. C. (2014). *Our sacred maíz is our mother: Indigeneity and belonging in the Americas.* Tucson, AZ: University of Arizona Press.

Ryan, C. (2013). Language use in the United States: 2011. U.S. Census Bureau. American community survey reports. Retrieved June 5, 2014, from www.census.gov/prod/2013pubs/acs-22.pdf.

Thomson, A. (2007). Four paradigm transformations in oral history. *Oral History Review, 34*(1), 49–70.

Tonatiuh, D. (2013). *Pancho rabbit and the coyote: A migrant's tale.* New York, NY: Abrams Books for Young Readers.

———. (2014). Personal blog. Retrieved July 8, 2014, from https://duncantonatiuh.wordpress.com/.

Vásquez, O. A., Clark, E. R., & Flores, B. B. (2014). *Una pedagogía transmundial*/A transworld pedagogy: Anchoring theory to the sacred sciences. In B. B. Flores, O. A. Vásquez, & E. R. Clark, *Generating transworld pedagogy: Reimagining* La Clase Mágica (pp. 17–32). Lanham, MD: Rowman & Littlefield.

Vásquez, O. A., Flores, B. B., & Clark, E. R. (2013). *Consejos: Un diálogo respetuoso:* Critical and respectful dialogue. *Journal of Social Foundations, 27*(1–2), 111–18.

Wallace, C. (2014). *Literacy and the bilingual learner: Texts and practices in London schools.* Basingstoke, UK: Palgrave Macmillan.

Zentella, A. C. (1997). Latino youth at home, in their communities, and in school: The language link. *Education and Urban Society, 30*(1), 122–30.

DISCUSSION QUESTIONS

1. Discuss ethnic identity. What is it? How would you define? What is ethnicity? What is identity? What is culture?
2. Why do you think there is a dearth of children's Latino literature?
3. Discuss the following statement in small groups and share your thoughts with other groups. Deleuze and Guattari (1986) note that "a minor literature doesn't come from a minor language; it is rather that which a minority constructs within a major language" (59). What do they mean?
4. Why is it important for the literary canon to recognize and include Latino literature?
5. Reflect on the notions of biculturalism and bilingualism. How can an English-dominant child be bicultural and/or bilingual?

ACTIVITIES

A. Have your class read Clark and Flores (2001), "Who Am I? The Socio-construction of Ethnic Identity and Self-Perception of Bilingual Preservice Teachers" (see "Suggested Professional Readings" below). On a sheet of paper, have your students write "Who am I?" and the numbers 1 through 20. Give your students fifteen minutes to answer the question "Who am I?" twenty times with a single word or very short phrase. Make sure they write twenty responses. When they finish, ask them to record their ethnic identity at the bottom of page. Have them categorize their responses into areas such as physical makeup, beliefs, relationships, etc. Have them discuss in groups their categories and ethnic identity labels.

B. Develop a list of children's Latino books that your students read as children. In addition, have them conduct a survey of five teachers, five parents, five colleagues, five professionals including a librarian, and five friends of the Latino books they have read. Create a graph and discuss your findings.

C. Assign groups to conduct a "book collection" survey (number of books, authors, genre, children's books, etc.) of school libraries, community libraries, and five homes. Compile the information and discuss findings.

D. Select five to ten Latino children's books from the appendix and have your students each write a book review of one of the books. On the class website, post all of the book reviews.

E. Ask class members to volunteer to read at a school or library one of the books reviewed.

SUGGESTED PROFESSIONAL READINGS

Banks, J. (2004). Teaching for social justice, diversity, and citizenship in a global world. *Educational Forum*, *68*(2), 289–98.

Clark, E. R., & Flores, B. B. (2001). Who am I? The social construction of ethnic identity and self-perceptions of Latino preservice teachers. *Urban Review*, *33*(2), 69–86.

———. (2014). The metamorphosis of teacher identity: An intersection of ethnic consciousness, self-conceptualization, and belief systems. In P. Jenlink, *Teacher identity and struggle for recognition: Meeting the challenges of a diverse society* (pp. 3–14). Lanham, MD: Rowman & Littlefield.

Clark, E. R., Jackson, L. G., & Prieto, L. (2011). Identity: A central facet of culturally efficacious bilingual teachers. In B. B. Flores, R. H. Sheets, & E. R. Clark (Eds.), *Teacher preparation for bilingual student population:* Educar para transformar (pp. 40–58). New York, NY: Routledge.

Freire, P. (1971). *Pedagogy of the oppressed.* New York, NY: Herder and Herder.
Freire, P. (2014). Pedagogy of hope: Reliving pedagogy of the oppressed. New York, NY: Bloomsbury Academic.
González, N. (2005). Beyond culture: The hybridity of funds of knowledge. In N. González, L. Moll, & C. Amanti (Eds.), *Funds of knowledge: Theorizing practices in households, communities, and classrooms.* Mahwah, NJ: Lawrence Erlbaum Associates.
Sheets, R. H. (2005). *Diversity pedagogy: Examining the role of culture in the teaching-learning process.* Boston, MA: Allyn & Bacon.

Chapter Two

Exploring the Traditions of Latino Children's Literature: Beyond Tokenism to Transformation

Howard L. Smith, Belinda Bustos Flores, and
Daniel Alejandro González

INTRODUCTION

Children's literature can have a lasting effect on young readers. Thoughtfully chosen children's books can make an important contribution to the academic and emotional development of Latino children (Steiner, Nash, & Chase, 2008). As Barry (1998) notes, "Multiethnic literature increases minority children's self-esteem" (p. 631). It enhances ethnic pride and influences how children view themselves and their culture, while scaffolding their language and literacy development (Nieto, 2010; Wilkens & Gamble, 1998). Research also shows that such literature supports the "validation of minority students' heritage, greater self-esteem, and increased respect and appreciation for diverse cultures" (Nilsson, 2005, p. 535). This helps "children develop positive attitudes and respect for individuals in all cultures" (Wilkens & Gamble, 1998, p. 28). When any cultural group is excluded or poorly represented (Guerena & Erazo, 2000), the clear implication is that the group is not valued by society. Authentic children's literature demonstrates and validates the contributions that Latinos have made to the U.S. and the world. Similar to African American children's literature (Bishop, 2012), we suggest that Latino children's literature presents both the universality of human life and the uniqueness of the Latino experience.

Despite the indisputable contributions that such literature makes to the social, emotional, and cognitive well-being of young readers, there is a dearth of Latino children's literature in schools, libraries, and bookstores (Guerena & Erazo, 2000; Nilsson, 2005). The growing Latino population notwithstanding, there are several impediments to the production and acquisition of quality Latino children's literature. In this chapter, we explore the critical elements and define critically, culturally conscious books for and about Latino children and the process for their selection. Through our discussion, we also problematize the structural, ideological, and cultural realities that contribute to the status and vitality of present-day Latino children's literature.

THEORETICAL FRAMEWORK

While book publishers categorize any books with non-white characters as multicultural (Hill, 1998), authentic children's literature for Latino youth should be "culturally conscious." According to Harris (1990), culturally conscious texts "have major characters who are members of a particular ethnic group, textually identified as members, with a story set in an ethnic community or home . . . [and] told from the perspective of a member of that ethnic group" (p. 550). It is not the mere presence of an ethnic name or a character with a typical "ethnic phenotype" (e.g., features, skin color, hair) that creates a culturally conscious text. Hill (1998) elaborates on the important characteristics and objectives of this literature:

> Culturally conscious material presents children with accurate, non-stereotypical depictions [that] instill pride in children of the same ethnicity by validating and affirming cultural attributes. . . . [Such] books make children of all ethnicities aware that history was written by the dominant group and alert them to oppression in history and the present. . . . This literature also gives children an appreciation of the contributions of many cultural groups. (p. 37)

Prior research has used this notion of culturally conscious books as a metric for selecting appropriate literature for various minority groups (e.g., Yokota, 1993). Beyond culturally conscious, Martínez-Roldán (2013) posits:

> Approaching children's literature from a critical multicultural perspective implies that, when reading and analyzing the literature, we attend not just to its literary quality as art but also to issues of power and representation of people of various cultural backgrounds. (p. 6)

In our volume, we recommend that in addition to critical multicultural perspectives, we must also critically examine the use of language(s) and bilingualism representation in selecting authentic Latino children's literature. In the following discussion, we present theories that explicate the efficacy of children's literature for psychosocial, conceptual, and academic purposes. We also discuss the components (i.e., cultural and linguistic) of authentic, critically conscious Latino children's literature.

Identity Development

As mentioned in the first chapter, Latino children's literature can assist with ethnic identity development and affinity (see also chapters 3, 9, and 13). When texts mirror the child's life experiences, geographic roots, or cultural legacies, cultural and linguistic critically conscious children's literature connects with Latino readers in a way not possible through Eurocentric texts (Morgan, 2009: Naidoo, 2011a). In this volume you will read reflections of children's authors and illustrators as well as read the editors' *testimonios* (see chapter 14) in which they speak about the lack of Latino children's books. These speak to the importance of Latino children's literature. Such stories not only engage the imagination but also fortify the child's sense of well-being. Literature that affirms their culture helps Latino children and youth construct a healthy identity (Ghiso & Campano, 2013; Groenke et al., 2015; Naidoo, 2011b; see chapter 3). Al-Hazza (2010) finds that culturally conscious literature, such as Latino children's books, is not only for minorities. She suggests that multicultural children's literature also benefits mainstream children because it helps them to "understand commonalities of shared values, beliefs, and customs of people, whether the cultural commonalities are the same or dramatically different" (64).

We suggest that cultural and linguistic critically conscious Latino children's literature has the power to engage Latino children beyond functional literacy, such as reading and writing, into a deeper appreciation of their world and beyond. Further, when accompanied by critical engagement (e.g., reflective writing, dialogue) such culturally and linguistically based texts become a tool to overcome the sociopolitical and economic barriers that impede the academic and social achievement of Latino children (Martinez-Roldán, 2013; Naidoo, 2011b).

Conceptual Development

Clearly, culturally grounded Latino children's literature provides aesthetic and emotional enjoyment to the reader (Freeman, Feeney, & Moravcik, 2011). In addition, stories that faithfully represent Latino culture and traditions can also be purveyors of new information that promote conceptual and academic development (see chapter 1). In the hands of a skilled educator, linguistic and cultural critically conscious literature supports explorations of what is already known and those concepts that exist beyond the child's local understanding (Moll, Amanti, Neff, & González, 1992). In this way, Latino children's literature functions as a critical element for effective instruction. For Latinos and all children, literature that reflects their culture and the values of their community increase the likelihood of thoughtful engagement. As the chapters in part III of this volume will attest, children's literature supports learning in all the content areas, including the sciences (Ediger, 2010), mathematics (Iliev & D'Angelo, 2014), social studies (Alamillo & Arenas, 2012), and the language arts (DeNicolo & Fránquiz, 2006).

Critical Elements of Latino Children's Multicultural Literature

So that selected literature contributes to a Latino child's psychosocial, conceptual, and academic development, teachers and other professionals must be cognizant of certain vital components and ensure their presence in the texts. Several elements merge to create a good, critically conscious children's book. Authors must blend the literary elements of characterization, plot, point of view, setting, style, and theme to create an engaging tale appropriate for the age they are trying to reach (Ada, 2003). More importantly, perhaps, stories for Latino children must demonstrate an appreciation for their worldview and cultural values (Alamillo & Arenas, 2012; Escamilla & Nathenson-Mejía, 2003). As they read stories that reflect their traditions and family values, Latino and other minority children "come to realize that their culture also makes important contributions to the world, thereby improving their own self-concepts, while nurturing pride in their heritage" (Wilkens & Gamble, 1998, p. 28). Though relatively new in the U.S., children's literature has a long tradition in the countries of Latin America. Following is a brief account of major events in the development of Latino children's literature.

Brief History of Children's Literature in Latin America

During the pre-Columbian era, Mesoamerican indigenous groups had oral traditions, which included poetry, songs, and stories. Some oral traditions were expressed through hieroglyphs or pictographs. After the Spanish Conquest, friars collected, transcribed, and translated poems, songs, and stories into Spanish (Restall, Sousa, & Terraciano, 2005). The *Popol Vuh*, the premier example of Mayan poetry telling the story of the earth's creation, was translated into Spanish as well as many other languages (Christianson, 2007; Powell, 2005; Salter, 1989). Also, Brinton's Library of Aboriginal American Literature, number 7 (circa 1400–1800), published a collection of poems written both in Nahuatl and Spanish (Anonymous, 1890). While many indigenous poems and songs were eradicated during the conquest (Powell, 2005), oral traditions, such as *dichos, adivinanzas, consejos*, and *cuentos* continue to be evident in our Spanish-speaking communities (Acevedo, 1984).

Starting in the late 1800s and through the early 1900s, Latin American authors produced several remarkable works. Of special note was *Azul* (1888), a collection of short stories and poems penned by Nicaraguan poet Rubén Darío. Praised for its vivid imagery as well as its unfettered linguistic elegance, *Azul* was groundbreaking. Through its innovative lyrical structure it signaled the beginning of *modernismo* in Latin America (Montaldo, 1997).

Also, during this *modernismo* or boom period, stories of lush, verdant forests, wild animals, and breathtaking landscapes were en vogue throughout Latin American literature (Montaldo, 1997). Kane (2010) suggests that this was spurred on as a reaction to modernity and U.S. imperialism. Authors and critics wrote stories that paid homage to the indigenous people and their contributions (Montaldo, 1997). An exemplar of this "indigenous pride" genre written for children was *Cuentos de la selva* [Stories from the Forest] (1918) by Uruguayan Horacio Quiroga. Much like the tales of Rudyard Kipling, Quiroga's stories depicted wild animals and adventure. Arreguín-Anderson (see chapter 9) speaks to the use of the oral traditions as cultural relevant resources, such as *adivinanzas* (riddles) and *dichos* (sayings) to support children's acquisition of scientific concepts that are found in their natural surroundings.

Another great contributor to Latin American literature was Chilean writer and the 1945 Nobel Prize for Literature winner, Gabriela Mistral (see chapter 15). Much of her work, including poems and short stories, addressed social inequality and the plight of disadvantaged children in the Americas. She was a poet and recognized for her literary talent, her writing about children, and her social politics. An example of Mistral's recognized work is *Ternura: Canciones de niños* (1945).

Less indigenous in style was Colombian author Rafael Pombo (Orjuela, 1965), who produced his first works for children very much in the European tradition in 1854. His two-volume set of Spanish translations of English nursery rhymes titled *Cuentos pintados para niños* and *Cuentos morales para niños formales* was published in New York. So popular was this work that countless editions have been published since (e.g., *Cuentos pintados*, Pombo, 2008). Later he published a long list of titles, including the children's fables "Michín," "Juan Chunguero," "La pobre viejecita," "Simón el bobito," "El gato bandido," and "El renacuajo paseador," which were included in the 1916 anthology *Fábulas y verdades*. Though more than one hundred years old, they remain popular throughout Latin American to the current day and have been reproduced in a variety of multimedia.

In 1889, Cuban author and revolutionary José Martí created and edited a children's magazine titled *La edad de oro* [The Golden Age] (Martí, 2010; Montero, 2004) in New York. Groundbreaking in its appearance, in the four issues that were published, Martí wrote and selected original stories, folktales, essays, and biographies of people important to the Latin American community. Martí was both author and political activist, and many of the pieces he wrote or selected for publication included ideas of social transformation, objection to social stratification between the rich and the poor (*Los zapaticos de Rosa*), racism (*La muñeca negra*), pride in the indigenous culture of Latin America, and respect for foreign rights (Martí, 2010).

Despite *La edad de oro* and its effect of advancing dialogue on social issues for young audiences, literary creativity, and providing a Spanish publication outlet for children's authors in the U.S, there were notably few developments for Latino children's literature until the 1980s (Ada, 2003; Martínez-Roldán, 2013). Children's literature scholar Alma Flor Ada (2003) addresses this situation:

> For almost a hundred years, with the exception of a very few significant Latino writers, literature published for young audiences on Latino themes was virtually nonexistent. In the few instances in which non-Latino writers touched on Latino themes in the first seven decades of the century, Latino people were, at best, treated in a romanticized manner or as exotic creatures and most often in a very stereotypical and pejorative manner. (p. 41)

While there were innumerable titles of children's literature published in Latin America and Spain throughout the twentieth century, until the 1980s in the U.S., there was a dearth of children's books featuring Latino themes or images.

Children's Literature in the U.S.:
Conspicuous Absence of Minorities

In 1965, Nancy Larrick published *The All-White World of Children's Books* regarding African American children's literature. In her essay, she noted that "across the country 6,340,000 nonwhite children are learning to read and to understand the American way of life in books which either omit them entirely or scarcely mention them" (Larrick, 1965, p. 63). Several factors contributed to the power of Larrick's message. Publishers of children's books recognized Larrick as a prolific children's author. She was the president of the International Reading Association—a major voice in literacy circles with thousands of members. Finally, her critique emerged during the U.S. civil rights era (1954–1968), a time in which society was confronting structural inequalities within major institutions, including schooling, the media, and publishing. While there had been earlier critiques on the lack of representation (e.g., Baker, 1963; Rollins, 1959), based on Larrick's advocacy, "publishers took notice of their practices of exclusion and stereotyping" (Harris, 1990, p. 74). Even so, the initial focus was primarily on African American literature as Yokota surmises (1993), and there was less attention placed on other minority groups, such as Native Americans and Latinos. Varlejs (1978) recognizes this historical exclusion: "Somewhere in the sixties we woke up to the realization that minorities had been grossly misrepresented—when represented at all—in literature for young people. . . . For whatever reasons, specific discussions of Hispanic literature have been neglected." (p. 233).

In response, some publishers reviewed their extant inventories and multiculturized subsequent editions of more popular children's stories. Textually, this tokenism was accomplished through changing the name of a secondary character (e.g., "Mary" to "Maria"). Visually, some publishers inserted the face of a new "minority" character not present in the original edition. Baronberg's (1971) classic preschool picture book study noted that the illustrations of children were not distinguishable in terms of color or were shown as shadowed faces. These tactics preserved the original content and structure of the stories without capturing an authentic minority experience. Even as minority characters were added, research indicates that the internal structure of the stories (e.g., plot, worldview, cultural values) did not reflect Latinos or other minority groups presented in the children's stories (Botelho & Rudman, 2009; Harris, 1990; Morgan, 2011).

In the 1970s, as major publishers hired authors and illustrators from minority groups, some change was noted. As Micklos (1996) contends, "Children's books in general became more reflective of the world around them. In addition to better representing ethnic diversity, books for young people—especially in the new 'young adult' genre—began to address real-world issues such as death, divorce, and sex" (p. 61). During this same period, several new small presses opened, publishing children's books with a focus on specific ethnic and cultural groups (Micklos, 1996). In an attempt to gauge the success of "integrated" texts, in the late 1970s, Jeanne Chall and colleagues (Chall, Radwin, French, & Hall, 1979) replicated Larrick's study by reviewing 4,775 children's trade books published by the children's book presses between 1973 and 1975. The result: 689 books or 14.4 percent included one or more African American characters. This was more than a 100 percent increase from Larrick's (1965) survey. Glaringly missing, however, was any mention of Latinos or other marginalized groups (Micklos, 1996). Micklos (1996) elaborates:

> After signs of progress during the 1970s, the number of books written by minority authors leveled off and even began to drop in the early and mid-1980s. . . . Furthermore, books by and about Hispanics, Native Americans, Asians, and other ethnic minorities were even fewer. (p. 62)

In the U.S., social capital that promotes social mobility (Bourdieu & Thompson, 1991) includes skin color (e.g., white versus brown; Hunter, 2002), language (e.g., English versus Spanish; Clark, 2006); parental educational attainment (e.g., college versus grammar school), and immigration status (Valdez, Padilla, & Valentine, 2013). In the case of children's literature, Van Gelder (1996) notes that these forms of capital are linked to literacy competencies constructed in schools (e.g. print-based literacy, scientific literacy, and mathematical literacy). In so doing, these texts present minority groups as laborers or working-class individuals.

More than twenty-five years after Larrick's work, studies continue to find that children's books with Latino themes are a small percentage of books published or contain negative and stereotypic images (Barry, 1998). In her synthesis of the research on books with Latino characters or those written on Latino-related themes, Nilsson (2005) found that "a majority of investigators suggested the number of books with Hispanic representation written for children from preschool through high school age remains deplorably lacking" (p. 543). Even while there appears to be an increase in the absolute number of publications featuring Hispanics (Nilsson's term) "compared to the proportion of Hispanics who presently make up the United States population, there is indication that the relative proportion of Hispanic representation in children's literature has lost major ground" (Nilsson, 2005, p. 545). The consensus is that despite the slight advances of the last forty years, more improvements are necessary (Alamillo & Arenas, 2012; Bredegg, 2001; Hill, 1998; Jiménez-García, 2014; Micklos, 1996).

When studied from a global perspective, that is, all available titles published within a given period, the research indicates a paucity of children's books representing the Latino experience. Moreover, as Martínez-Roldán (2013) notes,

> Because of the many differences among Latinos, in language practices, social class, country of origin, and so forth, it is not possible for a children's book to accurately represent all Latinos as a group. Rather, teachers and children should have access to a variety of books that collectively represent students from various backgrounds and communities. (p. 13)

The goal of this volume is to present the rich, multicultural Latino children's literature that can be used in home, classroom, or library settings. In the following section, we give a brief historical account of books selected for honors by various organizations, or more specifically, award-winning children's books. Important to note is the limited number of awards received by authors of Latino children's books.

BRIEF HISTORICAL ACCOUNT OF CHILDREN'S BOOK AWARDS

Children's Literature Awards

A variety of agencies or literacy councils have selected and evaluated children's books published in the United States for almost one hundred years, including the Children's Book Council (CBC), the National Council of Teachers of English (NCTE), the International Literacy Association (ILA), and the American Library Association (ALA). While each organization has specific criteria, awards bestowed connote quality (e.g., outstanding writing style, poignant artwork) or exceptional engagement with a particular feature (e.g., artwork, genre; ALA, 2015a). The oldest book award in the U.S. is the Newbery Medal, awarded to notable children's literature since 1922 (Kidd, 2007). Eponymous with the eighteenth-century Englishman John Newbery (the first publisher and seller of children's books in the U.S.), the Newbery Medal is managed and conferred through the Association for Library Service to Children, a division of the ALA, and it is given to the book that makes the best contribution to children's literature that year (Thompson, 1988). Starting in 1938, the ALA initiated a companion honor, the Caldecott Medal, which was named for the nineteenth-century English illustrator Randolph Caldecott. This medal recognizes outstanding artwork in children's books. These awards are considered the premier achievements in children's literature (Thompson, 1988). In each successive decade, agencies developed new children's book awards with new criteria and perspectives (Morgan, 2011).

Van Gelder reviewed Newbery Medal award winners from 1986 to 1996 for the number of Latino-themed children's books recognized (Marks, 2006). Her study found that within the ten-year period, none of the winners "portrayed Hispanics as either major or minor characters" (Van Gelder, 1996). Iwamoto (1996) analyzed the content of award-winning children's literature from 1938 through 1995 by an examination of different social categories, including the ways different ethnic groupings were described and the themes of the books selected for the study. Using mixed methods (e.g., frequency, percentage, and thematic analysis), Iwamoto found that while some change had occurred over time, there continued to be an over-representation of white males as characters in stories and stereotyping in the areas representative of different cultures.

Children's Book Awards Reflecting Critically Conscious Literature

Certain specialized children's book awards recognize an author or illustrator who represents an ethnic or cultural group in an especially notable way (ALA, 2015a). Those texts considered for such awards invariably demonstrate the highest literary standards and possess an engaging story. At the same time, awarded books typically possess a "message" that dignifies the sociocultural experience of the designated cultural group in a manner appropriate for young readers. Starting in the mid-twentieth century, several national book awards were created to recognize stories that respectfully represented particular cultures or ethnic groups in children's literature (ALA, 2015a).

In 1950, less than ten years after the last Nazi concentration camp was closed, the Jewish Book Council (2015) created the National Jewish Book Award for Children's and Young Adult Literature and also the Louis Posner Memorial Award. Shortly thereafter, the Jane Addams Children's Book Award for children's books was created to honor children's literature that focused on "peace, social justice, world community, and the equality of the sexes and all races" (Jane Addams Children's Book Awards, 2015). This award was named for Nobel Peace Prize winner (1931) Jane Addams, who worked with immigrants and the underprivileged. Several decades later in 1970, the ALA awarded the first Coretta Scott King Book Award (ALA, 2015b), named after the wife of slain civil rights activist, Dr. Martin Luther King Jr. This honor recognizes outstanding stories by African American authors that focus on positive depictions of African Americans (ALA, 2015b). In 1978, a similar ALA award would be conferred upon outstanding African American illustrators (ALA, 2015a).

There are three notable honors for children's literature that fosters a positive image of Latino cultures or that affirms the social, cultural, linguistic, or historical contexts of Latino children: the Américas Award, the Tomás Rivera Mexican American Children's Book Award, and the Pura Belpré Award. The appellation of the first honor is derived from the Americas' geographic region and those connected to the same. The second and third pay homage to outstanding individuals from Latino cultures who have made significant contributions to society and who serve as role models for Latino children and educators.

The Américas Book Award for Children's and Young Adult Literature is a recognition given to fiction and nonfiction works created in the United States that portray the countries and cultures of Latin America or its people in a positive way. Inaugurated in 1993, the Américas award is conferred upon the authors of poems, folklore, stories, and other varieties of children's literature, written in English or Spanish.

In 1995, Texas State University at San Marcos established the Tomás Rivera Mexican American Children's Book Award. The honor was named after the late Mexican American writer and scholar Tomás Rivera, who rose from humble economic means to become chancellor of the University of California, Riverside, in 1979 until his death in 1984. The award was crafted to encourage authors and illustrators who created literature that authentically reflected the lives of Mexican American children and young adults in the Southwest (Byrd, 2005).

The Pura Belpré Award was named for the Puerto Rican writer/librarian Pura Belpré who worked tirelessly in the New York City Public Library system from 1921 until 1968 to bring joy to children through her puppet shows, story readings, poems, folktales, and librarianship (Hernández-Delgado, 1992). Besides invigorating library services for the Puerto Rican patrons of New York City, Belpré's accomplishments also include writing the first Puerto Rican folktale, "Pérez and Martina" (Hernández-Delgado, 1992) to be published in the United States. The Pura Belpré Award recognizes an original work that portrays, affirms, and celebrates the Latino cultural experience (Hernández-Delgado, 1992).

For over fifty years, children's book publishers have made efforts to produce texts that are more representative of cultural diversity and that include the perspectives of Latinos. A reasonable assumption is that children's literature awarded for literary excellence should be concomitantly culturally inclusive and affirming. Accordingly, many of the studies regarding critically conscious literature look to the published lists of award-winning children's books for insight into degrees of inclusion.

PRAXIS: APPLICATION OF THEORY

The inclusion of a Latino character or Spanish phrases is not sufficient to make a good Latino children's book. Latino children's literature should reflect both the distinctiveness of Latino cultural experiences and the universality of human experience. Also vital is that the experiences reflected do not perpetuate stereotypes in terms of linguistic or cultural referents (Chappell & Faltis, 2006). Several researchers and resources provide guidance for the selection of appropriate Latino children's literature (Botelho & Rudman, 2009; Garrison, 2012; Naidoo, 2011a; Smolen & Oswald, 2010; see chapter 6).

A perusal of the extant research on multicultural or Latino literature (Bishop, 2012; Levin, 2007; Louie, 2006; Morgan, 2011; Yokota, 1993) suggests four broad, overlapping categories for consideration when selecting Latino children's literature: (1) literary merit, (2) artistic (i.e., visual) merit, (3) cultural authenticity, and (4) critical consciousness. Outstanding or recommended Latino children's literature will have several elements from more than one category. Excellence within a single category is insufficient. Each of these elements as they pertain to Latino children's literature is discussed in the subsequent section.

Criteria for Selecting Latino Children's Literature

Literary Merit

Though there is no consensus, a good story is distinguishable by its aesthetic values, which include emotional complexity, originality, and the credibility of the story (Ada, 2003). In addition to an engaging plot or storyline, outstanding Latino children's literature contains realistic characters who are involved in plausible activities within an affirming cultural context (Meeker & Willis-Rivera, 2002). There are several notable examples: *The Revolution of Evelyn Serrano* (2012) a novel written by "Maria" of Sesame Street fame, tells the story of a fourteen-year-old Nuyorican Rican girl during the 1960s (Phil, 2007). Carmen Tafolla's *What Can You Do with a Rebozo?* (1998/2004) and later, *What Can You Do with a Paleta?* (1998; see part V) are engaging texts for all children but especially those with Mexican roots because they talk about two common items—the *rebozo* (shawl) and the *paleta* (popsicle).

Artistic Merit

Like literary merit, artistic merit refers to aesthetic considerations. The term in this context refers to the ways in which the images in a text stimulate the imagination and enhance the reading experience. To be effective, the artistic expressions used in Latino children's literature must support the message conveyed through the written system, that is, the illustrations must echo the meanings of the text. Just as important, the same images must also incorporate visual semiotics (i.e., signs, symbols, use of space) that complement the meanings of the text (Hosterman, 2005; see chapter 13).

When evaluating the illustrations of a Latino children's story, it is important to observe whether there is diversity among the populations represented. Does the illustrator make one character indistinguishable from another? Successful illustrators avoid stereotypes (Iwamoto, 1996). Also, conscientious illustrators create characters that realistically and genuinely represent people from the culture. Illustrator Elivia Savadier in her artwork for *I Love Saturdays y domingos* by Alma Flor Ada (2004) creates a variety of characters depicted in a positive manner. Conversely, illustrators who are indifferent may fabricate caricatures with exaggerated features designed to mock or dehumanize the culture depicted (Nilsson, 2005). Illustrations found in any book, especially literature destined for children's use, should stimulate the imagination in positive ways and avoid harmful stereotypes (see chapter 13).

Since 2000, the number of artists who collaborate on Latino children's literature has risen. In many cases, individuals are recognized both as authors and as illustrators. One example of a dually talented artist is Duncan Tonatiuh, who illustrated the cover for this textbook. His 2013 book titled *Pancho Rabbit and the Coyote: A Migrant's Tale* won the 2014 Tomás Rivera Mexican American Children's Book Award. The same book was awarded two honorable mentions, one for the illustrations and one for the text, from the Pura Belpré Award. Tonatiuh's *Separate Is Never Equal* (2014; see part V), most recently won the Jane Addams Children's Book Award under the Younger Readers Category.

Another prolific author and illustrator is Yuyi Morales, who provided the illustrations for such titles as the children's biography *Harvesting Hope: The Story of Cesar Chavez* (Krull & Morales, 2003; see part V), *Mi abuelita* (Johnston, Morales, & O'Meara, 2009; see part V), and some of her own stories such as *Just a Minute: A Trickster Tale* as well as *Counting Book* and *Nino Wrestles the World* (see chapter 13 and part V).

Authenticity

When discussing key elements in a text, literary scholars use the word "verisimilitude" to indicate the degree to which the author conveys the qualities of truth, credibility, or plausibility in the story (Martínez-Roldán, 2013). The same qualities apply to the concept of cultural authenticity (Yoo-Lee, Fowler, Adkins, Kim, & Davis, 2014). In multicultural literature, this refers to stories told from an insider's perspective, that is, the perspective of one who has been raised in, or who has extensively studied the community. In the case of Latino children's literature, cultural authenticity creates that verisimilitude in the text through three interrelated elements: plot, language, and character.

Plot

The plot of a story is the sequence of events that form the narrative. For cultural authenticity, a member of the culture should recognize the events as plausible for those within the culture. Authors who achieve this are able to present the universality and uniqueness of the Latino culture. For example, in the children's story *Family, Familia* by Diane Bertrand, she narrates the experience of Daniel González who gripes about attending a family reunion. He does not anticipate young people being present and, consequently, he does not expect to have any fun (Bertrand & Howard, 1999; see part V). Fortunately, he is pleasantly surprised. The story's primary theme, the joy and importance of family, will be recognized as a traditional value by Latino readers and appreciated by readers outside the Latino community.

Borrowing her plot structure from the Brothers Grimm, author/illustrator Bobbi Salinas-Norman (1998; see part V) puts a Southwest spin on the classic "The Three Little Pigs" with her protagonists Nacho, Tito, and Miguel. The story has the universal message that those who seem powerful may not be as powerful or scary as they would have you believe. Salinas keeps the trope of a "wolf wanting to eat the pigs" (he plans to turn them into *carnitas* and *chicharrones* for supper), but she resolves the conflict in a nonviolent, "vegan" way. This highly recommendable book garnered the Tomás Rivera Mexican American Children's Book Award in 1999 for its critically conscious story and the colorful, amusing illustrations. While brothers Nacho and Tito are depicted as Latino stereotypes (one brother sleeps in a hammock), brother Miguel, the hero-protagonist, is a Latino nerd who is shown working on his computer while surrounded by books with titles and authors.

Another book that has authenticity and is critically conscious is *My Very Own Room/Mi propio cuartito* by Amada I. Pérez and illustrated by Maya Christina González (Pérez & González, 2000; see part V), which tells the tale of a Mexican America girl who longs for a space of her own. What gives this story its authenticity is the notion of *familismo*—the idea that members of a family network engage in mutual support (see chapter 5). With the help of her various family members, the girl acquires her dream. Throughout the story, the narrator and protagonist of the story vacillates between the love she has for her bothersome family members (e.g., her dad snores, and her baby sister elbows her in the eye) and the longing she has for privacy and a quiet space. The idea of longing for a space of one's own is common to children of all ethnicities and could serve to start a classroom discussion on extended family and personal space. This story describes a big family living in a small house—like many Latino families—with frequent visits from other relatives from Mexico.

Another story plot that focuses on family is *Super Cilantro Girl/La Super-niña del Cilantro* written by Juan Felipe Herrera and illustrated by Honorio Robleda Tapia (2003; see part V). This fictional story centers on a Mexican American girl who fantasizes about being a superhero and who wants to save her mother who is trapped on the other side of the border. Universality comes from the longing that Super Cilantro Girl has for her mother. The cultural authenticity in this story comes from the problem: the U.S.–Mexican border that separates the daughter from the mother she misses. Stories like these present common challenges among some Mexican families without demeaning the culture or suggesting that the solution should come from someone outside the Latino community (see chapter 4).

Language

The great variation in the way Spanish is used within the Latino community is reflected in the way authors incorporate Spanish into their children's literature. One common approach is to translate mainstream texts from English into Spanish. Classic tales from the European tradition of Grimms' Fairytales and Hans Christian Andersen were perhaps the first to be translated (Andersen, Nadal, & Rackham, 1933). Countless others translations were to follow. One example by Babette Cole (1988; see part V) is *The Smelly Book/El libro apestoso*, in which the narrator uses rhyme to describe smelling things and situations.

There are Latino authors who write Latino-centric children's stories in English followed by a Spanish translation like Gary Soto's *Too Many Tamales/Qué montón de tamales* (Soto, Martinez, Ada, & Campoy, 1996; see part V). There are other, non-Latino authors like Joe Hayes who create engaging, authentic Latino-centric children's stories like *La llorona: The Weeping Woman* (2004; see part V), a traditional Mexican legend told in Spanish and English. Though dual-language books feature side-by-side English and Spanish translations, however, the mere presence of Spanish is not necessarily the best indicator of cultural authenticity.

The use of Spanish, in various forms, is one of the cultural markers found in Latino children's literature. In their attempt to represent the lived experience of Latinos, authors have "infused their works with various levels of Spanish language references in order to communicate the relationship between English and Spanish in their everyday lives" (González, 2009, p. 176). The language use and proficiency of Latinos is the result of historical, social, and cultural factors (Arteaga, 1997; González, 2009), which can be viewed as a bilingual continuum (Hornberger, 2004). At one extreme we find Latinos who speak only Spanish, and at the other extreme those who speak only English (González, 2009; Zentella, 2005). While a few are completely bilingual or *equilingual* (strong in both languages), most bilingual individuals have varying degrees of proficiency, including those who speak a few "catch phrases" and those who code switch (Dicker, 2003). Studies on language use in Latino children's literature find that authors use Spanish words and phrases for cultural flavor with varying degrees of success. "Spanish words and phrases hold considerable potential for enhancing the realism and cultural authenticity of English-based text, specifically by creating powerful bilingual images of characters, settings, and themes" (Barrera & Quiroa, 2003, p. 247). As Martínez-Roldán notes, "Literary realism and cultural authenticity can be advanced in English-based Latino children's literature through a modest number of carefully selected Spanish terms that are well integrated, rather than by a large number of ill-selected words" (2013, p. 8).

In their review of Spanish-language use in *Rainbow Tulip* by Pat Mora and illustrated by Elizabeth Sayles (Mora & Sayles, 2003; see part V), Barrera and Quiroa (2003) note that language choice is used to demarcate social distance between the main character and others. For example, they find the word *mamá* to be "the more intimate term reserved for the child's dialogue with her mother . . . [while its] English equivalent is a more public form for communicating with the reader and pointing to the girl's developing bilingualism." Barrera and Quiroa maintain that the judicious use of even a limited lexicon in Spanish could contribute to a positive imaging of Latinos in a children's text. Again, the author's respect and understanding of the culture is reflected in word choice.

This contrasts with another approach to infusing culture into a story, an approach termed "mock Spanish" (Hill, 1995). Martínez-Roldán (2013) defines this as the "borrowing or incorporation of particular Spanish words or elements into English in a way that strategically misrepresents and stereotypes the subordinated group" (p. 8). The result of this process is that a minority culture is demeaned. Researchers would agree that whether the use of mock Spanish is intentional or not, it serves to reproduce racist ideology (Hill, 1995; Martinez-Roldán, 2013). In Latino children's literature, mock Spanish is constructed in one of two ways, either through (1) affixation of morphemes to English words (e.g., "no problem-o," "el cheap-o," and "bird-ito") or through (2) "bold mispronunciation" of English words (e.g., "none of your beezness"; Martínez-Roldán, 2013).

The quintessential example of mock Spanish in children's literature is the *Skippyjon Jones* book series, written by Schachner (2005). The protagonist, Skippyjon Jones, is a white Siamese cat with blue eyes who longs to be a Mexican Chihuahua dog. In an attempt to give her stories Latino "flair," the author infuses each story with exaggerated Spanish pronunciation and ill-placed "ito" endings; for example, "I get the job done, yes indeedo" (Schachner, 2005).

Though such words are relatively few, the author's intentional misuse of Spanish vocabulary reinforces stereotypes and "creates negative images of Mexicans, the places they live, and the language they speak" (Martínez-Roldán, 2013, p. 11). Another example that promotes stereotypes is MacDonald's *You Wouldn't Want to Be an Aztec Sacrifice: Gruesome Things You'd Rather Not Know* (2013). This author has a series of books that perpetuates stereotypes of various groups and distorts historical accounts through its texts and illustrations. While not every author outside of the community writes egregiously bad Latino children's books, teachers, librarians, and curriculum developers should take care when making their selection of children's books for Latino children.

Using these guidelines, while also considering that children's literature should be critically conscious, we have developed a checklist for selecting authentic, critically conscious Latino children's literature that can be found at the end of this chapter. We have also identified quality Latino children's literature that meets these criteria, which that can be found in part V of this volume.

CONCLUSION

Studies cited indicate that publications of Latino children's literature are more inclusive of the Latino reality and may have fewer stereotypes. Yet this type of negativity and tokenism is still found as demonstrated in the examples cited in this chapter. Latino children need to read literature that "represents the excellence of their culture, demonstrates their culture's powerful award-winning texts, shows identifiable role models and proves accomplishments of [their] people" (Hasse, 2002, p. 15). When selecting critically conscious literature, educators should pay attention to illustrations, the plot, and the selected languages. There is a rich history that represents the wisdom, the victories, and the values of our Latino culture that should be presented in Latino children's literature. We concur with Chappell and Faltis (2007) that "the impact of stories lies both in their ability to create imagined worlds of experience and to craft messages about the values, attitudes and beliefs people embody in both imagined and . . . lived worlds" (p. 260). While it may challenge educators to locate high-quality literature that authentically presents the Latino experience, the benefit for students is well worth the effort.

REFERENCES

Acevedo, M. (1984). *La novela centroamericana: Desde el "Popol-Vuh" hasta los umbrales de la novela.* Reviewed by Joan E. Ciruti. *Hispanic Review, 52*(1), 107–8.

Ada, A. F. (2003). *A magical encounter: Latino children's literature in the classroom* (2nd. ed.). Boston, MA: Allyn & Bacon.

Al-Hazza, T. C. (2010). Motivating disengaged readers through multicultural children's literature. *New England Reading Association Journal, 45*(2), 63.

Alamillo, L. A., & Arenas, R. (2012). Chicano children's literature: Using bilingual children's books to promote equity in the classroom. *Multicultural Education, 19*(4), 53–62.

American Library Association (2015a). ALA Book, Print and Media Awards. Retrieved from www.ala.org/awardsgrants/awards/browse/bpma?showfilter=no.

American Library Association (2015b). Coretta Scott King Book Awards. Retrieved from www.ala.org/emiert/coretta-scott-king-book-awards-illustrations-gallery.

American Library Association (2015c). Pura Belpré Award. Retrieved from www.ala.org/awardsgrants/pura-belpr%C3%A9-award.

Andersen, H. C., Nadal, A., & Rackham, A. (1933). *Cuentos de Hans Andersen.* Barcelona, Spain: Editorial Juventud.

Anonymous. (1890). *Ancient Nahuatl poetry, containing the Nahuatl text of XXVII ancient Mexican poems.* (Original work circa 1400–1800). *Ancient Nahuatl poetry, number VII.* (D. G. Brinton, trans.). London, UK: Briton's Library of Aboriginal American Literature.

Arteaga, A. (1997). *Chicano poetics: Heterotexts and hybridities.* New York, NY: Cambridge University Press.

Baker, A. (1963). *Books about Negro life for children.* New York, NY: New York Public Library.

Baronberg, J. (1971). Black representation in children's books. New York, NY: ERIC Information Retrieval Center on the Disadvantaged, Teachers College, Columbia University.

Barrera, R., & Quiroa, R. (2003). The use of Spanish in Latino children's literature in English: What makes for cultural authenticity? In D. Fox & K. G. Short (Eds.), *Stories matter: The complexity of cultural authenticity in children's literature* (pp. 247–65). Urbana, IL: National Council of Teachers of English.

Barry, A. L. (1998). Hispanic representation in literature for children and young adults. *Journal of Adolescent and Adult Literacy, 41*(8), 630.

Bishop, R. S. (2012). Reflections on the development of African American children's literature. *Journal of Children's Literature, 38*(2), 5–13.

Botelho, M. J., & Rudman, M. K. (2009). *Critical multicultural analysis of children's literature: Mirrors, windows, and doors.* New York, NY: Routledge.

Bourdieu, P., & Thompson, J. B. (1991). *Language and symbolic power.* Cambridge, MA: Harvard University Press.

Bredegg, P. S. (2001). *Portrayal of Hispanics in state-adopted textbooks, grades one, three, and five: A content analysis.* (Dissertation/Thesis). ProQuest Digital Dissertations.

Brown, M. I. (1996). *Multicultural youth materials selection.* (Dissertation/Thesis). ProQuest, UMI Dissertations Publishing.

Chall, J. S., Radwin, E., French, V. W., & Hall, C. R. (1979). Blacks in the world of children's books. *Reading Teacher, 32*(5), 527–33. doi:10.2307/20194821.

Chappell, S., & Faltis, C. (2007). Spanglish, bilingualism, culture and identity in Latino Children's Literature. *Children's Literature in Education, 38,* 253–62.

Center for Latin American and Caribbean Studies (2015). Américas Book Award. Milwaukee, WI: University of Wisconsin, Milwaukee. Retrieved from www4.uwm.edu/clacs/aa/.

Christenson, A. J. (2007). Popol Vuh: Sacred book of the Quiché Maya people. Translated and commentary. Electronic version of original 2003 publication. Retrieved May 10, 2015, from www.mesoweb.com/publications/Christenson/PopolVuh.pdf.

Clark, T. (2006). Language as social capital. *Applied Semiotics, 8,* 29–41.

Darío, R. (1888). *Azul.* Argentina.

DeNicolo, C. P., & Fránquiz, M. E. (2006). "Do I have to say it?" Critical encounters with multicultural children's literature. *Language Arts, 84*(2), 157–70.

Dicker, S. J. (2003). *Languages in America: A pluralist view* (vol. 42). Cleveland, OH: Multilingual Matters.

Ediger, M. (2010). Children's literature and the science curriculum. *Journal of Instructional Psychology, 37*(2), 117.

Escamilla, K., & Nathenson-Mejía, S. (2003). Preparing culturally responsive teachers: Using Latino children's literature in teacher education. *Equity and Excellence in Education, 36*(3), 238. doi:10.1080/714044331.

Freeman, N. K., Feeney, S., & Moravcik, E. (2011). Enjoying a good story: Why we use children's literature when teaching adults. *Early Childhood Education Journal*, *39*(1), 1–5.

Garrison, K. L. (2012). "This intense desire to know the world": Factors influencing the selection of multicultural children's literature. (Dissertation/Thesis). ProQuest, UMI Dissertations Publishing.

Ghiso, M. P., & Campano, G. (2013). Ideologies of language and identity in U.S. children's literature. *Bookbird: A Journal of International Children's Literature*, *51*(3), 47–55.

González, T. (2009). Art, actvism and community: An introducation to Latina/o literature. In M. P. Stewart & Y. Atkinson (Eds.), *Ethnic literary traditions in American children's literature* (pp. 171–89). New York, NY: Palgrave Macmillan.

Groenke, S. L., Haddix, M., Glenn, W. J., Kirkland, D. E., Price-Dennis, D., & Coleman-King, C. (2015). Disrupting and dismantling the dominant vision of youth of color. *English Journal*, *104*(3), 35–40.

Guerena, S., & Erazo, E. (2000). Latinos and librarianship. *Library Trends*, *49*(1), 138–81.

Harris, V. J. (1990). African American children's literature: The first one hundred years. *Journal of Negro Education*, *59*(4), 540–55.

Hasse, K. (2002). Beware of harmful Latino male stereotypes in children's literature. *Delta Kappa Gamma Bulletin*, *68*(4), 15.

Hernández-Delgado, J. L. (1992). Pura Teresa Belpré, storyteller and pioneer Puerto Rican librarian. *Library Quarterly*, *62*(4), 425–40. doi:10.2307/4308742.

Hill, J. (1995). *Mock Spanish: A site for the indexical reproduction of racism in American English.* Paper presented at the Language and Culture, Symposium 2. Binghamton University, Binghamton, New York.

Hill, T. J. (1998). Multicultural children's books: An American fairy tale. *Publishing Research Quarterly*, *14*(1), 36–45. doi:10.1007/s12109-998-0004-9.

Hornberger, N. H. (2004). The continua of biliteracy and the bilingual educator: Educational linguistics in practice. *International Journal of Bilingual Education and Bilingualism*, *7*(2/3), 155–71.

Hosterman, A. (2005). Transmediation in the classroom: A semiotics-based media literacy framework. *American Journal of Semiotics*, *21*(1–4), 140.

Hunter, M. L. (2002). "If you're light you're alright": Light skin color as social capital for women of color. *Gender and Society*, *16*(2), 175–93. doi:10.1177/08912430222104895.

Iliev, N., & D'Angelo, F. (2014). Teaching mathematics through multiculture literature. *Teaching Children Mathematics*, *20*(7), 452.

Iwamoto, V. V. (1996). *The portrayal of ethnicity, gender, ages, character roles and themes in award-winning children's literature from 1938 through 1995.* (Dissertation/Thesis). ProQuest, UMI Dissertations Publishing.

Jane Addams Peace Association (2015). Jane Addams Children's Book Awards. Retrieved from www.janeaddamspeace.org/jacba/.

Jewish Book Council (2015). National Jewish Book Award. Retrieved from www.jewishbookcouncil.org/awards/national-jewish-book-award.html.

Jiménez-García, M. (2014). Pura Belpré lights the storyteller's candle: Reframing the legacy of a legend and what it means for the fields of Latino/a studies and children's literature. *Centro Journal, 26*(1), 110.

Kane, A. T. (Ed.). (2010). *The natural world in Latin American literatures: Ecocritical essays on twentieth-century writings.* Jefferson, NC: Mcfarland & Company.

Kidd, K. B. (2007). Prizing children's literature: The case of Newbery gold. *Children's Literature, 35*(1), 166–90.

Larrick, N. (1965). The all-white world of children's books. *Saturday Review of Literature,* 63–65.

Levin, F. (2007). Children's books: Encouraging ethical respect through multicultural literature. *Reading Teacher, 61*(1), 101–4. doi:10.1598/RT.61.1.13.

Louie, B. Y. (2006). Guiding principles for teaching multicultural literature. *Reading Teacher, 59*(5), 438.

MacDonald, F., & Antram, D. (2013). *You wouldn't want to be an Aztec sacrifice: Gruesome things you'd rather not know.* Danbury, CT: Franklin Watts.

Marks, D. F. (2006). *Children's book award handbook.* Westport, CT: Libraries Unlimited.

Martí, J. (2010). *La edad de oro.* Barcelona: Linkgua Ediciones. (Original work published 1889).

Martínez-Roldán, C. M. (2013). The representation of Latinos and the use of Spanish: A critical content analysis of *Skippyjon Jones. Journal of Children's Literature, 39*(1), 5–14.

Meeker, M., & Willis-Rivera, J. (2002). *De qué colores*: A critical examination of multicultural children's books. *Communication Education, 51*(3), 269–79. doi:10.1080/03634520216515.

Micklos, J., Jr. (1996). Thirty years of minorities in children's books. *Education Digest, 62*(1), 61.

Mistral, G. (1945). *Ternura: Canciones de niños.* Buenos Aires, Argentina: Espasa-Calpe Argentina.

Moll, L. C., Amanti, C., Neff, D., & González, N. (1992). Funds of knowledge for teaching: Using a qualitative approach to connect homes and classrooms. *Theory into Practice, 31*(2), 132–41.

Montaldo, G. (1997). *Sobre Rubén Darío, Azul . . . Cantos de vida y esperanza. Revista Iberoamericana, 63*(180). doi:10.5195/reviberoamer.1997.6214.

Montero, O. (2004). *José Martí: An introduction.* London, UK: Palgrave Macmillan.

Morgan, H. (2009). Gender, racial, and ethnic misrepresentation in children's books: A comparative look. *Childhood Education, 85*(3), 187.

———. (2011). Over one hundred years of misrepresentation: American minority groups in children's books. *American Educational History Journal, 38*(1–2), 357.

Naidoo, J. C. (Ed). (2011a). *Celebrating cuentos: Promoting Latino children's literature and literacy in classrooms and libraries.* Santa Barbara, CA: Libraries Unlimited.

———. (2011b). Embracing the face at the window: Latino representation in Latino children's literature and the ethnic idenity development of Latino children. In J. C. Naidoo, *Celebrating cuentos: Promoting Latino children's literature and literacy in classrooms and libraries* (pp. 19–44). Santa Barbara, CA: Libraries Unlimited.

Nieto, S. (2010). *The light in their eyes: Creating multicultural learning communities.* New York, NY: Teachers College Press.

Nilsson, N. L. (2005). How does Hispanic portrayal in children's books measure up after 40 years? The answer is "It depends." *Reading Teacher, 58*(6), 534–48. doi:10.2307/20205519.

Nobel Prize for Literature. Retrieved June 12, 2015, from www.nobelprize.org/ nobel_prizes/literature/laureates/1945/mistral-facts.html.

Orjuela, H. H., & Ortiz, R. P. (1965). *Biografía y bibliografía de Rafael Pombo.* Institutto Caro y Cuervo.

Phil, H. (2007). "Where am I?" A call for "connectednes" in literacy. *Reading Research Quarterly, 42*(3), 420.

Pombo, R. (1916). *Fábulas y verdades.* Bogotá, Colombia: Imprenta Nacional.

———. (2008). *Cuentos pintados.* Bogotá, Colombia: Babel Libros.

Powell, T. B. (2005). Recovering precolonial American literary history: "The origin of stories" and the Popol Vuh. In S. Castillo & I. Schweitzer (Eds.), *A companion to the literatures of Colonial America.* Oxford, UK: Blackwell Publishing.

Quiroga, H. (1918). *Cuentos de la selva para los niños.* Argentina.

Restall, M., Sousa, L., & Terraciano, K. (2005). *Mesoamerican voices: Native-language writings from Colonial Mexico, Oaxaca, Yucatan, and Guatemala.* New York, NY: Cambridge University Press.

Rollins, C. (1959). Books about negroes for children. *ALA Bulletin, 53*, 306–8.

Salter, M. A. (1989). Leisure-time pursuits of the Quiché Maya: Perspectives from the "Popol Vuh." *Aethlon, 6*(2), 239.

Schachner, J. B. (2005). *Skippyjon Jones in the dog house.* New York, NY: Dutton Children's Books.

Smolen, L., & Oswald, R. (2010). *Multicultural literature and response: Affirming diverse voices.* Santa Barbara, CA: Libraries Unlimited.

Steiner, S. F., Nash, C. P., & Chase, M. (2008). Children's books: Multicultural literature that brings people together. *Reading Teacher, 62*(1), 88–92. doi:10.2307/ 20204665.

Tafolla, C., & Córdova, A. (2008). *What can you do with a rebozo?* Berkeley, CA: Tricycle Press.

Thompson, R. A. (1988). Children's books: Awards and medals. *Children's Literature Association Quarterly, 13*(2), 96–96.

Tomás Rivera Organization (2015). The Tomás Rivera Mexican American Children's Book Award. Retrieved from http://riverabookaward.org/.

Valdez, C. R., Padilla, B., & Valentine, J. L. (2013). Consequences of Arizona's immigration policy on social capital among Mexican mothers with unauthorized immigration status. *Hispanic Journal of Behavioral Sciences, 35*(3), 303–22.

Van Gelder, M. (1996). Multiethnic representation in Newbery award books. (Unpublished master's thesis). Lawrence, KS: University of Kansas.

Varlejs, J. (Ed.). (1978). Young adult literature in the seventies: A selection of readings. Metuchen, NJ: Scarecrow Press.

Wilkens, J., & Gamble, R. (1998). Evaluating multicultural literature for use in the classroom. *Educational Considerations, 26*(2), 28–31.

Yokota, J. (1993). Issues in selecting multicultural children's literature. *Language Arts, 70*(3), 156–67.

Yoo-Lee, E., Fowler, L., Adkins, D., Kim, K.-S., & Davis, H. N. (2014). Evaluating cultural authenticity in multicultural picture books: A collaborative analysis for diversity education. *Library Quarterly, 84*(3), 324–47. doi:10.1086/676490.

Zentella, A. C. (2005). *Building on strength: Language and literacy in Latino families and communities*. New York, NY: Teachers College Press.

Checklist for Authentic, Critically Conscious, Latino Children's Literature

1. Story
   a. Are the stories interesting to children?
   b. Are there various conflicts for the children to explore?
   c. How are the conflicts resolved?
2. Characters
   a. Do the characters represent a variety of socioeconomic levels and vocations?
   b. Do "good" characters reflect a variety of backgrounds?
   c. Are females as well as males depicted in leadership roles?
3. Themes
   a. Does the story reflect the social, cultural, and historical reality of Latinos?
   b. Are values being explored instead of preached?
   c. Are there lessons to be learned?
4. Settings
   a. Do the stories reflect a variety of settings?
   b. Are urban, suburban, and rural settings represented realistically?
   c. Are cultural settings represented realistically?
5. Illustrations
   a. Is there diversity represented within cultural groups?
   b. Are characters realistically and genuinely represented?
   c. Do the illustrations avoid reinforcing societal stereotypes?
6. Other considerations
   a. Does the story present an "insider's" perspective?
   b. Are children exposed to multiple perspectives and values?
   c. Do the stories promote understanding of our diverse society?
   d. Is the language used authentically? (Hasse, 2002, p. 15)

DISCUSSION QUESTIONS

1. As we stated in this chapter, Latinos are not all the same. How do you decide whether a children's story selected for a class reflects the experiences of your Latino students? What kinds of feedback do you take from your students to be sure the text is connecting with them?

2. Just as there are different varieties of English (e.g., American, British, Australian), there are different varieties of Spanish (e.g., Puerto Rican, Peninsular, Guatemalan, Mexican). While some have tried to construct these differences as problematic or a hindrance to enjoyment of the literature, they should be seen as rich regional synonyms. What instructional strategies do you utilize when an author uses a variety of Spanish that is different from that of your students?

3. Despite the criticism leveled against books like the *Skippyjon Jones* series, they remain popular. What might teachers (and parents) find so appealing? How would you explain to a colleague or parent the adverse effects of this text? What authentic Latino children's texts would you suggest as an alternative?

4. When trying to infuse your classroom instruction with culturally authentic Latino children's literature, what resources (e.g., websites, bookstores, libraries) do you find most helpful? What are the titles that you would recommend to your library?

ACTIVITIES

A. Create an "author set" by selecting four or more titles written by the same author with a Latino theme. Evaluate each of the books in the set using the guidelines presented in this chapter and create a presentation that demonstrates whether the author provides an insider's or an outsider's perspective in their story.

B. Create an "illustrator set" by selecting four or more titles illustrated by the same artist with a focus on the Latino community. Review and analyze the illustrations to see how the images support an appreciation of Latino culture.

C. Select a children's book written primarily in English with Spanish words occasionally mixed in. Review the use of Spanish in the text. Using the guidelines from this chapter, analyze the authenticity of the use of Spanish in the text.

D. Select a children's story from the European tradition (e.g., "Cinderella" and "The Three Little Pigs") and a similar text with a Latino perspective.

Compare and contrast the two books. Create a visual display using a Venn diagram.

E. Search each of these organization's websites: Children's Book Council (CBC), the National Council of Teachers of English (NCTE), the International Literacy Association (ILA), and the American Library Association (ALA). Also explore the criteria for each of these awards: the Américas Award, the Tomás Rivera Mexican American Children's Book Award, and the Pura Belpré Award. Create a table and organize the information for each award and identify the current Latino children's book author and illustration award winners.

Part II

MULTICULTURAL CHILDREN'S LITERATURE REPRESENTING LATINO REALITIES

Figure 3.1.

Multicultural literature serves many important roles; one of them being that it allows Latino children to see that they are reflected in the very books that they read. It seems like a simple concept, right? All children should be able to see themselves reflected in the very stories that they read, right? But more often than not that hasn't been the case. Another important role for multicultural literature is that it educates us about cultures that are different from our own.

—Xavier Garza, November 5, 2014

Chapter Three

Beyond *Calaveras* and *Quinceañeras*: Fostering Bilingual Latino Students' Identity Development with Culturally Relevant Literature

Jamie Campbell Naidoo and Ruth E. Quiroa

I saw and heard myself in the characters and stories in this book. I wasn't then, nor am I now a Puerto Rican Kid growing up in New York City, but man, if those Latino characters weren't telling my very own story in my very own language, there wouldn't be a character in the world of books who could.

—René Saldaña Jr. (2013, ii–iii)

INTRODUCTION

Bilingual Latino children and youth come from heterogeneous cultural backgrounds representing diverse facets of the Latino cultural experience in the U.S. Some may be second-generation immigrants while others might be newcomers, and still others may be the children of Latino parents whose ancestors have been in the U.S. for decades. These youth all fall under the U.S. umbrella definition of "Latino" and can represent cultural heritages from Mexico, Puerto Rico, Cuba, or any number of countries in Central and South America and portions of the Caribbean. For these youth to truly make connections with literature that will inform their identity development, the books and digital media they encounter in classrooms and libraries must include diverse Latino characters from a variety of linguistic, socioeconomic, and cultural perspectives. At the same time, it is important that educators give Latino youth the space to navigate their cultural identities with the literature/media and not attempt to match perceived readers' heritages with those of characters in books.

Children's and young adult literature, particularly books about diverse Latino cultures, can be very influential in assisting Latino youth as they develop their ethnic identities. The history of youth literature available in the U.S. about the various Latino cultures indicates a marked distinction in quality, ranging from cultural stereotypes and omissions to celebrations of diverse cultural heritages (Naidoo, 2011; Ada, 2003). The quality of a particular piece of literature and its portrayal of Latino cultures can have either a positive or negative impact upon the self-esteem and identity development of young Latinos. For instance, if children encounter books that depict Spanish-speaking Latino characters as poor or unintelligent, then they will assume speaking Spanish is a hindrance to success. Fostering such attitudes is problematic, even more so when a child's home language is Spanish or a variation of Spanish, and the school environment promotes English-only communication. The children may develop feelings of unworthiness when instructed to speak Spanish or feel a disconnection between their home and school contexts.

The above examples ostensibly focus on the idea that youth will be exposed to Latino cultures in the school curriculum. What happens if a child never encounters their language or culture in the educational and recreational materials at school? Numerous authors—such as Esmeralda Santiago, Isabel Quintero, Maya Christina González, and René Colato Laínez—have described feelings of inadequacy during childhood due to the cultural absence of Spanish-speaking, bilingual, or Latino characters in the books they either were assigned to read in school or encountered in the classroom or library. Often many of these authors express anger at having their voices silenced and urge educators to include Latino youth literature in the school curriculum to assist students with their identity development (Santiago, 2000; Quintero, 2014).

Many well-meaning teachers, librarians, and other educators understand the importance of including literature on diverse topics in the curriculum but may not be aware of the body of Latino youth literature currently available, or they may simply relegate its use to Hispanic/Latino Heritage Month. Unfortunately, the highest quality materials and culturally authentic activities are irrelevant if Latino youth learn that their language and culture are not good enough to study or talk about throughout the year. Other educators may rely on the Five Fs approach to exploring cultural diversity: food, fashion, festivals, famous people, and folklore (Begler, 1998). While this educational practice is not completely objectionable, it cannot be the only way to introduce students to Latino culture. It is important for teachers and librarians to be sensitive when using the Five Fs to avoid cultural stereotyping. Often this approach tends to focus on Latino cultural elements that are flamboyant, mysterious, or charming rather than introducing learners to the contemporary, daily experiences and values of Latino youth. When educators rely on the Five Fs to explore Latino cultural diversity, it is extremely problematic if any of the Fs are not culturally accurate or reinforce outdated stereotypes. Sharing only folktales, such as "La llorona" or "Juan Bobo," with children can give them a distorted view of Latino culture and reinforce stereotyped beliefs. Introducing students to books where Latinos *only* wear peasant outfits or traditional "costumes," such as Mariachi outfits or *folklórico* dresses, can reinforce a sense of exoticism rather than fostering positive identity formation. Discussing Latino culture within the context of celebrations such as *El día de los muertos* or *Quinceañeras* is certainly an acceptable way to integrate cultural aspects into the curriculum. Students can make candy *calaveras* to celebrate *Día de los muertos* [The Day of the Dead], but they also need opportunities to see Latinos engaging in daily activities and facing common problems that bilingual youth encounter. We advocate for incorporating diverse Latino youth literature in the school curriculum throughout the year while also focusing on topics relevant to Latinos' lives, such as stories highlighting daily life experiences in all types of settings. These can include celebrating family and cultural roots; focusing on friendships, peer relationships, and school life; presenting informational narratives and biographies; examining immigration experiences; and exploring bilingual and bicultural experiences in texts that may also incorporate contemporary issues present in general literature for youth.

THEORETICAL FRAMEWORK

Multiple theoretical lenses have been used to explore factors that influence the cultural identity and experiences of youth (Hallowell, 1955; Vygotsky, 1986; Cummins, 2001). These theories explain how the print and digital media that youth consume along with their everyday encounters at home, school, or within the community can augment students' thoughts and feelings toward their cultural group. The review of the literature on reader response theory further indicates that youth can exhibit multiple responses to the text and illustrations of a book and construct meaning based upon numerous factors (Rosenblatt, 1995; Sumara, 1996; Cai, 2002). These include the cultural background(s) and prior experiences of the reader, the social context of the reading encounter, the reader's motivation for textual and visual engagement, and the presence of gaps between the text and illustration of the picture book. Considering this perspective, it is evident that Latino and non-Latino youth undergo numerous experiences, construct countless meanings, and generate multiple responses when they encounter a picture book, novel, or digital media about Latinos.

Besides Latino cultural content, the positive, negative, or even ambivalent use of language presented in a text can have an impact on the way Latino youth respond to literature. The tripartite framework for language planning outlined by Ruíz (1984) serves as a useful tool to better understand three complex, unconscious, and even pre-rational linguistic orientations evidenced in youth literature, namely, language-as-problem, language-as-resource, and language-as-right.

Dispositions toward bilingual and multilingual individuals are incorporated within primarily English-language books for youth in natural or didactic ways that develop the story plot and setting or simply indicate the cultural and linguistic background of the protagonists. The manner in which Spanish or Latin American indigenous languages are inserted, omitted, translated, or paraphrased can raise or even obstruct the literary and cultural quality of a book. Additionally, misspelled words, missing or ill-placed accents and articles, and incorrect terms in relation to the story setting and/or ethnic background of the protagonists, can cause unnecessary confusion and embarrassment for bilingual readers. Such problematic textual features speak to readers, whether intended or otherwise, and a repeated lack of care and attention to the inclusion of protagonists' heritage language within Latino-themed books can result in inconsiderate texts. This can have a cumulative effect, leading Latino students to internalize that their language is not important enough to be included appropriately in institutionally condoned books. Such subtleties not only injure Latino children but also encourage ignorance and prejudice on the part of non-Latino children (Cai, 2002). Thus, the misuse of Spanish or even the didactic values and themes relegated to it in a narrative often presents an underlying "language-as-problem" orientation (Ruíz, 1984). Sadly, many teachers and librarians not literate in Spanish, or not cognizant of the cultural underpinnings of specific terms and idiomatic expressions, may not be able to identify the problematic nature of these books and may naively propagate their use without mediating the linguistic and cultural aspects quietly embedded within.

In sum, Latino youth live in two disparate realities involving their home and school lives. The values of their heritage culture and its language may not be recognized or valued at school. This disconnect can cause undue stress for Latino students and negatively influence their school performance and identity development. Strongly linked to their self-conceptions, the ethnic identity of Latino youth comprises their beliefs and appreciation for the unique traits that encompass their cultural heritage. The major influence on the development of ethnic identities is the students' social and contextual surroundings or their everyday worlds that include family values and desires, unique Latino cultural traditions, teacher perceptions, print and digital media, and learning atmospheres (Vera & Quintana, 2004), not to mention the language in which they think and express themselves.

In the subsequent section we provide specific examples of culturally relevant texts and describe the potential influences these books can have on identity development of Latino youth. We attempt to provide books representing diverse Latino experiences to create a space for all Latino youth to explore their identities, whether they are emergent or fully bilingual (Spanish/English), dominant in Spanish or English, multilingual (indigenous languages), or speakers of different variations of Spanish.

PRAXIS: APPLICATION OF THEORY

Authors have written on a multitude of topics relevant to the cultural experiences of Latino youth. Some of these topics are more salient in the lives of contemporary Latino bilingual youth, thereby holding greater potential to influence their identity development. These themes include citizenship and immigration issues, shame and pride in linguistic and cultural heritage, multilingualism and language as a right, and cultural elements in everyday life experiences. We address each of these topics, providing examples of literature on multiple reading levels, discussing the possible effects they can have in the identity formation process. At the end of the chapter, we suggest activities in both the classroom and school library media center that will foster student engagement with this literature.

Citizenship and Immigration

While most Latinos are native born or naturalized U.S. citizens (U.S. Census Bureau, 2013), there is a preponderance of rhetoric in the media suggesting many Latinos are in the country illegally. The topic of illegal immigration in youth literature has the potential to negatively influence the ethnic identity development of Latino students, particularly when stereotypes and broad generalizations are made. Youth could leave with an impression that racial profiling puts them in danger of deportation and that the use of Spanish could aggravate the situation. However, when addressed appropriately in the curriculum, undocumented immigration provides a forum to discuss what it means to be a U.S. American and allows opportunities for students to discuss how deportation influences their lives or the lives of peers.

Julia Alvarez, recipient of the 2010 Pura Belpré Award for Latino children's literature, wrote *Return to Sender* (2009). The story follows eleven-year-old

Tyler whose family has hired a family of Mexican farm workers to save their Vermont farm from closure. He befriends Mari, the family's daughter, who is his age. After an Immigration and Customs Enforcement (ICE) raid on the farm threatens the Latino family, Tyler learns that only Mari's two younger sisters are here legally—Mari, her uncle, father, and mother are all undocumented immigrants scheduled for deportation. Because of his relationship with Mari, the event significantly alters Tyler's view of undocumented immigration. This middle-grade novel humanizes the experiences of Latino immigrant youth with undocumented family members. Its realistic portrayal serves as a forum for discussing the rights of these youth, as well as immigration legislation. Mari's character struggles to negotiate her pride in being Mexican while also adopting U.S.–American traditions. Her borderland experience of not quite belonging, along with the experience of losing family members to deportation, could serve as a source of comfort for students in similar situations.

A similar topic is covered in the bilingual Spanish-English picture book *From North to South/Del norte al sur* by René Colato Laínez (2014). This book describes the longing a young boy, José, has for his deported mother. José and his father travel from San Diego, California, to Tijuana, Mexico, to visit her in a shelter for recently deported women. The narrative, loosely based upon the experiences of first-grade students in Colato Laínez's classroom, authentically depicts the child's anxious fears about when his mother will receive her proper immigration papers to travel back to *El Norte* to be with the family. It also emphasizes the close bond that mothers have for their children even when they are unable to be together. The book provides an opportunity for primary-age children to discuss how it feels when a loved one is deported and offers comfort to those who might be suffering from such an event. The author focuses on the human emotions rather than the legal ramifications associated with undocumented immigration.

Another novel that successfully covers the topic is *Gaby, Lost and Found* by Angela Cervantes (2013). In this intermediate-level novel, eleven-year-old Gaby's life has been uprooted after her mother is deported to Honduras and her absent father moves in to unsuccessfully serve as caregiver. While this underlying plot provides the tension in the narrative, the book also follows Gaby and her Catholic school friends as they volunteer at an animal shelter, finding homes for unwanted pets. Gaby falls in love with a sickly cat and attempts to save it from its heartless owners, who have returned for the pet they abandoned. Whereas previous books overtly focus on undocumented immigration, Cervantes's novel addresses Gaby's feelings of abandonment through the parallel plot of the orphaned pets. The focus of the book on a Honduran American demonstrates the broader scope of illegal immigration, which is often characterized as only being a problem for Mexicans. The book also profiles a strong sense of community among Latinos and explores what happens to the children left behind, particularly when there is no hope of being reunited.

While the three books mentioned here were created with the purpose of humanizing the *undocumented* immigrant experience and propagating understanding, they don't provide easy answers and are written with children's sensitivities in mind. Each book explores Latino identity within the larger context of U.S. culture, with children trying to understand what it means to be Latino and a U.S. citizen. Both *Gaby, Lost and Found* and *Return to Sender* feature characters who struggle with how language influences cultural identity. In *Return to Sender*, Mari is disheartened that her sisters are becoming Americanized and do not want to learn or use Spanish. In *Gaby, Lost and Found*, the mother speaks *good* English and Gaby believes that if the border control officers could hear her mother speak, they would let her return to the U.S. The assumption by the characters in both of these books is that English is the force that empowers someone and keeps them in the country. Yet Gaby is also bilingual, and her ability to speak English and Spanish is not seen as a hindrance to her success. In fact, she treasures the sheet music of Spanish lullabies that her mother used to sing to her and finds comfort in the songs when she is distressed. *Gaby, Lost and Found* also directly focuses on the search for identity and the process of creating a new life while navigating the universal experiences common to all youth such as community, bullying, pet ownership, friendships, and school assignments. Topics such as these help Latino students navigate their experiences and build bridges between their home and school cultures.

Language: Problem, Resource, and Right

Two recently published picture books, all with strong female protagonists, serve as examples of differing language orientations. First, in Susan Middleton Elya's *Home at Last* (2006), Ana Patiño's family moves from rural Mexico to a corn-growing locale in the U.S. where she and her father begin to learn English right away at school and work. They do not seem to have negative experiences in relationship to language acquisition, unlike Ana's mother who stays home with the twin babies and is homesick for her relatives and home in Mexico. Ana and Papá tell Mamá that she can learn English as well, but she feels this is impossible until some difficult experiences serve to change her mind. She is initially overcharged at the grocery store and cannot clearly communicate the error to a clerk, who responds with "Speak English, lady" (Elya, 2006, n.p.). Later, Mamá worries because she cannot read a note Ana receives from school, and finally, she cannot procure assistance when one of the babies becomes ill with a fever. A neighbor responds, "I don't understand what you're saying" (Elya, 2006, n.p.), paying no attention to the crying baby in Mamá's arms. She finally accepts that the family will not return to Mexico and begins attending English classes. After four weeks, she is able to correct the store clerk when again overcharged, as well as triumphantly announcing in English, "We're home" (Elya, 2006, n.p.) The Spanish words and phrases included in the story are concurrently translated for the reader, with the Spanish dialogue in quotation marks, and the unquoted English terms directly following.

Language is viewed as a problem in Ana's new community, a disposition commonly experienced by many Latinos. As such, it is an important theme to explore in the classroom or library, meeting socioemotional goals of promoting empathy in monolingual English-speaking children for Latino children learning English as a new language. At the same time, the Latino child may identify with Ana: her excitement to learn a new language, her feelings of worry and concern for her mother and the safety of the family, as well as her joy when Mamá begins to learn English. To read oneself in a book can be very powerful, particularly when these textual themes are accompanied by warm, realistic illustrations that make the text come alive, as evidenced in this book. In addition, the inclusion of Spanish lends authenticity to the protagonists, although the technique employed to ensure understanding for monolingual readers and listeners tends to undermine this effort producing characters who use double-speak, which in texts is separated by quotation marks not visible during a read aloud.

Another book with similar themes is *Carmen Learns English* by Judy Cox (2010), which uses a first-person narrative by Carmen, a young girl wise beyond her years. Carmen explicates her experiences learning English at school and the resulting responsibility she feels to teach her younger sister and mother this new language. In fact, she spends time doing so after school each day to ensure that her sister is able to "speak English good like I do" (Cox, 2010, n.p.). Carmen describes her fear on the first day of school, saying that her heart felt sad because no one spoke Spanish, and that "they talked *muy* fast and I did not understand" (Cox, 2010, n.p.). Just as the tears start to fall, her classroom teacher, a white woman, greets her in Spanish and makes extra efforts throughout the day to teach her critical English vocabulary. Despite a fairly positive start to the year, Carmen is frustrated and angry when she does not have the English words to respond to a peer's accusation of incorrect counting, even though she read the numbers correctly in Spanish. The teacher then has the class count in Spanish and asks Carmen to instruct the students in Spanish every day. However, two older boys still tease her during recess, saying, "You got a funny accent" (Cox, 2010, n.p.). Carmen responds with hands on hips, "Excuse me? I don't got an accent. It's you who got the accent!" (Cox, 2010, n.p.).

The representation of language in *Carmen Learns English* includes aspects of both language-as-problem and language-as-resource orientations. The teacher views Carmen's heritage language as positive, important enough to include in the official curriculum, as she empowers the child to be an expert and teach others to speak words from her heritage language. Carmen values learning English as a new language and shares her growing knowledge with her family, while also defending the way she speaks in both English and Spanish. Yet her language-acquisition process is made painful by the thoughtless cruelty of two older, monolingual, English-speaking boys who seem to view their own command of English with great superiority, viewing any second-language use or influence on English as a problem. Italicized Spanish words and phrases are incorporated into the English narrative, and the protagonist makes use of exaggerated code-switching of Spanish words into English communication. Additionally, the book addresses accent in both English (Carmen) and Spanish the (teacher), as well as the socially constructed nature of language perspectives on "standard," accented, and bilingual speech.

Young bilingual Latino children may identify with protagonists in some way when reading these picture books, even though each proffers some form of language-as-problem orientation (Ruíz, 1984) on the part of secondary characters toward the protagonist, or by the protagonist herself. Young Latino children will need a more knowledgeable, culturally/linguistically sensitive other (Vygotsky, 1978) to scaffold discussions that highlight important identity issues in books that may also employ inconsiderate methods of inserting or translating language. Such dialogue is particularly important to promote the critical thinking skills expected by the Common Core State Standards (see chapter 6), and to highlight language-as-resource dispositions, so that students do not simply absorb subtle language-as-problem orientations.

Although Latino youth literature commonly includes themes related to Spanish/English, a few books also reference or include indigenous languages. One intermediate title, *Star in the Forest* by Laura Resau (2012), presents eleven-year-old Zitlally, whose Nahuatl name means *estrella* in Spanish, or "star." The story begins just after the girl's father has been deported to Mexico when his illegal status is discovered during a traffic ticket. Her parent's first language is discussed in the text as the language of soft sounds that her father speaks to her, and three different terms are incorporated into the primarily English text. Two inclusions are simply names, the protagonist's name and the family's village of origin in Mexico. Nahuatl is associated with Zitlally's happy memories of family and home in Mexico, and of her father's "*Ni-mitz nequi*" (Resau, 2012, p. 127), or "I love you," whispered in her

ear. Spanish is also woven into the text, set off in italics and generally representing commonly known words such as *Señora*; cognates like *deportado*
(deported) and *nervios* (nerves); and terms of endearment such as in *mi amor*
and *mi'ja*. Longer phrases (*Feliz cumpleaños*) are translated immediately,
although the simultaneous use of English and Spanish to express birthday
greetings is common for many bilingual and multilingual families living in
the U.S. At times, Spanish is skillfully woven into the text so that the reader
can easily infer meaning from its context: "Can you be quieter than a mouse
and if I say *suelo* can you drop to the ground and shut your eyes so *la migra*
can't see the light shining off them? (Resau, 2012, pp. 25–26). Once, Zitlally
expresses embarrassment at her mother's English abilities:

> "She said in English, 'I forget license in my home. I very sorry, very sorry,
> mister." My face got hot. She talked like a baby in English. . . . The cop talked
> slowly, like she was a little kid. . . . "Ma'am, are you aware you have a headlight
> out?" Mamá didn't understand. My mouth was stuck shut, so Dalia translated.
> (Resau, 2012, p. 66)

Most of the Spanish terms provided in the text are left untranslated, but consideration is given to the non-Spanish or non-Nahuatl speaker through the
provision of a glossary for each of these languages.

While the themes in *Star in the Forest* focus on the complex issues surrounding undocumented immigration to the U.S., the use of languages serves
to highlight the way Zitlally lives on the literal and figurative borders of different countries, cultures, and languages, together with the realistic social climate of middle school. As in other texts, language is presented as a problem
when Mamá's broken English is an embarrassment and potentially a threat
should her undocumented status be discovered, but it is also a resource as
Papá's Nahuatl brings comfort, care, and the identity of her family's indigenous Mexican heritage.

The idea that language is a right, as discussed by Ruíz (1984), is often
linked to legal action taken to ensure equality and justice for bilingual and
multilingual individuals, particularly in regard to education. Few titles for
youth tackle the legalities and rights of language and culture for Latinos,
which makes Duncan Tonatiuh's picture book, *Separate Is Never Equal:
Sylvia Mendez & Her Family's Fight for Desegregation* (2014), and the
intermediate-level chapter book *Sylvia & Aki* (2011) by Winifred Conkling
important publications. In differing degrees, both texts focus on the 1945 and
1946 court cases that eventually resulted in the integration of all-white public
schools in the state of California. Tonatiuh's well-researched picture book
reports the school district's rationale for barring Latino children from white
schools, quoting the school district superintendent's multiple racist excuses,

one of which is focused on language; namely, to improve Spanish-speaking students' English. Conkling's book provides more detail to his testimony:

> "The [school board] policy does read that for Spanish-speaking students and students who need help, we have set up Hoover School. . . . What do you mean by 'Spanish-speaking students'?" asked Mr. Marcus [the Mendez attorney]. "Those children who come to school with a language handicap. . . . That applies just to the Mexican children, doesn't it?" Mr. Marcus asked. "So far, yes," Mr. Kent said. (pp. 109–10)

The lawyer for the school system informs the judge that separate schools benefit Mexican children as they can take "Americanization" instruction to learn "American values and customs" (Conkling, 2011, p. 111). All of these statements make Sylvia angry, of course, as she wants to expose his lies, to say that she is a native English speaker and able to speak two languages, not just one. Both of these books clearly reveal the language-as-problem orientation of the public school and society in general which required legal action to ensure Spanish-speaking children in the state of California received equal educational opportunities as their monolingual English-speaking peers.

In Monica Brown's *Marisol McDonald Doesn't Match/Marisol McDonald no combina* (2011), red-haired, brown-skinned Marisol determines to wear colorful, mismatched clothing and eat foods not often found together, such as peanut butter burritos. She appreciates her Peruvian-Irish heritage and "speaking Spanish, English, and sometimes both" (Brown, 2011, p. 8). Yet she is affected by comments from teachers and schoolmates, and decides that she will have to match, a feat that proves exceedingly boring until her art teacher cannot think of a single reason to have to match. In fact, she reveals her own special name with its ties to two different ethnicities, "Ms. Tamiko Apple" (Brown, 2011, p. 42). Suddenly, Marisol is back to her sunny self and announces, "My name is Marisol McDonald and I don't match because . . . I don't want to!" (Brown, 2011, p. 26). This bilingual book provides a complete storyline in both English and Spanish, and it incorporates a few Spanish terms in the English narrative, none of which are translated since meaning can be inferred from the text and illustrations. Unlike the previous titles in which language is specifically targeted as a problem, this book focuses instead on how a biracial child navigates her world, combining what she likes into her identity—which includes two languages. Thus Marisol McDonald goes beyond a tripartite orientation toward language as a problem/resource/right because she is empowered to navigate her world, combining aspects from her ethnicities, cultures, and languages, into her identity as she pleases.

Latino youth need to be aware of the history surrounding their rights in the U.S., and the racism and unjust institutionalized practices of the past, in order to think critically about how some of these themes may still exist in subtle ways today. The language-as-problem orientation evidenced in several of the books discussed in this chapter is primarily associated with the dispositions of monolingual, white individuals. If it is exhibited by a Latino protagonist, it is often the result of his/her stressful experience at being taunted and shamed, or simply tired of assuming the role of a translator and language broker. When language is presented as a resource, as well as a right, *and* when it is skillfully woven into a text, rather than translated as doublespeak, Latino youth can better see the many benefits and advantages to their linguistic and literate gifts that cross two or more languages. They can also move toward finding individuality and biracial/bicultural/bilingual/biliterate identities. Consequently, the linguistic themes and language used in English-based and bilingual Latino youth literature, such as Spanish or Nahuatl (see box on p. 67), are important to explicitly include in the school curriculum and instruction, as well as in library programming.

Elements in Daily Life Experiences

While it is important to focus on themes such as immigration and language development and use, it is equally important to provide Latino youth with books that are light-hearted and less issue-driven. Books that highlight the daily experiences in a Latino student's life are important in identity formation as they demonstrate to Latino youth the universality of family, community, and school. At the same time, these books provide opportunities for non-Latino students to make connections with their Latino classmates over exciting topics, such as favorite sports or more mundane subjects such as a loose tooth.

In *Confetti Girl* by Diana López (2009), sixth-grader Lina Flores is wild about crazy socks, volleyball, and her friend Luis. These distractions keep her from focusing too much on the death of her mother a year ago and the drama of middle-school life that fills her days. Along with best friend Vanessa, Lina decides to play matchmaker between her book-obsessed father and Vanessa's recently divorced mother—who seems to have an unending supply of *cascarones* (confetti-filled eggs). Peppered with Spanish *dichos* (sayings), this lighthearted coming-of-age tween novel successfully captures the angst of a bicultural, bilingual Latino adolescent while seamlessly imbuing elements of Mexican American culture. It provides opportunities for Latino students to meet a cast of well-adjusted youth much like themselves. The integration of cultural elements can also help Mexican American students develop a sense of cultural pride.

Another middle-school book that successfully infuses elements of Mexican and Mexican American cultures into a humorous story about the daily experiences of a Latino adolescent is *Maximilian & the Mystery of the Guardian Angel: A Bilingual Lucha Libre Thriller*, written by Xavier Garza (2011). This novel follows eleven-year-old Max, a huge fan of *lucha libre* wrestling, as he attempts to solve a mystery about his favorite masked *luchador*—the guardian angel. While at one of the guardian angel's wrestling matches, Max discovers that his uncle and the *luchador* look very similar in appearance. Soon the boy discovers that the guardian angel is his mother's long-lost brother, who has returned to find someone in the family to carry on the *luchador* tradition. With a perfect title for reluctant readers, particularly boys, Max's adventure provides an opportunity for students to learn about Mexican wrestling and make intercultural connections with wrestlers and heroes from other cultures. At the same time, the book contains numerous references to Latino folklore and underscores the closeness of family in the Latino culture. Refreshingly free of heavy issues, the book offers the perfect forum for Latino students who are wrestling aficionados to take pride in being class experts, thus strengthening their identity development.

A book for older students by René Saldaña Jr. that captures the humor, angst, and mix of emotions of Latino youth is *¡Juventud! Growing Up on the Border: Stories and Poems* (2013). In this edited collection of eight stories and sixteen poems, readers are introduced to a wide cast of characters who are multilingual, bicultural, and multifaceted. The collection captures the experiences of adolescent and teens living in the borderlands of the Rio Grande Valley, exploring ways that physical, linguistic, and cultural barriers influence Latino youth on a daily basis. Much like the other books, *¡Juventud!* serves as a mirror for some Latino youth and a window for others who come from different Latino backgrounds. Nonetheless, many of the experiences described hold universal appeal.

Finally, a book for younger elementary children that describes a universal experience is *The Tooth Fairy Meets El Ratón Pérez*, by René Colato Laínez (2010). In this engaging picture book, Miguelito has just pulled his loose tooth and placed it under his pillow. The Tooth Fairy is on her way to collect his tooth for her castle, unbeknownst to *El Ratón Pérez*, who has come to collect the tooth to help build his rocket to the moon. Chaos ensues as each character vies for rightful claim of the tooth. The Tooth Fairy insists the tooth belongs to her because Miguelito lives in the U.S. and not in Latin America where Pérez has a monopoly on the tooth-collecting market. On the other hand, the mouse insists that the tooth belongs to him because he has collected the teeth of Miguelito's mother, father, and grandparents. Since the child is bicultural, both tooth stealers have dibs and learn a lesson in cooperation and crosscultural relations. Latino children will delight in this magical story that seamlessly presents biculturalism in an easy-to-understand and natural manner. The universality of a loose tooth can bridge the experiences of students from diverse cultural backgrounds and provide opportunities for Latino children to share their stories about tooth traditions in their families.

Collectively these books hold the potential to support the ethnic-identity development of Latino students. Their depictions of bilingual and bicultural Latino youth engaged in daily life or solving exciting mysteries serve as conduits for cultural pride, particularly when other elements of Latino cultural are seamlessly integrated into the text and illustrations.

CONCLUSION

Throughout this chapter, we have provided examples of how Latino literature in the school curriculum can influence the identity development of Latino youth, particularly from a linguistic and cultural perspective. We have highlighted specific picture books and novels, discussing the potential messages that readers might take away from the books. It is crucial that teachers and librarians develop an awareness of this literature, include it in classroom and school library collections, and integrate it into culturally responsive instruction. To facilitate further exploration into the use of Latino youth literature with students, we provide recommended readings, and activities as well as action-oriented discussion questions. Recommended children's books, including titles not mentioned in this chapter, are provided in part V with a goal to provide a wider selection of books for educators.

REFERENCES

Ada, A. F. (2003). *A magical encounter: Latino children's literature in the classroom* (2nd ed.). Boston, MA: Allyn & Bacon.

Alvarez, J. (2009). *Return to sender.* New York, NY: Knopf Books for Young Readers.

Begler, Elsie. (1998). Global cultures: The first steps toward understanding. *Social Education, 62*(5), 272–75.

Brown, M., & Palacios, S. (2011). *Marisol McDonald doesn't match/Marisol McDonald no combina.* New York, NY: Children's Book Press/Lee & Low Books.

Cai, M. (2002). *Multicultural literature for children and young adults: Reflections on critical issues.* Westport, CT: Greenwood Press.

Cervantes, A. (2013). *Gaby, lost and found.* New York, NY: Scholastic.

Colato Laínez, R., & Cepeda, J. (2014). *From north to south/Del norte al sur.* New York, NY: Lee & Low Books.

Colato Laínez, R., & Lintern, T. (2010). *The tooth fairy meets el ratón Pérez.* Berkley, CA: Tricycle Press.

Conkling, W. (2011). *Sylvia and Aki.* Berkeley, CA: Tricycle Press.

Cox, J., & Dominguez, A. (2010). *Carmen learns English.* New York, NY: Holiday House.

Cummins, J. (2001). *Negotiating identities: Education for empowerment in a diverse society.* Ontario, CA: California Association for Bilingual Education.

Elya, S. M., & Dávalos, F. (2006). *Home at last.* New York, NY: Lee & Low Books.

Garza, X. (2011). *Maximilian & the mystery of the Guardian Angel: A bilingual lucha libre thriller.* El Paso, TX: Cinco Puntos Press.

Hallowell, A. I. (1955). *Culture and experience.* Philadelphia, PA: University of Pennsylvania Press.

López, D. (2009). *Confetti girl.* New York, NY: Little, Brown Books for Young Readers.

Naidoo, J. C. (Ed). (2011). *Celebrating cuentos: Promoting Latino children's literature and literacy in classrooms and libraries.* Santa Barbara, CA: Libraries Unlimited.

Quintero, I. (2014). Making my self visible. *Diversity in YA* blog. Retrieved November 10, 2014, from http://diversityinya.tumblr.com/post/102284723605/making -my-self-visible.

Resau, L. (2012). *Star in the forest.* New York, NY: Random House Children's Books.

Rosenblatt, L. M. (1995). *Literature as exploration* (5th ed.). New York, NY: Modern Language Association of America.

Ruíz, R. (1984). Orientations in language planning. *Journal for the National Association of Bilingual Education, 8*(2), 15–34.

Saldaña, R., Jr., & Garza Johnson, E. (2013). *¡Juventud! Growing up on the border: Stories and poems.* Donna, TX: VAO Publishing.

Santiago, E. (2000). A Puerto Rican existentialist in Brooklyn: An interview with Esmeralda Santiago. In B. Kevane & J. Heredia (Eds.), *Latina self-portraits: Interviews with contemporary women writers* (pp. 130–40). Albuquerque, NM: New Mexico University Press.

Sumara, D. J. (1996). A life that includes reading: Understanding reading as embodied action. In D. J. Leu, C. K. Kinzer, & K. A. Hinchman (Eds.), *Literacies for the 21st century: 45th yearbook of the national reading conference* (pp. 385–97). Chicago, IL: National Reading Conference.

Tonatiuh, D. (2014). *Separate is never equal: Sylvia Mendez and her family's fight for desegregation.* New York, NY: Abrams Books for Young Readers.

U.S. Census Bureau (2013). 2012 American community survey. Table: S0201. Accessed November 19, 2014, from http://factfinder2.census.gov/bkmk/table/1.0/en/ ACS/12_1YR/S0201//popgroup~400.

Vera, E. M., & Quintana, S. M. (2004). Ethnic identity development in Chicana/o youth. In R. Velásquez, L. Arellano, & B. McNeill (Eds.), *The handbook of*

Chicana/o psychology and mental health (pp. 43–59). Mahwah, NJ: Lawrence Erlbaum Associates.

Vygotsky, L. (1978). *Mind in society.* Cambridge, MA: Harvard University Press.

———. (1986). *Thought and language.* Cambridge, MA: MIT Press.

DISCUSSION QUESTIONS

1. Consider your own orientation toward other languages and the children and families for whom they are a first language. How do these dispositions impact instruction overall? How do they affect the reading materials made available to students? How might your language orientation influence your students' learning and your communication with parents?

2. Make a list of the Latino-themed books for youth that you are familiar with, and then consider how they present language, culture, and other themes of importance to Latinos. How did you respond to these books? How did your students respond (monolingual English; Latino youth)? Describe how you may have scaffolded/mediated the cultural and linguistic content of these books for your students. How can you improve upon this instruction in the future?

3. It is beneficial to all students if Latino-themed books are incorporated into lesson plans, bibliographies, and displays in classrooms and school libraries throughout the academic year. Brainstorm specific instances when you can use these books with your students. Try to think of at least one example for each month of the school year.

ACTIVITIES

A. Make Latino youth literature available and easily accessible in school and classroom libraries.

B. Ensure parents and teachers are familiar with Latino youth titles through home-school communication.

C. Provide opportunities for retelling, storytelling, and authoring in the curricula.

D. Offer book clubs and literature circles using Latino youth literature.

E. Develop a Reading Buddies Program, pairing older students with younger children.

F. Plan reading and writing instruction that makes use of Latino youth literature in guided reading, read-alouds, shared reading, interactive reading, independent reading, written responses to books, and writing with Latino-themed mentor texts.

G. Implement home-school connections such as homework reading and parent read-alouds in the classroom or school library.

H. Participate in classroom and library collaborations such as family literacy events (parent nights, *El Día de los niños/El día de los libros* [Children's Day/Book Day] and *Noche de cuentos*) and thematic bibliographies with Latino youth literature.

I. Encourage students' artistic, aesthetic responses to Latino literature: drawing, readers' theater/dramatic response, etc.

J. Create thematic units of study or author/illustrator studies focused on Latino youth literature.

Common Language-Related Themes and Trends in Latino Youth Literature

More than one of these themes may be evidenced in a single Latino-themed text, with many picture books presenting didactic or mixed messages about bilingualism/multilingualism, identity, and the value of acquiring and learning English.

- new-language acquisition and literacy learning
- painful learning experiences for U.S. newcomers, with consequent feelings of loneliness and loss and the inability to perform daily routines or seek assistance
- feelings of humiliation, shame, and anger for a parent or oneself due to monolingual English characters' insults and insinuations of low intelligence
- exaggerated accents and code-switching (Spanish into English) or inappropriate code-switching (English into Spanish)
- appreciation of white peers or adults who attempt to speak broken Spanish to befriend or assist
- salvation, often by a white female teacher, who ensures peers are "kind" and who may use culturally responsive pedagogy
- language brokering (translation) for adults and peers
- negative attitudes toward bilingualism, especially translation, on the part of bilingual protagonists
- desire to teach parents, siblings, friends, and extended family English to avert potential or future shame and embarrassment for them
- a positive shift in protagonists' or parents' attitudes toward valuing bilingualism and learning English
- bilingualism and multilingualism presented as the norm

PROFESSIONAL READINGS

Chappell, S., & Faltis, C. (2007). Spanglish, bilingualism, culture and identity in Latino children's literature. *Children's Literature in Education, 38*(4), 253–62.

Cummins, A. (2013). Border crossings: Undocumented migration between Mexico and the United States in contemporary young adult literature. *Children's Literature in Education, 44*, 57–72.

Martínez-Roldán, C. M. (2013). The representation of Latinos and the use of Spanish: A critical content analysis of *Skippyjon Jones. Journal of Children's Literature, 39*(1), 514.

Naidoo, J. C. (Ed.). (2011). *Celebrating cuentos: Promoting Latino children's literature and literacy in classrooms and libraries.* Santa Barbara, CA: Libraries Unlimited.

Quiroa, R. E. (2013). Promising portals and safe passages: A review of pre-K–12 Latino/a–themed literature. In J. C. Naidoo & S. P. Dahlen (Eds.), *Diversity in youth literature: Opening doors through reading* (pp. 45–61). Chicago, IL: American Library Association.

Chapter Four

Cruzando Fronteras: Negotiating the Stories of Latino Immigrant and Transnational Children

Patricia Sánchez and Maité Landa

INTRODUCTION

How Do We View Transnational Immigrant Latino Students?

When we think of Latino education in the U.S., we must remember that a significant portion of young Latinos are the "new majority" in their communities (Sánchez & Machado-Casas, 2009; Wortham, Murillo, & Hamann, 2002); this is largely due to demographic shifts brought about by immigration and birth rates. Thus, we can safely say that issues surrounding immigration or immigrant families largely shape the Latino student experience, which inevitably includes aspects related to transnationalism. Transnationalism is when immigrants maintain ties to their new country and country of origin (Sánchez & Kasun, 2012). Even so, there is still a misperception about the transnational experiences or lifestyles of Latino immigrants in the U.S.

I (Sánchez) can recall the prevalence of these misperceptions when I was a second-grade bilingual education teacher during the mid-1990s. I taught in Houston, Texas. In my classroom, the majority of my twenty-six students (or their parents) were from Mexico, either from the state of San Luis Potosí or Tamaulipas—a few others were from El Salvador, Guatemala, or Nicaragua. During the winter holiday each year, about six or seven students would leave a couple of days early and another six or seven would return to school a few days after the January start date. Overall, about a third of my classroom left (and came back to) the U.S. each holiday season, embarking upon return trips to their families' countries of origin.

Several teachers and I would comment on this transnational activity, prompted by the familial, economic, social, organizational, religious, and political ties that immigrant families maintain across two nation-states (Glick Schiller, Basch, & Blanc-Szanton, 1992). Some teachers felt that these return trips were a detriment to the students' academic progress. A few even said, "They're going to lose their English when they go down there." Others were concerned about the possibility of students not being promoted because some of these absences could be marked as unexcused. In other words, these annual trips could have a negative impact on a student's attendance record because promotion in a public school district required a certain number of total attendance days each year, regardless of solid academic performance. Another educator (in a different school district and years later) remarked that the children were treated "like luggage" and lugged around on these return visits at the parents' will. She seemed to imply that the students' gained little (if anything) by going to visit their parents' natal communities.

The overwhelming majority of teachers framed their remarks and beliefs about this back-and-forth movement from a deficit perspective (Valencia & Solórzano, 1997). That is, they perceived these transnational trips as having an overall subtractive effect on the children in their schools. Gibson (1995) provides evidence of a high school teacher who exemplifies this "deficit thinking" in describing why he thinks "large numbers of young Hispanic males do not want to buy into the [U.S.] culture": "I think if Mexico were where India is, we would not have that problem. I think it's this constant re-indoctrination by these periodic visits [to Mexico]. . . . The Asian kids tend to move fairly well into the system (p. 99).

While some of the teachers' actual words may convey concern for students' academic achievement, in reality, this is a discourse of hegemonic U.S. schooling practices. This exemplifies how some teachers only see their students in terms of the (U.S.) schooling or education that is imparted to them through the state—anything that may interfere with this process is seen as subtractive. These notions do not treat a child as a whole person who spends an entire lifetime learning inside and outside of the classroom.

In addition, a hegemonic stance such as this obscures the other roles, persons, or selves that a student is—child, son, daughter, immigrant, brother, niece, grandson, transnational cousin, consumer, etc. In schools, children are often seen only as students—or as Paulo Freire (1970) remarks, as an "empty vessel" to be filled—while the many other roles they play and the knowledge gained in such roles is minimally addressed or ignored. This holds true as well as for the *educación* that their families, other relatives, and community members may impart to them (Villenas, 2002). In many cases, teachers express notions of knowing what is best for children, often implying they know better than the students' parents themselves.

Another intriguing aspect embedded in this dynamic is that some bilingual educators have felt that transnational students "lose" something in this movement between nation-states. Teachers who have acquired theoretical and practical knowledge regarding the lives of culturally and linguistically diverse students can also succumb to the hegemonic notions of U.S. schooling. Students' success in the bilingual education program can conflict with the pressure to transition them to the mainstream all-English classroom and can lead to viewing education in a limited way, thus devaluing the education that takes place outside of the school.

In this chapter, we call for educators who work with Latino bilingual children to seek texts that depict migration, border crossings, and transnational ties in a humanizing and authentic manner. We explore multicultural literature that authentically portrays immigrant and transnational issues from multi-sited perspectives; our analysis highlights books that bravely address challenging topics such as deportation, the criminalization of undocumented migrants, and the resiliency of immigrant families and children. To do this we use three frameworks to analyze twenty texts related to Latino immigration and transnationalism: cultural consciousness, funds of knowledge, and bibliotherapy.

THEORETICAL AND CONCEPTUAL FRAMEWORKS

Cultural Consciousness

The ways in which educators bring the "unofficial" world of their students into the official world of the classroom (Dyson, 1993, 1994) is critical in the public school classroom. Anne Haas Dyson describes students' unofficial worlds as consisting of peers, homes, and communities. She critically investigates how children negotiate these worlds in their writing (and school behavior), which is often mediated by adults and their beliefs showing how multiple literacies shape our interactions within the world.

As educators, then, it is important for us to understand the true power of story in the classroom and that it comes from a variety of sources, including traditional literature such as published children's picture books; inventive stories from the worlds of children and their child culture as well as the (oral) stories of their immigrant families, communities, and countries of origin.

Researchers who have looked at cultural consciousness in the stories of children's picture books (Day, 1996; Lent, 1983; Moore, 1985; Nodelman,

1988; Thompson, 2001) do so to determine the cultural authenticity of both the text and illustrations. In other words, cultural consciousness is the awareness or presence of culturally authentic words and images—the author conscientiously paid close attention to the culture being represented in the story and depicted it in an accurate manner. In our review of children's literature that addresses the immigrant experience—from departure of origin country, to crossing the border, to adapting to a new community and school, to living a transnational existence—we define the parameters of cultural consciousness based on our own experience as critical educators/scholars, as women who were raised in U.S.–Mexican border towns, and as mothers raising young girls of color. We use the cultural consciousness framework to remind us to assess children's picture books and young adult novels in a manner that is reflective of local immigrant/transnational/transborder communities. In other words, would our own extended families and networks of transborder and transnational migrants truly see themselves in these texts? Because of the increasingly globalized and transnational lives that many Latino immigrant children are experiencing in our schools today, transnational literacy (Sánchez, 2009) may well become a new category used to study the language, literacy, and ways in which children understand their lives across borders.

Funds of Knowledge

Too often, we use deficit frameworks to view certain students, their families, and activities; these limit the possibilities and type of teaching we can engage in within our classrooms. Funds of knowledge, on the other hand, help us see the assets or bodies of knowledge and skills that students derive from their households and communities; these funds of knowledge can be incorporated into the classroom to support and enhance students' educational experiences (González, Moll, & Amanti, 2005). If we could see immigrant transnational students through an assets-based lens, then we could harness their outside-of-school experiences and funds of knowledge. For example, when Latino immigrant students return from seeing their grandparents and visiting the rural communities (*los ranchos*) of their extended families, they have an extraordinary amount of rich material for oral language development, literacy activities, and creative expression. Their experiences during their return trips to Mexico are deep and run the gamut of working in small family businesses, exchanging currency, sharing in the duties of subsistence farming, and participating in community-wide social-religious-familial celebrations (Sánchez, 2009). If we as teachers could see these events as "international field trips," where students are constantly learning and expanding their knowledge, then all that the students and families do and learn in Mexico could be used as part of a curriculum infused by transnationalism, or as a broader funds of knowledge (González, Moll, & Amanti, 2005; Mercado & Moll, 1997; Moll, Amanti, Neff, & González, 1992; Sánchez, 2009; Vélez-Ibáñez & Greenberg, 1992).

Schools do not engage transnationalism or the Latino experience in the curriculum. But if we use a funds of knowledge framework to appreciate and examine the learning that takes place in transnational immigrant homes, then our classrooms can become spaces where we examine multicultural texts that corroborate what many Latino children and youth feel: it is rewarding—not detrimental—to be a transnational immigrant.

Bibliotherapy

As many of us know, children's picture books and young adult literature can both entertain and educate—as do all kinds of books. We also know that certain stories can help students cope with tough issues, like the loss of a family member, dealing with a major life change, or another traumatic event. The importance of children's literature cannot be underestimated when used as a form of bibliotherapy (Berns, 2004; Gomm, 2012).

Berns (2004) defines bibliotherapy as "the use of any kind of literature by a skilled adult or other interested person in an effort to normalize a child's grief reactions to loss, support constructive coping, reduce feelings of isolation, and reinforce creativity and problem solving" (p. 234). In his study *Content Analysis of 50 Picture Books for Latino Immigrant Children: Implications for Supportive Bibliotherapy*, Robert J. Gomm (2012) contends that the "benefits of using a bibliotherapeutic approach to support immigrant children include providing a safe distance for children to discuss their challenges, reducing isolation (feeling alone, that his or her situation is unique), and fostering expression and conversation" (p. 6). For some Latino immigrant students, the journey to the U.S. was a traumatic and difficult event. For others, having to leave family, friends, and a community behind in Latin America was the most challenging aspect of their migration story. And yet for some Latino students, there is a daily fear or trauma that does not dissipate because either they or their parents are undocumented immigrants in this country. Therefore, bibiotherapy serves as a useful tool with which to analyze literature about Latino immigration.

In the following section, we detail the application of cultural consciousness, funds of knowledge, and bibliotherapy in selecting and using children's multicultural books in the classroom.

PRAXIS: APPLICATION OF THEORETICAL AND CONCEPTUAL FRAMEWORKS

In this section, we offer readers a starting point for the selection and use of texts that touch upon Latino immigration and transnationalism as its own genre. Toward the end of this section, we also discuss what is missing in this genre and challenge teachers and other aspiring writers to create much-needed multicultural literature with these and other missing but pertinent themes of the larger umbrella of Latino immigrant experiences.

We organized the twenty books we selected (fourteen picture books and six young adult novels, listed in part V) into six themes—coincidentally, the twenty texts also have a publication range of twenty years, from 1993 to 2013. These themes reflect the experiences that Latino immigrant children undergo as well as the daily challenges they face as culturally and linguistically diverse students.

1. The hardships of leaving home and the difficulties in crossing the border.
2. The challenges of adjusting to the U.S. while maintaining your culture.
3. Keeping your name against all odds.
4. Serving as a language broker for your family.
5. Returning to your (or your parents') home country.
6. The bravery and resiliency of undocumented or mixed-status families.

Using Cultural Consciousness as a Litmus

Before we organized selected books into these six themes, we carefully read the books to ensure that they met our most important criteria: Are they culturally authentic? Do they demonstrate cultural consciousness when depicting Latino immigrant children and families? Of these published works, we feel that one lacked our seal of approval for cultural consciousness: *Chave's Memories*, by María Isabel Delgado (1996; see part V). Our critique of this story, which depicts a Mexican-American or Mexican immigrant family returning to visit their grandmother in rural Mexico for a weekend, lies mostly with the book illustrations.

- The white picket fence around the grandmother's humble home in Mexico does not seem common for such rural areas; instead it is more reminiscent of fencing around U.S. homes.
- The grandmother's garden looks more like a U.S. suburban home garden; *abuelitas* in Mexico often use recycled materials like coffee cans as flowerpots.

- The grandmother's kitchen does not look authentically Mexican: the tablecloth is white and red checkered, like one used for a U.S. mainstream picnic; the grandmother is not wearing an apron at all, which is often a common practice among *abuelitas* who work in their kitchens.

In addition, the storyline of *Chave's Memories* does not include a scene or the mention of a geopolitical border that needs to be crossed to travel from the U.S. to Mexico. For these reasons, we caution readers in their use of *Chave's Memories*—otherwise, the story itself is a good one as it is one of the very few texts available bilingually that depicts the physical transnational maintenance of familial ties across borders.

Applying Funds of Knowledge

The next conceptual framework that we considered in our review of multicultural literature when seeking works on Latino immigration and transnationalism was funds of knowledge. Of these six themes, where anywhere from two to five books are listed, we found that two of our themes directly demonstrate the knowledge and skills that Latino immigrant children and their households possess. These include the practices of (4) serving as a language broker for your family, and (5) returning to your (or your parents') home country. When young Latino immigrant children serve as language brokers, they are not only translating from English to Spanish for their parents, they are also brokering the two cultures. This is a practice or fund of knowledge that is often overlooked by classroom teachers; we do not realize the adult work that our students often do for their families.

Under the former theme, we found two children's picture books that depict how young bilingual children serve as interpreters for their families: *Speak English for Us, Marisol!* (2000) by Karen English and *A Day's Work* (1994) by Eve Bunting (see part V). These two stories show how family members of young Latino immigrant children may rely on them for their language brokering skills (Orellana, 2009) because they have more advanced English-speaking skills than the adults. Sometimes, school officials see such brokering as a form of bad parenting because the adults have not learned to speak English; these authors, however, demonstrate how this practice is not a deficit but a skill set appreciated and useful to the adults. And in *A Day's Work*, the grandfather offers a greater lesson to his grandson, Francisco, who serves as his language broker.

In the latter theme of children and their families taking return trips to their country of origin communities, the authors of three picture books and one young adult novel provide us with stories of family, nostalgia, celebrations, and cultural readjustments. While we previously mentioned *Chave's Memories*, the other picture books under this theme—*Going Home* (1996) and *Remembering My Roots and Living My Traditions* (2004; see part V)—depict journeys to Mexico that are more nuanced and detailed. *Going Home* has wonderful illustrations that show the magical excitement of traveling through small Mexican pueblos preparing for Christmas, and the story ends with Carlos and his sisters seeing their parents socialize, relax, laugh, and even dance in the middle of the night. That's when they realize why their parents' home community of *La Perla* is so special, and the realization re-energizes them after their long drive and the fatigue of the U.S. assimilation process.

In *Remembering My Roots and Living My Traditions* (2004; see part V), the family in this story travels to Mexico to celebrate their oldest daughter's *quinceañera* (fifteenth birthday). We see how Pepito and Xiridiana, the eight-year-old main characters, divide their time while in the rancho, learning about the different worlds of their grandparents and cousins. It is not difficult to surmise how much the fraternal twins learn while on this trip and why they find it difficult to leave and return to their U.S. community.

The last book under the theme of transnationalism is a young adult book by Julia Alvarez (2010; see part V), *How the Garcia Girls Lost Their Accents.* This collection of fifteen stories offers insight into the transnational social space of Dominican New Yorkers. It spans a greater amount of time than the picture books mentioned previously as it is not based on one sole trip to a country of origin but on a lifetime of adjusting to the U.S. with interspersed summer trips to the Dominican Republic. It also illustrates the gender roles and expectations in each country that are imposed upon the four Garcia sisters as they navigate their immigrant identity.

In the process of acquiring transnational funds of knowledge, many Latino children and youth also stretch their cultural flexibility in belonging to two distinct places. In the U.S., kids and teens may participate as members of multi-ethnic inner-city neighborhoods or predominantly white public school campuses. And then in their families' natal communities, they balance the challenges of integrating into communities with gendered divisions of labor, the latter possibly being more difficult due to their own acculturation trajectories which include Western notions of gender equality. Henry Trueba (2002) explains how such complexities require dexterity from transnational participants:

> Simultaneous multiple identities (not serial or sequential identities) require a unique skill and flexibility on the part of immigrant youths from all ethnic groups. The "new" and rapidly evolving postmodern society is more than ever led by a new youth that does not accept ethnic boundaries as a red light in the development of their potentialities. . . . What is new [in the most recent U.S. immigration wave] is its magnitude and the adaptive strategies of immigrants and migrants. (p. 8)

Latino transnational immigrants utilize their experiences with cultural (and gender) flexibility to inform their understanding of actors who move across borders and continue the circuit of migration not only in their local communities but globally as well. This understanding of complex lives both locally and globally surely helps them develop a broader consciousness of transnational families or a critical literacy of how the stories of their own lives should be recognized and expressed in multicultural literature. They possess much of what Shor (1999) defines as critical literacy:

> Critical literacy, then, is an attitude towards history, as Kenneth Burke (1984) might have said, or a dream of a new society against the power now in power, as Paulo Freire proposed (Shor & Freire, 1987), or an insurrection of subjugated knowledges, in the ideas of Michel Foucault (1980), or a counter-hegemonic structure of feeling, as Raymond Williams (1977) theorized, or a multicultural resistance invented on the borders of crossing identities, as Gloria Anzaldúa (1990) imagined, or language used against fitting unexceptionably into the status quo, as Adrienne Rich (1979) declared. (n.p.)

As educators of transnational Latino children, we have the potential to harness our students' transnational funds of knowledge and to continue to develop their critical literacies in a world that too often depicts the immigrant as less-than or criminal. But we need to access texts that depict these realities in a culturally authentic manner and eventually encourage our students to write their own.

Using Bibliotherapy

Finally, if we turn to bibliotherapy as an analytical tool in selecting children's works, we find that in recent years, there has been an uptick in books that depict (1) the hardships of leaving home and the difficulties in crossing the border; as well as (2) the bravery and resiliency of undocumented or mixed-status families. This is promising because authors are aware of the arduous journeys that many Latino immigrant adults and children undertake to reach the U.S., and instead of criminalizing such decisions and events, these multicultural texts humanize experiences sensationalized by the media.

One particular picture book that stands out to us is René Colato Laínez's *From North to South* (2013; see part V), in which José's mother is deported to Mexico for not having the proper paperwork to stay in the U.S. His home is a mixed-status household, meaning that some members are U.S. citizens or residents while others are undocumented. Children who struggle with feelings of loss or detachment, even a temporary loss like that of José whose mother now lives in a shelter in Tijuana, Mexico, will find a certain level of solace and connection with this story. This picture book validates a child who has similar difficult experiences (Berns, 2004).

Similarly, a young adult immigrant can reduce feelings of isolation by reading *Enrique's Journey* (2013; see part V) by Sonia Nazario or Alma Flor Ada's *Love, Amalia* (2013). Because Enrique's experience is tragic and dangerous, the importance of his story is evident. Enrique travels through Mexico with his younger sister aboard the roof of the train *Mata Gente* [Killer of People], commonly known as *La Bestia* [The Beast]. These experiences may be too traumatic to talk about even with family members. They are traumatized and scarred for trying to reunite with their family already residing in the U.S. When Latino immigrant students read a story like *Enrique's Journey*, their feelings about similar experiences and being alone because of these is greatly reduced.

For child immigrants, multicultural books about the immigration experience are not solely for entertainment but can often serve as a type of therapy that allows them to understand that their experience is not something they need to fear or something of which to be ashamed.

What's Still Missing?

While this chapter offers readers a good starting point in selecting and bringing multicultural texts about Latino immigration and transnationalism to the classroom, we found along our journey that the majority of authors who write about Latino immigrants focus on characters who are farm workers. This often-neglected student population and lifestyle deserves quality books; however, we also need more transnational immigrant literature that depicts families who work in other spaces, such as stores, factories, and restaurants. In addition, we are short on published works that highlight Latino immigrant families who work in non-blue-collar jobs.

We also need books for children and youth that celebrate the rich exchanges present in a Latino transnational household. Immigration and other real-life, challenging experiences can inform children's literature. There are many Latino immigrant families that reach varying levels of success and maintain healthy ties to two places at once. Why not have books that show family members from their home country coming to visit immigrant homes in the U.S.? Why not depict stories of transborder families that live alongside the U.S.–Mexico border? There is still so much children's literature that can be written on these topics.

CONCLUSION

In this chapter we discussed multicultural children's literature that touches upon themes and experiences important in the lives of Latino immigrant students and families. We explored children's and young adult texts that authentically portray Latino immigration and transnationalism using three lenses: cultural consciousness, funds of knowledge, and bibliotherapy. These books address challenging topics such as deportation, the criminalization of undocumented migrants, the resiliency of immigrant families and children, and the experiences of those of a mixed status family or community. We need to ensure that classrooms and libraries contain books that depict meaningful Latino experiences in a humanizing manner and encourage a new generation of Latino authors.

REFERENCES

Ada, A. F., & Zubizarreta, G. W. (2013). *Love, Amalia*. New York, NY: Simon & Schuster.

Berns, C. F. (2004). Bibliotherapy: Using books to help bereaved children. *Omega: Journal of Death & Dying, 48*(4), 321–36.

Day, K. S. (1996). The challenge of style in reading picture books. *Children's Literature in Education, 27*(3), 153–66.

Dyson, A. H. (1993). *The social worlds of children in an urban primary school.* New York, NY: Teacher's College Press.

———. (1994). "I'm gonna express myself": The politics of story in the children's worlds. In A. H. Dyson & C. Genishi (Eds.), *The need for story: Cultural diversity in classroom and community* (pp. 155–71). Urbana, IL: National Council of Teachers of English.

Freire, P. (1970). *Pedagogy of the oppressed.* New York: Continuum.

Gibson, M. A. (1995). Additive acculturation as a strategy for school improvement. In R. G. Rumbaut & W. A. Cornelius (Eds.), *California's immigrant children: Theory, research, and implications for educational policy* (pp. 77–105). La Jolla, CA: Center for U.S.–Mexican Studies, University of California, San Diego.

Glick Schiller, N., Basch, L., & Blanc-Szanton, C. (1992). Transnationalism: A new analytic framework for understanding migration. In N. G. Schiller, L. Basch, & C. Blanc-Szanton (Eds.), *Towards a transnational perspective on migration (*pp. 1–24). New York, NY: New York Academy of Sciences.

Gomm, J. (2012). *Content analysis of 50 picture books for Latino immigrant children: Implications for supportive bibliotherapy.* Thesis, Department of Counseling Psychology and Special Education, Brigham Young University.

González, N. E., Moll, L. C., & Amanti, C. (2005). *Funds of knowledge: Theorizing practices in households, communities, and classrooms.* Mahwah, NJ: Lawrence Erlbaum Associates.

Lent, B. (1983). There's much more to the picture than meets the eye. In R. Bator (Ed.), *Signposts to criticism of children's literature* (pp. 156–61). Chicago, IL: American Library Association.

Mercado, C., & Moll, L. C. (1997). The study of funds of knowledge: Collaborative research in Latino homes. *Centro, 9*(9), 26–42.

Moll, L. C., Amanti, C., Neff, D., & González, N. (1992). Funds of knowledge for teaching: Using a qualitative approach to connect homes and classrooms. *Theory into Practice, 31*(2), 132–41.

Moore, O. J. (1985). Picture books: The un-text. In D. MacCann & S. Woodard (Eds.), *The black American in books for children: Readings in racism* (2nd edition, pp. 183–91). Metuchen, NJ: Scarecrow Press.

Nodelman, P. (1988). *Words about pictures: The narrative art of children's picture books.* Athens, GA: University of Georgia Press.

Orellana, M. F. (2009). *Translating childhoods: Immigrant youth, language, and culture.* Mahwah, NJ: Rutgers University Press.

Sánchez, P., & Kasun, G. S. (2012). Connecting transnationalism to the classroom and to theories of immigrant student adaptation. *Berkeley Review of Education, 3*(1), 71–93.

Sánchez, P., & Machado-Casas, M. (2009). Introduction: At the intersection of trans-nationalism, Latina/o immigrants, and education. *High School Journal, 92*(4), 3–15.

Shor, I. (1999). What is critical literacy? *Journal of Pedagogy, Pluralism, and Practice, 1*(4). Retrieved on April 25, 2015, from www.lesley.edu/journal-pedagogy-pluralism-practice/ira-shor/critical-literacy/.

Thompson, A. (2001). Harriet Tubman in pictures: Cultural consciousness and the art of picture books. *The Lion and the Unicorn, 25*(1), 81–114.

Trueba, H. T. (2002). Multiple ethnic, racial, and cultural identities in action: From marginality to a new cultural capital in modern society. *Journal of Latinos and Education, 1*(1), 7–28.

Valencia, R. R., & Solórzano, D. G. (1997). Contemporary deficit thinking. In R. R. Valencia (Ed.), *The evolution of deficit thinking: Educational thought and practice.* New York, NY: Falmer Press.

Vélez-Ibáñez, C. G., & Greenberg, J. B. (1992). Formation and transformation of funds of knowledge among U.S.–Mexican households. *Anthropology & Education Quarterly, 23*(4), 313–35.

Villenas, S. (2002). Reinventing *educación* in new Latino communities: Pedagogies of change and continuity in North Carolina. In S. Wortham, E. G. Murillo Jr., & E. T. Hamann (Eds.), *Education in the new Latino diaspora: Policy and the politics of identity.* Westport, CT: Ablex Publishing.

Wortham, S., Murillo Jr., E. G., & Hamann, E. T. (2002). *Education in the new Latino diaspora: Policy and the politics of identity.* Westport, CT: Ablex Publishing.

DISCUSSION QUESTIONS

1. Describe any transnational practices that involve you, your family, or your students. Transnationality is a similar phenomenon among Puerto Ricans and other Latino groups. Circumstances such as seasonal occupation and weather can also affect transnational travel.

2. Why do you think that some teachers do not like their bilingual students traveling to their home countries? How can this chapter help inform teachers about the value of transnational practices in students' lives?

3. What is your experience with language brokering (personally, at your school, etc.)? How can schools better serve students who act as language brokers for their families?

4. What are the main challenges of living as an undocumented person in this country? What challenges exist for members of a mixed-status family?

5. To help fill in what's missing in the genre of Latino immigration and transnationalism, design the title and abstract of a multicultural children's text based on the experiences of student(s) in your classroom.

6. Create five to seven hashtags that represent the main concepts of this chapter.

7. Create two tweets (of 140 characters or less each) where one praises the content of this chapter and one critiques it.

ACTIVITIES

A. After reading *My Shoes and I* by René Colato Laínez (2010), create a large map in your classroom with the U.S. and Latin America. Attach a piece of yarn connecting each person's country of origin to their new home. You will have yarn pieces all over Mexico or Central America that should end up in the same location in the U.S. You could also add a piece of string for Mario (the main character in *My Shoes and I*), who comes to the U.S. from El Salvador.

B. Read both of the following children's picture books: *My Diary from Here to There,* by Amada Irma Pérez (2002), and *Pancho Rabbit and the Coyote,* by Duncan Tonatiuh (2013). Have your students create a diary based on Pancho Rabbit's journey and struggles to cross the border.

C. Compare and contrast the two picture books *My Name Is María Isabel,* by Alma Flor Ada (1993), and *My Name Is Jorge: On Both Sides of the River,* by Jane Medina (1999). Use a Venn diagram to document the similarities and differences.

D. "María" or "Mary": What's the difference? After reading *My Name Is María Isabel,* write down your full name on a piece of paper. Pass it to the person to your left. Take their name and change it in some way. You can make it longer, shorter, or change it completely. Read that name back to your peer. Tell her/him that this is their new "American" name and s/he is to answer to it for the remainder of the class. Only you call out the new name. (The name is only relevant to the teacher and not to the student's life. Also, note how many times s/he will ignore you.)

E. After reading *La Línea* by Ann Jaramillo (2008), ask students to search for online articles, news reports, or recorded stories about Central American youth who each enter the U.S. as unaccompanied minors. As an additional project, ask students to write welcome letters to the unaccompanied youth, waiting in local shelters to be released and reunited with family.

F. Create an imaginary dialogue between Enrique (from *Enrique's Journey*) and Esperanza (from *Esperanza Rising*). What would they talk about to each other? How would they compare their experiences, their relationship with their mother, and how would they rate their new lives in the U.S.? Make sure to include no less than five questions/answers between both teens.

PROFESSIONAL READINGS

Brochin, C. (2010). Review of *Felita*. New York, NY: Library Journals.

——. (2012). Literacies at the border: Transnationalism and the biliteracy practices of teachers across the U.S.–Mexico border. *International Journal of Bilingual Education and Bilingualism, 15*(6), 687–703.

Mangual Figueroa, A. (2012). "I have papers so I can go anywhere!": Everyday talk about citizenship in a mixed-status Mexican family. *Journal of Language, Identity, & Education, 11*(5), 291–311.

Mohr, N. (1999). *Felita*. New York, NY: Puffin Books.

Sánchez, P. (2007). Cultural authenticity and transnational Latina youth: Constructing a metanarrative across borders. *Linguistics and Education, 18*(3–4), 258–82.

——. (2007). Urban immigrant students: How transnationalism shapes their world learning. *Urban Review, 39*(5), 489–517.

——. (2009). Even beyond the local community: A close look at Latina youths' return trips to Mexico. *High School Journal, 92*(4), 49–66.

——. (2014). Dignifying every day: Policies and practices that impact immigrant students. *Language Arts, 91*(5), 363–71.

Sánchez, P., & Kasun, G. S. (2012). Connecting transnationalism to the classroom and to theories of immigrant student adaptation. *Berkeley Review of Education, 3*(1), 71–93.

Chapter Five

Using Children's Literature to Understand Values, Traditions, and Beliefs within Latino Family Systems

Mari Riojas-Cortez and Raquel Cataldo

INTRODUCTION

A quintessential element of the Latino community is *la familia* (family), and for that reason, *la familia* is a focal point of countless Latino children's stories. Families are unique in structure, size, genders, ages, and stage of family development (Berger & Riojas-Cortez, 2015). The family structure is the social setting where "young children's care and socialization takes place" (Wen, 2008, p. 1492). The U.S. Census (2010) provides a very formal definition of family as "a group of two or more people who reside together and who are related by birth, marriage or adoption" (n.p.). Despite the "official" definitions that may be offered, in the real world, families exist with a variety and number of individuals who may or may not be connected by birth, blood, marriage, or adoption. These configurations may not be readily understood or accepted by educators. Moreover, the conventional, mainstream notion of family lacks some of the elements associated with the definition of a Latino family or *la familia*.

Some educators and others outside of the community judge the Latino family using a very traditional, conservative perspective (López, 2015). There is a long tradition of studies normed on white, middle-class culture that reinforces misinterpretations and misunderstandings of Latino family practices. Fuller and Coll (2010) explain:

A half-century ago, Latino families were set in stark relief against the White middle-class mainstream. The fixed personality traits of "Mexican" children allegedly stemmed from the (equally uniform) practices and cultural traits of their parents,

typically cast as harmful deficits when compared with Whites. Scholars helped
to legitimate popular conceptions of "culturally deprived homes" that turned out
children who saw themselves as "more externally controlled," and took on fixed
personalities infused with "mistrust, shame, and doubt. (p. 559)

Moreover, for those whose family structure stands in contrast to the traditional family, they may find themselves at odds with others' opinions. For
example, a colleague once commented on a situation where a Mexican American teacher candidate was having difficulty with her mentoring teacher, who
was assigned to guide and support her during observation or practicum. The
colleague believed that the cooperating teacher did not like the teacher candidate because of her "lifestyle." The student was a single parent who was
"living with" the father of her children. Citing this example, the colleague
strongly believed that teacher candidates should not share their family "situation" with their mentoring teachers, as they may not agree with their lifestyle.
While acknowledging different opinions regarding family structure, it is evident from this comment that perhaps a more open understanding of families
is needed, particularly among teachers.

It would appear that the conventional, mainstream notion of family lacks
some of the elements associated with the Latino family or *la familia* (López,
2015). In this chapter, to counter deficit or traditional perspectives, we discuss the idea of *la familia* as it exists in the Latino community and the ways
in which its values, beliefs, and traditions are represented through Latino
children's literature.

THEORETICAL FRAMEWORK

We approach our research from a sociocultural perspective in which *la familia* is viewed as a unit in which children are socialized in term of beliefs,
values, and mores. In addition, for many Latinos it is in the home and from
their family that children acquire their bilingualism and biculturalism. Moreover, within the household it is *la familia* who assist children in acquiring
their funds of knowledge (González, Moll, & Amanti, 2005) and cultural
capital (Delgado Bernal, 2002).

La Familia: Different Families, Different Issues

The term "Latino" describes a population with a common cultural heritage
and often a common language, but it does not refer to a specific race or a

common ancestry (González Burchard et al., 2005). For Latinos, the family is a highly valued source of joy and support. Latinos are commonly described as having a sense of *familismo* or, in particular, "familial collectivism" (Fuller & García Coll, 2010). Members within *la familia* commonly share resources to benefit other members. Often there is a sense of collective pride when a group member succeeds or a sense of shared shame when a group member embarrasses or fails to positively represent the group.

Latino families are often composed of an extended family network that may include close friends who may be referred to as *tías* (aunts), *primos* (cousins), or *tíos* (uncles). All types of family structures have functions. Families have the responsibility to love, nurture, meet the physical needs of, and be role models for children. Olsen and Skogrand (2009) surmise,

Many [Latinos] would also say the family is central to one's identity. . . . Family members typically provide social, emotional, and financial support as needed and promote close relationships among family members. There is an emphasis on cooperation and interdependence among family members and individuals are encouraged to sacrifice individual needs for the benefit of the family. (n.p.)

Families engage children in socialization practices that are important in their culture (Bridges, Cohen, Scott, Fuller, Anguiano, & Livas-Dlott, 2015). Culture acts as a blueprint that largely dictates those values (Nieto, 2008). Since culture is dynamic, values, traditions, and beliefs often change for varying reasons. For instance, interethnic or interracial marriages are more common today than fifty years ago in the U.S. In 2008, among all newlyweds of Latino descent, 28 percent married someone different from their race or ethnicity (Passel, Wang, & Taylor, 2010). In the Latino community today, teen mothers are not being sent away *para evitar el que dirán* (to avoid others talking about them in shame) and rather are being embraced by their families. Latino attitudes toward teen pregnancy vary, based on acculturation level (i.e., affinity toward native or host-country values), as well as attitudes toward familism, gender roles, and other factors (East & Chien, 2010). Other social issues that may affect the family structure include homelessness, two-income parents, single fathers, and low income.

A reality of Latino family households is the increasing number of single-parent households and "other relatives" (e.g., aunts, uncles, cousins, older siblings) who become the legal guardian of school-age children (Marotta & Garcia, 2003). Studies show that grandparents now have the responsibility of raising their grandchildren, with one in ten living permanently with them (Livingston & Parker, 2010).

In the case of Latino families, additional issues such as immigration and generational status can contribute to the change of family structure, dynamics, values, and traditions. For example, a unique characteristic of Latino families, especially in the Southwest, is that their members may refer to more than one country as "home" (Punch, 2012). At times a child may live with one parent in the U.S., while the other parent lives in a different country as the result of immigration issues (Fuller & Coll, 2010; Henderson & Baily, 2013). Children from migrant families may reside in one geographic space with a grandparent or other relative while their parents work in another (Dreby, 2007; Molina, 2015). Legal issues may also divide families. Among siblings, one child may have legal U.S. residency, while another is forced to remain outside the country. As immigrant families (documented and undocumented) learn how to acculturate and navigate different systems of U.S. society, this very often occurs at the expense of their traditions and values (Olivos & Mendoza, 2010).

Though by some standards, the Latino community remains more conservative in gender roles and marital status (Fischer, Harvey, & Driscoll, 2009; Oropesa, 1996), there is an increase in the number of households shared or headed by openly lesbian, gay, bisexual, trans-gendered or gender-questioning parents (LGBTQ; Gray, Mendelsohn, & Omoto, 2015). Even teachers who are allies of the LGBTQ community may appreciate Latino children's texts that address potentially controversial issues with clarity, maturity, and sensitivity. These are difficult to find in the current offering of Latino children's literature but may be found in Latin American and Spanish literature.

The use of authentic, culturally relevant children's literature is not new, but often educators may struggle to find literature that aligns with the values and beliefs of their students and their families. Children's literature offers a way for teachers to critically reflect and validate children's experiences (Keis, 2006). According to renowned author and illustrator Yuyi Morales (2004), "books should inspire" the child. Thus, it is important to find literature where children find themselves to help them with their identity, but also to validate their experiences of their family without judgment.

It is important for teachers to understand that social issues faced by families may not necessarily impede the child's success, especially if there is support for the family. Educators can become important advocates for the rights of children and their families if they have an open mind and a commitment to educational equity. The use of transworld pedagogy, including authentic Latino children's literature, nurtures the child and scaffolds their learning while accepting and affirming their cultural identity (see chapters 1 and 14).

PRAXIS: APPLICATION OF THEORY

Learning about Family through Oral Traditions

Latino families often use the oral tradition (nursery rhymes, songs, *cuentos*, etc.) as a literacy tool when interacting with their young children (Riojas-Cortez & Flores, 2010; see chapters 2 and 11). In the early childhood classroom, educators often begin the school year teaching children about families and the roles that adults assume for the child's care. Some teachers use classic nursery rhymes during circle time that mention some type of family relation, such as the traditional Mexican oral rhyme: *Tortillitas para Mamá*. Also used are traditional songs that highlight the concept of family, such as *"Cinco patitos salieron a nadar, sobre las olas del inmenso mar. La mamá pata dijo: "cuac, cuac, cuac" y cuatro patitos regresaron con mamá"* [Five little ducks went out for a swim, on the waves of the great big sea. Mama duck said, 'Cuac, cuac, cuac,' and four little ducks came a-swimming back]. There are classic Mexican children's songs by renowned Mexican composer and performer of children's songs Gavilondo Soler, better known as *Cri-Crí, el Grillito Cantor* [The Little Singing Cricket], who would often sing songs about families. The song *Los tres cochinitos*, in which a mother puts her *cochinitos* to bed with lots of kisses, conveys the notion of a caregiver providing love and tenderness. Another of his compositions was *"Abuelito"* [Grandfather], in which a grandchild beckons his *abuelito* to come and tell him a bedtime story "from the thousands that he knows." These nursery rhymes and songs highlight the oral traditions of Latino families and the contributions that family members make to the child's literacy development through stories (Riojas-Cortez & Flores, 2010; Riojas-Cortez, Flores, Smith, & Clark, 2003).

La Familia in Latino Children's Literature

There are several children's books that speak to *la familia* capturing festive events, as well as sociocultural issues such as identity and diversity. Other books attend to social issues that impact the family structure, such as transborder and immigration issues (see chapter 4). In the following paragraphs, we highlight some examples of these books.

Festive Cultural Traditions

Among Latinos, family celebrations (e.g., birthdays and anniversaries) are often international affairs with grandparents, uncles, aunts, and cousins arriving from outside the country. In *Family, Familia* (Bertrand, Howard, & Castilla,

1999), a young man reluctantly goes to a family picnic and discovers the joy of being *entre familia* (among the family). He meets his cousins for the first time and finds much more in common with them than he had anticipated.

Sandra Cisneros explores the notion of physical diversity within a girl's family in the Latino children's story *Hairs/Pelitos* (Cisneros & Ybáñez, 1994). Each member of her family has hair that looks and acts differently, from Papa's broom-like hair to her mother's tresses that have "the sweet smell of bread before it's baked" (Cisneros & Ybáñez, 1994, n.p.). Similarly, *Fiesta Babies* (Tafolla & Córdova, 2010) demonstrates diversity within the Latino community. Tafolla and Córdova's characters are a rainbow of young faces that go from fair-skinned to warm-brown. As the title suggests, the five babies celebrate *fiesta* with colorful, traditional clothing, dancing, waving the Mexican flag, and eating traditional *antojitos* [snacks] with their family.

Immigration and Transborder Experiences

Latino children's literature can help children understand the mixed emotions associated with forced separation and the experiences of transnationalism (see chapter 4). *Waiting for Papá/Esperando a Papá* (Laínez, 2004) is a story about a young boy and his mother who come to the United States from El Salvador, leaving his father behind. The boy longs to be reunited with his father and devises a way to show him how much he cares. In *Super Cilantro Girl* (Herrera & Robledo, 2003), Esmeralda lives with her grandmother after her mother is denied reentry into the U.S. following a visit to Mexico. The young heroine imagines being transformed into a superhero flying off to rescue her mother. In *Dear Primo: A Letter to My Cousin* (Tonatiuh, 2010) two cousins—one from New York the other from Mexico City—write about the events in their lives. Through their correspondence they discover commonalities and a sense of closeness despite the distance that separates them.

Author Jorge Argueta's story *Xochitl and the Flowers/Xóchitl, la niña de las flores* (2003) is about an El Salvadorian family that immigrates to San Francisco to start a new life. Xóchitl, the young protagonist, is sad to be away from her homeland but is excited at the opportunity to sell beautiful, colorful flowers as she used to do back home. In a demonstration of "familial collectivism" (Fuller & Coll, 2010), her family receives support for the new flower business venture from relatives and other immigrants from the neighborhood including "Mr. Awad, the Arab American man" (Argueta, 2003, n.p.).

Single-Caretaker Families

Arthur Dorros has written a series of Latino children's books that highlight the relationships between a child and one adult. Among his excellent works are *Abuela* (Dorros & Kleven, 1991); *Papá and Me* (Dorros & Gutierrez, 2008); and *Abuelo* (Dorros & Colón, 2014). Each portrays a warm and loving relationship between a child and a caretaker. These are examples of Latino children's books that demonstrate different adults in a child's life may be the provider of love, nurturing, and protection.

Although we all have different beliefs and opinions regarding family structure, the reality is that families are diverse in many different aspects. As educators, we must ensure that children's experiences are represented in the materials and activities that value their background. In addition to reading these books with children, we can also ask them to draw a picture of their family or a picture showing one day in the life of their family, possibly doing a family activity. We can be proactive and select books that reflect their realities (see chapters 2 and 6). In doing so, we acknowledge each child's family structure.

Socialization Practices in Latino Children's Literature

Teachers need to develop cultural competence in order to carefully examine children's literature that critically engages children in literacy practices (Montiel-Overall, 2014). In addition, teachers need to know how to utilize well-selected children's literature to contribute to their overall development (see chapters 2 and 6). Knowledge regarding a family's socialization practices such as values, traditions, and beliefs serves as a starting point (Bridges et al., 2015). Such practices may include: *familismo* (family ties), *cariño* (affection), and *biculturismo* (biculturalism) as well as beliefs such as *respeto* (respect) and *ser bien educados* (have good manners). Each of these notions corresponds to values and expectations of behavior within *la familia*. As socialization practices, these may be present in all family structures to different ways and degrees. Importantly, while ethnic minority families may change through time, many of their basic values last as they are passed down through different generations (Treas & Carreon, 2010). These practices can be validated in Latino children's literature and demonstrated in the following sections.

Familismo

Strong family ties are important to many Latino families. Family members care for each other and enjoy each other's company (Berger & Riojas-Cortez, 2015). Teachers need to think about how to best expand the concept of *familismo* within the context of their classroom. In order to understand *familismo*, one must understand the important role that family members play in all aspects of child development, particularly the socioemotional. It is not unusual for families to visit their grandparents every weekend or spend holidays and vacations with one another (some children live with their grandparents or their grandparents with them). Grandparents often do something special with their grandchildren, as in the case of *Magda's Tortillas* (2000), written by Becky Chavarria-Chairez and illustrated by Anne Vega, where the grandmother, or *abuelita*, creates a special event for Magda's birthday, who is turning seven years old. The *abuelita* helps Magda learn how to make flour tortillas, which is a way to pass down cultural knowledge from one generation to the next. Magda's *abuelita* also makes Magda feel good about herself by involving the entire family in giving Magda encouragement in the tortillas she is making.

Often teachers use this book to reinforce "math" concepts because of the different shapes of Magda's tortillas. However, *Magda's Tortillas* can be used to actually look beyond the academic focus and extend deeper into the value of strong family ties, particularly for a child who is very young. To bring *familismo* to the classroom, teachers can have students share the preparation of a dish, or any other activity that they do with a special member of their family. Teachers can send home index cards and ask families to write their favorite *receta de la familia*, or family recipe. Once all the cards are collected, the teacher can have each child illustrate their recipe on their card. The teacher can send home a copy of the cookbook and have families discuss similarities and differences among the recipes provided. The teacher can also have the children discuss what their families do when they make the special recipe, thus enhancing the topic of *familismo*.

As mentioned, for some Latino families, particularly those of immigrant status, it is common for several families to provide support for one another and at times to live in the same house. The issues that surround these families vary, but the reality of not having enough room for everyone to live comfortably and to have private spaces is presented in *Mi propio cuartito* (2001) by Amada Irma Pérez and illustrated by Maya Christina González. A young Mexican American girl has to share the room and her bed with her younger siblings. Although she loves her brothers, she yearns for a room of her own so that she can read and dream. With the help of her mother, she finds a small closet in their house that becomes her *cuartito*. The *familismo* in this story happens when this young girl's uncles and siblings become involved in making sure that this place becomes special for her, even painting a color "stronger than pink, Magenta!" (p. 17). Students may not have the option of having their own *cuartito*, as the young girl does in this text; however, students can easily design and write about their own special place. Simply having a journal or diary could be that special place for a child to go to share family stories. As an excellent example of familial collectivism, this may be the fertile ground students need to share an event on how their own family comes together to achieve a task, to plan an event, or to solve a problem.

Respeto

The Spanish word *respeto* infers a deep feeling of love and admiration toward someone, particularly in one's family. Latino families show *respeto* for adults such as mothers, fathers, grandparents, aunts, and uncles. We show *respeto* for family members and neighbors. *I Love Saturdays y domingos* (2004), written by Alma Flor Ada and illustrated by Elivia Savadier, portrays a young girl of Mexican American and European-American background visiting her grandparents on Saturdays and Sundays. On Saturdays, the protagonist visits her paternal grandparents, and she engages in practices from a Eurocentric perspective. On Sundays, *domingos*, she visits her maternal *abuelos* (grandparents), *Abuelito* and *Abuelita*, from Puerto Rico and learns *Boricua* (i.e., Puerto Rican) cultural practices. In the book, it is evident that the granddaughter has respect for each family's traditions and language as she uses the language that is spoken by the grandparents. This child navigates in two worlds *con respeto* for both heritages, which also supports biculturalism as a value whereby an individual identifies with and understands two different cultures (Fielding & Harbon, 2013).

Too Many Tamales (1993) by Gary Soto creates a story about obedience and *respeto* with a funny twist. Although the story focuses largely on making *tamales* (a traditional dish consisting of corn-based dough filled with pork or other ingredients) during Christmas, the notion of *respeto* and the consequences that occur when children do not have *respeto* are evident. María is asked not to "play" with her mother's ring and she ignores this request. Disobedience is a sign of "*no tener respeto*" for many Latino families. The story comes alive when all of the cousins get together for a common cause of "finding the ring," which also depicts familial collectivism. It is evident that an important lesson about *respeto* is learned. Most children can tell a story of a time they learned an important lesson, perhaps of not listening to their parents or not having *respeto*. Having children work in groups to share their stories can help jog their memory of similar experiences.

Ser bien educados

An important value in Latino families is to be *bien educado*, which refers to children becoming well-rounded individuals. *Ser bien educados* does not mean having a good education; rather, it is an expectation of how the individual utilizes a socially accepted comportment (e.g., politeness, respect for elders, etc.) in various settings. This expectation benefits children in their socioemotional development. For example, families often tell children to express gratitude by saying "Thank you" or *"Gracias"* when something is given to them. When greeting others, children are expected to have a cordial process for greeting others, such as *beso y abrazo* (kiss and hug), shaking hands, or saying a welcoming greeting. Early on, many children in Latin America hear the traditional song "Pimpón" about a little boy doll who has very good manners. José Luis Orozco includes the song in his children's book *Diez deditos/Ten Little Fingers* (1997). Families often sing this song to encourage children to be like Pimpón and keep good hygiene, stay clean, refrain from crying when something hurts, be friendly, and go to sleep early. These are all values for many Latino families. Author Pat Mora writes a simple book about giving thanks for everything we have, titled *Gracias/ Thanks* (2005) illustrated by John Parra. Another book that subtly promotes *ser educado* through greeting is *Dear Primo: A Letter to My Cousin* (2010) by Duncan Tonatiuh. In this book, Carlitos (in Mexico) and Charlie (in the U.S.) always begin writing their letters by using a formal salutation: "Dear," or *Querido* in Spanish.

Behavior is another expectation of *ser bien educado*. Families often tell children, *Pórtate bien, como un niño bien educada* (behave like a well-edu-cated child). This encourages the child to follow the appropriate social rules, including listening to adults and following their commands. The Latino bi-cultural experience often includes fear of less-than-perfect behavior expected by our families. The individuals' behavior is a reflection of their families, who tell stories about *El Cucuy* to help children think before engaging in unacceptable behavior, *"Si no te portas bien te va a llevar el Cucuy"* (If you don't behave, the *Cucuy* is going to take you away). Very young children from infancy in many Latin American countries and the U.S. are told about the mythical character *El Cucuy, El Coco, or El Cuco*, which is similar to the bogeyman. A traditional Mexican lullaby says, *"Duérmete mi niño, duérmete ya, porque viene el Cuco y te comerá"* (Go to sleep my child, go to sleep now, for if you don't the Cuco would come and eat you). In the book *Mayte y el Cuco/Mayte and the Bogeyman* (2006) by Ada Acosta González and il-lustrated by Christina Rodríguez, Mayte suspects Don Aparicio is *El Cuco*. She comes to this conclusion because Don Aparicio is always complaining about children who misbehave or are naughty and insists that they be taught a lesson. Another version of the *Cucuy* is one written by Joe Hays and illus-trated by Honorio Robledo. *¡El Cucuy! A Bogeyman Cuento in English and Spanish* (2001) recounts the traditional story of how disobedient children get a good scare from *El Cucuy*. It is important for teachers to remember that these stories are set in a mythical context to teach the importance of having good manners. It is a tradition that is not intended to scare or hurt children. Scaring children is never acceptable. Within the context of mythical characters, teachers can discuss the importance of having good manners. In order to conquer the children's fears, as a class the children can make a *Cucuy* collage because *El Cucuy* is different for every child, and *y no es de veras* (it is not real).

Ser bien educados also encompasses being good neighbors in our communities, such as in the book *Quinito's Neighborhood: El vecindario de Quinito* (2013) by Ina Cumpiano and illustrated by José Ramírez. Quinito knows that a *vecindario* (neighborhood) is more than just houses and stores: it is a place where people value and take care of each other. These values are largely embedded in the Latino experience of the importance of looking out for your neighbors and friends out of a sense of solidarity and *el ser bien educados*. We can provide opportunities for children to construct their own neighborhood with blocks. They can add items to their structure such as trees, plants, cars, and even their neighbors! Encourage children to engage in sociodramatic play in the block center. If the children allow the teacher to engage in their play, she or he can act out different roles in order for children to share their experience growing up in their *vecindario* (neighborhood).

Cariño

The feeling of *cariño* comes from love toward anyone who has an important part in your life. For Latinos, *cariño* is more than just an expression; it is a deep feeling toward others that are almost *como familia* (like family). A good example of showing *cariño* toward a family member is in *Antonio's Card/ La tarjeta de Antonio* (2005) by Rigoberto González and illustrated by Cecilia Concepción Álvarez. The focus of this book centers around Antonio, a boy whose family has a different structure—his mother has a partner named Leslie. Although Antonio loves both of his mothers, he struggles when other children start making comments about Leslie's appearance. His reaction is to change the routine and not let the other children see Leslie, but then when Mother's Day comes around, he writes Mother Day's cards for both of his mothers. This book shows the tensions that children may feel when their family's structures are considered nontraditional.

Cariño for the different traditions and values of a family is also shown in the classic children's picture book by Carmen Lomas Garza *Cuadros de familia/Family Pictures* (2005). In this book, Carmen Lomas Garza celebrates a strong sense of family and community and the *cariño* the author has for each. Stories such as the one depicted in these books allow for positive representations of Latino children and their families (Naidoo, 2008). This is the perfect occasion to allow students to share their family structure modeled in the form of a tree. The trunk can be used to write the child's name, while one branch can be added for each member of the family they want to include. Adding leaves with words to describe that family member can show a beautiful representation of their family. The leaves can be different colors to point out the differences in each of their family members.

An interesting book that depicts how *cariño* grows in different situations is *Featherless/Desplumado* (2004) by Juan Felipe Herrera with illustrations by Ernesto Cuevas Jr. This story is about a young boy named Tomasito who is in a wheelchair due to spina bifida. Tomasito at first doesn't like his *desplumado* (featherless) bird. Over time, *cariño* emerges as Tomasito learns to connect with *Desplumado* by talking to him every time the kids in the soccer team ignore Tomasito because he is in a wheelchair. Eventually, the kids in the soccer team learn to be with Tomasito and use his talent of hitting the soccer ball with his head. Tomasito, in turn, learns to appreciate *Desplumado* for who he is. This book is one of the few books that depict Latino children with disabilities. Teachers can see how children without disabilities learn to include children who are different from them. In learning more about children with disabilities, children can share *cariño* with one another. Teachers can share their own personal strengths and weaknesses on a t-chart and invite students to create their own t-chart. This allows students to begin to see that no one is perfect and can help them improve an area or find an area where they can lend support to a classmate.

El Biculturalismo

Latinos differ in their biculturalism depending on their generational status (e.g., recently immigrated, native born of immigrant parent, native born of a native born parent, etc.). Biculturalism is often discussed in relation to language because of the presence of bilingualism within the family. Yet becoming bicultural can present difficulties because of the pressure to conform. It is important for teachers to note that bilingual learners value their bilingualism and also their biculturalism. Thus, the discussion in this section will highlight language in a bicultural world. For instance, author Ofelia Dumas Latchman in *Pepita Talks Twice/Pepita habla dos veces* (1995) gives us an example of a child (Pepita) growing up bilingually and who, although she loves and appreciates her family, finds speaking two languages (English and Spanish) tiring. After a series of events, Pepita decides not to speak Spanish anymore, but eventually she comes around after her dog Lobo does not respond to her when she calls him "Wolf." She finds the benefits of bilingualism by experiencing the need to speak two languages.

An issue that often confronts bicultural children is their Spanish names. In the book *Me llamo María Isabel/My Name is María Isabel* (1996) by Alma Flor Ada with illustrations by Dyble Thompson, a third grader moves from Puerto Rico to the U.S. In her new class, there are two other girls named "María" and the teacher asks her if she can start calling her "Mary." María Isabel wants to fit in, but she is not willing to change her identity as she was named after her grandmothers. Although María Isabel knows that names can be translated, the issue goes deeper to that of the meaning behind the name. For example, when I was a teacher (Riojas-Cortez), a parent specifically asked me during a home visit at the beginning of the school year to make sure that the name of his son, "Esteban," be used and not to translate it to "Stephen" as many would do. The father explained that Esteban was named after his grandfather, who had been promised that his name would always be used. Latino children must learn how to navigate in this bicultural world while always fighting to keep their identity. Jans-Thomas (2009) underscores the importance of teachers studying the heritage of a name in order to better understand children and families. Being bicultural does not mean that children and families must change their identity. A person's name is the sweetest word to their ears and their identity. Teachers can have students discover the meaning and origin of their own name. Children can interview their parents or other family members to learn the origin of their name. Afterward, you can provide children with art materials so that they can use these to decorate their names. This activity can be done at the beginning of the school year. After the children write and decorate their names, they can share their stories with each other or in a small group.

Many Latino authors such as René Colato Laínez tell us personal stories that help us identify the dichotomy of two cultures that immigrant children experience once they immigrate to the U.S. An example is Colato Laínez's book *The Tooth Fairy Meets el Ratón Pérez* (2010). This wonderful story shows one tradition in two cultures that has been adapted in different settings. The tooth fairy traditionally leaves coins for children under their pillow and she takes the fallen tooth. The *ratón* also does the same; so when Colato Linez brings both characters together, it is truly a tug of war very similar to what Latino bicultural children face every day in many contexts. For example, this can be compared to the cultural conflict a child may encounter because of the clash between traditions. Learning the traditions from their culture will first allow children to understand the traditions of the new culture in the U.S. After reading *The Tooth Fairy Meets el Ratón Pérez*, children can choose to make puppets so that they can dramatize conversations that might occur between the two characters.

CONCLUSION

The diversity of families is seen in their different structures and experiences. Latino families in the U.S. have complex experiences. While Latinos have commonalities regarding their notion of family, dependent on various social issues (e.g., generational status and family structure), Latinos may display different types of families. All families have the responsibility of meeting children's physical and emotional needs and providing children with the most fulfilling experiences that can derive from their cultural practices. Teachers must become culturally efficacious (see chapters 1 and 14) and find ways to understand those different notions in the experiences of children. The use of authentic Latino children's literature to critically engage children in issues that they and their friends face every day becomes essential so that children can see their families valued and respected.

REFERENCES

Ada, A. F., & Savadier, E. (2002). *I love Saturdays y domingos*. New York, NY: Atheneum Books for Young Readers.

Argueta, J. (2003). *Xochitl and the flowers/Xóchitl, la niña de las flores*. San Francisco, CA: Children's Book Press.

Bazemore, S. G., & Noblit, G. W. (1978). Class origins and academic achievement: An empirical critique of the cultural deprivation perspective. *Urban Education, 13*(3), 345–60. doi:10.1177/0042085978133006.

Bertrand, D. G., Howard, P. R., & Castilla, J. M. (1999). *Family*. Houston, TX: Piñata Books.

Cisneros, S., & Ybáñez, T. (1994). *Hairs/Pelitos*. New York, NY: Knopf.

Crafter, S. (2012). Parental cultural models and resources for understanding mathematical achievement in culturally diverse school settings. *Educational Studies in Mathematics, 81*(1), 31–46. doi:10.1007/s10649-011-9359-5.

Crawford, J. (1995). *Bilingual education: History, politics, theory, and practice*. Los Angeles, CA: Bilingual Educational Services.

Delgado Bernal, D. (2002). Critical race theory, Latino critical theory, and critical raced-gendered epistemologies: Recognizing students of color as holders and creators of knowledge. *Qualitative Inquiry, 8*(1), 105–26.

Dorros, A., & Colón, R. I. (2014). *Abuelo*. New York, NY: Harper.

Dorros, A., & Gutierrez, R. (2008). *Papá and me*. New York, NY: Rayo/HarperCollinsPublishers.

Dorros, A., & Kleven, E. (1991). *Abuela*. New York, NY: Dutton Children's Books.

Dreby, J. (2007). Children and power in Mexican transnational families. *Journal of Marriage and Family, 69*(4), 1050–64.

East, P. L., & Chien, N. C. (2010). Family dynamics across pregnant Latina adolescents' transition to parenthood. *Journal of Family Psychology*, *24*(6), 709–20. doi. org/10.1037/a0021688.

Fielding, R., & Harbon, L. (2013). Examining bilingual and bicultural identity in young students. *Foreign Language Annals*, *46*(4), 527–44.

Fischer, C., Harvey, E. A., & Driscoll, P. (2009). Parent-centered parenting values among Latino immigrant mothers. *Journal of Family Studies*, *15*(3), 296–308. doi:10.5172/jfs.15.3.296.

Fuller, B., & Coll, C. G. (2010). Learning from Latinos: Contexts, families, and child development in motion. *Developmental Psychology*, *46*(3), 559.

González Burchard, E., Borrell, L. N., Choudhry, S., Naqvi, M., Tsai, H.-J., Rodriguez-Santana, J. R., & Risch, N. (2005). Latino populations: A unique opportunity for the study of race, genetics, and social environment in epidemiological research. *American Journal of Public Health*, *95*(12), 2161–68.

González, N. G., Moll, L. C., & Amanti, C. (Eds.). (2005). *Funds of knowledge: Theorizing practices in households, communities, and classrooms.* Mahwah, NJ: Lawrence Erlbaum Associates.

Gray, N. N., Mendelsohn, D. M., & Omoto, A. M. (2015). Community connectedness, challenges, and resilience among gay Latino immigrants. *American Journal of Community Psychology*, *55*(1), 202–14.

Gutierrez, D. S. (2014). *Illustrated identity: Race and classification in colonial Mexican Casta paintings.* (Dissertation/Thesis), ProQuest, UMI Dissertations Publishing.

Henderson, S. W., & Baily, C. D. R. (2013). Parental deportation, families, and mental health. *Journal of the American Academy of Child and Adolescent Psychiatry*, *52*(5), 451–53. doi:10.1016/j.jaac.2013.01.007.

Herrera, J. F., & Robledo, H. (2003). *Super Cilantro Girl.* San Francisco, CA: Children's Book Press.

Hoffman, E. (2003). *Los mejores colores/Best colors.* St. Paul, MN: Redleaf Press.

Ladson-Billings, G., & Tate, W. F. (2006). *Education research in the public interest: Social justice, action, and policy.* New York, NY: Teachers College Press.

Laínez, R. (2004). *Waiting for Papá/Esperando a Papá.* Houston, TX: Piñata Books.

López, O. S. (2015). Averting another lost decade: Moving Hispanic families from outlier to mainstream family research. *Journal of Family Issues*, *36*(1), 133–59.

Marotta, S. A., & Garcia, J. G. (2003). Latinos in the United States in 2000. *Hispanic Journal of Behavioral Sciences*, *25*(1), 13–34.

Molina, R. S. (2015). Caring while missing children's infancy: Transnational mothering among Honduran women working in Greater Washington. *Human Organization*, *74*(1), 62–73.

Nicholls, L., & Gómez, R. (2014). *Nicolás tiene dos papás.* Santiago de Chile: MOVILH.

Niska, K. J. (1999). Mexican American family processes: Nurturing, support, and socialization. *Nursing Science Quarterly*, *12*(2), 138–42.

Olsen, C. S., & Skogrand, L. (2009). Cultural implications and guidelines for extension and family life programming with Latino/Hispanic audiences. *Forum for Family and Consumer Issues, 14*(1). Retrieved from http://ncsu.edu/ffci/publications/2009/v14-n1-2009-spring/olsen-skogrand.php.

Oropesa, R. S. (1996). Normative beliefs about marriage and cohabitation: A comparison of non-Latino whites, Mexican Americans, and Puerto Ricans. *Journal of Marriage and Family, 58*(1), 49–62.

Pérez, A. I., & González, M. C. (2000). *My very own room*. San Francisco, CA: Children's Book Press.

Punch, S. (2012). Studying transnational children: A multi-sited, longitudinal, ethnographic approach. *Journal of Ethnic and Migration Studies, 38*(6), 1007–23.

Riojas-Cortez, M., & Flores, B. B. (2010). Música, versos y juegos: Familias Latinas desarrollando el lenguaje oral con sus niños *Novedades Educativas: Publicación de Nivel General y Educación, 22*(230), 46–49.

Riojas-Cortez, M., Flores, B. B., Smith, H. L., & Clark, E. R. (2003). Cuéntame un cuento: Bridging family literacy with school literacy. *Language Arts, 81*(1), 62–71.

Tafolla, C., & Córdova, A. (2010). *Fiesta Babies*. Berkeley, CA: Tricycle Press.

Tonatiuh, D. (2010). *Dear primo: A letter to my cousin*. New York, NY: Abrams.

U.S. Census Bureau. (2010). Current Population Survey Glossary. Retrieved from www.census.gov/cps/about/cpsdef.html.

DISCUSSION QUESTIONS

1. How do children learn their beliefs, values, and traditions? How can you incorporate these into your lessons?
2. What makes Latino families unique? Select and identify books from part V that can be used to teach *familismo*.
3. Discuss different family structures found in your neighborhood community.
4. Why do you think Latino families are often the focal point of Latino children's literature?
5. Think about your own family experiences. How were family values taught to you?

ACTIVITIES

A. In addition to reading books in which the focus is the family with children, we can also ask them to draw a picture of their family, or a picture showing one day in the life of their family, or a picture of a family activity or event.
B. To bring *familismo* to the classroom, teachers can have students share the preparation of a dish, or any other activity that they do with a special

member of their family. Teachers can send home index cards and ask families to write their favorite *receta de la familia* or family recipe. Once all cards are collected, the teacher can have each child illustrate their recipe on their card. The teacher can send home a copy of the cookbook and have families discuss similarities and differences among the recipes provided. The teacher can also have the children discuss what their families do when they make the special recipe, thus enhancing the topic of *familismo*.

C. Have children tell a story of a time they learned an important lesson, perhaps of not listening to their parents or adult, or of not having *respeto*. Having children work in groups to share their stories can help jog their memory of similar experiences.

D. Have children discover the meaning and origin of their own name. Children can interview their parents or other family members to learn the origin of their name. Afterward, provide children with art materials they can use to decorate their names. This activity can be done at the beginning of the school year. After the children write and decorate their names, they can share their stories with each other or in a small group.

E. Select a book that deals with immigration issues and design an activity that can help children understand or cope with living apart from a family member or hardships of crossing the border.

PROFESSIONAL READINGS

Riojas-Cortez, M., & Flores, B. B. (2009). Sin olvidar a los padres: Families as collaborators within the school and university partnership. *Journal of Latinos and Education, 8*(3), 231–39.

———. (2009). Supporting preschoolers' social development in school through funds of knowledge. *The Journal of Early Childhood Research, 7*(2), 185–99.

Riojas-Cortez, M., Flores, B. B., & Clark, E. R. (2003). Los niños aprenden en la casa: Valuing and connecting home cultural knowledge with the school's early childhood education program. *Young Children, 58*(6), 78–83.

Riojas-Cortez, M., Flores, B. B., Smith, H. L., & Clark, E. R. (2003). Cuéntame un cuento: Bridging family literacy with school literacy. *Language Arts, 81*(1), 62–71.

Chapter Six

Using Culturally Relevant Literature for Latino Children in the Early Childhood Classroom

Ysaaca Axelrod and Cristina Gillanders

INTRODUCTION

The Latino population in the United States is increasingly larger and more diverse (Pew Research Hispanic Trends Project; U.S. 2012 Census Report; see chapter 1), and there is a need for children's books in classrooms that represent the multiple and diverse experiences of Latinos. While there has been a slight increase in books written in English and Spanish that represent authentic Latino experiences, as well as more translations of books into Spanish, there continues to be a dearth of such books, particularly for children under the age of five (Rich, 2012; see chapter 1).

There are few board books (books printed on thick paperboard, designed for very young children who are learning how to handle books) in Spanish for young children, and most are translations of well-known books such as *Brown Bear, Brown Bear, What Do You See?* by Bill Martin Jr. and Eric Carle (1983); *The Very Hungry Caterpillar* by Eric Carle (1979); and *Good Night Moon* by Margaret Wise Brown (1947). While these books are much loved, they do not reflect the cultural and linguistic practices of Latino children. For children ages 5–7, there are more options; in addition to translations of well-known English books, there are several authors, such as Alma Flor Ada, Monica Brown, Maya Christina González, Duncan Tonatiuh, and Pat Mora, who portray Latino children and families and who incorporate Spanish through translanguaging practices (including words in Spanish in text or fully translated stories; García, 2009; see chapter 1).

In spite of the increased number of books that are culturally and linguistically relevant for Latino bilingual learners, it is still a challenge for teachers to find ways to select texts that are authentic for the children in their classrooms and to then incorporate these books into their curriculum. The most important factor for teachers is to build relationships and learn about the students in their classroom in order to be able to select books that are culturally and linguistically authentic and reflect their students' experiences. Given the diversity within Latino students, this is a challenge; however, the purpose of this chapter is to offer some suggestions and guidance for selecting texts for young children as well as offering examples of existing literature and ways to use this literature in classrooms.

The focus of this chapter is to examine children's books that are appropriate for early childhood classrooms and discuss ways to incorporate these authentically into the curriculum. We use the term "teacher" in this chapter to refer to anyone who is interacting with children and literature, so this might include a classroom teacher, librarian, tutor, paraprofessional, and even a parent. We will examine the formal aspects of texts such as the use of language and vocabulary, text formatting, and visual stereotyping in illustrations. We will then offer suggestions of ways to include these texts within the classroom curriculum, both as part of explicit literacy instruction, as well as part of creating a classroom that engages in culturally relevant pedagogy.

THEORETICAL FRAMEWORK

In this chapter, we rely on two theoretical frameworks to guide our ideas of the importance of using culturally and linguistically authentic texts with young bilingual learners. The first framework we use is a sociocultural framework, drawing primarily on the work of Levi Vygotsky (1978) and Jerome Bruner (1986). One of the primary tenets of sociocultural theory is that it supports the notion that children learn through social interactions with others, and their development occurs first on a social level and then on an individual level. Vygotsky (1978) talks about the ways that children learn from each other, a more skilled peer, or an adult. In the classroom context, we see the ways that teachers and peers support learning by introducing new concepts, modeling behaviors or skills, and sharing experiences. Children learn language through conversations and through reading and writing texts. Young bilingual learners are learning and negotiating the process of learning two (and sometimes more) languages and cultures. They are learning these languages from their families, communities, teachers, and peers.

Because of the social nature of learning, the community, culture, and context within which children are developing are important factors in a child's development. Children are not just learning skills; rather, they are also learning cultural practices and norms. Bruner writes, "It is not just that the child must make his knowledge his own, but that he must make it his own in a community of those who share his sense of belonging to a culture" (Bruner, 1986, p. 127). Children who are bilingual learners are learning the cultural practices and norms that are associated with the languages that they speak. They are learning the contexts where they speak each language; for example, at home they might speak Spanish, but at the supermarket they speak English. Teachers who work with young bilingual learners need to recognize and understand the complex process involved in learning and negotiating multiple languages. In order to support the development of children, we must acknowledge and recognize their cultural and linguistic experiences outside of the classroom and use these as resources within the classrooms. In this chapter, we will describe strategies to help teachers select texts that build on children's linguistic and cultural capital, and offer suggestions for how to use these within the classroom.

The second theoretical framework that guides our work in this chapter is a critical multicultural approach to language and literacy development. Many scholars focus on multicultural education and have different definitions of what constitutes multicultural education (Souto-Manning, 2013). In this chapter, we are focusing on two goals of multicultural education: (1) the inclusion of culturally and linguistically diverse content (in our particular case, Latino children's literature), and (2) the ways that this literature can be used to help empower children and challenge deficit orientations of the language and literacy skills of children who speak languages other than English. Scholars who focus on children's literature argue that "it is critical for children of color to be afforded opportunities to see themselves, their cultural norms, and perspectives included in the books that they read" (McNair, 2013, p. 193); we argue that this is also true for language practices. It is important for children to see representations that they can identify with in stories so they can build connections to the text and feel that their language and cultural experiences are important and relevant. In addition, we argue that literature that represents the experiences of Latino children and their language practices are important for any classroom given the increased number of Latinos in the U.S. and given our increasingly globalized society. "Multicultural teaching is good teaching for all students" (Souto-Manning, 2013, p. 5); all children and teachers benefit from literature that authentically represents the language and cultural practices of different groups within our society. While the focus of this chapter is helping teachers to select and develop a literacy curriculum that is authentic to the young Latino children they serve, we believe that all classrooms benefit from a critical multicultural approach.

PRAXIS: APPLICATION OF THEORY

The purpose of this chapter is to both offer some suggestions of texts that portray Latinos, including language practices of Latinos, as well as provide suggestions for how to select literature that is culturally and linguistically relevant for particular groups of children. While we are using the term "Latino" to refer to a group of people, it is important to acknowledge the diversity within the group, based on country of origin, language practices, immigration patterns, and history, as well as individual differences among children and families. What we offer are aspects to consider when deciding which books to integrate in the curriculum and instruction. Ultimately, early childhood educators will make the most appropriate decisions based on their deep knowledge of the children and families.

Authenticity

The power of using multicultural literature in the early childhood classroom not only lies on its literary characteristics but also on its potential as a pedagogical tool (Fox & Short, 2003) for developing children's language, reading comprehension, socioemotional development, and ability to become participants in their sociocultural contexts. In order to maximize the potential of literature as a pedagogical tool, authenticity should become critical. A common notion of authenticity is the idea that the reader senses that there is truth in how a cultural experience is represented in the book (Fox & Short, 2003). Take for instance using authentic texts for promoting reading comprehension. In his book *The Life of Pi*, Martel (2012) writes, "The world isn't just the way it is. It is how we understand it, no? And in understanding something, we bring something to it, no? Doesn't that make life a story?" (p. 302). In order to understand a text, a reader must intentionally interact with the reading and "bring something to it." Books that are completely alien to Latino children's experiences will hinder their ability to make connections to their prior knowledge. For bilingual Latinos, stories that show similarities to their own lives will aid their ability to comprehend the text even when they may not have the vocabulary to understand each word.

In her work with African American children's literature, Jonda McNair (2008) focuses on the importance for African American children and their families of reading books that portray African Americans, their cultural practices, and perspectives in helping develop children's literacy skills. Reading culturally relevant books helps students better understand and engage more deeply with texts. The use of culturally and linguistically authentic texts has potential for increasing Latino children's achievement in classrooms (see chapters 1 and 2).

Furthermore, authenticity in the text can have implications for children's self-identity. Beginning in early childhood, children start the process of developing their self-concept (Brown, Mangelsdorf, Neff, Schoppe-Sullivan, & Frosch, 2009). A positive self-concept is paramount for children's social and emotional development. Participation in sociocultural practices with family and friends inform children's self-discovery. Similarly, children obtain information about their identity through portrayals of "people like them" in books and media. Stereotypical and negative images of the self can misrepresent how children define themselves. McNair (2008) also discusses the benefits of culturally relevant literature for children's identity and identity development as well as their overall literacy skills. Authentic literature can provide a realistic depiction of Latino children and their families and therefore contribute to a more positive development of their identity and self-concept (see chapters 1 and 3).

Therefore, authenticity should be considered in light of the function of the literature in the lives of the readers (Fox & Short, 2003). How can we decide if a book is authentic or not? Our position is that authenticity will be determined by the sociocultural practices of the children, families, and communities in the classroom. In the U.S., Latinos can trace their heritage to more than twenty Spanish-speaking nations worldwide (Pew, 2013). Furthermore, within these groups' histories of immigration, socioeconomic status, education, and life, stories vary widely. Thus, even children's literature with a "Latino theme" can be inauthentic if it does not reflect the vast array of experiences of Latino children and families in the U.S. For example, the book *Los Tres Pequeños Jabalies/The Three Little Javelinas* by Susan Lowell (1992) uses the tale of "The Three Little Pigs" for describing the adventures of three javelinas (southwestern cousins of pigs) living in homes built out of tumbleweeds and saguaro, and running from a hungry coyote, who hopes to eat them with red chile sauce. Latino children from the southwest and with a Mexican heritage will probably identify important elements of this story, while those living in Puerto Rican communities in New York City will be unfamiliar with its humorous subtleties.

Consequently, to decide if a book is authentic or not, we believe that rather than examining which aspects in children's books seem to represent Latinos,

teachers should focus on the cultural practices in which the children participate in their everyday lives with their families and communities. As Gutierrez
and Rogoff (2003) recommend,

> By focusing on the varied ways people participate in their community's activi-
> ties, we can move away from the tendency to conflate ethnicity with culture,
> with assignment to ethnic groups made on the basis of immutable and often
> stable characteristics such as Spanish surname or country of birth. Equating
> culture with race, ethnicity, language preference, or national origin results in
> overly deterministic, static, weak, and uncomplicated understandings of both
> individuals and the community practices in which they participate. (p. 21)

As an example, Cappiello and Savage (2013) describe the challenge the
teachers at East Migrant Head Start faced to find children's books that
reflected the experience of Mexican migrant families in the Southeast.
Therefore, they developed a series of children's books based on the cultural
practices of Mexican workers in the farmland. Teachers organized a series of
focus groups in which they learned about the parents' sociocultural practices,
stories of immigration, and work and life in the farmland. Using this information, teachers created several children's books that had themes related to
working in the farmland and migrating. Parents were asked their opinions
about the books and if they really reflected their lives. They also asked parents to relate their experiences growing up in Mexico, their hopes and dreams
for their children, their current work, and what they enjoy about their jobs.
Children and parents created books that were then used in the classroom for
promoting early literacy (Cappiello & Savage, 2013). A point to consider was
that the Head Start teachers had established a positive relationship with the
families that allowed them to explore more deeply the families' sociocultural
experiences and co-construct the books that they were going to use.

In another example from a bilingual (Spanish/English) Head Start classroom in New York City, the teachers often found themselves unable to find
books that accurately reflected the demographics of all their students (Dominican, Puerto Rican, Mexican, Mixtec) within a single book. Many children's books address a particular group of Latinos, such as Gary Soto's *Too
Many Tamales* (1992), which tells a story about a Mexican girl at Christmas
making a traditional Mexican dish, tamales. This book is a popular and much
loved story; however, the cultural practices that it highlights are specific to a
particular community, and not all Latinos share these practices. The teachers
at Head Start also struggled to find books that accurately portrayed the reality of living in a large city, such as a New York City, with Latino characters.
In their classroom, the teachers "resolved" this issue by creating books every
year using photographs of the children in the class and having the children

write the captions for the photographs. The captions were sometimes in English, sometimes in Spanish, and sometimes a combination of both, reflecting the children's linguistic skills and preferences. By using the children's images and voices, the teachers were able to create books in the classroom that accurately portrayed and reflected the experiences of their students. The children loved reading these books, pointing out their friends and commenting on what they were doing. These classroom-made books allowed the children to see their experiences and lives in print.

The teachers' concerns in these examples highlight the challenges of finding literature that accurately reflects the diversity of the Latino population. In classrooms where children come from a variety of backgrounds, it is a challenge to find books that are inclusive of many nationalities and sociocultural experiences. Another way that the teachers in this classroom worked to make books inclusive was by highlighting the particular cultural or language practice shown in books and using these as discussion points for the children. During a read aloud about a kite, for example, the teacher stopped at the word "*cometa*," which is the word for "kite" in the story. The teacher asked the children, pointing to the picture of the kite, what they would call this object. The children called out *chiringa, papalote, papagayo,* and *volantín,* all of which are words for kite in different countries in Latin America. These words then became the impetus for a discussion where the teacher would talk about the different varieties of Spanish in the classroom. While the teacher in this classroom was a Spanish-speaker, in these conversations both teacher and students were positioned as learners. Teachers had similar conversations when reading about particular cultural practices, such as the making of *tamales* and *piñatas* at birthdays, which is not shared by all Latinos (see chapter 3). The teachers would ask children to share what their family would do for special occasions, such as birthdays and holidays, foods that they would prepare together with their families, and places they would visit with their families (either trips back to see family members or visits to local parks or attractions). These conversations were ways for the teachers and children to get to know each other as well as ways for the teachers to help the children make connections to texts that perhaps might not otherwise be culturally relevant to them.

Language

Another aspect to consider when examining a children's book is how language is used. Barrera and Quiroa (2003) have pointed out that in the last few years, Spanish has been introduced in many Latino children's books. Some authors have used a few Spanish words in the text to introduce a "cultural flavor" to the story, while others create bilingual books that include both the English and Spanish complete texts. Unfortunately, it is common to find misspellings, incorrect grammar, and typographical errors in books that are English-based and incorporate Spanish words in the text, and in bilingual books. In books that are bilingual—that is, books with the same text in English and another language—it is important to consider if the translations are grammatically correct and if they maintain the main goal and stylistic properties of the original text. When words in Spanish are used in an English-based book, the authors attempt to illustrate the way that many Latino immigrants in the U.S. use code-switching or translanguaging practices (see chapter 2).

In some cases, in order to maintain the authenticity of the narrative, it might be essential to use words in Spanish or English that do not have translation. For example, words for foods such as *tamales, tacos, empanadas,* and *arroz con leche* do not have English equivalents. Some kinship words frequently used are *mamá, papá, abuela,* and *tío,* among others (Barrera & Quiroa, 2003). These words are introduced to reflect emotional connection or an intimate relationship with members of the family. In many Latino families who have become English monolinguals through the generations, they may continue to maintain Spanish terms of kinship even though they use mainly English to communicate among themselves. We agree with Barrera and Quiroa (2003) that the use of some well-selected words in English-based books can bring some authenticity to a book because they can reflect language practices in specific sociocultural settings. However, introducing Spanish words without a cultural understanding of how these words are used in authentic settings can lead to stereotypical views of Latinos (Martínez-Roldán, 2013). More research is needed to determine the potential benefits of books that use well-chosen words in Spanish or English for young bilingual Latino learners.

Research evidence exists, however, that bilingual books have benefits for literacy development. Naqvi, Thorne, Pfitscher, Nordstokke, and McKeough (2013) conducted an experimental study in which teachers and native language readers read bilingual books for fifteen weeks to a group of kindergarten children with diverse language backgrounds. Results indicated that those children in the experimental group who were read to in English, French, Punjabi, and Urdu showed greater gains in graphophonemic knowledge than those who were read to in English only. Findings such as these indicate that bilingual books have great potential for literacy development in young Latino dual-language learners. Furthermore, in another experimental study, Mendez, Crais, Castro, and Kainz (2015) compared the effectiveness of a vocabulary development intervention in which one group of Latino Spanish-English bilingual preschoolers were exposed to readings aloud of culturally relevant bilingual storybooks, while another group were exposed to the same books but only read in English. Children in the group exposed to the bilingual condition learned more words in both English and Spanish than the children in the English only condition.

For those teachers who are monolingual English speakers, evaluating the quality of the Spanish translations in bilingual books or the use of Spanish words might be a daunting task. These teachers may be interested in creating an advisory group of parents or community members who can provide insights about the authenticity of the book and the quality of the language used. Another safeguard is selecting books that have received awards for Latino children's literature such as the Américas Book Award, the Tomás Rivera Mexican American Children's Book Award, and the Pura Belpré Award (see chapters 1 and 2).

Another aspect to consider regarding language is the text or script in which the language has been written. In some books the text or script in each language demonstrates a different status. Reyes (2006) describes how Spanish-English bilingual young children create "theories" to explain the differences between English and Spanish in books. A four-year-old participant in her study, for example, explained that a text was written in English because "*están las letras grandes*" (the letters are big) and the one in Spanish "*porque están las letras chiquitas*" (the letters are small). Reyes (2006) further explains that in some bilingual books the script might show more importance in terms of size, boldness, position on the page and spacing between lines. Some authors choose to differentiate texts using different colors to represent each language. What is clear is that an important consideration when choosing Latino literature is that Spanish should not be portrayed as a less-important language in comparison to English.

Illustrations

The most important role of the illustrations in a picture book is to enrich the story to engage the reader in the life of the characters. As mentioned earlier, illustrations can also have implications for children's development of their self-concept and identity. Consequently, illustrations need to depict realistically the experiences of children in their everyday lives. There is also another reason for presenting illustrations that are realistic, especially for the very young. In a study of fifteen- and eighteen-month-olds, Ganea, Pickard, and DeLoache (2008) found that when children were presented with realistic pictures of a novel object (i.e., realistic photographs and drawings rather than realistic cartoons), they tended to have less difficulty transferring the label from the picture to the novel object. Very young children are more likely to

identify the new vocabulary in real objects when illustrations are more realistic (see chapter 13).

Another aspect to consider with slightly older children is that when interpreting illustrations, they often ignore the text in a book and rely mostly on
their personal experiences (Schickedanz & Collins, 2012). The teacher's role
is to clarify these misconceptions through explanations. In these explanations,
the teacher can model the process of integrating various sources of information, including children's background knowledge and experiences, especially
with young children (Schickedanz & Collins, 2012).

Stories

The search to achieve authenticity should not be detrimental to creating an
interesting story. Stories should engage and spark children's imagination.
Boring stories will not capture children's attention even if they are authentic.
Cognitive scientists have indicated that interest level in a story can benefit
children's recall and reading comprehension (Hidi & Baird, 1986). Traditional folk and fairy tales are often of high interest to children (see chapter
7). They also can provide emotional, cognitive, and linguistic benefits to
bilingual children (Gregory, 2009). In the book *The Uses of Enchantment*
(2010), famous psychoanalyst Bruno Bettelheim suggests that children can
use fairy tales to solve interpersonal and moral problems. Since most folk
and fairy tales use a traditional narrative structure, children learn that stories
have a beginning, middle, and end and also have specific language forms (i.e.,
"Once upon a time"). This knowledge will help them in the future to comprehend more sophisticated texts. For bilingual Latino children, folk stories can
help them become socialized into the traditions and oral storytelling of their
families and communities (see chapters 5 and 11).

At times teachers believe that narratives with intricate story lines may
be difficult for young children to follow, especially if they are bilingual.
However, in our experience, stories that have suspense, unexpected events,
and are centered on important questions about life are usually quite popular
among young children. For example, the book *La Cucaracha Martina*, retold
and illustrated by Daniel Moreton (1999) and available both in English and
Spanish, tells the story of a ravishing cockroach who is determined to find the
source of the one beautiful noise she has heard among the loud city sounds.
In her search she receives several marriage proposals until she finds the true
source of the beautiful noise, a cricket, which she ends up marrying. This
story is based on a Caribbean folktale and can be found in different versions
in Latin America (e.g., La ratoncita presumida/*The Vain Mouse*). Moreton's
version is thirty-one pages long, which could be considered a long book for

four-year-olds. However, in our work with teachers, we have found that this book is of great interest to children, especially when they are provided with opportunities to retell the story in their dominant language or to reenact it in the dramatic play area (Gillanders & Castro, 2011). In one classroom, the teacher arranged the dramatic play area with pictures of the children's parents' weddings and included props such as wedding veils and ties. Children created invitation cards for the wedding and played "getting married," deepening their comprehension of the story and extending into their play the vocabulary used in the book.

SELECTING AND USING
YOUNG CHILDREN'S LITERATURE

In the following section, we highlight some books and authors that offer culturally and linguistically relevant literature for Latino children, and we offer suggestions for how these might be used with young children (see also table 6.1 at the end of this chapter). We have organized this section according to different language practices within books: books appropriate for very young children; books with their text translated into both English and Spanish; and books that include translanguaging within the text. All of these books represent different aspects of Latino culture, nationalities, and language practices. We have attempted to present a collection of literature that is inclusive of the diversity among Latino families and communities.

Books for Very Young Children

Author Ginger Foglesong Gibson and illustrator René King Moreno have collaborated on several bilingual books that are appropriate for very young children (the books are available in paperback as well as board book format). We will focus on two of their books, *¡Fiesta!* (2003) and *¡Siesta!* (2005), and some ways to use these in classrooms. *¡Fiesta!* focuses on preparations for a party, and on each page the children add new items, *una canasta* (one basket), *dos trompetas* (two horns), *tres animalitos* (three little animals). Similarly, *Siesta* focuses on preparing for a nap outdoors, and on each page the children grab different items a *mochila azul* (blue backpack), *chaqueta roja* (red jacket), *flauta verde* (green flute). Both books focus on concepts that are part of the early childhood curricula: counting, colors, and early literacy skills, such as repetitive text. However, these books offer the possibility of teaching and talking about these concepts in ways that are culturally and linguistically relevant to young Latino children. The text in both English and Spanish helps support young learners who are learning English by providing them with conceptual knowledge in Spanish, while developing their vocabulary in both languages. The simplicity of the text and its repetition, exact translation, and visual support allow teachers who might not be familiar with Spanish to support the language development of young bilingual learners.

The themes of these books—naps and a party—are familiar and relevant to most young children's lives. The books' illustrations depict what appear to be Latino children; however, neither book makes specific reference to a particular ethnicity or nationality. In the book *¡Fiesta!*, we do see particular references to Latino culture, such as the *piñata* (which is most strongly associated with Mexican culture; however, it has been adopted by other cultures too), and many of the images of the market portray objects that are associated with various Latino cultures, such as *maracas*, woven blankets, and ceramics.

These books could be used as starting points for conversations with children about their home lives and traditions. Both books center around activities that are part of children's home lives, celebrations, and day-to-day activities. After reading *¡Siesta!*, teachers can ask children to talk about what they might take with them on a nap—for example, something that is important to them, like a favorite toy—songs they might sing with their families, places they might want to go to take a nap. After reading *¡Fiesta!*, teachers can ask children how they and their families celebrate special events in their homes (being sensitive to the fact that some families might not celebrate holidays or birthdays; see chapter 5). Using this knowledge, teachers can have children create their own books about objects they would want to bring for a nap, or objects they would place in a *piñata*. Children could also write a book together, mimicking the style of the mentor texts, focusing on some of the concepts presented in each of the books, such as numbers and colors.

These books, while quite simple, offer the possibility of showing children images in books that might be relevant and familiar to them as they learn basic concepts. Teachers should be mindful of the importance of using culturally and linguistically relevant texts even when teaching basic concepts such as numbers, colors, and shapes in order to engage and help all children make connections to their lives and experiences (see part III).

Bilingual Books

Some books include both texts in English and Spanish on the same page, which gives the opportunity to teachers to read the book in both languages. Two books by Diane Gonzáles Bertrand and illustrated by Alejandro Galindo worth mentioning are *The Empanadas That Abuela Made/Las empanadas que hacía la abuela* (2003) and *The Party for Papá Luis/La fiesta para Papá*

Luis (2010). These books highlight the importance of extended family celebrations in the context of cooking and birthday parties. An interesting aspect of these books benefitting bilinguals is that the text cumulatively includes a new phrase. For bilingual learners, the repetition provides the opportunity to learn "chunks of language" (Gregory, 1996) that will serve as a basis for creating syntactic constructions in the new language. The script used in the book has an equal status in English and Spanish, and children can learn new vocabulary in both languages. These books also represent important values for Latino families such as the importance of the extended family and working together toward a common goal.

Teachers can also engage young children in role-playing. For example, during the reading aloud of *The Party for Papá Luis* (Gonzáles Bertrand & Galindo, 2010), children can be encouraged to represent each one of the characters of the story. Children can also use the book as a reference to plan a party for the class (e.g., writing invitations, preparing decorations, counting the candy for the *piñata*, preparing a cake, etc.). Similarly, *The Empanadas That Abuela Made* (2003) can become a springboard for conversations about the food that children eat in their homes. The book includes a recipe for empanadas that can be reproduced on chart paper so children can make these in the classroom.

Translanguaging in Books

"Translanguaging" is a term used to refer to the dynamic processes of bilinguals whereby they draw from their full linguistic repertoire through blending of their language practices (García, 2009). An example of translanguaging in texts is when authors include words in the text that are in another language as a way to emphasize particular words; or because the word in the other language is more appropriate; or because there is not a good translation of the particular word. This technique of translanguaging in texts is often used (as we describe in the language section above) when the majority of the text is written in English, with interspersed words in Spanish for emphasis. In most cases, the meaning of the words in Spanish can be figured out through context clues, although on occasion the author will provide explanations (see chapter 7). In this section, we will present several books and authors that use this technique. Arthur Dorros's book *Isla* (1999) talks about a young girl's adventure with her *abuela* (grandmother) when they fly over the island from which her grandmother originated. This book is available in English with Spanish phrases and in Spanish with English phrases. In the book, the child and her grandmother "visit" an island in the Caribbean and see different parts of the island—the markets, the beaches—and visit family.

The phrases in the "non-dominant" language in the text are used for family members, grandmother, aunt, and uncle, and to highlight different aspects of the text.

Alma Flor Ada's *I Love Saturdays y domingos* (2004) tells the story of a little girl and her two sets of grandparents. She spends Saturdays with her English-speaking grandparents and *domingos* (Sundays) with her Spanish-speaking grandparents. The dialogue is written in Spanish when she talks about Sundays, demonstrating that she and her grandparents speak in Spanish. Throughout the book, the main character talks about the different things she does with each set of grandparents, highlighting the different cultural practices of each and also demonstrating the ways in which she blends and navigates across and between them.

We have decided to include books written primarily in one language but blending in a second language in order to highlight the language practices of some Latino children, who might engage in translanguaging practices, using both English and Spanish, depending on context and audience. Both of these books focus on family, and the selection of words to be translated are purposeful and add emphasis to the stories (see chapter 5). *Isla* does not mention a particular island; however, it does highlight aspects of the culture of Spanish-speaking countries in the Caribbean (Cuba, the Dominican Republic, Puerto Rico). As the reader, we are led to assume that the young child has created this imaginary adventure based on the stories she has been told by her grandmother. This would be a great way to start a conversation with young children and their families about where they are from, and what stories they might want to share. It is an opportunity to invite family members to share stories about their home countries (or towns; see chapter 4). After reading this story in a Head Start classroom in New York City, many of the children (who were from the Dominican Republic and Puerto Rico) decided to play that they were going on a trip. They rearranged the chairs in the classroom to be an airplane and took a trip to the islands, recreating scenes from the book during their play. In early childhood classrooms, teachers can incorporate elements of traveling and of children's home countries into the dramatic play area in order to encourage children to play and act out what it might be like to visit different countries.

I Love Saturdays y domingos is a book that explicitly talks about different cultural practices across two cultures, as well as the ways that some individuals navigate between different cultures. This book is particularly useful to have in early childhood classrooms with a diverse group of children as it opens up a conversation about different languages. It offers the possibility of discussing language and cultural practices, such as who speaks what language with whom and what are some of the different things that we might do in our homes, as well as differences within families themselves.

CONCLUSION

Our goal in this chapter is to offer suggestions and guidance for selecting children's literature for young Latino bilingual early childhood learners; however, while we can provide a framework for selecting literature, the most important component for selecting literature is to know the children and families in your classroom or coming to your library (Zapata, 2013). In order to be able to pick books that are relevant to the experiences of the children in your classroom or library, you must be familiar with their lives, experiences, linguistic practices, and homes and communities. In his work on "funds of knowledge," Moll and his colleagues (1992) discuss the importance of teachers getting to know and learning about the resources within the families of the children in their classrooms. They argue that learning about funds of knowledge within a community is important because it positions the teacher as the learner and the families as experts, and with this new knowledge, teachers can better help students leverage their prior knowledge and skills in the classroom context and with the curriculum. An important component of children's cultural capital is language, and books that are written in Spanish and English offer early childhood students the possibility of drawing from their full linguistic repertoire in classrooms, as well as developing language and literacy skills in both languages. Teachers who are monolingual often feel that they are unable to support children's home-language development because of their lack of familiarity with the languages; however, bilingual books in classrooms and libraries are a way to support children's language development, and teachers have the opportunity to learn language skills from their students.

Through children's literature, teachers position themselves as learners too, learning from children and texts about cultures/languages that they might not be familiar with. Nathenson-Mejía and Escamilla (2003) describe a study in which they used Latino children's literature in a teacher preparation course. Most of the teacher candidates in these courses were white, middle-class, monolingual females with little previous experience working with Latino children and families. Using bilingual books that reflected sociocultural practices of mostly Mexican-American children, teacher candidates found connections between their lives and those of the children they were teaching. Teacher candidates were also able to observe children's enthusiasm toward these books and reflect on the influence of the books in children's comprehension.

Culturally and linguistically relevant texts must be part of the early childhood classroom curriculum and not seen as "add on" activities for special occasions, such as holidays. Students must feel like their experiences and linguistic practices are part of the daily curriculum in order for them to see themselves as part of the classroom community and to see the relevance of the curriculum to their lives.

REFERENCES

Ada, A. F., & Savadier, E. (2004). *I love Saturdays y domingos.* New York, NY: Aladdin Paperbacks.

Barrera, R., & Quiroa, R. (2003). The use of Spanish in Latino children's literature in English: What makes for cultural authenticity? In D. L. Fox & K. G. Short (Eds.), *Stories matter: The complexity of cultural authenticity in children's literature* (pp. 247–65). Urban, IL: NCTE.

Bertrand, D. G., DeLange, A. P., Ventura, G. B., & Gruenbeck, L. (2003). *The empanadas that abuela made.* Houston, TX: Piñata Books.

Bertrand, D. G., Galindo, A., & Ventura, G. B. (2010). *The party for Papá Luis.* Houston, TX: Piñata Books.

Bettelheim, B. (2010). *The uses of enchantment: The meaning and importance of fairy tales.* New York, NY: Vintage Books.

Brown, G. L., Mangelsdorf, S. C., Neff, C., Schoppe-Sullivan, S. J., & Frosch, C. A. (2009). Young children's self-concepts: Associations with child temperament, mothers' and fathers' parenting, and triadic family interaction. *Merrill-Palmer Quarterly, 55*(2), 184–216.

Brown, M. W., & Hurd, C. (1947). *Goodnight moon.* New York, NY: Harper.

Bruner, J. (1986). *Actual minds, possible worlds.* Cambridge, MA: Harvard University Press.

Cappiello, C., & Savage, K. (2013, June). *No tengo límites: Who I become when parents and schools partner in bicultural education.* Paper presented at the National Institute for Professional Development of the National Association for the Education of Young Children, San Francisco, California.

Carle, E. (1979). *The very hungry caterpillar.* New York, NY: Philomel Books.

Dorros, A., Kleven, E., & Dorros, S. M. (1999). *Isla.* New York, NY: Puffin Books.

Fox, D., & Short, K. (Eds.). (2003). *Stories matter: The complexity of cultural authenticity in children's literature.* Urbana, IL: National Council of Teachers of English.

Ganea, P. A., Pickard, M. B., & DeLoache, J. S. (2008). Transfer between picture books and the real world by very young children. *Journal of Cognition and Development, 9*(1), 46–66.

García, O. (2009). *Bilingual education in the 21st century: A global perspective.* Malden, MA: Wiley-Blackwell.

Gibson, G. F., & Moreno, R. K. (2005). *¡Siesta!*. New York, NY: Greenwillow Books.

———. (2003). *Fiesta!* Columbus, OH: SRA/McGraw-Hill.

Gillanders, C., & Castro, D. C. (2011). Storybook reading for young dual-language learners. *Young Children, 66*(1), 91–95.

Gregory, E. (2008). *Learning to read in a new language: Making sense of words and worlds.* Thousand Oaks, CA: Sage Publishers.

Gutierrez, K. D., & Rogoff, B. (2003). Cultural ways of learning: Individual traits or repertoires of practice. *Educational Researcher, 32*(5), 19–25.

Hidi, S., & Baird, W. (1986). Interestingness—A neglected variable in discourse processing. *Cognitive Science, 10*(2), 179–94.

Lowell, S., & Harris, J. (1992). *The three little javelinas.* Flagstaff, AZ: Northland Publishing.

Martel, Y. (2012). *Life of Pi: A novel.* New York, NY: Mariner Books.

Martin, B., & Carle, E. (1983). *Brown bear, brown bear, what do you see?* New York, NY: Holt, Rinehart, and Winston.

Martínez-Roldán, C. M. (2013). The representation of Latinos and the use of Spanish: A critical content analysis of *Skippyjon Jones. Journal of Children's Literature, 39*(1), 5–14.

McNair, J. C. (2008). The representation of authors and illustrators of color in school-based book clubs. *Language Arts, 85*(3), 193–201.

———. (2013). "I never knew there were so many books about us": Parents and children reading and responding to African American children's literature together. *Children's Literature in Education, 44*(3), 191–207.

Méndez, L. I., Crais, E. R., Castro, D. C., & Kainz, K. (2015). A culturally and linguistically responsive vocabulary approach for young Latino dual-language learners. *Journal of Speech, Language, and Hearing Research, 58*, 93–106.

Moll, L. C., Amanti, C., Neff, D., & González, N. (1992). Funds of knowledge for teaching: Using a qualitative approach to connect homes and classrooms. *Theory into Practice, 31*(2), 132–41.

Moreton, D. (1999). *La cucaracha Martina: A Caribbean folktale.* New York, NY: Turtle Books.

Naqvi, R., Thorne, K. J., Pfitscher, C. M., Nordstokke, D. W., & McKeough, A. (2013). Reading dual-language books: Improving early literacy skills in linguistically diverse classrooms. *Journal of Early Childhood Research, 11*(1), 3–15.

Nathenson-Mejía, S., & Escamilla, K. (2003). Connecting with Latino children: Bridging cultural gaps with children's literature. *Bilingual Research Journal, 27*(1), 101–16.

Pew Research Hispanic Trends Project. (2012). Statistical Portrait of Hispanics in the United States, 2012. Retrieved May 15, 2015, from www.pewhispanic.org/2014/04/29/statistical-portrait-of-hispanics-in-the-united-states-2012/.

———. (2013). Diverse Origins: The Nation's 14 Largest Hispanic-Origin Groups, 2013. Retrieved May 1, 2015, from www.pewhispanic.org/2013/06/19/diverse-origins-the-nations-14-largest-hispanic-origin-groups/.

Reyes, I. (2006). Exploring connections between emergent biliteracy and bilingualism. *Journal of Early Childhood Literacy, 6*(3), 267–92.

Rich, M. (2012, December 4). For young Latino readers, an image is missing. *New York Times.* www.nytimes.com/2012/12/05/education/young-latino-students-dont -see-themselves-in-books.html.

Schickedanz, J. A., & Collins, M. F. (2012). For young children, pictures in story-books are rarely worth a thousand words. *Reading Teacher, 65*(8), 539–49.

Soto, G., & Martinez, E. (1992). *Too many tamales.* New York, NY: Putnam.

Souto-Manning, M. (2013). *Multicultural teaching in the early childhood classroom: Approaches, strategies, and tools, preschool–2nd grade.* New York, NY: Teachers College Press.

Vygotsky, L. (1978). *Mind in society: The development of higher psychological processes.* Cambridge, MA: Harvard University Press.

Zapata, A. (2013). "No, I don't want to!" Nurturing contexts for sharing culturally specific literature. *World of words stories: Connections from the classroom.* Retrieved from http://wowlit.org/on-line-publications/stories/storiesiv6/3/.

DISCUSSION QUESTIONS

1. What are some of the ways that you currently select texts for your classroom or library? Based on this chapter, what might be some new criteria for selecting books that are culturally and linguistically authentic for young bilingual learners?

2. What do you think are the benefits of having culturally and linguistically authentic texts in your classroom or library?

3. What do you think might be some challenges to finding culturally and linguistically authentic texts and how might you work around these challenges?

4. Think back to children's books that you read when you were younger. What were your favorite books? What were your favorite characters? Why? Using your same reasons (e.g., I identified with the main character; I wanted to be like the main character when I grew up; I liked the pictures), talk about how children in your classroom might see the same book based on their life experiences.

5. What are some activities or ways that you could use to make existing texts in your classroom more culturally and linguistically authentic for your students?

6. What are some resources in your school community that you might seek out in order to learn more about the cultural and linguistic experiences of the children in your classroom or coming to your library?

ACTIVITIES

A. Bring in examples of children's books and have the students in your class look through the books and think about what are the elements of culture and cultural experiences that the book portrays. Then have your students think about which children in a classroom might identify with the book and who might not identify with the book. What might be some strategies or ways to make the book more culturally relevant to a diverse group of children?

B. Divide your class into small groups and ask the students to think about what might be some activities to get to know the members of their group that could be used in an early childhood classroom? What are some ways to get to know families, the community where they live? What activities worked? What were some of the challenges?

C. Using the Internet, ask students to create a list of books that they would want to have in their classroom that they believe would be culturally and linguistically authentic for their children (they can use their student teaching placements or any classroom that they are familiar with as their example).

D. Give students examples of books that portray Latino children and ask them to identify cultural elements within the book; then ask them who would find this book culturally and linguistically authentic.

Table 6.1. Aspects to Consider When Selecting Books for Young Bilingual Latino Children

Authenticity
- What sociocultural beliefs and practices does the book describe?
- How do these sociocultural beliefs and practices reflect the children's experiences at home and in their community?
- How are these sociocultural beliefs and practices depicted in the book? Do they reflect stereotypical views of people of specific cultural and ethnic groups?

Language
- How is Spanish used in the book?
- Does the book introduce sophisticated vocabulary in both English and Spanish?
- If the book uses translation, are the spelling and grammar correct without any typographical errors?
- If two languages are used, are they shown with equal importance?

Illustrations
- Do the illustrations enrich the children's reading experience of the book?
- Do the illustrations depict authentic images of Latino children and families?
- For very young children, are the illustrations realistic?
- What are possible misconceptions that can emerge from the illustrations of the book?

Stories
- Is the story engaging and interesting for the audience?
- Is the story appropriate for the ages of the audience?
- Does the story include topics that are important and meaningful for children in the class?

E. Select a book that is culturally and linguistically relevant to a group of children. Create a list of lessons/activities that could be designed around the book. How would this book address a variety of linguistic needs? How might this book fit into a unit or series of lessons in a classroom?

PROFESSIONAL READINGS

Ada, A. F., & Campoy, F. I. (2013). *Yes! We are Latinos.* Watertown, MA: Charlesbridge.

Botelho, M. J., & Rudman, M. K. (2009) *Critical multicultural analysis of children's literature: Mirrors, windows, and doors.* New York, NY: Routledge.

Fox, D., & Short, K. (Eds.). (2003). *Stories matter: The complexity of cultural authenticity in children's literature.* Urbana, IL: National Council of Teachers of English.

Naidoo, J. C. (Ed.). (2011). *Celebrating cuentos: Promoting Latino children's literature and literacy in classrooms and libraries.* Santa Barbara, CA: Libraries Unlimited.

Part III

MULTICULTURAL LITERATURE IN THE CONTENT AREAS: LANGUAGE ARTS, SOCIAL STUDIES, SCIENCE, AND MATHEMATICS

Figure 7.1.

When a young person sees a world in a book that appears familiar, it helps them navigate their own. A Latino child offered the opportunity to readily see self in a book is validated that their journey through life can be also be navigated. By default, without examples that a young Latino reader can relate to, her participation in society at large seems less valid. . . . Authenticity, in craft, in content.

—Joe Cepeda, illustrator, April 9, 2015

Chapter Seven

Embracing the Complexity of Language: Bringing All Forms of Knowledge into the Language Arts through Latino Children's Literature

Christina Passos DeNicolo

INTRODUCTION

Multicultural children's literature by Latino authors can be an instrumental tool to highlight the diversity of language use and the complexity of language learning and to support students in connecting what they are learning in English to their home languages or dialects. Children's literature can provide a cultural foundation or backdrop from which to identify their prior knowledge, teach comprehension strategies, and introduce academic concepts and vocabulary. This pedagogical approach is in contrast to language arts curricula that often reflect current educational reform movements more so than the existing research on literacy practices that build on students' linguistic and cultural knowledge (Reyes de la Luz & Halcón, 2001). For the majority of bilingual learners, the curricular focus is on English language learning and a transition to an English-only classroom environment. This focus limits teachers' ability to connect literacy with students' lives (Freire & Macedo, 1987) and to employ a curriculum that reveals the complexity of students' multilingualism (Ball & Farr, 2003), and it is based on monolingual language practices (García & Flores, 2014). The Common Core State Standards (National Governors Association Center for Best Practices & Council of Chief State School Officers, 2014) are one example of this type of limitation and have been critiqued for being developed based on research on monolingual English speakers (García, 2010; DeNicolo & García, 2014). At the same time, the standards have been noted for positioning languages as situated, interconnected (van Lier & Walqui, 2012), and requiring attention to each domain, all of which are beneficial for bilingual learners. Thus, language arts teachers are faced with the challenge of becoming creative in negotiating standards, instruction, cross–cultural understanding, and children's needs, particularly their need to build on the forms of knowledge they develop outside of school—languages, literacies, and popular culture (Dyson, 2003; Hull & Shultz, 2002)—while thinking about topics that matter to them.

In this chapter, I will highlight instructional methods for using multicultural children's literature to promote literacy and language learning for bilingual learners within elementary language arts classrooms. Literature discussion, textual connections, *testimonio* (personal narrative), and bilingual stories draw on students' cultural and linguistic repertoires of knowledge while providing opportunities to develop and use language across domains and languages.

THEORETICAL FRAMEWORK

To examine the ways that Latino children's literature promotes critical literacy and language arts instruction for social justice, I utilize the frameworks of critical race theory (CRT), Latino critical race theory (LatCrit), and literacy as social practice, or sociocultural perspectives on literacy. Critical race theory (CRT) acknowledges the persistent and pervasive role of race in U.S. society and institutions (Bell, 1995; Solórzano & Yosso, 2002). Central to this theory is the understanding of how inequities are maintained through the normalizing of practices and policies that position the knowledge and interests of the dominant cultural group as superior, leading to the erasure, silencing, and distortion of the history and voices of communities of color (see chapters 8 and 14). *Majoritarian tales* (Solórzano & Yosso, 2002), also referred to as *master narratives* (Montecinos, 1995), are stories that are told from the perspective of the dominant culture about historically marginalized groups and equity. These types of narratives or stories are at times perceived as facts or justification for the advancement of the dominant cultural group. One example of a majoritarian tale is the notion that Mexican Americans do not value education (Valencia, 2002). This majoritarian tale is used to explain differences in educational outcomes between Mexican American students and their European American counterparts. If educators agree with this thinking, they may interpret the behavior of Latino students and families as confirmation that they do not care about education and fail to see the role that policies, instructional practices, or curriculum play in educational success. The tale would mask the underlying beliefs regarding knowledge and equality and place blame for educational success solely on students and their families. Critical race scholars challenge these tales and ideologies through the voiced experiences of people of color that illustrate the distortions of majoritarian tales (Delgado Bernal, 1998; Solórzano & Yosso, 2002; Yosso, 2006; Ladson-Billings, 2009; Willis, 2008).

Latino critical race theory, also known as LatCrit, builds on and extends CRT through a focus on issues that shape the lives of Latinos in the United States, such as language, immigration status, and culture (Delgado Bernal, 2002; Espinoza & Harris, 1997; Yosso, 2006). Scholars who have applied LatCrit to education examine the ways in which Latino students, parents, and communities acknowledge the subtractive nature of schooling for Latinos (Valenzuela, 1999) and challenge what types of knowledge are seen as valid (Delgado Bernal, 2002) through counternarratives. Presenting real-life examples of the ways Mexican American parents provide *consejos* (advice) to encourage their children to do their best in school counters the majoritarian tale that holds that they do not value education (Valencia, 2002). Counternarratives function as a tool for action and social justice (Willis, 2008) by unmasking the unchallenged truths of the majoritarian tale and centering the lived experiences and knowledge of communities of color as a point of reference for understanding societal inequities (Delgado Bernal, 2002; Yosso, 2006).

Sociocultural Perspectives on Literacy

Literacy instruction that connects with what is meaningful to children is particularly important for bilinguals and bilingual learners (García, Kleifgen, & Falchi, 2008), who are developing reading and writing skills across multiple languages. Activating prior knowledge about what is being read supports reading comprehension (Anderson & Pearson, 1984) and the building of new knowledge (Walqui, 2008). Sociocultural perspectives on literacy, which view literacy as complex, purposeful, and collaborative interactions involving texts (Street, 1984; Bartlett, 2007), are a useful lens through which to explore the role of multicultural children's literature in the language arts classroom. Vital to this perspective is an understanding that literacy is social practice, and individuals engage with texts in different ways based on the form (e.g., writing an essay or texting), the purpose, the participants, and the context. Barton and Hamilton (2000) write, "Literacy practices are the general cultural ways of utilizing written language which people draw upon in their lives. In the simplest sense literacy practices are what people do with literacy" (p. 7). Understanding literacy practices as cultural practices means there is not only one form of literacy (e.g., reading and writing standard English). Through our looking at literacy events, insight can be gained into the literacy practices that contribute to the formation of those literacy events. Literacy events that are meaningful and promote interaction can show the thoughts, feelings, prior experiences, and beliefs that underlie engagement with texts or the literacy practices that shape the literacy event (Barton & Hamilton, 1998).

The work of Vygotsky (1978) supports our understanding of literacy development. For Vygotsky, learning does not occur in isolation but through interactions with others that are shaped by participation within and across the cultural contexts of people's lives. Amidst interaction within these contextual layers, meaning develops first at the interpersonal level through speech and practices of participation, and then on an intrapersonal level. Children's interactions with others who are more knowledgeable than they are promote their language development as well as their learning, particularly if their learning is within the zone of proximal development: beyond what they have mastered but not at a level of difficulty that disengages them (Vygotsky, 1978). A child's learning is directly related to his or her interaction with the mediational tools accessed in a given environment. Tools and artifacts such as speech, symbols, writing, and texts mediate students' interaction with self and with others. School, according to Vygotsky, is important because the classroom environment provides multiple opportunities for interaction with a range of tools and artifacts.

Other scholars in the area of sociocultural perspectives on literacy have demonstrated how children maintain and utilize linguistic and cultural knowledge developed in their homes and communities inside and outside of school (Gutiérrez, Bien, Selland, & Pierce, 2011; Martínez, 2010; Martin-Beltrán, 2010). For example, a significant contribution from this work is how students access all of their repertoires of knowledge when hybrid spaces for language use are created in the classroom. Spaces are formed when learners express themselves through multiple languages and dialects. Language practices may include code-switching, or the use of more than one language or language variation in a communicative act (Martínez, 2010; Zentella, 1997, 2003), reflecting the sociohistorical context and bilinguals' emerging identities. Language practices are also referred to as *translanguaging*, which García (2009, p. 45) defines as "multiple discourse practices in which bilinguals engage in order to make sense of their bilingual worlds." Using various forms of linguistic knowledge is a natural part of bilingualism, and studies have shown that multiple language practices in school promote academic learning (Gutiérrez, Baquedano-López, Alvarez, & Chiu, 1999; Gutiérrez et al., 2011; see chapters 1 and 2).

Multicultural Children's Literature

Multicultural children's literature in the elementary language arts classroom can function as a bridge that enables students to form connections between academic learning and their cultural and linguistic knowledge. This form of literature is often written by authors of the cultural group represented in the text or those with in-depth knowledge of the group, and it addresses themes that are not commonly available or fairly represented in the school curriculum (Harris, 2003), while promoting critical and complex examinations of human experience (Nieto, 1997). Multicultural literature supports student development of a positive sense of self by allowing students to experience their cultural background and language in texts, while also bringing a broader range of voices into the classroom (Jiménez, Moll, Rodríguez-Brown, & Barrera, 1999). When Latino emergent bilingual learners read literature by and about Latinos, they are more likely to be able to build on knowledge from home, develop crosscultural awareness, and form textual connections. These benefits are more attainable when the literature is of high literary quality, meaning that representations of cultural and linguistic groups are authentic and non-stereotypical (Bishop, 1997).

Multicultural children's literature may also include critical fictions (Mariani, 1991), a form of literature that offers the reader a way to examine the lives and histories of individuals from culturally and linguistically diverse backgrounds to gain insight into the societal implications of those realities (Enciso, 2001; Medina, 2006). Medina (2006) writes, "Critical fictions often feature the voices of those authors from underrepresented and marginalized communities where their writing works as an agent of liberation to claim a space in society, including a literary community that has been dominated by white male perspectives" (p. 72). Common to this genre is the author's voicing of a reflective and reflexive positionality vis-à-vis cultural and linguistic identity, racialization, linguicism, and racism. One example of this is from the bilingual picture book *My Diary from Here to There* (Pérez, 2002). In the beginning of the story, the main character writes in her diary of her fears about moving to the U.S. from Mexico, pondering whether she will be allowed to speak Spanish. At the end of the story, she writes of how she carries her home town, family, and friends within, "They're inside my little rock, they're here in your pages and in the language that I speak, and they're in my memories and my heart" (p. 30). Through her diary entries, readers can envision how the main character is navigating her understanding of discrimination, place, and identity.

Examining multicultural children's literature through these frameworks means looking for the ways literature disrupts ideologies of cultural deficit, meritocracy, and colorblindness through the authentic voices of Latinos in the U.S., representative of the many nationalities, ethnicities, and histories that fall under the umbrella of Latino. Through a lens informed by CRT, LatCrit, and sociocultural perspectives on literacy, it becomes evident how Latino children's literature can mediate students' knowledge production. Children's literature can promote literacy and language learning through the reading, listening, and discussing of topics that hold cultural relevance and significance for Latino students. Opportunities to reflect, question, and critically consider issues of importance engage students in using their linguistic knowledge, which is key to learning for both monolinguals and bilingual learners.

Multicultural Children's Literature as a Resource

Multicultural children's literature provides students whose experiences are not aligned with the dominant cultural group with opportunities to draw from their funds of knowledge (Moll Amanti, Neff, & González, 1992) as a resource for making sense of academic content and showing teachers what they know and understand (Gutiérrez et al., 2011; Enciso, 2001). Literature discussion is one method for seeing the schemas students possess and have available to support their comprehension of texts (Anderson & Pearson, 1984). Pilonieta and Hancock (2012) examined students' comprehension of literature that addressed social issues relevant to their lives. They worked with first-grade teachers to identify the types of efferent and aesthetic responses (Rosenblatt, 2005) to literature that were reflective of students' lived experiences. The study findings indicated that students made connections to the texts and that their young age did not cause them to react to the social issues in the texts, such as homelessness or racism, with fear but with insight and wisdom.

A growing body of scholarship (López-Robertson, 2012a, 2012b; Martínez-Roldán & López-Robertson, 1999; Martínez-Roldán, 2003) has shown the ways that Latino children's literature and small-group discussion create pathways for the storytelling abilities bilingual students learn at home to function as a tool for making meaning of texts in school. Martínez-Roldán (2003) conducted a case study of a second-grade student's participation in Spanish and English literature discussion groups and identified how Isabel, the focal participant, took on different roles within the groups depending on the language of the discussion. In literature discussions that occurred in Spanish, she drew on knowledge of narratives and storytelling to understand text and talk, while during the English groups she was more focused on supporting the flow of the discussion. Building on this work, López-Robertson (2012a) examined ways that second-grade students in a bilingual class drew on their knowledge of storytelling while reading and talking about children's literature that centered on the experiences of migrant workers in the U.S.

Through analysis of the responses across *pláticas literarias* (literary conversations) of four students, López-Robertson found that students engaged in storytelling based on their lived experiences better understood what they were reading, responded more to the text, and formed text-to-life connections. Analysis of the discussion transcripts showed how students used storytelling as a meditational tool for exploring the meaning and complexity of their lived experiences when talking about books that resonated with their lives. Medina (2010), in a study with fifth-grade students, identified ways that popular imaginaries transcended space and time in literature discussion groups reading literature by Latino authors that centered on migrant experiences. Findings from the study showed how Latino children's literature reflective of students' lived experiences invited critical discussions that moved beyond individual cultural connections with texts and brought insight into students' understanding of the multiple worlds in which they lived. The relevance of the literature and meaningful talk worked together to make visible students' funds of knowledge, complex understandings of their multiple worlds, and their individual and collective experiences within those worlds.

The studies above have demonstrated the value in pairing quality multicultural children's literature with small-group discussion in bilingual classrooms. DeNicolo and Fránquiz (2006) conducted a study of bilingual learners' participation in literature discussion groups in an English language arts class. They found that students' cultural and linguistic knowledge was activated when they read about social issues relevant to their lives. The study findings indicated that when students had critical encounters with text, when they read something that surprised, frightened, or intrigued them, the format for interaction in the small groups shifted. These shifts resulted in discussions that were more critical and complex and moved the groups to greater levels of understanding of both talk and text. The authors illustrated this through the literature circle discussion of four girls reading *Felita* by Nicholasa Mohr (1979). Participation in the literature circle changed after the group read about the racism that Felita, the main character, experienced upon moving to a new neighborhood. The four girls, who were Puerto Rican, African American, Mexican American, and Mexican, experienced a critical encounter with the text when reading that Felita was insulted with a racial slur and blocked from walking to her home. This critical encounter led the girls to go beyond the question-answer format they were using to talk about the text to reflecting on their own experiences in order to identity potential responses to that type of violence. One significant finding was that the shift in how the students participated enabled the student with the most emergent level of English proficiency to engage more fully by sharing her thoughts and opinions. The combination of forming and discussing textual connections provided opportunities for peer modeling of language use and linguistic mediation; however, when critical encounters emerged, it enabled the bilingual learners to take on new roles in the discussion groups (DeNicolo & Fránquiz, 2006; DeNicolo, 2010).

PRAXIS: APPLICATION OF THEORY

In this section, I explore what it means to consider CRT, LatCrit, and socio-cultural perspectives on literacy when thinking about language arts instruction at the elementary level.

These frameworks highlight the need to challenge deficit perspectives of Latinos and advocate for social justice through the selection of instructional materials and practices that function as counternarratives while also promoting dialogue and knowledge production.

Literature Discussion

A starting point for teachers when identifying instructional methods and planning lessons utilizing children's literature is to identify the learning objectives for the lessons and reflect on the role that literature will play toward helping students meet those objectives. The learning goals and purpose will, in turn, influence the literature selection. According to Medina (2006), one important step in selecting children's literature by Latino authors is to learn about the author to more fully understand the text. Reading several selections by an author can deepen one's understanding of the author's perspective and can aid in assessing the cultural authenticity of the story (Naidoo, 2011).

Rosenblatt's (1978) transactional reading theory contributed widely to the use of children's literature in the language arts classroom. Reader response centers on the transaction between the reader and the text when the reader draws on their prior knowledge and life experiences while reading and interpreting literature. Textual understandings from this perspective are individual and varied, as what each person brings to and takes away from the reading of literature will be different (Wolf, 2004). Reader response critics argue that at the classroom level this approach becomes reduced to solely text-to-self connections without analysis of other features of literature such as language, sociohistorical context, and issues of power.

One approach to reader response is through small-group literature discussion. Literature groups can provide opportunities for textual understandings and critical analysis of literature through discussion. Groups can be organized in a variety of ways and paired with a range of activities depending on the instructional goal and grade level of the learners. They may select books for literature discussion from a group of books that have a common theme and/

or genre. Teachers or librarians can organize text sets that consist of six to eight books that address a specific concept (Short, Kauffman, & Kahn, 2000), present different perspectives of a topic (Robb, 2002), or are written by the same author. Teachers/librarians working with younger learners may have small groups reading the same book at one time. Literature discussion with older elementary students may involve multiple groups reading different books from a text set at one time. There are several benefits to using text sets with bilingual learners. Exposure to a concept across a range of texts provides bilingual learners with the opportunity to build schema (Walqui, 2008) and deepen their understanding of the concept and related vocabulary (Hadaway, Young, & Ward, 2011). These benefits of the transactional approach to reading are multiplied when students are critically examining textual understandings and concepts through discussions with peers.

Text selection is one major aspect of literature discussion groups, and the role of the teacher or librarian in the discussion is another important consideration. Teachers/librarians may take on a facilitator role in discussion groups or observe student-led groups. The role of the facilitator may evolve as learners become familiar with the process for reading and discussing texts. There are also multiple formats for student-led groups, and as with all other considerations, the determination for group formation must be made in relation to the learning goals.

Literature Discussion and Language Use

Having students with a range of language proficiency levels may be beneficial if all students are encouraged to participate across both languages (DeNicolo, 2010). If there is not a value for Spanish in the English language arts classroom, an emergent bilingual may not be able to participate in a way that allows them to benefit from a discussion group. It is important that teachers work with students to identify the norms for discussion, language use, and language for reading. For example, the following excerpt is from a literature discussion in a fourth-grade English language arts class of three girls reading *My Name Is María Isabel* (Ada, 1995) and *Me llamo María Isabel* (Ada, 1996). Two group members had selected the Spanish version of the text and one the English version. The girls were all bilingual learners of varying proficiency levels in English and diverse nationalities (Puerto Rican, Mexican, Salvadoran-Dominican). Mari decided to read the text in Spanish.

Mari: Let's read in Spanish.

Sol: No, you don't know English, so the book is in English.

Mari: We need to try Spanish.

Sol: You need to try *inglés.*

Ana: *Voy a estar leyendo ahora* [I will be reading now].

Sol: *Ella no va a estar leyendo ahora* [She will not be reading now].

This brief exchange between the three students highlights the different goals the students had for participating in the literature discussion. For Mari, it was important for them to try the discussion in Spanish, but Sol, who identified as having more knowledge of English, believed that English was the language that Mari needed. To ensure full student participation, teachers should establish parameters for equitable language use.

Small-group discussion that supports student identification of textual connections with children's literature promotes increased engagement and student sharing of language practices from home such as storytelling (López-Robertson, 2012a; Martinez-Roldán, 2003). Reading texts that reflect students' cultural backgrounds allows bilingual learners to tap into the funds of knowledge (Moll et al., 1992) developed in their homes and communities across formats for literature response. Monolingual English-speaking teachers may encourage students to use Spanish in responding to children's literature (Iddings, Risko, & Rampulla, 2009; Fránquiz & de la Luz Reyes, 1998). Even though they may not have the language skills to understand all of what students are saying, it communicates to students a value for their knowledge (DeNicolo & Fránquiz, 2006). Through discussion and identification of connections, teacher and students can build an understanding across languages (DeNicolo, 2010).

Textual Connections

Identifying texts that portray realistic experiences and address social issues reflects one of the premises of critical race theory and LatCrit: the value for the lived experiences of those who have been subordinated told in authentic forms as a tool for disrupting myths regarding student learning and potential. *Testimonio* is one such form that has been used to challenge dominant myths or majoritarian tales in the form of a counternarrative. *Testimonios* are personal narratives regarding lived experiences and struggles that are shared orally or in writing with the goal of supporting and promoting solidarity among others who may be part of a similar struggle (Delgado Bernal, 2002; Fránquiz, 2003; Acevedo, 2001; Saavedra, 2011).

DeNicolo, González, Morales, and Romaní (in press) analyzed the written *testimonios* of bilingual learners in a third-grade classroom. After reading, listening to, and discussing children's literature and the *testimonios* of Latino graduate students, the students wrote their own narratives. The literature and the *testimonios* functioned as mentor texts (Dorfman & Cappelli, 2007), texts that model specific features of writing. The children's literature and *testimonios* illustrated ways the third-grade students could talk about their experiences as Latinos, becoming bilingual, and navigating school. The unit began with students forming textual connections with the text *La Mariposa* (Jiménez, 1998), an autobiographical account of the author's first experiences in school in the U.S. and not knowing English. For example, through one of the third-grade students' reflections and illustrations, we can see the textual connection she made after reading the story. She writes of the text, "When Mrs. Scalopino, the teacher presents Francisco to the class all the kids stared at him," and she draws a child with an anxious face. The child's illustrations also capture the emotional context. She then makes the following text-to-life connection as she also illustrates with a child looking less than happy, "When my sister had to go to pre-K but it was her first day and she was scared all the kids stared at her."

Many of the students showed how *La Mariposa* resonated with them through writing and illustrations. Veronica (all names are pseudonyms) described that the part of the story where the teacher told Francisco to speak in English and he did not understand, reminded her of when she was with a group of friends and did not understand what one of her friends said. These examples show how forming textual connections with children's literature supported learners' understanding of what they were reading. The task of forming textual connections guided students' reflection on their memories of navigating school and bilingualism.

Textual connections with literature that are reflective of students' lives can also serve as a model or mentor text for students' writing. In the same unit, the third-grade students formed text-to-self connections with *testimonios* about bilingualism written by three graduate students who, like the third graders, were of Mexican American descent and grew up bilingual. Brenda noted that she formed a connection with Lucía's narrative, particularly because Lucía did not know English when she was younger and felt a sense of accomplishment as she developed bilingualism. Brenda then expanded on this point in her written *testimonio* where she described how she helped her father by translating for him. *Testimonios* provided students with the opportunity to redefine their abilities and demonstrate their agency.

Similar to identity texts (Bernhard, Cummins, Campoy, Ada, Winsler, & Bleiker, 2006), this form of writing can provide validation and healing for bilingual learners, particularly when their languages and cultures have been positioned as problematic for learning in school. According to Bernhard et al. (2006), identity texts are books written by children where they define who they are and where they are from through images, writings in English and their home language, and photographs. These texts supported young learners' engagement with literacy through validation of their identities and shared participation in developing and using the texts in the classroom.

Language Practices

In addition to opening a door for students to respond to text and write about their own lives, children's literature by Latino authors presents an alternate perspective through language practices that go beyond the monolingual language use that is commonly depicted in children's literature. Bilingual, multilingual, and bidialectical learners all have unique ways of using language across the contexts of their lives, and their language use varies based on their participation in those contexts (Rogoff, 2003). In a context of linguistic hegemony, texts that highlight the variation in how bilinguals and multilinguals use their languages can be both validating and informative for language arts students. Current literature by Latino authors includes texts that are written in Spanish and English and incorporate Spanish words or phrases, highlighting how bilinguals use their languages in their daily lives. Translanguaging (García, 2009) reflects the natural, dynamic, and fluid nature of language practices for bilinguals, such as code-switching and code mixing. When bilingual learners are offered the opportunity to see their language practices in texts, it counters the prevailing message that standard language forms, particularly English, are the most effective or preferred form of communication.

In a study of third-grade Latino students in a bilingual classroom (DeNicolo et al., in press), the teacher had been directed to use English only for language arts instruction. When students read *testimonios* written by university students that incorporated Spanish in a variety of ways, they began using Spanish in their own writing. One student wrote of her textual connection, "When her mom said to her échale ganas. Everyday when I wake up my mom wakes me up to give me breakfast and she kiss[es] me and my sister on the cheek and said to us échale ganas." The use of the Spanish term *échale ganas* was essential to convey the connection and encouragement that is expressed when saying Give it your all! Prior to being exposed to texts with Spanish, the bilingual learners had rarely used Spanish in their writing.

Dual-language books have texts in English and another language either for students to read bilingually or to read in only one of the languages (Naqvi, McKeough, Thorne, & Pfitscher, 2012). The text is generally the same in both languages, and at times key words in the non-English language are used in the English section. One benefit of dual-language books is that they provide students with an opportunity to read with access to two linguistic codes and/or to practice reading in their less proficient language. Amada Irma Pérez is the author of three texts that are written in English and Spanish: *Nana's Big Surprise* (Pérez, 2007), *My Very Own Room* (Pérez, 2000), and *My Diary from Here to There* (Pérez, 2002). Each of the stories contains themes that are very relevant for all students—family, moving, and finding space—and reflect the experiences of many Latinos in U.S. *Antonio's Card* (González, 2005) is an example of a dual-language text that combines cultural relevance with the universal theme of acceptance. González challenges standard notions of family through the experiences of Antonio, a young boy faced with the heteronormative beliefs of his classmates when his mother's partner picks him up from school (see chapter 5). This text, while primarily focused on perceptions of family, provides opportunities to examine intersectionality and what it means to be Latino, to be Spanish-speaking, and to have two mothers. Thus, dual-language texts offer multiple opportunities for students to examine the complexities of themes such as these while activating what they know about the topics across their developing languages.

When identifying children's literature that uses bilingual language practices, it is important to note how and why Spanish is used as well as the underlying messages conveyed regarding language and language speakers (Chappel & Faltis, 2007). René Colato Laínez in *My Shoes and I* (2010) uses Spanish to highlight the power of the rhyme *Sana, sana, colita de rana* and how it helps the main character persevere on his journey from El Salvador to the U.S. The rhyme is not translated directly in the text but is written in English in the back of the book. Yuyi Morales, in *Los Gatos Black en Halloween* (2006) uses Spanish words within the English rhymes that are not translated but easily understood through illustrations. In *My Abuelita* (Johnston, 2009), the word "*abuelita*" is used throughout but other Spanish words in the story are followed by the English translation. *Dear Primo. A Letter to My Cousin* (Tonatiuh, 2010) is written in English. Spanish words are utilized to signal important cultural activities or traditions and detailed illustrations are used instead of English translation to ensure understanding of the cultural comparison between the cousins' lives in the U.S. and Mexico. Children's literature that uses multiple linguistic codes provides validation to students regarding their own language use and also functions as a model for writing.

Multimodal Responses

In addition to literature response through discussion and writing, visual arts and music may be a more engaging format for bilinguals' knowledge production in the language arts.

Rodríguez-Valls, Kofford, and Morales (2012) describe a powerful project creating graffiti walls with migrant secondary students. The students first developed cultural tags similar to identity texts that represented their identities, stories of themselves, and heritage. After reading poetry addressing social issues, the students studied graffiti and street art. After this exploration, as a group they discussed how their individual representations of themselves could be merged to convey a collective message. This can also be done with elementary students (see chapter 14).

Graphic boards involve students creating visual representation of aspects of a story or text that are meaningful or interesting to them. This type of response is beneficial to bilingual learners as it reduces the linguistic load involved with reading a text and responding in writing. The visual illustrations or symbols mediate students' language learning, enabling students to demonstrate their comprehension of text and use of language skills to convey thoughts and understandings to others (Medina & Martinez-Roldán, 2011). In a similar vein, graphic novels can support students' understanding of concepts (Yang, 2008). Yuyi Morales's book *Niño Wrestles the World* (2013) is ideal for younger ages. Utilizing a graphics approach, Morales (2013) depicts through the story of a young boy the passion that many children hold for Mexican professional wrestling.

Creating responses through comic strips, graphic boards, graffiti walls, and visual interpretations allows students to build language while learning. These formats invite students' visual and artistic knowledge to scaffold language and literacy practices. Allowing students to find their own voices in responding to children's literature may enable more critical deconstruction of the themes present in the literature. The following discussion of two fourth-grade students who began freestyling while discussing *The Circuit* (Jiménez, 1997) highlights the value of performative responses (DeNicolo, 2004). Slim Shady asked JZ (self-selected pseudonyms) to translate a word he had not read or heard before, "*la frontera.*"

JZ: The cool thing I see is that how they pass *la frontera* [the border].

Slim Shady: Hey yo, by the way since, you know Spanish yo, what's *la frontera*? Shoot, I don't know what the heck is *la frontera. . . .*

JZ: *La frontera* is where the immigrants pass when they don't have papers. Immigrants, immigrants. Okay, yo, I think we have a snoop doggy.

Although both boys attended a Spanish/English two-way immersion program, Slim Shady, who was English dominant, was unfamiliar with the term "*la frontera,*" leading JZ, an emergent bilingual, to provide a definition, rather than a translation, that was rooted in his knowledge of immigration.

This definition demonstrated JZ's understanding of "*la frontera*" as he did not provide a one-word translation such as "frontier" or "border" but instead explained the purpose for this place to deepen Slim Shady's understanding of *The Circuit*. Through freestyling as a way to talk about the text, the boys talked about the themes present in the story—moving, crossing the border—in a more complex manner. For JZ, finding creative ways to talk about what he was reading functioned as a pathway for showing what he knew from his home life. The back-and-forth nature of freestyling allowed him multiple attempts to express in English his understanding of the cultural themes that were unfamiliar to Slim Shady. The combination of the text and format for talking about the text made JZ's knowledge and language skills essential for engaging and learning in the literacy event.

CONCLUSION

Literature response, intertextuality, and multimodal interactions with text are three examples of integrating children's literature by Latino authors into the language arts classroom. While each of these methods could benefit bilingual learners in all English general-education classrooms, transitional bilingual, and two-way immersion programs, the strength of the approach is dependent on the clarity of the purpose. In identifying the purpose for using children's literature, teachers should reflect on how the literature connects with the curricular goal and objectives, extends or highlights the topic being studied, and enables the teacher to identify students' background knowledge. The selection of literature requires a deep reading and critical analysis regarding how Latinos are portrayed in the text, the quality and realistic representation of characters and events, and the historical and social context (Medina, 2006; Naidoo, 2011).

Multicultural children's literature that is authentically responsive to a particular cultural group has long been valued as an important resource to engage learners and enable them to see aspects of their own lives and ways of being (Bishop, 1997; Cai, 2002; Harris, 2003). Topics that resonate with students are more likely to promote engagement with the text (DeNicolo & Fránquiz, 2006) and perseverance when challenges in comprehension or reading arise. When students are reading and discussing across cultures and languages, critical encounters with texts have the potential to move learners into deeper levels of discussion and open up opportunities for cultural and linguistic mediation (DeNicolo, 2010).

Children's literature by Latino authors can function as mentor texts (Dorfman & Cappelli, 2007) for introducing features of writing such as voice and organization. Bilingual texts and children's literature that incorporates Spanish words and phrases to portray authentic language practices can also model for learners how they can utilize all of their linguistic knowledge in their responses to literature. Through opportunities to see a range of ways that languages are used to tell stories, learners can be inspired to draw on the funds of knowledge from their homes and communities to produce new understandings.

REFERENCES

Acevedo, L. del Alba (2001). *Telling to live: Latina feminist testimonios.* Durham, NC: Duke University Press.

Ada, A. F., & Thompson, K. D. (1995). *My name is María Isabel.* New York, NY: Aladdin Paperbacks.

———. (1996). *Me llamo María Isabel.* New York, NY: Aladdin Paperbacks/Libros Colibri.

Anderson, R. C., & Pearson, P. D. (1984). A schema-theoretic view of basic processes in reading comprehension. In P. D. Pearson, R. Barr, M. L. Kamil, & P. Mosenthal (Eds.), *Handbook of reading research* (pp. 255–91). New York, NY: Longman.

Ball, A. F., & Farr, M. (2003). Language varieties, culture, and teaching the English language arts. In J. Flood, D. Lapp, J. R. Squire, & J. Jensen (Eds.), *Handbook of research on teaching the English language arts* (2nd ed., pp. 435–45). Mahwah, NJ: Lawrence Erlbaum Associates.

Bartlett, L. (2007). To seem and to feel: Situated identities and literacy practices. *Teachers College Record, 109*(1), 51–69.

Barton, D., & Hamilton, M. (1998). *Local literacies: Reading and writing in one community.* New York, NY: Routledge.

———. (2000). Literacy practices. In D. Barton, M. Hamilton, & R. Ivancic (Eds.), *Situated literacies: Theorising reading and writing in context* (pp. 7–15). New York, NY: Routledge.

Bell, D. A. (1995). Who's afraid of critical race theory? *University of Illinois Law Review, 4*(1995), 893.

Bernhard, J. K., Cummins, J., Campoy, F. I., Ada, A. F., Winsler, A., & Bleiker, C. (2006). Identity texts and literacy development among preschool English language learners: Enhancing learning opportunities for children at risk for learning disabilities. *Teachers College Record, 108*(11), 2380–405.

Bishop, R. S. (1997). Selecting literature for a multicultural curriculum. In V. J. Harris (Ed.), *Using multiethnic literature in the K–8 classroom* (pp. 1–20). Norwood, MA: Christopher-Gordon Publishers.

Cai, M. (2002). *Multicultural literature for children and young adults: Reflections on critical issues.* Westport CT: Greenwood Publishing Group.

Chappel, S., & Faltis, C. (2007). Spanglish, bilingualism, culture and identity in Latino children's literature. *Children's Literature in Education, 38,* 253–62.

Colato Laínez, R. (2010). *My shoes and I.* Honesdale, PA: Boyds Mill Press.

Delgado Bernal, D. (1998). Grassroots leadership reconceptualized: Chicana oral histories and the 1968 East Los Angeles school blowouts. *Frontiers: A Journal of Women Studies, 19*(2), 113–42.

———. (2002). Critical race theory, Latino critical theory, and critical raced-gendered epistemologies: Recognizing students of color as holders and creators of knowledge. *Qualitative Inquiry, 8*(1), 105–26.

DeNicolo, C. P. (2004). Connecting literacy, language, and lived experience: Examining the use of literature discussion circles in a fourth-grade classroom (unpublished doctoral dissertation). University of Colorado, Boulder, Colorado.

———. (2010). What language counts in literature discussion? Exploring linguistic mediation in an English language arts classroom. *Bilingual Research Journal, 33*(2), 220–40.

DeNicolo, C. P., & Fránquiz, M. E. (2006). Do I have to say it? Critical encounters with multicultural children's literature. *Language Arts, 84*(2), 157–70.

DeNicolo, C. P., & García, G. E. (2014). Examining policies and practices: Two districts' responses to federal reforms and their use of language arts assessments with emergent bilinguals (K–3). In P. J. Dunston, L. B. Gambrell, K. Headley, S. K. Fullerton, & P. M. Stecker (Eds.), *63rd Yearbook of the Literacy Research Association* (pp. 229–42). Oak Creek, WI: Literacy Research Association.

DeNicolo, C. P., González, M., Morales, S., & Romaní, L. (in press). Teaching through *testimonios*: Bringing linguistic and cultural wealth into a bilingual classroom. *Journal of Latinos and Education, 14*(4).

Dorfman, L. R., & Cappelli, R. (2007). *Mentor texts: Teaching writing through children's literature, K–6.* Portland, ME: Stenhouse Publishers.

Dyson, A. H. (2003). *The brothers and sisters learn to write: Popular literacies in childhood and school cultures.* New York, NY: Teachers College Press.

Enciso, P. E. (2001). Mediating multicultural children's literature. In J. E. Many (Ed.), *Handbook of instructional practices for literacy teacher-educators* (pp. 135–48). Mahwah, NJ: Lawrence Erlbaum Associates.

Espinoza, L., & Harris, A. P. (1997). Afterword: Embracing the tar-baby-LatCrit theory and the sticky mess of race. *La Raza Law Journal, 10,* 499–599.

Fránquiz, M. E. (2003). Literacy reform for Latina/o students. *Reading Research Quarterly, 38*(3), 418–30.

Fránquiz, M. E., & de la Luz Reyes, M. (1998). Creating inclusive learning communities through English language arts: From *chanclas* to *canicas. Language Arts, 75*(3), 211–20.

Freire, P., & Macedo, D. P. (1987). *Literacy: Reading the word and the world.* South Hadley, MA: Bergin & Garvey Publishers.

García, G. E. (2010, April). *National literacy standards and assessments for Spanish speakers and English learners: Policy and instructional implications.* Featured research presentation at the annual convention of the International Reading Association, Chicago, Illinois.

García, O. (2009). Bilingual education in the 21st century: A global perspective. Malden, MA: Blackwell.

García, O., & Flores, N. (2014). Multilingualism and the common core state standards in the United States. In S. May (Ed.), *The multilingual turn: Implications for SLA, TESOL and bilingual education* (pp. 147–66). New York, NY: Routledge.

García, O., Kleifgen, J. A., & Falchi, L. (2008). From English language learners to emergent bilinguals. *Equity matters: Research review 1, Campaign for educational equity*. New York, NY: Teachers College, Columbia University.

González, R., & Alvarez, C. C. (2005). *Antonio's card*. San Francisco, CA: Children's Book Press.

Gutiérrez, K. D., Baquedano-López, P., Alvarez, H. H., & Chiu, M. M. (1999). Building a culture of collaboration through hybrid language practices. *Theory into Practice, 38*, 87–93.

Gutiérrez, K. D., Bien, A. C., Selland, M. K., & Pierce, D. M. (2011). Polylingual and polycultural learning ecologies: Mediating emergent academic literacies for dual-language learners. *Journal of Early Childhood Literacy, 11*, 232–61.

Hadaway, N. L., Young, T. A., & Ward, B. (2011). Passing on and preserving our stories: Universal experiences in children's literature around the world. *Childhood Education, 87*(6), 381.

Harris, V. J. (2003). The complexity of debates about multicultural literature and cultural authenticity. In D. L. Fox & K. G. Short (Eds.), *Stories matter: The complexity of cultural authenticity in children's literature* (pp. 116–34). Urbana, IL: National Council of Teachers of English.

Hull, G., & Schultz, K. (2002). *School's out: Bridging out-of-school literacies with classroom practice*. New York, NY: Teachers College Press.

Iddings, A. C. D., Risko, V. J., & Rampulla, M. P. (2009). When you don't speak their language: Guiding English language learners through conversations about text. *Reading Teacher, 63*(1), 52–61.

Jiménez, F. (1997). *The circuit*. Boston, MA: The Horn Book.

———. (1998). *La mariposa*. New York, NY: Houghton Mifflin Company.

Jiménez, R. T., Moll, L. C., Rodríguez-Brown, F. V., & Barrera, R. B. (1999). Latina and Latino researchers interact on issues related to literacy learning. *Reading Research Quarterly, 34*(2), 217–30.

Johnston, T. (2009). *My abuelita*. New York, NY: Harcourt Children's Books.

Ladson-Billings, G. (2009). Just what is critical race theory and what's it doing in a nice field like education? In E. Taylor, D. Gillborn, & G. Ladson-Billings (Eds.), *Foundations of critical race theory in education* (pp. 18–36). New York, NY: Routledge.

López-Robertson, J. (2012a). *Esta página me recordó*: Young Latinas using personal life stories as tools for meaning-making. *Bilingual Research Journal, 35*(2), 217–33.

———. (2012b). *Oigan, tengo un cuento*: Crossing *la frontera* of life and books. *Language Arts, 90*(1), 30–43.

Mariani, P. (1991). *Critical fictions: The politics of imaginative writing* (no. 7). Seattle, WA: Bay Press.

Martin-Beltrán, M. (2010). Positioning proficiency: How students and teachers (de) construct language proficiency at school. *Linguistics and Education, 21*, 257–81.

Martínez, R. A. (2010). Spanglish as literacy tool: Toward an understanding of the potential role of Spanish-English code-switching in the development of academic literacy. *Research in the Teaching of English, 45*(2), 124–49.

Martínez-Roldán, C. M. (2003). Building worlds and identities: A case study of the role of narratives in bilingual literature discussions. *Research in the Teaching of English, 37*, 491–526.

Martínez-Roldán, C. M., & López-Roberston, J. (1999). Initiating literature circles in a first-grade bilingual classroom. *Reading Teacher, 53*(4), 270–81.

Medina, C. L. (2006). Interpreting Latino/a literature as critical fictions. *ALAN Review* (Winter), 71–77.

———. (2010). Reading across communities in biliteracy practices: Examining translocal discourses and cultural flows in literature discussions. *Reading Research Quarterly, 45*, 40–60.

Medina, C. L., & Martinez-Roldán, C. (2011). Culturally relevant literature pedagogies: Latino students reading in the borderlands. In J. C. Naidoo (Ed.), *Celebrating cuentos: Promoting Latino children's literature and literacy in classrooms and libraries* (pp. 259–72). Santa Barbara, CA: ABC-CLIO.

Mohr, N., & Cruz, R. (1979). *Felita.* New York, NY: Dial.

Moll, L. C., Amanti, C., Neff, D., & González, N. (1992). Funds of knowledge for teaching: Using a qualitative approach to connect homes and classrooms. *Theory into Practice, 31*(2), 132–41.

Montecinos, C. (1995). Culture as an ongoing dialogue: Implications for multicultural teacher education. In C. Sleeter & P. McLaren (Eds.), *Multicultural education, critical pedagogy, and the politics of difference* (pp. 269–308). New York, NY: State University of New York Press.

Montes, M., & Morales, Y. (2006). *Los gatos black on Halloween.* New York, NY: Henry Holt and Company.

Morales, Y. (2013). *Niño wrestles the world.* New York, NY: Roaring Book Press.

Naidoo, J. C. (2011). Reviewing the representation of Latino cultures in U.S. children's literature In J. C. Naidoo (Ed.), *Celebrating cuentos: Promoting Latino children's literature and literacy in classrooms and libraries* (pp. 59–78). Santa Barbara, CA: ABC-CLIO.

Naqvi, R., McKeough, A., Thorne, K. J., Pfitscher, C. (2012, July 2). Dual-language books as an emergent-literacy resource: Culturally and linguistically responsive teaching and learning. *Journal of Early Childhood Literacy.* doi:10.1177/1468798412442886.

National Governors Association Center for Best Practices & Council of Chief State School Officers. (2014). *Common Core State Standards.* Washington, DC: Authors. Retrieved from www.corestandards.org.

Nieto, S. (1997). We have stories to tell: Puerto Ricans in children's books. In V. J. Harris (Ed.), *Using multiethnic literature in the K–8 classroom* (pp. 59–93). Norwood, MA: Christopher-Gordon Publishers.

Pérez, A. I. (2000). *My very own room/Mi propio cuartito.* San Francisco, CA: Children's Book Press.

———. (2007). *Nana's big surprise/Nana, ¡Qué sorpresa!* New York, NY: Children's Book Press.

Pérez, A. I., & González, M. C. (2002). *My diary from here to there/Mi diario de aquí hasta allá.* San Francisco, CA: Children's Book Press.

Pilioneta, P., & Hancock, S. D. (2012). Negotiating first graders' reading stance: The relationship between their efferent and aesthetic connections and their reading comprehension. *Current Issues in Education, 15*(2), 1–8.

Reyes de la Luz, M., & Halcón, J. J. (2001). *The best for our children: Critical perspectives on literacy for Latino students.* New York, NY: Teachers College Press.

Robb, L. (2002). Multiple texts: Multiple opportunities for teaching and learning. *Voices from the Middle, 9*(4), 28.

Rodríguez-Valls, F., Kofford, S., & Morales, E. (2012). Graffiti walls: Migrant students and the art of communicative languages. *Journal of Social Theory in Art Education, 32*, 96–111.

Rogoff, B. (2003). *The cultural nature of human development.* New York, NY: Oxford University Press.

Rosenblatt, L. M. (1978). *The reader, the text, the poem: The transactional theory of the literary work.* Carbondale, IL: Southern Illinois University Press.

———. (2005). Literature—S.O.S.! *Voices from the Middle, 12*(3), 34–38.

Saavedra, C. M. (2011). Language and literacy in the borderlands: Acting upon the world through "testimonios." *Language Arts, 88*(4), 261–69.

Short, K. G., Kauffman, G., & Kahn, L. H. (2000). "I just need to draw": Responding to literature across multiple sign systems. *Reading Teacher*, 160–71.

Solórzano, D. G., & Yosso, T. J. (2002). Critical race methodology: Counter-storytelling as an analytical framework for educational research. *Qualitative Inquiry, 8*(1), 23–44.

Street, B. (1984). *Literacy in theory and practice.* Cambridge: Cambridge University Press.

Tonatiuh, D. (2010). *Dear primo: A letter to my cousin.* New York, NY: Abrams Books for Young Readers.

Valencia, R. R. (2002). Mexican Americans don't value education! On the basis of the myth, mythmaking, and debunking. *Journal of Latinos and Education, 1*(2), 81–103.

Valenzuela, A. (1999). *Subtractive schooling: U.S.–Mexico youth and the politics of caring.* New York, NY: State University of New York Press.

Van Lier, L., & Walqui, A. (2012). *How teachers and educators can most usefully and deliberately consider language.* Paper presented at the Understanding Language Conference, Stanford, California.

Vygotsky, L. S. (1978). *Mind in society: The development of higher psychological processes.* Cambridge, MA: Harvard University Press.

Walqui, A. (2008). Scaffolding instruction for English language learners: A conceptual framework. *International Journal of Bilingual Education and Bilingualism, 9*(2), 159–80.

Willis, A. I. (2008). Critical race theory. In B. V. Street & N. H. Hornberger (Eds.), *Encyclopedia of language and education* (vol. 2, pp. 15–28). New York, NY: Springer.

Wolf, S. A. (2004). *Interpreting literature with children.* Mahwah, NJ: Lawrence Erlbaum Associates.

Yang, G. (2008). Graphic novels in the classroom. *Language Arts, 85*(3), 185–92.

Yosso, T. J. (2006). *Critical race counterstories along the Chicana/Chicano educational pipeline.* New York, NY: Routledge.

Zentella, A. C. (1997). *Growing up bilingual: Puerto Rican children in New York.* New York, NY: Wiley.

———. (2003). José, can you see? Latin@ Responses to racist discourse. In D. Sommer (Ed.), *Bilingual games: Some literary investigation* (pp. 51–66). New York, NY: Palgrave Macmillan.

DISCUSSION QUESTIONS

1. What are the essential factors that should guide teachers in selecting multicultural literature by Latino authors?
2. What specific issues related to Latinos in the United States are addressed in children's literature by Latino authors? What perspectives underlie the themes addressed?
3. What are ways that emergent bilingual learners can respond to children's literature in the language arts classroom?
4. What is important to consider in regard to how languages are portrayed and used in children's literature?

ACTIVITIES

A. Identify concepts in the curriculum for your grade level that could be addressed through a text set.
B. Review the resources that are available in your school or community to conduct an author and/or illustrator study. In your school or community library, look for multiple texts by one author. How could you begin to read the work of different authors and identify possible topics or themes to discuss with students?
C. Find colleagues and form a critical reading group.
D. Explore the opportunities that exist in your school to read and discuss literature with students' parents and family members. Consider how engaging in family literacy groups might provide you with insight into children's literature that is culturally relevant for your students.

PROFESSIONAL READINGS

Ada, A. F. (2003). *A magical encounter: Latino children's literature in the classroom* (2nd ed.). New York, NY: Pearson.

Barrera, R., & Quiroa, R. (2003). The use of Spanish in Latino children's literature in English: What makes for cultural authenticity? In D. Fox & K. Short (Eds.), *Stories matter: The complexity of cultural authenticity in children's literature* (pp. 247–65). Urbana, IL: National Council of Teachers of English.

Bishop, R. S. (1992). Multicultural literature for children: Making informed choices. In V. J. Harris (Ed.), *Teaching multicultural literature in grades K–8* (pp. 37–58). Norwood, MA: Christopher-Gordon Publishers.

California State Department of Education (1998). *10 quick ways to analyze children's books for racism and sexism.* Adaptation of brochure by the Council on Interracial Books for Children. Retrieved from www.chil-es.org/10ways.pdf.

Dorfman, L. R., & Cappelli, R. (2007). *Mentor texts: Teaching writing through children's literature, K–6.* Portland, ME: Stenhouse Publishers.

Harris, V. J. (2003). The complexity of debates about multicultural literature and cultural authenticity. In D. L. Fox & K. G. Short (Eds.), *Stories matter: The complexity of cultural authenticity in children's literature.* Urbana, IL: National Council of Teachers of English.

Medina, C. L. (2006). Interpreting Latino/a literature as critical fictions. *ALAN Review* (Winter), 71–77.

Naidoo, J. C. (2011). *Celebrating cuentos: Promoting Latino children's literature and literacy in classrooms and libraries* (pp. 59–78). Santa Barbara, CA: Libraries Unlimited.

Nieto, S. (1997). We have stories to tell: Puerto Ricans in children's books. In Violet J. Harris (Ed.), *Using multiethnic literature in the K–8 classroom* (2nd ed., pp. 59–93). Norwood, MA: Christopher-Gordon Publishers.

Chapter Eight

En Aquel Entonces y Hoy en Día: Using Latino Children's Literature to Situate Social Studies Education

Mary Esther Soto Huerta and Carmen Tafolla

INTRODUCTION

Teachers of social studies education are charged with designing instruction that guides student learning about *en aquel entonces y hoy en día* (the past and the present). Today, many encounter systematic conflicts for designing culturally relevant pedagogy, having to compete with the value given to student performance on state-mandated assessments perceived as reliable measures of their knowledge, critical thinking, and skills (Valenzuela, 2005). Teachers and other decision-makers are left to determine how these performance outcomes correlate to the competencies required by Latino students to navigate their life in the twenty-first century.

While the National Curriculum Standards for Social Studies (NCSS, 2015) and research-based findings continue to provide evidence and push for the reorganization of curricula that create relevant and authentic learning spaces, learning scripts and the use of traditional academic curriculums remain intact. Bias is still evident when considering the emphasis given to Columbus and to the October 12 designated holiday, celebrating the day that he "discovered" America. The implication is that the indigenous inhabitants of the continent required a European-based discovery and written annals to authenticate their existence (Elbow, 2015). The children's book *In 1492* (Marzollo, 1948) exemplifies this European-based perspective by touting European accomplishments and portraying the indigenous people only as props. This ideology, of colonization, continues to represent indigenous populations as unintelligent and primitive, discounting their history, cultural practices, languages, and complex knowledge. Latino students are burdened by the implications of these biases when they discover that indigenous peoples were conquered and that their defeat completes the story. By logical extension, and as descendants of those defeated indigenous peoples of the past, Latinos are also burdened by the implications of "scripted" biases embedded in school curriculums.

A reorganization of the social studies curriculum would evoke critical thinking by including texts explaining that Columbus, the Puritans, and other early colonizers were all immigrants who did not speak the languages of the Americas (see chapter 14). Teachers could use *Encounter*, written by Jane Yolen (1992), to learn about Columbus's arrival from the perspective of a young Taino boy. A more realistic depiction of the arrival of Columbus's expedition and its consequences, the narrative more accurately describes the moment of encounter between two world cultures. For those who lament the loss of a classic tale as traditionally told about Columbus's great discovery, teachers should examine the accounts of Spanish priest Fray Bartolomé de las Casas (1992), who lamented the death of 3 million native peoples in the span of fourteen years. Even Columbus's (2003) own diaries from 1451 to 1506 casually document that with Christian piety, he raped and beat native women as well as mutilated and murdered adolescents and adults who did not pay enough gold tribute. An important poem to also consider is Tafolla's *Voyage* (1975). This poem counters traditional biases when it challenges the reader to predict the outcome with the arrival of a fourth ship, used to signify an alternative to the invasion of the new world and the forced collision, conquest, and repression of robust cultures.

Guiding student inquiry through the use of literature and academic texts is an instructional approach that is supported by the National Association for Multicultural Education (NAME) 2013 position statement. The NAME position statement calls for schools to prepare students to become active participants in a democracy and advocate for a socially just society through a curriculum that addresses individual differences including race, ethnicity, language, class, gender, ability, ageism, religion/spirituality, and sexual orientation. To accomplish this, NAME proposes that students, their life histories, and experiences be placed at the center of the teaching and learning processes. Additionally, the pedagogy that students receive should occur in a context that is familiar and address multiple ways of thinking. Further, NAME tasks teachers and students to critically analyze oppression and power relations in their communities, society, and the world (2013).

These guiding principles situate social studies education as a critical pathway that can guide students' discovery and understanding of origin, place, character, responsibilities, and rights. Each facet can inform students about connections to their community and how to read the world (Freire, 1970).

When stories become the groundwork for analysis, questioning, and drawing meaning about self, texts, and the world, they enable students to impose order on the many and varying experiences that they encounter in their daily lives and to situate their positionality in the world (Gee, 2015; Wolf, 2004).

Culturally relevant pedagogy also leverages students' cultural capital and funds of knowledge (González, Moll, & Amati, 2005) for learning and restructuring the curriculum. Gay (2010) argues that culturally relevant pedagogy requires teaching to students' personal and cultural strengths. When authentic Latino children's literature is incorporated in social studies education, Latino student engagement and learning can be enhanced through authentic dialogue that contradicts traditional teaching and learning "scripts" that promote a single point of view. These learning spaces also foster the co-construction of student-teacher knowledge (Gutiérrez, 2008). This approach to teaching and learning may be more critically significant for Latino students than for the student considered as more privileged by our society. In the latter case, privilege is designed by membership and participation in the mainstream culture based on social economic class where English holds a ubiquitous status that is mirrored by school curriculums. However, we contend that countering the traditional, colonial narrative supports the development of all students.

THEORETICAL FRAMEWORK

The history of the mainstream culture is disseminated and normalized daily, considering how public institutions are structured (Horkheimer & Adorno, 2001); how buildings, highways, and parks are named; how the media (through news reports and television dramas) associates ethnic minorities with such social conditions as poverty, low-levels of education, crime and mayhem; and how schools are organized. The seminal works of Macedo and Bartolomé (2001), Valencia (2010, 2012), and Valenzuela (1999) have outlined how biased assumptions that emerge from societal misrepresentations have permeated societal attitudes, and they have influenced the low expectations of Latinos and their potential to achieve academically. These deficit portrayals have engendered the silencing of Latinos, have created vacuums of learning negligent of critical analysis, have generated gaps of cultural knowledge, and have caused a perpetual disequilibrium of Latino students' sense of place.

Moreover, Latino children's history and identity have been largely ignored within U.S. children's literature. The Cooperative Children's Book Center report (2010) found that of the three thousand volumes of children's books published in 2009 and sent to the center by publishers, large and small nationwide, only sixty-one had significant Latino content, and of these, only sixty (or 2 percent) had been written by Latino authors and/or illustrators. The findings indicated that only American Indians ranked lower among the major ethnic groups (see chapters 1, 2, and 15). These statistics show the dismal under-representation of Latinos portrayed in children's literature as well as in the fields of social studies, science, mathematics, and the arts, which further minimizes Latino contributions. Lacking in children's literature have been references to Latino military contributions even though, according to Samora and Simon (2003), Latinos today represent the highest percentage of military Medal of Honor winners of any ethnic group in the U.S.

The low representation of Latinos in the world of books, both academic and literary, ignores the issues that Latinos and other ethnic minority students encounter throughout their schooling, including alienation and discrimination (Ada, 2003). The low representation of Latinos in the world of books creates social distance between the ethnic minority child and the educational system when the perceived distance from the world of books sustains the belief that it is not relevant to their life. Paulo Freire (1970) describes the effect of emptiness that emerges from transmissive modes of education: "The banking notion of consciousness [is] that the educator's role is to regulate the way the world 'enters into' the student . . . to 'fill' the student by making deposits of information" (p. 57). He continues describing the effects of social distances as "detached from reality, disconnected from the totality that could give them significance. Words are emptied of their concreteness and become a hollow, alienated, and alienating verbosity" (p. 52).

Teaching social studies to Latino students must be intentional. Teachers of social studies education are charged with designing culturally relevant pedagogy to situate Latino funds of knowledge at the center of teaching and learning (González, Moll, & Amanti, 2005). One way to do this is by utilizing authentic Latino children's literature to sustain knowledge about heritage and history (informal and formal), and to examine how sociopolitical contexts have impacted lived experiences and cultural practices.

These approaches describe transformative pedagogy (Cummins, 2000), which guides students' awareness and their agency to engage in social practices. Teaching to sustain the agency of Latino students to transform curriculum and co-construct knowledge through inquiry and dialogue requires that teachers purposefully embed *conscientizacao*, or consciousness-raising (Freire, 1990), in daily instruction. According to Freire (1990), an integrated process occurs as the word is read, and then the world is read. Additionally, Ada (2003) offers that through transformative education, learning must always emerge from a student's personal and emotional reality. Transformative pedagogy utilizes the lenses of critical literacy to probe issues of agency and social practice to attain equity, social justice, and change (Nagda, Gurin, & Lopez, 2003). Through the critical process of transformative pedagogy, according to Nagda et al. (2003), Latino students gain awareness about their positionality in their community and in their globalized society (see chapter 14).

What impact can Latino children's literature have on the learning of social studies and historical patterns of the human experience, especially for Latino children? Authentic Latino children's literature values Latinos as full actors and creators of history. The impact can be significant to Latino children's identity and self-esteem as well as a positive influence on how Latinos are perceived by other cultural groups (see chapters 1, 2, and 3). In a society where Latino children confront prejudice and discrimination for speaking a language other than English, using academic texts and quality multicultural literatures that value their heritage, their home culture, and their home language remains a vital instructional practice (Ada, 2003).

Latino children's literature reflects powerful topics that are an essential part of the teaching of the social sciences. This type of literature includes works that address conflicts between nations; the blending of cultures; the understanding of bias and prejudice; and the dynamics of leadership, revolution, protest, social justice, and social change (Barrera & Garza de Cortés, 1997). Furthermore, Latino cultural stories "are always interwoven with the stories that exist within our culture, both in content and in the style and structure of the telling" (Short, Lynch-Brown, & Tomlinson, 2014, p. 6).

Through transformative pedagogy, critical dialogue is always paired with reading and comprehending quality multicultural literature, guiding students to discover counternarratives through the presentation of conflicting viewpoints and by questioning traditional story events and resolutions. This constructivist approach to learning relies on critical thinking and the blending across cultures (home, school, and community). The co-construction of knowledge through inquiry and dialogue further provides a better understanding of ethnic group diversity marked by the dynamic nature of culture (Gee, 2015). Thus a transformative pedagogy approach to teaching social studies enables Latino students to perceive a personal and emotional connection to the deep-seated concepts associated with history, economics, geography, and civilizations, among other social studies concepts. As Latino students gain ownership of their learning through active engagement of social studies–related concepts, they critically understand their role in the world. With the integration of Latino children's literature, students can gain awareness and affirmation of their identities as multilingual and multicultural, considered the new "normal" in the twenty-first century (August, Shanahan, & Escamilla, 2009).

PRAXIS: IMPLEMENTING TRANSFORMATIVE PEDAGOGY

The integration of transformative pedagogy with social studies education is in line with the NCSS (2015). The standards promote the development of civic competence through the development of knowledge, intellectual processes, and democratic dispositions. This requires students to be active and engaged participants in public life. Additionally, this civic mission demands that instruction should include all students by addressing cultural, linguistic, and learning diversity by examining similarities and differences based on race, ethnicity, language, religion, gender, sexual orientation, exceptional learning needs, and other educationally and personally significant characteristics of learners. Combined, these standards pronounce that diversity among learners is a characteristic that embodies the democratic goal of embracing pluralism to make social studies classrooms laboratories of democracy (NCSS, 2015).

The use of authentic Latino children's literature can sustain the goal of developing civic competence as outlined by the NCSS (2015) when texts and illustrations are of the highest quality, when the portrayal and symbolic representations of Latinos are accurate and engaging, and when they avoid stereotypes and reflect rich characterization (see chapters 2, 6, and 13). These literary features, however, contrast with books that use Latinos as negative literary devices. Latinos are included more often than not in weak or ineffective roles in the narratives, while using only Eurocentric themes broadcasts negative messages about diversity throughout the storylines. These texts are also typified by themes proposing that in order to "fit into" the dominant culture, individuals must surrender their uniqueness and exceptionality. One example is the narrative *The Rainbow Fish and the Big Blue Whale* (Pfister & James, 1998), which garnered great financial success. This narrative is about a fish covered in beautiful glowing scales, but whom the other fish ridicule. The protagonist decides to give away all his scales to the other fish. *The Rainbow Fish* is left without a trace of his previous beauty or uniqueness. *Skippyjon Jones* (Schachner, 2009) is another book that continues to garner great financial gains at the expense of appropriating a stereotype associated with Latinos as a literary device (see chapter 2). The author uses the main character, a Siamese cat, to evoke humor by mocking the way that some Spanish-speakers speak English. While the themes may vary, both books undermine a respect for cultural and linguistic diversity.

The feature of appropriating stereotypes of ethnic minorities as a literary device is not supported by the NCSS (2015); conversely, standards are organized by strands that guide culturally relevant pedagogy. While not all strands are used, the following section categorizes authentic Latino children's literature with the relevant strand for teaching social studies. Teachers must expect that many of the books listed in the following section overlap across the different NCSS strands (2015). Each strand is framed by themes that are explicitly explained. They are also broad and generalizable. This enables teachers to integrate the strands with their instruction straightforwardly. The teacher's role is to make a variety of books available to students, books aligned with student interest and reading comprehension. Further, if bilingual learners (García, 2010) can be more successful readers in Spanish, the teacher is obliged to make these books available in order to sustain an equity of opportunities for all students to read and learn.

Additionally, for each social studies strand, ideas are provided for using literature to complement the social studies curriculum. The teacher is, therefore, tasked with reading and analyzing the literature that they select to appropriately enhance student awareness of how Latino children's literature explicitly connects to the social studies curriculum. These instructional processes scaffold students' critical thought about how the different concepts that they explore are relevant to their life.

Culture

The NCSS themes associated with this culture strand state that human beings create, learn, share, and adapt to culture; that cultures are dynamic, change, and blend over time. Through experience, observation, and reflection, students should be able to identify elements of culture as well as similarities and differences among cultural groups across time and place.

There are Latino children's books that describe the richness of Latino communities, the bilingual and bicultural experience, biculturalism, and present culture as dynamic (see part V). Latino multicultural books can guide student awareness of the heterogeneity and variability of the lived experiences of Latinos. For example, while the main character in *Just a Minute: A Trickster's Tale* (Morales, 2003) is *Señor Calavera*, or Mr. Death, Yuyi Morales makes the humorous character palatable (to general audiences) when considering that the cultural icon depicted represents a belief valued by many Latinos that death is part of the natural life cycle. The essential objective for using Latino children's literature, then, is to acknowledge and demonstrate that each culture is rich and reflects wisdom, and that cultural practices, beliefs, and values must be respected.

One book that describes the cultural capital existing in Latino neighborhoods located in the city is *What Can You Do with a Paleta?* (Tafolla & Morales, 2009). The author documents the many magical sights, sounds, and cultural treasures of the *barrio* (neighborhood and community) in the story, which is typically viewed by the public as a slum, a ghetto, and where diminished hopes reside. The delightful contradiction to these stereotypic expectations is that Latino children from these communities can easily relate to the images and role of the *paletero*, the *paleta* wagon, and the *frutería* (fresh fruit shop). The author also depicts the many treats and kindnesses bestowed by the neighbors, marking this book as a counternarrative to statements made about the barrio. The social studies teacher can guide students to explore social issues using Latino children's literature (see chapter 3 and 13).

To guide younger students to identify elements of cultural practices and beliefs that may be similar or different from their lived experiences, or across time and place, teachers can conduct read alouds. Teachers should first introduce or remind and guide students to attend to the posted, designated social studies strand—for example, culture—which they are currently studying along with the learning objective. After the selected book has been read aloud, the teacher will already have posted three guiding questions that enable students to draw explicit connections to the strand and to the learning objective. Possible guiding questions could include

1. How does this story explain something similar to what your family does?
2. How does this story describe something that is different?
3. Why do you think people are different (live differently, or have different ideas)?
4. How do you feel about those differences (or when you meet someone who is different)?
5. What questions do you have?

The teacher should scribe student responses to sustain a spiraling approach to instruction by continuously drawing connections between the social studies strand and the particular narratives that are read to students.

For older students, teachers can guide students to engage in an author study. The teacher should design a collection of the literary works of the designated authors and ensure that books are available to students either in the school or in libraries. Through a self-selected approach, each student can engage in studying the literary works of an author. Teachers can design time for peers studying the same author to share books and to discuss. Possible guiding questions can include Why does the author use this setting? What seems to be important to this author? What connections can you make with the author or the story? The role of the teacher-facilitator is to make explicit the various learning objectives and to guide students to draw connections between the social studies strand and the literacy activities that they engage. They must comprehensively explain the learning objectives, the expected learning outcomes, and any related products and/or performances that students will be asked to create.

Time, Continuity, and Change

The theme associated with this social studies strand guides students to understand the past in order to analyze the causes and consequences of events and developments, and to place these in the context of the institutions, values, and beliefs of the periods in which they took place. This strand also guides students to understand how past events influence the present.

It is essential that Latino students understand that it is not always the stronger or the largest army that wins a war. Tafolla's *You Don't Have to Be Bigger to Be Important: A Cinco de Mayo Poem* (Ada et al., 1993, p. 179) emphasizes that in their revolt against the well-armed and experienced French army, the new volunteer-based Mexican army, albeit victorious, encountered many disadvantages, including being much smaller than the French army. The theme of might vs. right is also addressed in another poem concerning bullying. Guadalupe Garcia McCall's *The Bully* (Vardell & Wong, 2012, p. 248) describes a young girl's rage and shame at the hands of a bully. The topic of bullying is especially relevant to children, who may often find themselves feeling small or inexperienced. Both of these works can be used to teach civic competency through teacher-guided discussion that explores the issue of might vs. right and the role of leadership in generating social change.

Literary works that focus on leadership include Juan Felipe Herrera's (2003) *Super Cilantro Girl* and *Doña Flor: A Tall Tale of a Giant Woman with a Great Big Heart* by Pat Mora (2005). Each book shifts the power from the norm, showing the enchantment of differences. The young super-heroine in *Super Cilantro Girl* transforms herself with "hair longer than a bus, and skin so green it could have only come from cilantro." This narrative represents a counternarrative to the traditional storylines that demote young girls to victims and damsels in distress. In this case, Super Cilantro Girl flies to the U.S.–Mexico border, picks up her mother, puts her in her pocket, and rescues her. The book addresses issues of immigration, the separation of families through deportation, and the intimacy lost by families separated by nation-state borders and governing policies (see chapter 4).

Teachers can use these and similarly themed books that provide a counternarrative to traditional perspectives and worldviews. Students can be guided to assess problems associated with a time and place and the expected outcomes. Students can then consider possible options in present-day social and political contexts to predict potential outcomes and their influence on social change. In a separate activity, students are encouraged to illustrate and write about the attributes of Super Cilantro Girl. Students could draw comparisons and similarities between the super heroine described in the book and a traditional superhero. Discussions can also guide students to consider and question traditional gender roles and assigned expectations for each gender based on cultural beliefs as well as societal assumptions and attitudes.

People, Places, and Their Environments

The theme associated with this social studies strand guides students to study people, places, and environments to understand the relationship between human populations and the physical world. For this strand there are critical literary works based on historical moments. In *Sylvia and Aki*, Winifred Conkling (2013) recounts how two young ethnic minority girls experience discrimination as a consequence of the after-effects of World War II. In *Esperanza Rising*, author Pam Muñoz Ryan (2000) describes the life of a young girl and her family during the Mexican Revolution. Other historical moments are represented in similar literary works (see part V).

Latino children's literature can assist in increasing student awareness and inspire critical thinking through inquiry. One approach to incorporate inquiry and dialogue with the social studies curriculum is through book clubs, also known as literature circles (Daniels, 2002). Literature circles enable students to explore and understand the complex contexts and perspectives associated with each narrative. Through small-group discussions, older children can explore temporal factors of the particular era, cultural practices and languages, the political climate, people's rights and responsibilities, geography, socioeconomic considerations, governance, and religion, among other influencing social factors. Literature circles sustain student agency when group members choose a book to read selected from a collection provided by the teacher. To draw multiple connections across the curriculum, the students must be aware of how the book collection that the teacher provides is aligned with the social studies learning objective and the social studies strand. Each member of the small group is tasked with reading the pages assigned by the group and with fulfilling a designated role, including leading the discussion at each meeting, scribing for the group, preparing questions, and gathering materials and resources.

The teacher-facilitator's role is to design and clarify the learning objectives and outcomes for each group meeting and for the overall literacy project; to model reading comprehension and how to ask questions; to create and explain the rubrics that will be used to guide the development of student products or performances; and to rotate between literature circles groups to facilitate inquiry through discussion. As aforementioned, the teacher must systematically make evident to students how the children's multicultural literature that they read connects to the social studies strand and the curriculum that they are currently studying.

Literature circles represent a constructivist, cooperative approach to making sense of texts, particularly when group members make decisions and problem-solve to ensure that they meet the literacy-based objectives and outcomes. As students generate multiple perspectives by thinking about what they read, each story can gain relevancy for students. Additionally, the longer that students engage in repeated readings of texts and use literacy to respond to what they read, the more they can enhance their reading comprehension and fluency over time (Pérez, 2003).

Individual Development and Identity

The theme associated with this social studies strand states that personal identity is shaped by an individual's culture, by groups, by institutional influences, and by lived experiences shared with people inside and outside the individual's own culture throughout his or her development. In the same vein, there is children's literature that provides a wide diversity of contemporary Latino realities and identities (see chapter 3 and part V).

Another set of literary works that complements this social studies strand addresses the experiences of immigrant or migrant children as they travel to new towns and new schools and encounter unfamiliar environments (see chapter 4). This set of works includes *Downtown Boy* (Herrera, 2005); *Tomás and the Library Lady* (Mora & Colón, 2000); *My Diary from Here to There: Mi diario de aquí hasta allá* (Pérez & González, 2013); and *The Circuit: Stories from the Life of a Migrant Child*, written by Francisco Jiménez (1999; see part V). The picture book *La leyenda de Mexicatl: The Legend of Mexicatl* (Harper & Casilla, 2000; see part V) is a tale that explains the origins of the Mexican indigenous people and infuses the concept of migration with great respect and historical significance.

Other literary works can offer a child's perspective about the difficult conditions and adjustments that immigrants encounter, including entering school not knowing how to speak English (see chapter 4). These works include Julia Alvarez's *Return to Sender* (2009); Margarita Robleda's (2005) *Paco: Un niño Latino en los Estados Unidos/Paco: A Latino Boy in the United States*; and *Esperanza Rising* by Muñoz Ryan (2000; see part V).

Teachers can use these resources to analyze the reasons why people migrate, considering their aspirations; the context of time, place, economics, and well-being; modes of travel available; items that they carried with them; and their plans and strategies. Older students can conduct research to draw historical and contemporary comparisons between people who migrate, including farm workers, undocumented immigrants, Puritans, Hernán Cortés, Columbus, and other migrants worldwide. Throughout history, migration has been a human experience, and using both academic texts and relevant literary works can guide students to examine the complex factors that drive migrations and the extenuating circumstances that can emerge from that experience (see chapter 4).

To explore how diverse lived experiences influence identity, Monica Brown (2013) describes the happy existence of an interracial child in *Marisol McDonald Doesn't Match/Marisol McDonald no combina*. In *Abuelita's Secret Matzahs*, Sasso (2005; see part V) describes the religious prejudice experienced by Spanish Jews, who could not reveal their religion and suffered the penalty of death as dictated by law. Seeking religious freedom, Spanish Jews migrated to the Americas, the new world (Santos, 2000). Once on the American continent, Spanish Jews kept many religious and culinary traditions. Today *el pan de semita* (unleavened bread), is a staple at Mexican *panaderías* (bakeries) in the Southwest (Santos, 2000). Teachers can expand on the theme of religious freedom when this book supplements a unit of study about the Pilgrims, who also traveled to the new world seeking religious freedom.

Another excellent approach to studying crosscultural experiences is Alma Flor Ada's (2013) *Nacer bailando*, which takes the reader through the process of friendship as two girls learn to accept and respect each other's culture. The teacher can read this book aloud to the whole group and then guide a discussion about the cultural attributes of each girl. A classroom activity can follow that guides students to generate listings of their family traditions, *dichos* (proverbs/sayings), legends, holidays, and other cultural expressions represented in the classroom (see chapters 7 and 9). After the teacher compiles the information, organizes it, and then posts the information on multiple chart papers mounted around the classroom, students can begin to "read around the room." The students' task is to place a red "sticky" star beside the item that is not represented in their own culture, and every time they encounter something familiar, they can place a gold star beside the item. A green star can be used to mark cultural activities that they would like to participate in and/or explore. When the whole group examines the postings, the teacher can guide student dialogue that considers how individual cultural practices and lived experiences are, and have been, influenced by many other cultures, and how cultures blend to create new traditions and ethnic identities (e.g., mestizo culture, Tex-Mex, Nuyorican). A useful poem to explore Puerto Rican celebrations in New York is Gloria Vando's *Puerto Rican Day Parade* (Ada et al., 1993).

Moreover, the topics addressed by each book listed for this social studies strand replace hollow stereotypes and make visible the multifaceted and dynamic nature of identity. Also, some literary works exemplify the diversity in family units within the Latino community through narratives that show how children can live with a grandmother, a single mother, two mothers, a father, no parent, many siblings, no siblings, or adopted families (see chapter 5). Beyond understanding how people are similar and different (see the social studies strand on culture), it is also important that students explore their own unique identity to understand how their perspectives are shaped by time, lived experiences, particular cultural practices, geography, and other factors that influence their social identity.

Teachers can also guide students to explore the cultural background of each main character by designing a cultural tree that explicitly lists a character's cultural attributes. The design should be a logical, visual cue, or graphic organizer, and reference for students. The graphic organizer that the teacher designs should remain posted throughout the unit of study. With the main character's name written at the top of a large chart paper, the text provides constant evidence during reading about the character's cultural attributes. Some of the cultural attributes that may emerge from the literature include gender roles, family units, geography/region, age, time, economic status, class issues, types of employment, and the influence of time. Each thread of evidence is used to further analyze character traits, story events, conflicts, consequences, and resolutions. When several books are included and analyzed, the cultural connections drawn between the academic and literary texts are enhanced.

The study of biographies is also included in the social studies strand. Teachers can use books such as *Portraits of Hispanic American Heroes* (Herrera, 2014) and multiple genres to help students understand the attributes of a biography. Students can then use published biographies as models to write their own introspective biographies.

Power, Authority, and Governance

One of the themes associated with this strand includes the study of the dynamic relationships between individual rights and responsibilities, the needs of social groups, and the concepts of a just society. It is expected that learners should become more effective problem-solvers and decision-makers when addressing the challenges, persistent issues, and social problems encountered in public life.

The literature aligned with this strand addresses issues of leadership, poverty, and social change. Some of the Latino children's literature that follows these themes is included in part V. This strand also emphasizes civic competence through the development of concepts associated with citizenship and community-building. Mora and Martinez (2014; see part V), in *I Pledge Allegiance*, uniquely provide multiple methods of learning the U.S. pledge of allegiance by emphasizing multigenerational, naturalized, and native-born approaches.

To explore the needs of social groups, and the concepts of a just society, both younger and older students can become more effective problem-solvers and decision-makers through a variety of activities. After hearing Amada Irma Pérez's (2013; see part V) *My Very Own Room/Mi propio cuartito*, read aloud, for example, young children can dictate their persuasive ideas to the teacher while older students can engage in persuasive writing activities to address self-selected issues. In each instance, the teacher makes explicit to students the strategies of persuasion modeled by the main character. Students learn that they can benefit from using multiple text genres as models for using literacy to create change. This is an example of implementing critical literacy.

Using books that address social inequalities and evoke social justice through change in collaboration with others, students can draw connections to their own lives. For example, teachers can hold a circle-time on the carpet to talk about conditions or actions occurring in their community that need to be changed. Huerta (1995) recalls such a discussion circle in a first-grade classroom. A young Latino child living in a low-SES community reported having to walk with his mother and younger sister past a smelly animal carcass each day on his way to school. During the circle discussion, the students and the teacher brainstormed about how to solve this problem. The teacher provided a telephone directory and demonstrated how she searched for the Department of Animal Control, and the students agreed that calling that office would be a good place to start. The student wrote the phone number and shared it with his mother later that evening. A week later, at the next circle-time, the young child reported that the carcass had been removed.

Teachers have used the book *That's Not Fair! Emma Tenayuca's Struggle for Justice/¡No es justo! La lucha de Emma Tenayuca por la justicia* by Tafolla and Tenayuca (2008; see part V) and a model developed by Tafolla (2010) to guide students to identify and describe situations they believed were unfair in their own life or in the lives of their families and communities and to generate strategies.

Older students are also keenly aware of conditions or actions occurring in their community that need to be changed, and they can use any of the literary works listed above to analyze the strategies used by the protagonists to create change; to analyze the consequences of the strategies applied; and to assess potential benefits and risks. Older students can then engage literacy-related activities to express the statement of the problem/issue, to conduct research, to propose strategies, and to generate written reports, letters, or performances.

While the teacher-facilitator continuously holds the responsibility of designing and managing both guided and open-ended approaches to teaching and learning, the described literacy-related activities sustain student leadership and agency. As the students use literature as models to broaden ideas and perspectives, the literature also supports their use of literacy-based knowledge and skills to generate products or performances. Using literature as models for literacy-based, open-ended learning activities can further enhance student ownership of their own learning.

Production, Distribution, and Consumption

This social studies strand guides students to acknowledge that people have wants that often exceed the limited resources available. One approach to exploring this strand is to have students gather and analyze data to critically think about how best to deal with scarcity of resources.

To teach the importance of natural resources to human settlements, students must consider and analyze the location of waterways, the availability of food, and the natural resources of wood, stone, metal, flora, and fauna that sustain the development of societies. Within the Latino context, our *mestizo* and indigenous values provide rich legends that emphasize the importance of the earth and its abundance. In *The Woman Who Outshone the Sun* (Zubizarreta, 1991), we read a powerful Zapotec legend that describes a village that takes for granted its surrounding natural resources, the beauty of nature, and the importance of diversity. Lucía, a large woman with an unusual rapport with the local river, arrives in the small village and is considered odd and strange. Each day when Lucía visits the river, the fish and the otters swim into her hair and the river rises to meet her. After being mistreated for being different, she decides to leave the village, and so do the river, the fish, and the otters. While the villagers realize how crucial their river was to their survival, the children also become aware of the consequences that emerged from the villagers' acts of cruelty. To rectify the situation, the children assume leadership and find a resolution (see chapter 9).

The concept of environmental guardianship and ecological responsibility can be taught by using Latino children's literature that also emphasizes traditional Latino values such as *respeto*. In *Baby Coyote and the Old Woman/ El coyotito y la viejita* (Tafolla, 2000), children learn respect for friendship, other species, and the environment. Respect for natural resources and agriculture can also be taught to early readers. *¡Ymm-MmMm-que rico! America's Sproutings* (Mora & López, 2007; see part V) traces the production and use of chocolate, tomatoes, and vanilla, among other popular crops, to their Mexican and South American roots. Other books, like *Grandma's Chocolate/El chocolate de abuelita* (Price & Fields, 2010; see part V), infuse modern resources and traditions with the enduring magic of their centuries-old, pre-Columbian heritage. This social studies strand can guide Latino students to explore how finite resources impact wants, needs, production, and consumption at home and within their globalized economy (see chapter 9).

CONCLUSION

One of the most crucial characteristics of an authentic, Latino-based story is that it promotes the concept of diversity. Conversely, the appropriation of the Latino culture to write stories about Latinos but omit the Latino perspective conveys notions of homogeneity and leverages messages of anti-diversity. In these narratives, Latinos, or images of Latinos, are used as a literary device only to recount traditional history, with Latinos remaining perpetually under-served, under-represented, and under-respected.

The teachers of social studies education are tasked with integrating the powerful messages presented through Latino children's literature to best describe, explain, and question consequences, implications, and connotations. This instructional approach reveals how vital literary works are to Latino students' engagement with schooling. Using the power of story and literacy-based tasks to guide students to understand and learn social studies concepts is beneficial because the process evokes critical thought. This engagement with multiple genres can determine whether students' history is learned, remembered, and used in their lives to influence change.

Children also need an emotional interaction with literary works that generate a point at which personal and emotional awareness permeates students' intellectual activities. This level of interaction with multiple and varied use of literacy permits students to more fully understand and contemplate the social studies concepts that they study.

It is also imperative that teachers explain and demonstrate how social studies–based concepts are relevant to Latino students. Knowledgeable teachers can guide deep interpretations of the texts that highlight students' cultural capital framed by their heritage, identity, culture, language, and talents. In the twenty-first century, a "just the facts" approach to instruction will not enable Latino students to apply civic competency in the contemporary global society in which they live.

Transformative pedagogy requires teachers of social studies education to use quality Latino children's literature with intentionality. Teachers are tasked with guiding student learning by engaging inquiry and using literacy to problem solve. The development of civic competency is at the core of social studies education, and stimulating engagement through quality multicultural literature that both complements and embellishes the social studies curriculum enables Latino students to generate authentic and meaningful connections. Drawing from the world of books further enhances students' existing worldviews, encouraging them to wonder about their world.

To accomplish these objectives, students must have ample opportunities to study and learn from a rigorous social studies curriculum framed by inquiry and problem solving. Culturally relevant, quality literature and literacy-based activities are the intellectual tools that provide Latino students with opportunities to transform a globalized society to a more egalitarian world.

REFERENCES

Ada, A. F. (2003). *A magical encounter: Latino children's literature in the classroom* (2nd ed.). White Plains, NY: Pearson.

Ada, A., Harris, V., & Hopkins, L. (1993). *A Chorus of cultures: Developing literacy through multicultural poetry*. Carmel, CA: Hampton Brown.

August, D., Shanahan, T., & Escamilla, K. (2009). English language learners: Developing literacy in second language Learners—Report of the National Literacy Panel on language-minority children and youth. *Journal of Literacy Research, 41*, 432–52.

Barrera, R. B., & Garza de Cortés, O. (1997). Mexican American children's literature in the 1990s: Toward authenticity. In V. J. Harris (Ed.), *Teaching multicultural literature in grades K-8* (pp. 20–242). Norwood, MA: Christopher-Gordon.

Columbus, C. (2003). Journal of the first voyage of Columbus. In J. E. Olson & E. Gaylord Bourne (Eds.), *The Northmen, Columbus and Cabot, 985–1503: Original narratives of early American history*. New York, NY: Charles Scribner's Sons. Retrieved June 4, 2015, from http://mith.umd.edu/eada/html/display.php?docs=columbus_journal.xml.

Conkling, W. (2013). *Sylvia & Aki*. New York, NY: Yearling.

Cooperative Children's Book Center (2010). Retrieved May 26, 2015, from https://ccbc.education.wisc.edu/.

Cummins, J. (2000). *Language, power, and pedagogy: Bilingual children in the crossfire* (vol. 23). Bristol, UK: Multilingual Matters.

Daniels, H. (2002). *Literature circles: Voice and choice in book clubs and reading groups*. Portland, ME: Stenhouse Publishers.

De las Casas, B. (1992) *The devastation of the Indies: A brief account* (H. Brifault, trans.). Baltimore, MD: Johns Hopkins University Press.

Elbow, P. (2015). Opting for the vernacular. In T. Kalmar, *Illegal alphabets* (pp. 127–30). New York, NY: Routledge.

Freire, P. (1970). *Pedagogy of the oppressed.* New York, NY: Continuum.

García, O. (2010). *Educating emergent bilinguals: Policies, programs, and practices of English language learners.* New York, NY: Teachers College Press.

Gay, G. (2010). *Culturally responsive teaching* (2nd ed.). New York, NY: Teachers College Press.

Gee, J. P. (2015). Ways with letters and sounds. In T. Kalmar, *Illegal alphabets* (pp. 137–40). New York, NY: Routledge.

Gibson, C. (1971). *The black legend: Anti-Spanish attitudes in the Old World and the New.* New York, NY: Random House.

González, N., Moll, L. & Amanti, C. (2005). *Funds of knowledge: Theorizing practices in households, communities, and classrooms.* Mahwah, NJ: Lawrence Erlbaum Associates.

Gutiérrez, R. (2008). A "gap-gazing" fetish in mathematics education? Problematizing research on the achievement gap. *Journal for Research in Mathematics Education, 39*(4), 357–64.

Herrera, J. F. (2014). *Portraits of Hispanic American Heroes.* New York, NY: Penguin.

Herrera, J. F., & Tapia, H. R. (2003). *Super cilantro girl/La superniña del cilantro.* New York, NY: Lee & Low Books.

Horkheimer, M., & Adorno, T. W. (2001). The culture industry: Enlightenment as mass deception. In M. G. Durham & D. M. Kellner (Eds.), *Media and cultural studies: Key works* (pp. 41–74). Malden, MA: Blackwell Publishers.

Huerta, M. E. (1995). Report to Edgewood ISD teachers' inservice. Unpublished manuscript.

Macedo, D., & Bartolomé, L. (2001). *Dancing with bigotry: Beyond the politics of tolerance.* New York, NY: Palgrave.

Marzollo, J. (1991). *In 1492.* New York, NY: Scholastic.

McCall, G. G. (2012). The bully. In S. Vardell & J. Wong, *The poetry Friday anthology: Poems for the school year with connections to the TEKS, K–5 edition* (p. 248). Princeton, NJ: Pomelo Books.

Mora, P., & Colón, R. (2005) *Doña Flor: A tall tale about a giant woman with a big heart.* New York, NY: Knopf.

Morales, Y. (2003). *Just a minute! A trickster tale and counting book.* San Francisco, CA: Chronicle Books.

Nagda, B. A., Gurin, P., & Lopez, G. E. (2003). Transformative pedagogy for democracy and social justice. *Race Ethnicity and Education, 6*(2), 165–81.

National Association for Multicultural Education (2013). Definition updated 2013. Retrieved May 30, 2015, from www.nameorg.org/2003_name_position_statements.php.

National Curriculum Standards for Social Studies (2015). Introduction. Retrieved May 26, 2015, from www.socialstudies.org/standards/introduction.

Pérez, B. (2003). *Becoming biliterate: A study of two-way bilingual immersion education.* Mahwah, NJ: Lawrence Erlbaum Associates.

Pfister, M., & Brown, B. (1998). *Rainbow fish and the big blue whale.* New York, NY: NorthSouth Books.

Ryan, P. M. (2000). *Esperanza rising*. New York, NY: Scholastic.

Samora, J., & Simon, P. (2003). *A history of the Mexican American people*. Retrieved from www.jsri.msu.edu/museum/pubs/MexAmHist/chapter16.html.

Santos, R. G. (2000). *Silent heritage: The Sephardim and the colonization of the Spanish North-American frontier 1492–1600*. San Antonio, TX: New Sepharad Press.

Schachner, J. (2009). *Skippyjon Jones lost in spice*. New York, NY: Penguin.

Short, K., Lynch-Brown, C., & Tomlinson, C. (2014). *Essentials of children's literature*. White Plains, NY: Pearson.

Tafolla, C. (1993). You don't have to be bigger to be important: A Cinco de Mayo victory poem. In *A chorus of cultures: Developing literacy through multicultural poetry* (p. 179). Carmel, CA: Hampton-Brown Books.

———. (2009) *What can you do with a paleta?/Que puedes hacer con una paleta?* San Francisco, CA: Tricycle Books.

———. (2010). *Report on reading rock stars*. Activities administered by ESC Region I to McAllen ISD, Mercedes ISD, and PSJA ISD. Edinburg, TX: Education Service Center I. Unpublished report.

———. (2012). *Voyage*. In C. Tafolla, N. E. Cantú, & R. Hinojosa, *Curandera, 30th anniversary edition* (p. 36). San Antonio, TX: Wings Press.

Valencia, R. R. (2010). *Dismantling contemporary deficit thinking*. New York, NY: Routledge.

——— (Ed.). (2012). *The evolution of deficit thinking: Educational thought and practice*. London, UK: Falmer Press.

Valenzuela, A. (1999). *Subtractive schooling: U.S.-Mexican Youth and the politics of caring*. Albany, NY: State University of New York Press.

———. (2005). Introduction: The accountability debate in Texas: Continuing the conversation. In A. Valenzuela (Ed.), *Leaving children behind: How "Texas style" accountability fails Latino youth* (pp. 1–32). Albany, NY: State University of New York Press.

Wolf, S. A. (2004). *Interpreting literature with children*. New York, NY: Routledge.

Yolen, J., & Shannon, D. (1992). *Encounter*. New York, NY: Harcourt.

Zubizarreta, R., Rohmer, H., & Schecter, D. (1991). *The woman who outshone the sun: The legend of Lucia Centeno*. (Story by R. Zubizarreta, H. Rohmer, & D. Schecter from a poem by A. Martinez). New York, NY: Scholastic.

DISCUSSION QUESTIONS

1. As a teacher, how would you conceptualize integrating your social studies curriculum with quality Latino children's literature?
2. What materials and resources (and teacher colleagues) do you anticipate needing?
3. Assess your grade-level social studies curriculum. Which NCSS strands will you select to teach throughout the school year? What Latino children's

literature featured in this chapter will you select to match each strand that you will teach? For each subsequent school year, which additional strands and books will you select to add to the social studies curriculum?

4. The next step in enhancing the social studies curriculum is to add literacy-based tasks. This means that while some students may benefit from reading academic and literary works in Spanish, they may also generate written products or performances in that language or in English (see García & Wei [2014] for information on teaching and learning through a *translanguaging* approach). How will you ensure that the literacy-based assignments are relevant and aligned with grade-level benchmarks? With the literacy and language development stage of each student (English and Spanish)? With the literacy and language development stage of each second language learner?

5. Consider how concepts across the curriculum intersect with the social studies curriculum. Identify these as you study the goals and objectives of other content areas across the school year.

6. Based on the anecdotal notes that you generate during the school year, what is your plan for assessing your success in integrating your social studies curriculum, and for refining and revising the learning activities that you designed? How will you continue to enhance your social studies curriculum?

ACTIVITIES

A. Select five multicultural books written about Latinos or that include a Latino character. Use the attributes of authentic literature. Rate the level of authenticity of each book.

B. Your classroom may include Latino students developing literacy in both Spanish and English. Assess your classroom library by determining the availability of authentic literature in Spanish for your students. Ensure that the regional dialect of Spanish represented in these books reflects the regional dialect spoken by your students.

C. Serve as a member on your campus leadership team to help expend the campus library budget. Work with other committee members and the campus librarian to purchase authentic multicultural literature each year for your campus library, with special attention to high-quality books recognized by such awards as the Pura Belpré Award, the Américas Award, the Tomás Rivera Mexican American Children's Book Award, and the International Latino Book Award.

D. Select an NCSS strand. Read each of the book selections listed for that strand. Identify those that your students can read independently. Also identify those that should be read aloud to facilitate comprehension through a guided reading approach.

E. To implement literature circles in your classroom, write a grant to purchase classroom sets of authentic Latino literature. Certain schools may also qualify for selection by such foundations as First Book and Reading Rock Stars, which provide free books to all participating students in the selected schools.

PROFESSIONAL READINGS

Acuña, R. (2015). *Occupied America: A history of Chicanos* (8th ed.). White Plains, NY: Pearson.

Ada, A., Harris, V., & Hopkins, L. (1993). *A chorus of cultures: Developing literacy through multicultural poetry.* Carmel, CA: Hampton Brown.

Botelho, J. M., & Rudman, M. K. (2009). *Critical multicultural analysis of children's literature: Mirrors, windows, and doors.* New York, NY: Routledge.

Horning, K., et al. (2010). *Cooperative Children's Book Center (CCBC) Choices 2010.* Madison, WI: University of Wisconsin-Madison, Cooperative Children's Book Center.

McCall, A. L. (2004). Using poetry in social studies classes to teach about cultural diversity and social justice. *Social Studies, 95*(4), 172–76.

Möller, M. (2003). Philadelphia's Mexican war workers. *Pennsylvania Legacies, 3*(2), 16.

Nagda, B. A., Gurin, P., & Lopez, G. E. (2003). Transformative pedagogy for democracy and social justice. *Race Ethnicity and Education, 6*(2), 165–81.

Portales, R., & Portales, M. (2005). *Quality education for Latinos and Latinas: Print and oral skills for all students, K–College.* Austin, TX: University of Texas Press.

Portes, P. R., Salas, S., Baquedano-López, P., & Mellon, P. J. (2014). *U.S. Latinos and education policy: Research-based directions for change.* New York, NY: Routledge.

Samora, J., & Simon, P. (2003). *A history of the Mexican American people.* Retrieved from www.jsri.msu.edu/museum/pubs/MexAmHist/chapter16.html.

Schell, E., & Fisher, D. (2007). *Teaching social studies: A literacy-based approach.* Upper Saddle River, NJ: Pearson Merrill Prentice Hall.

Thornton, S. J. (2005). *Teaching social studies that matters: Curriculum for active learning.* New York, NY: Teachers College Press.

Chapter Nine

Dichos y Adivinanzas: Literary Resources That Enhance Science Learning and Teaching in the Bilingual Classroom

María Guadalupe Arreguín-Anderson and
José Ruiz-Escalante

INTRODUCTION

Vignette

Tadeo is a five-year old Latino boy who loves plants and animals. He acquired this affection from his aunt and uncle whose oldest dog, Kiko, follows him around every time he visits, wanders around their immense yard, and gets lost among trees and leaves. Kiko is a thirteen-year-old dog and soon falls asleep on a garden section where Tadeo and his aunt had just planted some red oak seedlings out of acorns that they collected the previous fall during a nature walk. "*¿Qué vamos a hacer? ¿Podemos salvar los arbolitos?* [What are we going to do? Can we save the little trees?]" Tadeo wonders as he runs in dismay to tell his grandmother that Kiko laid on the plants and they are going to need more dirt. "*Está bien* [That is fine]," says his grandmother, as she replies with a Spanish proverb: "*Pero no hay que hacer una tormenta en un vaso de agua* [Do not make a mountain out of a molehill]."

What Is the Challenge?

Tadeo's natural inclination to explore nature is not unusual. This affinity with living things, or *biophilia*, as Wilson (1993) labels it, is reflected in most children's fascination with nature. It is an attraction that gradually fades as children perceive a disconnect between the way they learn about and explore science in their environment and the curricular structures, processes, and discourses that they find in school. Statistics show that Latino children like

167

Tadeo are very unlikely to choose a science field as their college major or to dedicate their life to the study of science. His teachers will face the challenge of breaking a cycle that shows a drastic underrepresentation of Latinos in the fields of science, technology, engineering, and mathematics (STEM). In general, Latinos represent only 5.2 percent of all employed scientists and engineers in the U.S. (National Science Foundation, 2014).

Educators in today's culturally and linguistically diverse schools will have a strong influence on children's academic performance and their perceptions of themselves as potential scientists, and just as importantly, they will be in a position to recognize experiential knowledge about science that children like Tadeo already possess when they enter the classroom, and the cultural resources that have contributed to their knowledge construction. Throughout this chapter, we take a critical look at the role that Latino children's literature—specifically, traditional cultural resources such as *dichos* (proverbs) and *adivinanzas* (riddles)—can play in the construction of children's scientific knowledge, and how these resources can supplement culturally relevant lessons. *Dichos* and *refranes* have become synonyms for some of Mexican background, and the word *dicho* has replaced *refranes*. With this in mind, this chapter will use both words interchangeably.

Intersections between Science Teaching and Learning and Latino Children's Literature

This chapter focuses on the intersections between science and Latino children's literary resources. Science teachers generally engage children in reading and writing endeavors to carry out scientific inquiries. Language arts teachers know that all areas of literacy (reading, writing, speaking, and listening) lay the foundation for success in all academic content areas. In many settings, especially at the elementary level, educators teach all subjects and plan interdisciplinary lessons knowing that science and language arts

- develop, extend, and refine the knowledge base of students;
- assist students in organizing knowledge into useful schemas or networks;
- learn vocabulary that is related to topics being studied; and
- supply many opportunities for practice and rehearsal in communication through writing, speaking, and representing things visually (Bass, Contant, & Carin, 2009, p. 244).

We emphasize the pursuit of meaning from a perspective that capitalizes on what children already know. Prior knowledge is constantly built on as children use their senses to explore and experience their surroundings and as they interact with other individuals within their environment. Because much of the process of knowledge construction is overwhelmingly situated in the context of the natural world, this chapter focuses on a discussion of symbolic experiences of nature and their relevancy to science learning and teaching in bilingual classrooms. The authors are interested in dissecting symbolic sources of traditional science knowledge that have been present in the lives and homes of Latino children. These sources include *dichos* and *adivinanzas*. The goal is to promote science and literacy instruction that is congruent with the cultural make-up of Latino children as they learn about science, formulate explanations of natural events, and utilize resources that support daily learning.

Physical, Intellectual, and Symbolic Affordances in Nature

Explanations of natural phenomena and depictions of nature such as myths, legends, songs, stories, sayings, and riddles have historically emerged in all cultures and are evidenced in people's traditions and practices. These depictions or symbolic connections with nature, however, do not emerge in isolation. They stem from an initial immersion in and direct experience with the natural world. We hypothesize that people, and specifically children, are attracted to nature because of the type of physical, intellectual, and symbolic stimulation that it affords. In other words, as children engage in active exploration of the natural world, they are guided by their senses to objects and organisms that they can physically see, touch, smell, hear, see, and often taste. Such will be the case with a rock that children can pick up and feel; a bug that can be examined; or a stick that can be used as a tool. Affordances of nature translate into very concrete relationships between the child and elements of the environment (Gibson, 1979). Physical engagement is inherently embedded in the act of "doing science," which implies active involvement in inquiry-based investigations. Direct manipulation is a crucial factor in the process of knowledge construction, but it must be supplemented with opportunities to ponder and think.

Children are intellectually stimulated by the observations of patterns in nature as well as natural events that entice their sense of wonder. Lawrence (1993) coined the term "cognitive biophilia" to explain people's need to employ symbols of nature to express figurative thinking, to illustrate the moral or lesson of a situation, and to engage in varied levels of mental activity. Cognitive activity, as proposed in the revised version of Bloom's taxonomy revolves around verbs including remembering, understanding, applying, analyzing, evaluating, and creating (Krathwohl, 2010). Continuous contact with nature exposes children to knowledge of multiple labels for organisms, objects, and events. By manipulating a rock by a river, for example, children may engage in a game like rock skipping, which might result in analysis, evaluation, and creation of techniques to achieve success as they test the water surface. Additionally, they can potentially learn and remember words such as "pebble," "smooth," and "flat."

Physical and cognitive experiences with nature fuel "the human need for metaphorical expression . . . as no other realm affords such vivid expression of symbolic concepts" (Lawrence, 1993, p. 301). A symbol of nature is an abstract representation of a concrete or tangible element. A poem about a bird or a riddle about a squash, for example, convey mental images or abstract referents to elements removed from direct experience. Much of the children's literature repertoire and the topics depicted in the different genres are strongly determined by context-specific environmental conditions. It is no coincidence that in Alaska there are regions in which forty different words can by employed to refer to snow. Specific terms for snow that is softly falling or good for sledding can be found in children books. Another example is the Sami people of Scandinavia and Russia who are said to have at least one thousand words for reindeer (Robson, 2013). In Latino cultures, children who grow up in the rural areas of northern Mexico are very likely to know a variety of words for cactus and its fruit as well as multiple words associated with domesticated animals such as goats. It is no surprise, Kellert (1993) states, that "animals constitute more than 90 percent of the characters employed in language acquisition and counting in children's preschool books" (p. 52). Animals and other elements of nature serve to link children's prior knowledge with aspects of the academic world. A story, riddle, or proverb depicting a tree and a cat, for example, provides a symbolic representation related to elements of nature that were initially experienced through direct physical contact.

Symbolic Experiences of Nature: Latino Children Literature, *Dichos* and *Adivinanzas*

Science education reform documents (American Association for the Advancement of Science, 1993; National Research Council, 2002) recommend the use of physically engaging and intellectually stimulating activities for all children. This directive is in line with principles of developmental direction indicating that children's learning advances from concrete to abstract, from exploratory to goal directed, and in this case, from enactive to symbolic. An enactive representation is evident when children use their body to represent a concept or an experience (Kostelnik, Soderman, & Whiren, 2011). For instance, after observing frogs, children may choose to demonstrate how they "can hop like a frog." This enactive representation of a concept may lead to more abstract or symbolic means of representing the same idea. Thus children might draw a duck or write about it. Kellert (2002) defines symbolic experiences as "representations or depicted scenes of nature that sometimes are realistic but that also, depending on circumstances, can be highly symbolic, metaphorical, or stylized characterizations" (p. 119). In this chapter, the intersections between science and literary Latino resources are illustrated through metaphorical representations of nature, specifically those that are found in Latino riddles and proverbs. This is how a "lady in a silk dress that goes through the air" is a metaphorical expression that when infused in a riddle seeks to challenge the interlocutor to guess that "the lady" is a butterfly.

Latino children's books, which provide cultural resources, are discussed as pieces that reflect and connect to children's experiential knowledge and cultural repertoire. Drawing from a critical perspective (Delgado Bernal, 2001; Yosso, 2002) these resources are dissected in terms of the ways in which they are central to children's prior knowledge, specifically in terms of culturally congruent science lessons that draw on children's funds of knowledge.

THEORETICAL FRAMEWORK

Connecting *Dichos* and *Adivinanzas* to Culturally Congruent Teaching

The lessons children learn from home are often discussed in terms of their moral value (Wong Fillmore 2000; Delgado Bernal 2001); that is, the cultural knowledge needed to successfully navigate the different contexts we often encounter and to endure through difficult circumstances. Additionally, Wong Fillmore (2000) asserts that families provide

> a sense of belonging; knowledge of who one is and where one comes from; an understanding of how one is connected to the important others and events in one's life the ability to deal with adversity, and knowing of one's responsibility to self-family and community. (p. 206)

The idea that children's homes are spaces in which one develops an identity and acquires tools for moral direction has been extended to a discussion of homes as spaces that also provide a knowledge foundation in different academic domains, including science. What is currently in place, critical scholars contend, is a system in which curricular structures, processes, and discourses are often "disguised as neutral and objective" (Yosso, 2002, p. 93). This system often presents science learning as impartial, automatically discounting what children already know and the repertoire of skills and the pedagogies they have been exposed to in their homes. Delgado Bernal (2001) defines pedagogies of the home as practices that "extend the existing discourse on critical pedagogies by putting cultural knowledge and language at the forefront to better understand lessons from the home space and local communities" (p. 624). Historically, traditional knowledge embedded in Latino children's literature and traditional cultural resources has not been considered a standard source from which to draw when learning science.

The need to make science accessible to all learners is highlighted by science education reform initiatives and documents indicating that less-privileged students, mostly from non-dominant groups, continue to be underserved. In our estimation, the Common Core State Standards adhere to Next Generation Science Standards (Lee, Quinn, & Valdés, 2013; NGSS, 2015) guidelines in terms of disciplinary core ideas, so we will focus on these guidelines in relation to bilingual learners. In the National Research Council (2002) Framework for K–12 Science Education, the NGSS favors approaches and strategies that (1) value and respect the experiences that all students bring from their backgrounds (e.g., homes or communities), (2) articulate students' background knowledge (e.g., cultural or linguistic knowledge) with disciplinary knowledge, and (3) offer sufficient school resources to support student learning (Lee & Buxton, 2010). These underlying themes and strategies prompt educators to deliberately connect with students' funds of knowledge related to the science lessons designed. Funds of knowledge "refer to these accumulated and culturally developed bodies of knowledge and skills essential for household or individual functioning and well-being" (González, Moll, & Amanti, 2005, p. 72). In the southwestern context of their work, González and Moll (2002) have found funds of knowledge represented in areas of traditional science knowledge such as mining and metallurgy, ranching and animal husbandry, ethnobotany, and transborder transactions. González and Moll (2002) propose, "What better way to engage students than to draw them in with knowledge that is already familiar to them and to use that as a basis for pushing their learning?" (p. 627). They suggest that classroom lessons "can build on the familiar knowledge bases that students can manipulate to enhance learning in mathematics, social studies, language arts, and other content areas" (2002, p. 43) such as science. In doing so, students will be more likely to perceive an authentic validation of the knowledge they possess.

One of our central goals as educators is to engage students in the process of knowledge construction. In the next section, we analyze the role of experiential knowledge and an interdisciplinary perspective in the process of teaching and learning science. Initially, educators must recognize bilingual learners as valuable contributors. Children's cultural identity is expressed in a variety of ways: (1) the games they play, (2) the language they use, (3) the activities they engage in, and (4) the foods they eat, for example. In this sense, we suggest that educators can begin their science teaching with children's "experiential knowledge," drawing from Latino children's literature along with traditional cultural resources, including *dichos* and *adivinanzas.*

Culturally Relevant Literature and Resources That Support Symbolic Science Learning

One way to address the disconnect or mismatch between the science that children learn and experience at home and the science they encounter in school is to infuse the curriculum with literary resources that are culturally relevant and support cognitive and linguistic growth. Extending Wilson's hypothesis related to people's general affinity with nature, Lawrence (1993) highlights the intersections between nature, thought, and language. Under this perspective, all living things and elements of the natural world shape people's cultural practices in different ways. In other words, "nature, as represented by the actual biological and behavioral traits of a particular animal, becomes transformed into a cultural construct that may or may not reflect the empirical reality concerning that animal but generally involves much embellishment" (p. 302). Examples of embellished views of animals and plants can be identified in *dichos, adivinanzas,* and children's books. Carmen Bravo-Villasante, one of the pioneers of children's literature in Spanish, considers oral traditions as the most popular genre of children's literature. This genre includes folklore, sayings, proverbs, tongue twisters, riddles, and other resources that foster connections between children's dreams and academic learning (Barker, 1982).

Dichos/refranes, or popular sayings, are defined as tools that convey cultural values, and they are often used in social conversations to encapsulate lessons learned, a piece of advice, or a perspective on life. *Dichos/refranes* represent a key aspect of cultural identity and are not only used within Latin American countries. As Espinoza-Herold (2007) states, "Mexican Americans share with Spanish speakers throughout the world a rich and varied repertoire of *dichos,* with a vibrant and ongoing communicative tradition that appears to contrast, at least in some aspects, with that of Anglo-American society" (p. 265).

In children's homes and communities, *dichos* are overwhelmingly inspired by people's encounters with nature. Often animals, plants, nature-related events, and life-like processes are embedded in *dichos* to metaphorically represent a situation of daily life. The popularity of *dichos* is evident in Latino songs, TV shows (e.g. *Como dice el dicho*), and media in general (Sánchez, 2009). In daily conversations, the use of animals and plants to convey a message is common. References include, for example, a turtle when indicating that a person works or acts slowly, or a pepper to describe a hot-tempered individual. We are, Wilson (1993) proposes, inherently attracted to nature. This attraction has led us to use nature, including all its elements, when speaking figuratively. Through *dichos*, children learn not only about life, but also about science. In his book titled *El porqué de los dichos: Sentido, origen y anécdota de los dichos, modismos y frases proverbiales de España con otras muchas curiosidades* (2002), José María Iribarren documented at least 671 examples of *dichos/refranes*, most of which symbolize through animals, plants, and elements of nature.

Similarly to *dichos*, *adivinanzas* convey knowledge and often make multiple connections with science concepts. However, in contrast to *dichos*, *adivinanzas* require "out of the box thinking" and are dialogic. In this dialogue, "the one who sets out the enigma knows the answer and demands the receptor to exercise his imagination and sense of interpretation, thus establishing an intellectual game between both" (Montalvo Castro, 2011).

According to Miaja de la Peña (2005), the structure of the riddle usually includes four elements:

1. Introduction formula. For example, (1) Tell me fortune teller, or (2) What will it be?
2. Concluding formula. For example, (1) Guess if you can, or (2) He who cannot guess is a big fool.
3. Orientating elements, which are usually within the text. For example, In the middle of the sky am I, yet I'm not a star. Answer: The letter *k* in "sky."
4. Disorientating elements, which are rhetoric or meaning traps. For example, What gets wetter the more it dries? Answer: A towel.

Both *adivinanzas* and *dichos* provide symbolic experiences with science. Kellert (2002) suggests that symbolic representations of nature permeate children's linguistic and social repertoire very early in life. With this in mind, sayings and riddles represent literary resources that have the potential to help teachers enhance students' connections with scientific concepts while providing a vehicle to enhance language development (see table 9.1).

REVIEW OF THE LITERATURE

Children's funds of knowledge in the science curriculum are scarcely addressed by the literature. *Dichos*, for example, have been explored as tools that teachers can utilize to learn about Latino children's culture and storytelling practices and as tools to enhance literacy development at home (Sánchez, 2009; Sanchez, Plata, Grosso, & Leird, 2010). Additionally, *dichos* have been

Table 9.1. Sample of *Dichos* and *Adivinanzas* and Their Connections to Science

Examples of Cultural Resources (children's literature: dichos and adivinanzas)	English Translation and Meaning	Connections to the Science Curriculum (concepts and skills)
Dicho—De tal palo tal astilla.	The apple does not fall far from the tree. (A son or daughter is like his or her parents in character or behavior.)	The inherited traits and learned behaviors of organisms
Dicho—No por mucho madrugar amanece más temprano.	Getting up at dawn will not make the morning come sooner. (Rushing will not make things happen faster.)	The patterns and rhythms of the cycles of life
Adivinanza—A cuestas llevo mi casa, / camino sin tener patas, / por donde mi cuerpo pasa queda un hilito de plata. Respuesta: El caracol.	I carry my home on my back. / I walk but have no feet. / My body leaves a trace of silver as it moves. Answer: The snail.	The connections between the external characteristics of organisms and how they move and survive (life science)
Adivinanza—Amarillo por fuera, / amarillo por dentro / y con un corazón en el centro. Respuesta: El durazno o el chabacano.	It is yellow on the outside, / it is yellow in the inside, / and it has a heart in its center. Answer: A peach or an apricot.	The parts of plants (life science)

dissected in terms of resiliency and as a central piece of funds of knowledge transmitted in mother-daughter relationships and in conversations related to educational attainment (Espinoza-Herold, 2007).

Studies that focus on the use of *adivinanzas* with children have explored this tool in audiovisual format. For example, Montalvo Castro (2011) asked students eight to nine years old to solve audiovisual riddles created in YouTube. The findings indicate that multimedia riddles require special attention to elements such as content and clues that elicit emotional satisfaction. Students' ability to solve riddles has also been explored in a group setting.

On average, children's sense of humor and the ability to use and enjoy figurative language develops early. By kindergarten, most children are likely to have developed to a level at which they enjoy using language for fun (Otto, 2014). This includes using riddles, word games, and other sources of figurative language such as proverbs and sayings.

PRAXIS: APPLICATION OF THEORY

Incorporating *Dichos* and *Adivinanzas* into the Formal Study of Science

A Lesson on Plants

An important goal in the study of organisms is the understanding that the survival of plants and animals is dependent on the ability to satisfy basic needs. In general, plants need air, light, water, and nutrients to ensure growth, survival, and reproduction (Bass, Contant, & Carin, 2009). K–2 students are expected to understand the characteristics, basic needs, and life cycles of organisms. In grades 3–5, students are expected to understand the structure and function of living systems, reproduction and heredity regulation and behavior, populations and ecosystems, and diversity and adaptations of organisms (National Research Council, 2002). Culturally, many Latino children have access to knowledge about plants in the context of planting, cooking, remedies, and other traditional activities.

This lesson follows the 5E (engage, explore, explain, elaborate, and evaluate) instructional model of inquiry that progresses from an initial phase in which students are engaged in the topic to an opportunity to actively explore and manipulate the concept in concrete, authentic ways (Arreguín-Anderson & Ruiz-Escalante, 2014; Bass, Contant, & Carin, 2009). Next, they have an opportunity to connect those explorations to an academic explanation of what is to be learned through those experiences. Subsequently, they expand by applying their just-learned knowledge and skills. This type of inquiry model seeks to capitalize on children's curiosity and natural inclination to explore their surroundings as they make connections to what they already know.

Engaging Students in the Study of Plants through Riddles

One of the keys to a successful introduction to a lesson is the degree to which educators connect with students' prior knowledge. Under a critical perspective, teachers can accomplish this goal by becoming researchers of their students. One idea is to communicate with parents to find out what riddles might be related to plants they know. These riddles can be connected to specific topics in the study of seeds, the life cycle of a plant, and its growth, characteristics, and functions, etc. Teachers can create a riddle bank that reflects the specific culture in their school. A suggested resource is *Spanish Riddles and Colcha Designs* by Reynalda Ortiz and Pino Dinkel

Table 9.2. Example of an *Adivinanza* and a *Dicho*

Adivinanza	Riddle	Dicho	Saying
Soy muy chiquita, pero de mí árbol o planta puede salir. Respuesta: La semilla	I am usually little, but from inside me, trees or plants can germinate. A seed	Al nopal solo lo van a ver cuando tiene tunas.	You only visit the cactus when it is bearing fruit.

(1988); this book includes riddles in Spanish and English. As you introduce a lesson related to plants, write a riddle or a saying on the board and let students think about it. Always make sure that there is a connection between the general idea of the riddle or proverb and the lesson's key concepts—in this case, the parts of a plant, the life cycle of a plant, or the characteristics of livings organisms. Examples of a *dichos* and an *adivinanza* can be found in table 9.2.

You may want to hold a discussion as a whole group regarding possible answers to the riddle. In pairs, students can figure out the meaning and connections of the riddle as well as produce an illustration. This can serve as an informal way to assess their knowledge prior to engaging in active exploration of the concept of seeds and plants.

Exploring Plants

To encourage student participation during the explore phase of the 5E model, hold a discussion regarding the meaning of the proverb previously introduced. What do people mean when they say that a cactus is only visited when it bears fruit? How can the cactus survive if no one takes care of it? Are there instances when people are also visited or sought after only when they have something to give? What are some examples? In preparation for students' exploration of the concept, have parent volunteers or students bring plants from home. Ask students to label the parts of the plant they brought from home and next to it to draw a tree or plant they choose from the school's garden or surrounding areas outside their classroom.

Explaining the Process

The explain phase of the inquiry cycle brings another opportunity to connect to Latino literature and to the curriculum and pedagogies of the home. As children share their explorations and discoveries, a group of parents can

Table 9.3.   A Traditional *Dicho* and Its English Translation

Dicho	Spanish	Translation
	Verde fue mi nacimiento / colorado mi vivir / y negro me estoy volviendo / cuando me toca morir. Respuesta: El higo.	I was green when I was born. / Red as I grew up. / And black as I died. Answer: The fig.

be asked to share the process they follow to care for plants and what those plants are used for at home. As a teacher, you can identify connections with the science standards in your district. This is an opportunity in which to ask for additional examples of cultural tools that connect with the topic.

Elaborating and Applying What Students Have Learned

During the elaborate phase of the 5E model, involve your students in a project that allows them to apply what they know and to extend their new understanding while addressing and utilizing a cultural resource. For example, students can engage in a project to propagate plants. They can interview a member of their family or community for information on a plant or tree to propagate. Then they can document their research and carry out the project by planting the seed or taking the cuts from a plant such as a fig tree and following the suggested methods of care. Additionally, they can extend their inquiry by researching proverbs or riddles related to a plant or its fruit. This information can come from home or their neighborhood. See table 9.3 for examples of symbolic representations of plants or parts of a plant.

Evaluation

Use a rubric or checklist to evaluate students' reports as they document the progress of their project (see table 9.4). As you explain the rubric or checklist to your students, make sure that expectations are clear. For example, indicate what academic words are expected. The words "tree," "plant," "propagation," "water," "embryo," "germination," "oxygen," "carbon dioxide," and "photosynthesis" should be included in their report. Additionally, you may want to include the expectation that the riddle or proverb includes an explanation. Observation skills may include careful examination of their seed; use of several senses to explore; identification of details. Finally, their explanation of the cultural resource may include the moral or lesson behind the saying or the solution of the riddle researched. Two websites that are useful in the

Table 9.4. Checklist: Plants in My Community Project

Checklist: Life Cycle and Basic Needs of a Plant

Knowledge and Skills	Yes/No	Expected behaviors
Observations		I used more than one sense to observe my plant/seed.
		I used technology to document the changes in my seed/plant.
		I discussed my observations with my team members.
Vocabulary		I used the words "tree," "plant," "propagation," "water," "embryo," "germination," "oxygen," "carbon dioxide," and "photosynthesis" in my report.
Research		I talked to adults in my community to investigate the type of plant that is suitable for the local climatic conditions.
		I used Internet sources to research my plant.
		I researched a dicho/adivinanza that relates to the life cycle of a plant.
		I talked to members of my community to provide an explanation related to the cultural connections of the dicho/adivinanza selected.
		I presented my project and findings to a real audience.

design of checklists and rubrics include pblchecklist4teachers.org and www.rubistar4teachers.org.

Teachers should be aware that experiential knowledge is a crucial first step in adopting and adapting pedagogies that can significantly enhance children's access to equitable science education. Spanish sayings, or proverbs, and riddles encapsulate communities' wisdom and are significantly reflective of peoples' tendency to symbolize through animals and plants. Science activities that incorporate cultural resources, often addressed in children's literature, encourage children to perceive their lives reflected in the curriculum. An inquiry approach that integrates science and all aspects of literacy, including reading, writing, listening, and speaking, can significantly enhance children's motivation to engage in the pursuit of new knowledge. One suggested way to design interdisciplinary science lessons that are culturally congruent with Latino bilingual learners is to infuse inquiry lessons such as those based on the 5E model with opportunities to connect with proverbs and riddles. A purposeful connection with traditional knowledge that bilingual learners acquire in the context of their families and their communities is key to establishing relevancy in the science curriculum that students encounter in school.

REFERENCES

American Association for the Advancement of Science (1993). *Benchmarks for science literacy.* New York, NY: Oxford University Press.

Arreguín-Anderson, M. G., & Garza, E. V. (2014). Bilingual pairs in teacher education: Exploring WILD strategies in an environmental education workshop. *Action in Teacher Education, 36*(2), 171–84. doi:10.1080/01626620.2014.898599.

Barker, M. E. (May, 1982). La literatura infantil en español y su papel en el desarrollo del autoconcepto del niño. *Hispania, 69*(2), 269–73.

Bass, J. E., Contant, T. L., & Carin, A. A. (2009). *Methods for teaching science as inquiry.* Boston, MA: Allyn & Bacon.

Delgado Bernal, D. (2001). Living and learning pedagogies of the home: The mestiza consciousness of Chicana students. *International Journal of Qualitative Studies in Education, 14*(5), 623–39.

Espinoza-Herold, M. (2007). Stepping beyond *sí se puede: Dichos* as a cultural resource in mother-daughter interaction in a Latino family. *Anthropology & Education Quarterly, 38*(3), 260–77.

Gibson, J. J. (1979). *The ecological approach to visual perception.* Boston, MA: Houghton-Mifflin.

González, N., & Moll, L. C. (2002). *Cruzando el puente*: Building bridges to funds of knowledge. *Educational Policy, 16*(4), 623–41.

González, N., Moll, L. C., & Amanti, C. (2005). *Funds of knowledge.* Mahwah, NJ: Lawrence Erlbaum Associates.

Iribarren, J. M. (1974). *El porqué de los dichos; sentido, origen y anécdota de los dichos, modismos y frases proverbiales de España, con otras muchas curiosidades* (4th ed.). Madrid, Spain: Aguilar.

Kellert, S. R. (1993). The biological basis for the human values of nature. In S. R. Kellert and E. O. Wilson (Eds.), *The biophilia hypothesis* (pp. 42–69). Washington, DC: Island Press.

———. (2002). Experiencing nature: Affective, cognitive, and evaluative development in children. In P. H. Kahn Jr. & S. R. Kellert (Eds.), *Children and nature: Psychological, sociocultural, and evolutionary investigations* (pp. 117–51). Cambridge, MA: MIT Press.

Kostelnik, M. J., Soderman, A. K., & Whiren, A. P. (2011). *Developmentally appropriate curriculum: Best practices in early childhood.* Boston, MA: Pearson.

Krathwohl, D. R. (2010). A revision of Bloom's taxonomy: An overview. *Theory into practice, 41*(4), 212–18.

Lawrence, E. A. (1993). The sacred bee, the filthy pig, and the bat out of hell: Animal symbolism as cognitive biophilia. In S. R. Kellert & E. O. Wilson (Eds.), *The biophilia hypothesis* (pp. 31–41). Washington, DC: Island Press.

Lee, O., & Buxton, C. A. (2010). *Diversity and equity in science education: Theory, research, and practice.* New York, NY: Teachers College Press.

Lee, O., Quinn, H., & Valdés, G. (2013). Science and language for English language learners: Language demands and opportunities in relation to Next Generation Science Standards. *Educational Researcher, 42*, 223–33.

Miaja de la Peña, M. T. (2005). La adivinanza. Sentido y perseverancia. *Acta Poética*, *26*(1–2), 443–63.

Montalvo Castro, J. (2011). Adivinanzas audiovisuales para ejercitar el pensamiento creativo infantil. *Comunicar: Revista Científica de Edocumunicación*, *36*(18), 123–30.

National Research Council (2002). *A framework for K–12 science education: Practices, cross-cutting concepts, and core ideas.* Washington, DC: National Academy Press.

National Science Foundation (2014). *Science and engineering indicators 2014.* Arlington, VA: National Science Foundation.

Next Generation Science Standards (2015). Retrieved from www.nextgenscience.org/next-generation-science-standards.

Ortiz y Pino de Dinkel, R., & Gonzáles de Martínez, D. (1988). *Una colección de adivinanzas y diseños de colcha/A collection of riddles and colcha designs.* Santa Fe, NM: Sunstone Press.

Otto, B. (2014). *Language development in early childhood education.* Boston, MA: Pearson.

Robson, D. (2013, January 14). There really are 50 Eskimo words for "snow." *Washington Post.* Retrieved from www.washingtonpost.com/national/health-science/there-really-are-50-eskimo-words-for-snow/2013/01/14/e0e3f4e0-59a0-11e2-beee-6e38f5215402_story.html.

Sánchez, C. (2009). Learning about students' culture and language through family stories elicited by dichos. *Early Childhood Education Journal*, *37*, 161–69.

Sánchez, C., Plata, V., Grosso, L., & Leird, B. (2010). Encouraging Spanish-speaking families' involvement through *dichos*. *Journal of Latinos and Education*, *9*(3), 239–48.

Wilson, E. O. (1993). Biophilia and the conservation ethic. In S. R. Kellert & E. O. Wilson (Eds.), *The biophilia hypothesis* (pp. 31–41). Washington, DC: Island Press.

Wong Fillmore, L. (2000). Loss of family languages: Should educators be concerned? *Theory into Practice*, *39*, 203–10.

Yosso, T. J. (2002). Toward a critical race curriculum. *Equity & Excellence in Education*, *35*(2), 93–107.

DISCUSSION QUESTIONS

1. What is a symbolic experience with nature? Explain the value of sayings, or proverbs, and riddles (in Spanish) as resources that extend children's connections with nature and science as a subject.
2. What is the value of the pedagogies and curriculum of the home in the teaching and learning of science?
3. What are the similarities between an *adivinanza* and a *dicho*?
4. What are the differences between an *adivinanza* and a *dicho*?

5. What are the characteristics of an *adivinanza*? What makes *adivinanzas* cognitively challenging?

ACTIVITIES

A. During your experience as a teacher, you probably have designed a variety of science lessons and activities. Take one of those lesson plans and analyze it with two questions in mind: How can I infuse children's literature and cultural resources such as *dichos* and *adivinanzas* into this lesson? and How can I add a connection to the home so that children extend both their knowledge of science and their knowledge of cultural wisdom within their communities?
B. Observe a bilingual elementary classroom for half a day. What clues do the environment and practices you observe provide about infusion of children's culture into science learning? Interview the teacher to learn about ways in which he or she infuses students' culture into general practices and specifically into the teaching of science.
C. Develop a chart that summarizes cultural resources, including riddles, tongue-twisters, and popular sayings that your parents, neighbors, and other relatives can share with you (see table 9.5). Which ones did you already know? How many of them make references to animals, plants, or events in nature? Highlight those in yellow. What do you notice? Compare your list with that of a colleague.

PROFESSIONAL READINGS

Costigan, S., Muñoz, C., Porter, M., & Quintana, J. (1989). El sabelotodo: *The bilingual teacher's best friend.* Carmel, CA: Hampton-Brown.

Lee, O., Quinn, H., & Valdés, G. (2013). Science and language for English language learners: Language demands and opportunities in relation to Next Generation Science Standards. *Educational Researcher, 42,* 223–33.

Table 9.5.

Dichos	Adivinanzas	Other Cultural Resources

Chapter Ten

Tiempo y Cultura: Exploring Latino Stories through Mathematics

Carlos A. LópezLeiva and Yoo Kyung Sung

INTRODUCTION

Mathematics education, literacy, and language arts are not frequently integrated at upper elementary grade levels despite the great learning opportunities that an interdisciplinary approach provides to students. From the language arts perspective, Braddon, Hall, and Taylor (1993) note,

> Reading is a process in which the reader's knowledge and textual information act together to produce meaning. . . . As proficiency develops, reading should be taught not so much as a separate subject in school, but as integral to learning mathematics, literature, social studies, and science. When connections among these subject areas develop, students are better able to understand motive and action, form and function, or cause and effect. The idea that reading instruction and subject-matter instruction should be integrated is an old one in education, but there is little indication that such integration often occurs in practice. (p. 2)

Thus, reading is a meaning-making process that becomes more meaningful when combined with other subjects. Moreover, from a mathematics education perspective, Janes and Strong (2014) argue that the integration of children's literature with mathematics is helpful in several ways. For instance, literature supports children's sense of connections between their lived experiences and the stories they read (p. 12). As a result, this combination motivates children's learning, develops and stretches children's imagination, and fosters communication, critical thinking, problem solving, and creative thinking in the classroom (Janes & Strong, 2014). One example of this combination is

Juanito's friendships in *Las Amistades de Juanito* (Alumnado de la Escuela de Magisterio, 2000). In one of the stories, Juanito wants to pick apples from a tree that is too tall, so his friends of different heights come to help him reach the fruit. The story's plot, mathematical representations, and interactions further the learning of mathematical concepts.

Despite these benefits, such integrations are not often available to all learners. In early childhood education (ECE), picture books are more commonly read for teaching mathematical concepts than in elementary children's classrooms (Thatcher, 2001). Thatcher recommends that teachers and curriculum designers recognize the power of children's literature, which has been utilized as an important tool in the mathematics curricula in early childhood programs. Contrastingly, learning processes in elementary education tend to be dichotomized, and mathematical concepts are separated from language arts and reading. Mathematics is deemed a "content" area and generally taught separately through expository texts.

The exploration of teaching content areas through children's books has constructed an unintended convention in terms of classroom applications and educational research. Attempts at promoting the integration of mathematics and literature mainly provide a succinct book list with an explicit context to explore mathematical concepts (McDonald & Rasch, 2004; Thatcher, 2001; Forrest, Schnabel, & Williams 2005; Krech, 2003). Few scholars, however, have attempted interdisciplinary connections. For example, Lake (2009) features a literature-based approach to teaching mathematics, and Hopkins and Barbour (1997) introduced poems for learning mathematics. Burns and Sheffield (2004) taught lessons in which stories were used to unpack mathematical concepts in children's literature. Despite these attempts at integrating mathematics and language arts, this practice is rare.

Cultural connections with mathematics are uncommon. Previous studies highlight the importance of equity in mathematics education for Latinos (Gándara, 2006; Gutiérrez, 2002; Gutstein, 2003), and the performance of Latino students in mathematics, which correlates to socioeconomic and linguistic status in the U.S. (Chang, Singh, & Filter, 2009; Lopez & Cole, 1999). While such approaches and information are essential to promote awareness and change, we also recognize the need for research on the integration of and interdisciplinary approaches to teaching and learning mathematics with explicit links to cultural perspectives. Latino children's literature represents a way for such a pedagogical perspective and classroom practice.

To that end, in this chapter we present an approach that reveals and highlights the mathematics embedded in children's stories. More specifically, concepts of time are explored as a means to bridge mathematics and literature and to enable readers to experience cultural connections in a wide range of contexts. This innovative work aims to challenge commonly practiced field separations by drawing on cultural connections in mathematics and literature, more specifically in relation to Latino children's literature. This work represents a new approach in two ways. First, we view mathematics as a lens through which children read and interpret multicultural stories so that they extend and clarify their current understanding of time with new and different concepts. In this way, young readers make meaning while learning about how different measures and uses of time play out within the events of the story. Second, we challenge the idea that only children's stories with embedded mathematical concepts (Clark, 2007) can support an integrated approach to teaching mathematics and language arts. We argue that through our approach, children can also learn about concepts of time, reading, and social studies (i.e., Latino cultures). Our approach invites children to make meaning of and personalize concepts of time and culture.

We propose an approach that connects the term *text to time*. Keene and Zimmerman (1997) observe that students' reading comprehension is enhanced when they make different types of connections, such as *text to self*, *text to text*, and *text to world*. Text is viewed as not only written words in a specific language script; instead, text is framed in broader types of formats and uses. In our case, text relates to different Latino cultures, mathematics, and children's stories. Through our approach, we believe that children can make connections of *text to time*, and then *time to self*. In this *text-to-time* approach, school-age readers are to interpret how characters in a specific context or culture spend time in practices, and how family, community, and friends participate in sharing these practices of using time. This set of practices, actions, and beliefs is linked to specific ways of talking in a culture or a community, namely, a *languaculture* (Agar, 2006), which constitutes a fit between language, speakers, and meaning-making within groups.

As children make sense of time linked to practices and actions within a story about a specific culture, they are reading and learning about cultures and uses of time. Additionally, to address the mathematical dimension of time, our approach makes use of elapsed time portrayed on an open timeline (Dixon, 2008). Children can track the time related to events in a story. Thus Latino children's literature becomes a vehicle for children to learn about concepts of time and people from other Latino cultures and communities. While Latino children learn about other people similar to and different from them, we believe that these children also learn about themselves.

Our approach addresses and expands on current concerns in mathematics education. For example, under the domain of Measurement and Data (MD), the Common Core State Standards for Mathematics (CCSS-M) describe a sequence for learning the concepts of time (see table 10.1). This sequence starts

Table 10.1. Standards across Grade Levels on Concepts of Time (National Governors Association, 2010)

Grade	CCSS-M Standards on Concepts of Time
1st	**1.MD.3.** Tell and write time in hours and half-hours using analog and digital clocks (p. 16).
2nd	**2.MD.7.** Tell and write time from analog and digital clocks to the nearest five minutes, using a.m. and p.m. (p. 20).
3rd	**3.MD.1.** Tell and write time to the nearest minute and measure time intervals in minutes. Solve word problems involving addition and subtraction of time intervals in minutes, e.g., by representing the problem on a number-line diagram (p. 24).
4th	**4.MD.1.** Know relative sizes of measurement units within one system of units including km, m, cm; kg, g; lb., oz.; l, ml; h, min, sec. Within a single system of measurement, express measurements in a larger unit in terms of a smaller unit. Record measurement equivalents in a two-column table.
	4.MD.2. Use the four operations to solve word problems involving distances, intervals of time, liquid volumes, masses of objects, and money, including problems involving simple fractions or decimals and problems that require expressing measurements given in a larger unit in terms of a smaller unit. Represent measurement quantities using diagrams such as number-line diagrams that feature a measurement scale (National Governors Association, 2010, p. 31).

in first grade with the goal of children learning to tell and write time in hours and half-hours using analog and digital clocks. Then in fourth grade, students are expected to use time intervals and convert time measurements from larger to smaller units and represent these quantities using a number line (National Governors Association, 2010).

The CCSS-M suggested learning sequence requires that concepts of time be part of mathematical operations by the third and fourth grades. It does not mention concepts of time in fifth grade and higher, presumably because students have mastered such concepts. Consequently, Kamii and Russell (2012) argue that previous studies have found this sequence to be disconnected from children's developmental maturation. For example, the same authors find that previous research results assert that concepts of time might remain difficult for children until sixth grade. Further, another study on national mathematics assessment found that 42 percent of eighth-grade students had difficulty establishing the equivalent of 2.5 hours in minutes (Jones & Arbaugh, 2004). This argues for more research to understand and organize a learning sequence on temporal relationships (Kamii & Russell, 2012).

In this chapter, we first provide a review of literature on Latino children's literature, storytelling, and mathematics. Then we describe the theoretical framework of our approach. Next, through a Guatemalan story as an example, we present the seven moments of the application of our approach and follow up with a discussion of this approach. Finally, we suggest readings and activities to enhance this approach.

THEORETICAL FRAMEWORK

Latino Cultures and Children's Literature

Stories, fictional or not, consist of narratives that demonstrate how we see others or ourselves living and coping with life (Alterio, 2003). While stories include a plot—beginning, conflict, and resolution—they also describe the context and factors that affect the story. Stories also help us "know, remember and understand" (Livo & Rietz, 1986, p. 2). Stories are ways to "learn with all the complexities of related issues in teaching, as in life" (Quintero, 2004, p. 10). In multicultural children's literature, several studies have explored Latino culture in children's literature (Barrera & Quiroa, 2003; Barrera, Quiroa, & Valdivia, 2003). Many of them use sociocultural theory in their research frameworks and present subjects embedded in power dynamics depicted through illustrations and texts (Barrera, Quiroa, & Valdivia 2003; Williams, 2005). Such sociocultural and political approaches often discuss cultural identities through representational aspects, bilingualism, and biliteracy development in multicultural children's literature (Barrera & Quiroa, 2003; Naidoo, 2008; Martínez-Roldán, 2013).

Multicultural approaches in the U.S. celebrating purported cultural differences tend to over-represent the Mexican or Mexican American background as stereotypically cultural and foreign. As a result, such perspectives undermine the fundamental ethical goal of promoting awareness of diversity in multicultural education (Levy & Hughes, 2009). While multicultural literature presents a well-intended social-justice purpose for promoting awareness of differences, books depicting stories of Latino children in the U.S. frequently present a narrow scope of the Latino diversity (i.e., mostly stories or information about children of Mexican descent). Thus, we urge the expansion of such representation in children's literature, especially those utilized at school, as well as research on the sociocultural and sociopolitical contexts of the multiple Latino cultures.

Storytelling and Mathematics

Stories are resources used to teach mathematics so that children can think about the issues and mathematical concepts embedded in the stories. Stories provide a context in which to apply and make meaning of mathematical operations and numbers. For English as a second language (ESL) classrooms, storytelling situates the mathematical meaning-making in contexts that include cultural and linguistic practices familiar to children so they can problem solve comfortably (Celedón-Pattichis & Musanti, 2013). By including familiar contexts, communication, and authentic use of language, storytelling eases the learning of mathematics, particularly for bilingual and ESL children. Through storytelling, then, teachers can provide a meaningful problem-solving context in which students think about and understand the problem then devise and share with peers strategies for the problem's solution (Turner, Celedón-Pattichis, Marshall, & Tennison, 2009).

Other examples of integrating storytelling include the use of family stories and pictures that bilingual Latino students create in relation to their everyday experiences and then mathematize to pose problems to their peers to solve (LoCicero, Fuson, & Allexsaht-Snider, 1999). This process helps students link the mathematics curriculum with their lives and community experiences. Another storytelling approach in mathematics is the use of children's books with embedded mathematical concepts, such as *Sir Cumference and the First Round Table* (Neuschwander & Geehan, 1997). Here, as students read the story, they explore both the plot and the embedded mathematical concepts. This combination motivates students and presents a meaningful context of applied mathematics. Often the reading of these stories is just an introduction to learning about the mathematical concepts (Clark, 2007). Consequently, storytelling supports greater mathematical achievement. In fact, O'Neill (2004) found that students who score highly on storytelling ability also do so in mathematics.

Storytelling and Time

Many scholars highlight the significance of storytelling in children's development (Carger, 2005; Spooner, 2003). In *Diciendo cuentos* [Telling Stories], López-Robertson (2012a) explores the role of young Latinas' stories in *pláticas literarias* [literature discussion]. López-Robertson's study reveals the power of stories based on lived experiences, as young Latinas sought to create meaning during *pláticas literarias*. She emphasizes the power of *cuentos* in that *pláticas literarias* provide an opportunity for students to connect to their cultural tradition of storytelling. López-Robertson (2012b) notes, "In telling *cuentos*, the young Latinas demonstrated the capacity to use language to create meaning from a book by carefully connecting it to their life experiences (book + life + *cuento* = intertextuality)" (p. 40). Based on positive outcomes such as López-Robertson's, we acknowledge the potential of stories to engage children in meaningful literature discussions that integrate explorations of time. This could mean the exploration of portions of a day (e.g., hours, evening, afternoon) as well as special occasions like a wedding or Christmas day. Storytelling can be a great way to uncover how time frames our cultures in present and past, as well as a meaningful way to enhance children's understanding of time concepts. People have told stories for centuries. Carger (2005) notes that stories are "the most time-honored way in which cultures preserve the past and shape the future" (p. 237).

Teaching about time includes also teaching an understanding of the calendar and concepts such as years, months, weeks, and days. Barnes (2006) challenges the classroom structured time to teach the calendar (e.g., counting the number of days school has run) and instead suggests authentic ways to use the calendar by having students raise questions and ideas about time. For example, "How long would it take the daffodils to bloom?" In this way, students make use of the calendar wall to record special events, which opens a window to talk about past and future weeks, days, and months, and students can thereby connect these concepts with their lives. Furthermore, children also need to identify other smaller-unit concepts such as morning, afternoon, and night, as well as time-related terms like *before*, *after*, *next*, *hours*, *minutes*, and *seconds*. While adults take the use of concepts of time for granted and as part of everyday life, in contrast, children are just starting to discover and understand time (McGuire, 2007). This is evident through children's arbitrary use of *tomorrow* and *yesterday*.

Teachers can better facilitate the learning of time when they have a greater sense of how students construct frameworks of time (Barnes, 2006). The strategies that best support children's understanding of time concepts are to (1) include a historical account of time, (2) promote use of estimation strategies connected to real-life experiences, and (3) make use of informal and formal time units (McGuire, 2007).

Accordingly, McGuire (2007) notes that current measurement of time derives from Babylonian perspectives and their sexagesimal numerical system. She describes the cultural nature of time and the reasons for the use of sexagesimal—instead of decimal—numbers to keep track of time. Her point challenges the idea that digital clocks better support learning on how to read time. Children need to understand that time is based on the 60-base system (McGuire, 2007). For example, 8:47 almost depicts a decimal number, but on an analog clock, the hands depict a better relationship between 47 minutes past the hour and the 13 minutes left to reach nine o'clock. Analog clocks conceptually represent a more transparent model for sexagesimal numbers.

Van de Walle, Karp, and Bay-Williams (in press) suggest a learning sequence and procedures to facilitate the learning of reading time by using an analog clock. Smith and MacDonald (2009) describe how drawing clocks provides insights into children's understanding of time and argue that guided observation of the clock and its drawing help students understand the clock better. Pagni (2005) suggests the use of clocks in middle school to teach angles. Also, Andrade (2011) describes the use clocks to teach gears and fractions. Another study reports how two third-grade students used the conventional terminology of time (e.g., 60 mins. = 1 hr., 60 secs. = 1 min.). However, their real-life sense of time did not align with their numerical knowledge of these concepts. This showed that their personal sense of time had to be reaccommodated to match conventional units of time. These connections were developed by thinking simultaneously about a clock along with real-life events, like jumping or drinking water (Aguilar-Valdez, LópezLeiva, Roberts-Harris, Torres-Velásquez, Lobo, & Westby, 2013).

Mestizo Theoretical Framework

Our *mestizo* framework to think about time and storytelling represents a combination of Mesoamerican and European perspectives. This framework includes three main perspectives: the Mayan *cosmovisión*, real-life mathematics, and culture, and it also combines them through the concepts of time, storytelling, and children's literature.

Time, Storytelling, and Culture

Multicultural children's books provide opportunities to learn about other cultures as they describe the context, values, and practices of the community presented in the story. Our approach explores a wide range of Latino children's stories so that a more comprehensive understanding about this group of people might be generated. This understanding would be beneficial to U.S. Latino children as well as to children from other backgrounds.

We understand *culture* as a plural noun because as we take up multiple roles (e.g., child, worker, cousin, citizen, parent) in our lives, we simultaneously live in and belong to multiple cultures (Agar, 2006). This perspective promotes a non-essentialistic view on culture; however, we also understand that in each culture in which we live, we share with others the values and practices held in that culture. Language helps us "make sense of what the others [and we] say and do" (p. 11) in a culture. *Languaculture* is a term that refers to this connection that includes the use a language (e.g., grammar and vocabulary) and cultural understandings, values, historical knowledge, and meanings created within a community (Agar, 2006).

Hence, when children read multicultural stories, they also engage in understanding the languaculture in the story. Reading requires a cultural translation even when the story is written in the reader's language (Smagorinsky, 2011). Encountering new languacultures happens through both reading and real-life situations. Cultures and differences often become apparent when outsiders encounter them. Agar (2006) uses the term "rich points" to describe these differences or surprises. Children finding rich points in a story represents learning opportunities about the new languaculture. To understand these points, they need a "translation" linked to the perspectives and values of the original languaculture and guidance away from deficit perspectives. When deficit or biased perspectives about a story emerge, they must be critically deconstructed and reconstructed into renewed understandings of the new languaculture (Janks, 2012). For example, a diverse set of stories or investigations on topics related to the biased perspectives might help children renew their perspectives of the issue.

Time, Storytelling, and the Mayan Cosmovisión

The Mayan *cosmovisión* interweaves mathematics and everyday lives through time and language (Duque Sánchez, 2013). This worldview understands humanity as an entity in which the physical and spiritual coexist in time, space, and movement (Matul, 1996), so that being a person is intricately connected to existing in a space and time, as in a story. While the Mayans did not use specific time terms, they viewed time as related to the movement of the cosmos, such as the position of the sun, moon, and stars (Cabrera, 1995). For instance, the Mayan referred to the beginning of the universe through silence or a zero (Matul, 1996). Further, Mayan terminology regarding the cosmos movement is inherently mathematical. For example, "*Oxij*" refers to "in three days" since its root, "*oxi*," means "three." Patterns and measures of the movement of the cosmos is what we understand today as time. Thus, like the Mayan *cosmovisión*, children's stories embed time in their plot.

Time, Storytelling, and Real-Life Mathematics

School curricula seldom connect mathematics to real life. Conversely, a realistic mathematics education (RME) perspective understands mathematics as an inherently human activity. Accordingly, children's everyday contexts such as lived experiences, stories, and society should be part of and support the learning and teaching of mathematics (Freudenthal, 1991). Considering the RME perspective, and to make more explicit connections between mathematics and children's lives depicted through stories, in our approach we include the concepts of elapsed time and an open number line. *Elapsed time* refers to a block or period of time for a particular event, or a measured duration of an event. Elapsed time and the open number line were used with children to make sense of and record their thought processes when they solved addition, subtraction, and elapsed-time problems (Dixon, 2008). In the problem "Marni started watching a movie at 3:30. It ended at 4:45. How long did Marni watch the movie?" (p. 20), children used an open number line to identify 3:30 as the starting time and moved along the line in leaps of time that made sense to them (e.g., 30 min. + 30 min. + 15 min.) to solve the problem.

Consequently, we use elapsed time to bridge events in a story with time. Children reason and identify the duration of events on an open number line and simultaneously track the story plot and timeline. In this way, children track their own thinking and then reflect on and manipulate concepts of time, a situation that in turn may support their understanding of temporal relationships (Kamii & Russell, 2012). Elapsed time may include qualitative (e.g., same age, older than, younger than) or numerical (e.g., thirty more minutes) quantifications. Such explorations and representations of concepts of time align with CCSS-M (Van de Walle et al., 2016).

PRAXIS: APPLICATION OF THEORY

Integrating Children's Stories and Mathematics

Our approach represents an innovative and integrative way to learning and teaching about mathematics (time, elapsed time), language arts (storytelling, reading), and social studies (multiple Latino cultures). Previous studies have integrated storytelling and mathematics (LoCicero et al., 2009; Turner et al., 2009); children's literature and mathematics (Bay-Williams & Martinie, 2008; Burns & Sheffield, 2004; Clark, 2007; Janes & Strong, 2014); elapsed time and problem solving (Dixon, 2008; Kamii & Russell, 2012); and children's literature and culture (e.g., López-Robertson, 2012a). However, no study has integrated all of these factors. Further, Van de Walle et al. (in press) reports a similar approach to ours in which children use elapsed time in real-life events of dog races to keep track of and compare the winning times of their favorite dogs (Lawrence & Straight, 2011).

In our approach, we use multicultural children's stories to explore the elapsed time of the events mentioned in the story. The duration of the events is represented on an open number line. This analytical process supports meaning-making about both the story plot and a specific concept of time. Plot analysis allows reflection on the context and culture of the story. Through a careful selection of Latino multicultural stories, we propose a way of exploring Latino cultures through this approach as well. According to CCSS-M, this approach is designed for children in the third and fourth grades, but older children may also benefit from this experience (Kamii & Russell, 2012). Through elapsed-time analysis of the story plotted on the timeline, our approach encourages children to explore and reflect on their sense of time and make connections across concepts of time. In the following sections, we present our approach by first describing our book selection criteria and then listing the four stories selected for this chapter. Next, we introduce and discuss the seven moments of our approach.

Book Selection

In order to provide a wider perspective on Latino cultures, we explored literature within and outside of the U.S. We chose realistic fiction picture books because they offer visual prompts to think about culture and time. We excluded nonfiction because of the lack a continuous narrative (e.g., books describing cultural traditions). Legends with substantial time leaps or complex, mythical language were also excluded, as were stories with flashbacks or flashforwards due to confusing time structure. Selected books were sorted by time categories, for example, an hour, a day, a week, a month, a year, and a lifetime.

Our Approach

Our approach includes seven moments. We use the term "moment" for two reasons: First, the concept of time is implicit in this term. Second, we want to highlight each phase as an opportunity for teachable *moments* to emerge rather than as following a list of steps to complete. These moments describe an inductive process of thinking about time and culture through a problem-solving process. It means that students will analyze the story as events, apply elapsed-time concepts to the events, and then plot them on a number line. The moments in our integrated approach described below will last several class periods.

Exploration of Time and Culture — Moment 1

Before the story is introduced, students' prior knowledge of the culture and of time concepts needs to be activated to explore the story. For example the story *Ri ajkem rik'in ri ti tz'unün/La tejedora y el colibrí/The Female Weaver and the Hummingbird* (Morales Santos & de Miranda, 2013) comes from the Kaqchikel culture in Guatemala. Students should explore information about the Kaqchikel culture and language. For this, they could search online for information, pictures, etc. about this culture. The teacher may also show a video about people speaking Kaqchikel. The teacher should support students' cultural understanding by being mindful of potential deficit perspectives of the culture as well as opportunities for critical reflection and dialogue. This process encourages familiarity, connectedness, and, hopefully, appreciation of Kaqchikel culture and values.

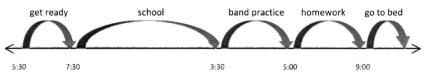

Figure 10.1. My Tuesdays Schedule

To introduce the specific concept of time embedded in the story—in this case, the hours in a day—the teacher needs to provide hands-on activities related to real-life events that help students develop a clearer understanding of the specific concept of time. Students are to think about how long a day is and how it feels as a set of hours. For example, students can brainstorm about activities that take about one hour such as a class period or a TV program. Students should also think about how many hours there are in parts of the day such as the morning or the afternoon. They can explore these time concepts in several ways. For example, children can share with each other their daily activities (see figure 10.1). Additionally, they can be asked to connect these activities to an open number line and count forward and back hours within a day to define the distances between numbers and determine the elapsed time for each activity (Dixon, 2008).

Story Introduction—Moment 2

This moment encompasses a brief exploratory process about the story and book. The process involves a review of the bibliographic elements of the book (e.g., the author and year of publication). Additionally, students are also asked to provide predictions or to guess the plot, location, and how long they think the story takes in terms of a targeted time concept. The processes enacted in this moment are geared toward creating expectation and motivation and building understanding of the story and its concept of time. In the case of *The Female Weaver and the Hummingbird* (Morales Santos & de Mi-

Table 10.2. Languages in the Story "The Female Weaver and the Hummingbird"

Kaqchikel	Spanish	English
Ruma k'a ri' wakami konojel ri q'opoji' taq ixoqi' nkib'än taq tz'unün chupam ri kipo't, koyob'en chi jun q'ij nitzolin pe ri kimetz' xtoqa pa kik'aslem (p. 14).	Por eso es que todas las mujeres jóvenes de la región hacen colibríes en sus huipiles, para esperar al novio que algún día vendrá a sus vidas (p. 14).	That is why all young women in the region make blouses with hummingbirds in them, hoping that one day a boyfriend will come into their lives.

Note: Adapted from Morales Santos & de Miranda, 2013.

randa, 2013), we suggest including table 10.2 to start a conversation about the languages included in the story. Furthermore, based on previous classroom exploration of the Kaqchikel culture and the title of the story, the teacher might ask, "What do you think the story will tell us about what happens in this culture?" and "Based on the illustration on the cover, what do you think the story is about?" Also in relation to time, some suggested questions are "Based on the name of the story, what do you think the story will tell us happens within a day?" and "How much can happen in a day?"

Individual Reading of Story—Moment 3

In this moment, children read the story. For *The Female Weaver and the Hummingbird*, students would read an English translation, but they should also be able to see the story in the other languages (Kaqchikel and Spanish). Before reading, a prompt that might provide initial support is "If the story title is *The Female Weaver and the Hummingbird*, then what should we pay attention to as we read?" As the children read, they will be encouraged to take notes on ideas related to time and culture. Other initial prompts might include "As we read, how can the words in the story tell us about ideas of time?" and "As we read, how does the story tell us about ideas or information about the Kaqchikel culture?" Keeping these ideas in mind and on the board, students would read independently and take notes on the plot and what they find relevant about culture and time in the story.

Location and Sequencing of Plot Events on Timeline—Moment 4

This moment encompasses a process of meaning-making with and analysis of the story. Students are provided with an open timeline to record the main events of the story. Figure 10.2 portrays how *The Female Weaver and the Hummingbird* timeline might look after the plot events have been identified. This process aims at understanding the story better by encouraging students to plot in pairs the story events on the timeline. When students plot the events, they may have questions about terms or ideas in the story, so they can consult other books, dictionaries, or the Internet in order to learn more about the story context or unclear terms. After plotting the story, the teacher would facilitate a whole-group discussion to explore children's understanding of the story and the related culture. It is important to promote a conversation that leads to productive linking of perspectives on issues of cultural, linguistic, and/or racial diversity. Rich points could be sources of collective investigation and discussion to develop clearer cultural understandings. Questions that might help the discussion include (1) What were the major issues in the story? (2) What things did we learn about the weaver, her family, her town, and the

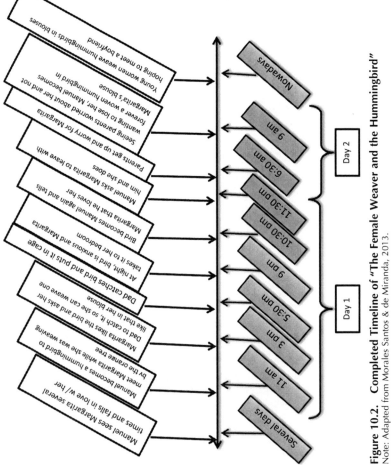

Figure 10.2. Completed Timeline of "The Female Weaver and the Hummingbird"
Note: Adapted from Morales Santos & de Miranda, 2013.

Kaqchikel culture or language? (3) What do you think the weather is like in this place? (4) What do weavers do? and (5) What are hummingbirds?

Assignment of Time Frames to Plot Events on a Timeline—Moment 5

Moment 5 complements moment 4. In this moment, children solve problems regarding the elapsed time of the events they have identified on their story timeline. For a productive understanding of elapsed time of the story events, the teacher would prompt student thinking about the plot. For example, the teacher would ask (1) How much time do you think the story took? (2) How long do people usually sleep at night? (3) How long do people's work shifts last? (4) How long does to it take to weave a *huipil*? (5) How old do you think Margarita is? and (6) How fast do hummingbirds fly? These questions aim at activating prior knowledge of time-related terms before students start assigning elapsed time to each story event. They should not only assign times to the events but also think of a rationale for their choices. We suggest that children work in pairs. This process makes the mathematical content more explicit and recontextualizes the story as students assign their own meaning in terms of time to the story events. We suggest that children track the elapsed time in the lower section of the timeline, as figure 10.2 shows.

Shared Reflection—Moment 6

Moment 6 promotes the sharing of findings and reflections on the story analysis. Each pair of children should volunteer to share their story timelines with everyone. During the sharing, others can elaborate on or contrast it with their findings. The goal should not be to determine a right or wrong understanding, but to learn how others thought about the story's plot, time, and culture. In order to guide the whole-group conversation toward reflecting on Latino cultures and time, we suggest the following discussion questions. These are broad enough to debrief various stories.

- What did we learn about what people in the story do?
- What did you learn about their culture, language, and values?
- What did we learn about time?
- What are some similarities or differences in comparison with your life?
- How did we learn about the Latino culture?

Written Reflection—Moment 7

The last moment addresses an individual reflective process by writing about what was learned of the story, time concepts, and culture. Students can present their reflections in conventional writing formats or develop more visual and creative representations like a poster, a digital story, or a slideshow presentation. Reflections may include questions students still have at this stage of the process. These questions reveal possible future steps, areas of reinforcement, or rich points that need a further work. Teachers should also use this moment as an assessment process.

CONCLUSION

Our approach represents a conceptual proposal of the integration of Latino children's stories and elapsed time to teach and learn about cultures and concepts of time. Language arts, social studies, and mathematics are integrated in a unit with multilayered goals. For Latino students, this approach—depending also on book selection—aims to expand the scope of literature, culture, language, and ideas that typically dominate the rhetoric about Latinos in the U.S. Through addressing the rich points that may emerge during discussions and readings, we suggest a critical literacy approach to learn about cultures (Janks, 2012). Thus children and teachers investigate and learn together through stories about their own and new cultures, practices, and values.

Mathematically, the identification and analysis of elapsed time may not only help students develop their sense of time (Kamii & Russell, 2012), but may also point to patterns of time-use in different events that could point to cultural perspectives on the use of time. Our approach also provides the opportunity to include diverse exploration of concepts of time, depending on what the timeframe of the story includes. We have identified a wide range of time concepts that could be explored, such as minutes, hours, days, weeks, months, seasons, years, decades, lifetime, and annual cycles. Teachers can select books that specifically target the time concept that they are to study with their students. This approach is not to replace specific mathematics instruction on time, but rather to complement and expand that instruction.

Our approach has moved beyond including only children's books that have embedded mathematical concepts in the story (Clark, 2007). This opens up a wide selection of books to be utilized, so possible units that teachers develop may incorporate not only a variety of Latino literature from different countries but also global children's literature beyond Latino literature in order to promote learning about cultures around the world. While a lesson could include one book or story for the whole class, there is also the option of adapting the same approach for small groups, so that at moment 6, students may share several stories instead of many perspectives of the same story. This opens another approach, since the selected stories could target one culture and different stories, several stories from a similar group in different contexts, or different groups with similar traditions. The combinations are innumerable, but they come together depending on the teaching goals and topics to be explored. We believe that integrated story and time analysis provides deeper insights into the story. Other ideas could be added to the process. For example, children could use maps and locate the places featured in the books they have read and then pursue studies about the climate, people, buildings, art, and other characteristics of those places.

We believe that reading should not be only about written text, but also about reading the texts embedded in the story, including mathematics. This integrative perspective supports greater levels of understanding. The construction of meaning that readers develop through an interactive process of connecting "the text with their broader life narrative, generat[es] new texts that in turn make that narrative more comprehensible" (Smagorinsky, 2011, p. 159). While we aim at supporting keener readers, users of mathematics, and culturally aware students, we strive through our approach to promote transformational educational practices that encourage learners to become creators of new texts, doers of mathematics, and facilitators of intercultural relationships.

REFERENCES

Agar, M. (2006). Culture: Can you take it anywhere? *International Journal of Qualitative Methods*, *5*(2), 1–12.

Aguilar-Valdez, J. R., LópezLeiva, C. A., Roberts-Harris, D., Torres-Velásquez, D., Lobo, G., & Westby, C. (2013). *Ciencia en Nepantla*: The journey of Nepantler@s in science learning and teaching. *Cultural Studies of Science Education*, *8*(4), 821–58.

Alterio, M. (2003). Using storytelling to enhance student learning. *Higher Education Academy*. Retrieved from www-new1.heacademy.ac.uk/assets/Documents/resources/database/id471_using_storytelling_to_enhance_learning.pdf.

Alumnado de la Escuela de Magisterio (2000). *Las amistades de Juanito*. Retrieved from www.uclm.es/profesorado/mvmarin/cuentos.html.

Andrade, A. (2011). The clock project: Gears as visual-tangible representations for mathematical concepts. *International Journal of Technology Design and Education*, *21*, 93–110.

Barnes, M. K. (2006). How many days 'til my birthday? Helping kindergarten students understand calendar connections and concepts. *Teaching Children Mathematics*, *12*(6), 290–95.

Barrera, R. B., & Quiroa, R. E. (2003). The use of Spanish in Latino children's literature in English: What makes for cultural authenticity? In K. G. Short & D. L. Fox (Eds.), *Stories matter* (pp. 247–68). Urbana, IL: National Council of Teachers of English.

Barrera, R. B., Quiroa, R. E., & Valdivia, R. (2003). Spanish in Latino picture storybooks in English: Its use and textural effects. In A. L. Willis, G. E. Garcia, R. Barrera, & V. Harris (Eds.), *Multicultural issues in literacy research and practice* (pp. 145–65). Mahwah, NJ: Lawrence Erlbaum Associates.

Bay-Williams, J. M., & Martinie, S. L. (2008). *Math and nonfiction.* Sausalito, CA: Math Solutions Publications.

Braddon, K. L., Hall, N. J., & Taylor, D. (1993). *Math through children's literature: Making the NCTM standards come alive.* Englewood, CO: Teacher Ideas Press.

Burns, M., & Sheffield, S. (2004). *Math and literature.* Sausalito, CA: Math Solutions Publications.

Cabrera, E. (1995). *Calendario Maya: En la cosmovisión Maya* (pp. 138–429). Guatemala: Liga Maya de Guatemala.

Carger, C. L. (2005). The art of narrative inquiry: Embracing emotion and seeing transformation. In J. Phillion, M. F. He, & F. M. Connelly (Eds.), *Narrative & experience in multicultural education* (pp. 231–45). Thousand Oaks, CA: Sage Publications.

Celedón-Pattichis, S., & Musanti, S. I. (2013). Grade 1: "Let's suppose that . . . ": Developing base-ten thinking with Latina/o emergent bilingual learners. In M. Gottlieb & G. Ernst-Slavit (Eds.), *Academic language in diverse classrooms: Promoting content and language learning. Grades K–2, Mathematics* (pp. 87–124). Thousand Oaks, CA: Corwin Press.

Chang, M., Singh, K., & Filer, K. (2009). Language factors associated with achievement grouping in math classrooms: A cross-sectional and longitudinal study. *School Effectiveness and School Improvement, 20*(1), 27–45.

Clark, J. (2007). Mathematics saves the day. *Australian Primary Mathematics Classroom, 12*(2), 21–24.

Dixon, J. K. (2008). Tracking time: Representing elapsed time on an open timeline. *Teaching Children Mathematics, 15*(1), 19–24.

Duque Sánchez, H. (2013). El sentido del número en la cultura Maya. (Unpublished Thesis). Universidad Tecnológica de Pereira, Colombia.

Forrest, K., Schnabel, D., & Williams, M. (2005). Math by the book. *Teaching Children Mathematics, 12*(4), 200.

Freudenthal, H. (1991). *Revisiting mathematics education: China lectures.* Dordrecht, The Netherlands: Kluwer Academic Press.

Gándara, P. (2006). Strengthening the academic pipeline leading to careers in math, science, and technology for Latino students. *Journal of Hispanic Higher Education, 5*(3), 222–37. doi:10.1177/1538192706288820.

Gutiérrez, R. (2002). Beyond essentialism: The complexity of language in teaching mathematics to Latino/a students. *American Educational Research Journal, 39*(4), 1047–88.

Gutstein, E. (2003). Teaching and learning mathematics for social justice in an urban, Latino school. *Journal for Research in Mathematics Education, 34*(1), 37–33.

Hopkins, L. B., & Barbour, K. (1997). *Marvelous math: A book of poems.* New York, NY: Simon & Schuster Books for Young Readers.

Janks, H. (2012). The importance of critical literacy. *English Teaching: Practice and Critique*, *11*(1), 150–63.

Janes, R. C., & Strong, E. (2014). *Numbers & stories: Using children's literature to teach young children number sense*. Thousand Oaks, CA: NCTM & Corwin.

Jones, D., & Arbaugh, F. (2004). What do students know about time? *Mathematics Teaching in the Middle School*, *10*, 82–84.

Kamii, C., & Russell, K. A. (2012). Elapsed time: Why is it so difficult to teach? *Journal for Research in Mathematics Education*, *43*(3), 296–315.

Keene, E. O., & Zimmerman, S. (1997). *Mosaic of thought: Teaching comprehension in a reader's workshop*. Portsmouth, NH: Heinemann Publishing.

Krech, B. (2003). Picture-book math: Read-alouds are great springboards to super math learning. *Instructor*, *112*(7), 42.

Lake, J. (2009). *Math memories you can count on: A literature-based approach to teaching mathematics in the primary classrooms*. Markham, ON, Canada: Pembroke Publishers.

Lawrence, K. (Producer), & Straight, A. (Producer & Director) (2011). *Great lesson ideas: The Iditarod & math*. United States: Tri-Film Production for Teaching Channel. Film retrieved from www.youtube.com/watch?v=WPvy4knZ_YY.

Levy, S. R., & Hughes, J. M. (2009). Development of racial and ethnic prejudice among children. In T. D. Nelson (Ed.), *Handbook of prejudice, stereotyping and discrimination* (pp. 23–42). New York, NY: Psychology Press.

Livo, N., & Rietz, S. (1986) *Storytelling: Process and practice*. Denver, CO: Libraries Unlimited.

LoCicero, A. M., Fuson, K. C., & Allexsaht-Snider, M. (1999). Mathematizing children's stories, helping children solve word problems, and supporting parental involvement in math learning. In L. Ortiz-Franco, N. Hernández, & Y. DeLa Cruz (Eds.), *Changing the faces of mathematics: Perspectives on Latinos* (pp. 156–67). Reston, VA: National Council of Teachers of Mathematics.

Lopez, A., & Cole, C. L. (1999). Effects of a parent-implemented intervention on the academic readiness skills of five Puerto Rican kindergarten students in an urban school. *School Psychology Review*, *28*, 439–47.

López-Robertson, J. (2012a). "*Esta página me recordó*": Young Latinas using personal life stories as tools for meaning-making. *Bilingual Research Journal*, *35*(2), 217–33.

———. (2012b). "Oigan, tengo un cuento": Crossing *la frontera* of life and books. *Language Arts*, *90*(1), 30–43.

Martínez-Roldán, C. M. (2013). The representation of Latinos and the use of Spanish: A critical content analysis of *Skippyjon Jones*. *Journal of Children's Literature*, *39*(1), 5–13.

Matul, D. (1996). Fibras del corazón. In *La cosmovisión Maya* (pp. 130–97). Guatemala: Liga Maya de Guatemala.

McDonald, S., & Rasch, S. (2004). *Picture books + math = fun*. Chicago, IL: Booklist Publications.

McGuire, L. (2007). Time after time. *Australian Primary Mathematics Classroom*, *12*(2), 30–32.

Morales Santos, F., & de Miranda, S. G. (2013). *Ri ajkem rik'in ri ti tz'unün/La tejedora y el colibrí/The female weaver and the hummingbird.* (P. Morejón Patzán, trans). Guatemala City, Guatemala: Prensa Libre.

Naidoo, J. C. (2008). Opening doors. *Children & Libraries, 6*(2), 27.

National Governors Association Center for Best Practices, Council of Chief State School Officers. (2010). Common core state standards for mathematics. Washington, DC: Author. Retrieved from www.nga.org/cms/home/special/col2-content/common-core-state-standards-init.html.

Neuschwander, C., & Geehan, W. (1997). *Sir Cumference and the first round table: A math adventure.* Watertown, MA: Charlesbridge Publishing.

O'Neill, D. (2004). Narrative skills linked to mathematical achievement. *Literacy Today, 41.*

Pagni, D. L. (2005). Angles, time, and proportion. *Mathematics teaching in the middle school, 10*(9), 436–41.

Quintero, E. P. (2004). *Problem-posing with multicultural children's literature: Developing critical early childhood curricula.* New York, NY: Peter Lang Publishing.

Smagorinsky, P. (2011). *Vygotsky and literacy research: A methodological framework.* Boston, MA: Sense Publishers.

Smith, T., & MacDonald, A. (2009). Time for talk: The drawing-telling process. *Australian Primary Mathematics Classroom, 14*(3), 21–26.

Spooner, M. (2003). The stories we are: Old Meshikee and the winter of 1929. In W. Bishop & H. Ostrom (Eds.), *The subject is story: Essays for writers and readers* (pp. 51–61). Portsmouth, NH: Heinemann Publishing.

Thatcher, D. H. (2001). Reading in the math class: Selecting and using picture books for math investigations. *Young Children, 56*(4), 20–27.

Turner, E., Celedón-Pattichis, S., Marshall, M., & Tennison, A. (2009). "Fíjense amorcitos, les voy a contar una historia": The power of story to support solving and discussing mathematical problems with Latino/a kindergarten students. In D. Y. White & J. S. Spitzer (Eds.), *Mathematics for every student: Responding to diversity, grades pre-K–5* (pp. 23–41). Reston, VA: National Council of Teachers of Mathematics.

Van de Walle, J. A., Karp, K. S., & Bay-Williams, J. M. (in press). *Elementary and middle school mathematics: Teaching developmentally* (11th ed.). Upper Saddle River, NJ: Pearson.

Williams, B. (2005). Home and away: The tensions of community, literacy, and identity. *Journal of Adolescent & Adult Literacy, 49,* 342–43.

DISCUSSION QUESTIONS

1. What are other forms in which you would like to implement and transform our approach?
2. If you find a children's book that is not in a language you understand, how can you learn more about this book and perhaps use it in your classroom?

3. If students have difficulty determining the elapsed time for an event, what are some possible ways to support their reasoning and understanding?
4. What are the benefits of learning and exploring cultural issues and concepts of time through stories?

ACTIVITIES

A. Use real maps or fictional ones to track events in the story.
B. Include videos related to the stories you select.
C. Invite guest speakers who may talk more about the story topics.
D. Invite families into your classroom to share children's stories that they know even if these take place in another country.
E. Interview children before and after this process to learn about what they are learning.
F. After students have participated with you in this process, let them pick the books they would like to read or use through this approach.
G. Use tools (e.g., chronometers, clocks, calendars, pictures) and activities that will provide multimodal ways to explore concepts of time and understand and measure elapsed time.
H. Apply our approach to the book titles listed in the appendix to the chapter.

PROFESSIONAL READINGS

Dixon, J. K. (2008). Tracking time: Representing elapsed time on an open timeline. *Teaching Children Mathematics, 15*(1), 19–24.

López-Robertson, J. (2012). "Está página me recordó": Young Latinas using personal life stories as tools for meaning-making. *Bilingual Research Journal, 35*(2), 217–33.

McGuire, L. (2007). Time after time. *Australian Primary Mathematics Classroom, 12*(2), 30–32.

APPENDIX

1. Bertrand, D. G., & Delange, A. P. (2008). *Sip, Slurp, Soup, Soup: Caldo, caldo, caldo.* Houston, TX: University of Houston, Piñata Groups. This story, written in Spanish and English, takes place in an urban area that could be in either the U.S. or Latin America, and it describes how Latino children in the same family observe their mom preparing soup for lunch. Then when their dad comes home, they go out with him to buy tortillas.

The whole family then shares and enjoys lunch. This story evolves within a few hours.

2. Dominguez, K. K., & Paterson, D. (2002). *The Perfect Piñata/La piñata perfecta*. (T. Mlawer, trans). Morton Grove, IL: Albert Whitman & Company. This story, written in Spanish and English, takes place in an urban area that could be in either the U.S. or Latin America, and it describes a girl who is preparing for her birthday party. Her parents take her to buy a piñata, and they find the perfect piñata, a butterfly. The girl develops an affection for the piñata as she spends a whole week with it. By birthday party time, the girl can't break her piñata, so her parents make instead a piñata out of a bag, placing candy in it. At the end, the girl has two perfect piñatas. This story evolves within a week.

3. Kurusa & Doppert, M. (1995). *The Streets Are Free*. New York, NY: Annick Press. This story, written in Spanish and English, takes place in a slum of Caracas, Venezuela, on the hills surrounding the city. The story describes how Cheo, Carlitos, and Camila grow up in this area, showing changes in their lives and the city. This story evolves within a lifetime.

4. Morales Santos, F., & de Miranda, S. G. (2013). *Ri ajkem rik'in ri ti tz'unün/La tejedora y el colibrí/The Female Weaver and the Hummingbird*. (P. Morejón Patzán, trans.). Guatemala City, Guatemala: Prensa Libre. This story is written in Spanish and Kaqchikel. (Kaqchikel is one of the twenty-three indigenous languages in Guatemala. This language is different from Spanish; it is a language derived from the ProtoMaya language. Speakers of Kaqchikel mostly live in the central area of Guatemala.) The story takes place in a rural area of Guatemala. It describes how Margarita, a young Kaqchikel woman, meets a boy who is in the form of a hummingbird. Once at home, in Margarita's room, the boy turns into human form and tells Margarita that he is in love with her. As the boy and girl are leaving, her parents wake up and worry about their daughter. Becoming aware of their suffering, the boy becomes a hummingbird woven into Margarita's blouse, where he stays forever. This story evolves within two days. For a description of Kaqchikel culture and people, see www.youtube.com/watch?v=kTByrFmp1IM.

Part IV

MULTIPLE MODES
OF MULTICULTURAL
CHILDREN'S LITERATURE

Figure 11.1.

Young Latino kids need to see themselves in books. Stories have a natural power to move an audience. Seeing a familiar character in a protagonist role will inspire confidence for their own dreams and goals. It is important to create and share literature that empowers a Latino audience through relatable characters and culture . . . sharing our worlds and words.

—Lindsey Olivares, author and illustrator, June 17, 2015

Chapter Eleven

Cultural Multiliteracies: Integrating Technology with Latino Children's Literature

Lucila D. Ek, Sonia N. Sánchez, and
Myriam Jimena Guerra

INTRODUCTION

Scholars and educators focusing on the literacy worlds of pre-K–12 students need to examine the various and diverse literacies that make up their students' daily lives. For Latino bilingual children, a significant concern lies in how multiliteracies connect with their cultural practices. In addition, educators and scholars must go beyond the traditional literacy curriculum and recognize that technology shapes and influences the kinds of literacies in which students engage. Palfrey and Gaser (2008) argue that children need to acquire and develop digital competency. Thus, this chapter uses a multiliteracies theoretical framework to focus on new digital literacies and on how educators can incorporate these along with Latino children's literature into the learning context.

Technology evolves so rapidly that children, teachers, and librarians around the world are constantly exposed to new software, technology applications, and video games. Integrating technology in today's curriculum is essential to meeting the educational needs of today's generation. Technological developments in today's global markets challenge educators to learn the newest technological trends to be able to reach out to students who belong to the so-called cyberkids generation (Facer & Furlang, 2001; Holloway & Valentine, 2003). Thus educators have to integrate multimedia and technology into Latino children's literature and other activities to enhance bilingual students' learning. In this chapter, we provide activities to develop the digital literacies of bilingual students utilizing Latino children's literature.

THEORETICAL FRAMEWORK

Scholars such as Gallego and Hollingsworth (2000) extend the traditional literacy landscape by highlighting community- or culturally based conceptions of literacy as well as those of lived experiences. In doing so, they move beyond traditional definitions of literacy as reading, writing, and speaking standard English—practices that are privileged in schools. The work of the New London Group (1996) on multiliteracies contributes to the theoretical framework for this chapter. Like that of Gallego and Hollingsworth (2000), this work moves beyond narrow definitions of literacy and instead focuses on the diversity of literacies that are found in different contexts. The New London Group (NLG) chose the word "multiliteracies" to address two important issues: "the multiplicity of communications channels and media, and the increasing saliency of cultural and linguistic diversity" (p. 63). These scholars assert, "Multiliteracies also creates a different kind of pedagogy, one in which language and other modes of meaning are dynamic representational resources, constantly being remade by their users as they work to achieve their various cultural purposes" (p. 64). This approach recognizes the multimodal realities of literacy practices that relate text to the audio, visual, spatial, and behavioral. In addition, the multiliteracies frame addresses the rich linguistic and cultural diversity that all learning and teaching contexts comprise.

We suggest that utilizing Latino children's literature along with a multiliteracies approach decenters literacy definitions that focus on only one standardized national language and its accompanying "authoritarian kind of pedagogy" (NLG, 1996, p. 64). According to the NLG, a pedagogy of multiliteracies focuses on broader forms of representation and differences in cultural contexts. Multiliteracies reflect the realities of diversity by underscoring the need to "interact effectively using multiple languages, multiple Englishes, and communication patterns that more frequently cross cultural, community, and national boundaries" (p. 64).

A multiliteracies approach can address the privileges of some literacies over others. Luke (1994) compares schools to a literacy marketplace that favors the dominant cultural practices over those of language minority students. Literacy capital has not been valued by traditional schooling. Poor, non-dominant language speakers have had limited access to school-like language and literacy practices (Heath, 1983). Hence, literacy is a key site for societal power struggles (Luke, 1994; Street, 2001) as evidenced in decision making over who gets to define literacy and determine literacy curriculum and pedagogy. Digital literacies are another valuable currency. Not all learners have equal access to these new technological literacies. Libraries too can be an important setting that shapes the literacy marketplace and that provides access to academic literacies for Latino children.

Digital Literacy

Literacy practices that are mediated by new technologies have been dubbed "digital literacies" (Knobel & Lankshear, 2007; Lam & Rosario-Ramos, 2009). These forms of communication have a complex multimodal, multimedia aspect (Lewis & Fabos, 2005). Scholarship on students' digital practices largely focuses on those who are monolingual or whose first language is English (Coiro, Lankshear, & Leu, 2008; Hagood, Leander, Luke, Mackey, & Nixon, 2003). However, the few studies that examine bilingual learners and technology document how digital literacies are key to identity formation, maintenance of the heritage language, and the acquisition of a second language (Lam & Rosario-Ramos, 2009; Sánchez & Salazar, 2012).

Incorporating cultural multiliteracies is even more complex for bilingual learners because they must navigate two languages. Educators, such as teachers and librarians of Latino bilingual learners, must attend to how they acquire language and literacy in both Spanish and English. Research emphasizes the importance of encouraging children's bilingualism and literacy to facilitate the development of their biliteracy (Moll, Saez, & Dworin, 2001; Reyes, 2006; Reyes & Azuara, 2008). Latino students' biliteracy development is also facilitated by parents, teachers, librarians, and peers who can scaffold the students' language and literacy learning in a variety of ways (Reyes, 2006; Reyes & Azuara, 2008). Educators can leverage children's bilingual language practices from their homes and communities in their literacy teaching. Bilingual learners, for example, engage in *code-switching*, which is the mixing of two or more languages (Ek, García, & Garza, 2014; Zentella, 1997), and *translanguaging* (see chapters 2 and 7), which includes all bilingual learners' complex language practices using their entire linguistic repertoire (García, 2009). Thus, educators must use these language practices as resources, and by doing so, they can be change agents.

PRAXIS: APPLICATION OF THEORY

Educators everywhere are challenged to design innovative activities that use technology as a resource while incorporating children's literature. The ideas in this section explore Latino children's media literacy and offer activities that promote twenty-first-century literacy skills in bilingual settings. Traditional practices like storytelling can be integrated into these activities. Storytelling as an oral tradition among Spanish-speakers has been one of the most important ways through which knowledge has been passed down through the generations (Riojas-Cortez, Flores, Smith, & Clark, 2003). Storytelling can help immigrant and bilingual children make sense of their new experiences. They can author their narratives using technology; thereby learners feel that their stories are welcomed into the learning context and displays.

Digital Storytelling

> Stories keep memories alive. Your life stories as well as your family's stories about the most memorable life experiences are worth preserving.

> —Bernajean Porter

Digital storytelling combines the art of telling stories with multimedia. Whether it be through a digital application or a computer-based program, digital stories engage the use of technical tools to blend audio, video, and graphics with the author's story. As with traditional storytelling, digital stories can be designed as narratives to mirror the rich oral practices shared within the Latino community. An example of a digital narrative is Barbara Renaud González's (2014) e-book on voting-rights activist Willie Velasquez, an interactive pop-up book that includes music and photos. Through narratives, students are able to preserve the cultural meanings behind the art of storytelling and share stories as a means of entertainment or the teaching of valuable lessons.

The impact of digital storytelling on learner engagement, language acquisition, and critical thinking skills has been shown to be a transformative technological tool in bilingual classrooms. Studies looking at the use of these digital literacies in settings with emergent bilinguals document the development of skills crucial for linguistic development (Skinner & Hagood, 2008; Verdugo & Belmonte, 2007; Yang & Wu, 2012). Like oral storytelling, digital storytelling creates a space where cultural tradition intersects classroom practice. Through retelling, learners are able to build on narrative skills acquired through practices at home. In addition, vocabulary is reinforced and the visualization found in the pictorial representation of the story provides students with the ability to build comprehension skills through interaction with non-written texts. Furthermore, digital storytelling provides students with opportunities to organize information in a way that is more familiar and echoes their use of technology outside of the classroom (Adams, 2009; Shelby, Caffey, Úbéda, & Jenkins, 2014). One example of this use of technology is through video-editing software applications that allow students to create digital stories. These applications are designed to edit photo and video clips by manipulating simple editing tools, allowing users to create video footage and import video, audio, and photo files. It is just one of many digital platforms where students, teachers, and librarians can combine literacy and digital practices to construct narrative and expository texts.

Storytelling using this technology facilitates and builds on multiple literacy skills through multimodal practices. Students are challenged to create narratives that tell a story for a variety of audiences while critically thinking about choosing and editing artifacts that will support the meaning of their stories. As an instructional tool in bilingual settings, digital storytelling taps into the cultural and linguistic resources of bilingual learners. The linguistic and cultural capital of Mexican American families was explored during a parent institute that expanded on the connections between home and school literacies through a storytelling session (Riojas-Cortez, Flores, Smith, & Clark, 2003). Some of the linguistic features of storytelling, which were identified, included the use of the native language to construct narratives embedded with literary and grammatical forms needed in school. Parents used a variety of literary forms connected to their cultural heritage. What their observations reveal about the oral traditions that exist in Latino families validate the importance of storytelling as a literacy practice (Riojas-Cortez et al., 2003).

Digital storytelling allows students to engage in authentic learning to develop linguistic skills. When engaging in both process-oriented (e.g., brainstorming, storyboard mapping) and product-oriented tasks (e.g., script writing, publishing), students are actively involved in the production of language associated with the task. Oral collaboration with peers to create stories or provide feedback during peer conferencing build on the linguistic skills required to successfully create and critically evaluate digital stories. Through script writing, learners are able to produce narratives using different linguistic variations, such as code-switching, Southwest Spanish, or Mexican Spanish. "Constructing stories in the native language allows for creativity in storytelling" (Riojas-Cortez et al., 2003, p. 67) and can include the use of different linguistic varieties.

The option to choose the language or languages with which to tell a story fosters students' use of both their home and school languages and encourages students to develop a sense of self as learner and problem solver (Vásquez & Durán, 2000; see chapter 3). In addition, digital storytelling applications incorporate the use of higher levels of cognitive processes as students learn to construct meaning from resources that require varying levels of reading, summarization, analysis, and discussion to develop their stories (Yang & Wu, 2012).

Digital storytelling can build on the rich oral literacies of Latino students and their families. Through digital stories, students can capture cultural practices by creating stories that teach moral lessons through *dichos* (sayings), *refranes* (proverbs), or *cuentos* (stories; Riojas-Cortez et al., 2003; Sánchez, Plata, Grosso, & Leird, 2010; see chapters 3 and 9). They can also share family stories that depict traditions, explain customs, or highlight memorable events.

Incorporating Latino Children's Literature

According to Naidoo (2011), "High-quality Latino children's literature can be a catalyst for new learning with new technologies" (p. 308). The interaction between traditional texts and new digital literacies creates a two-way process of knowledge sharing and building about Latino culture through multimodal texts (Naidoo, 2011). In the learning setting, this interaction allows Latino students to access background knowledge to create digital stories. The following are examples of digital storytelling activities that incorporate the cultural knowledge found in both Latino communities and Latino children's literature.

- Create a public service announcement or simulate a debate. Topics can include immigration policies, better community infrastructures, importance of bilingualism and/or biculturalism, better health services, and contributions of Latino local or world leaders. There are a number of Latino children's books and novels that inspire discussion on these topics.
  a. *Side by Side: The Story of Dolores Huerta and César Chávez/Lado a lado: La historia de Dolores Huerta y César Chávez* (Brown, 2009)
  b. *Pancho Rabbit and the Coyote: A Migrant's Tale* (Tonatiuh, 2013)
  c. *That's Not Fair! Emma Tenayuca's Struggle for Justice/¡No es justo! La lucha de Emma Tenayuca por la justicia* (Tafolla & Tenayuca, 2008)
  d. *Separate Is Never Equal: Sylvia Mendez and Her Family's Fight for Desegregation* (Tonatiuh, 2014)
  Note: These are books for young readers that describe the plight of migrant workers and the equality for Latinos in education. For older readers, books include *After Peaches* (Mulder, 2009), the story of a ten-year-old girl's struggles with the experience of being a political refugee from Mexico, and *Pocho* (Villarreal, 1989), the story of a young boy who moves to the U.S. and is caught between honoring his ancestral traditions and the traditions of his new home.
- Design a virtual guided tour of students' communities or family home countries using artifacts and family interviews. *Mayeros: A Yucatec Maya Family* (Ancona, 1997) looks at the traditions and history of a Mayan family.
- Reenact a historical event in Latino history. Teachers can choose to have students tell the story of the Battle of the Alamo from the perspective of the Mexican army or retell the Mexican War of Independence. *Enrique*

Esparza and the Battle of the Alamo (Brown, 2009) uses reader's theater to tell the story of a young man's experience during the Battle of the Alamo (see chapter 8). Students can also depict cultural traditions of Latino families. *The Fiesta Dress: A Quinceañera Tale* (McCormack, 2009) is a vividly illustrated picture book that depicts images of a little sister's day as her older sister is preparing for her *quinceañera* (see chapter 3). The book is written in English but is sprinkled with Spanish words that are defined in the glossary.

- Document a process or concept in a content-specific area. For science, this might include explaining what causes a volcano, earthquake, or flood and how these natural phenomena shape the earth (see chapter 9). Students can make connections to personal experiences or knowledge about these phenomena to their home country. *Hill of Fire* (Lewis, 1971) tells the story of a farmer who complains that nothing happens until one day there is a volcanic eruption in his small Mexican village.
- Use other software for digital storytelling. In addition to iMovie, there is a variety of other resources, websites, and applications that teachers can use for digital storytelling.
  a. Photostory: an application that is very child friendly and especially designed for storytelling. The stories can be told in five steps using multimedia and the software allows use of video and images, title, music, and narration.
  b. iMovie: an application designed to edit photo and video clips to create video footage and to import video, audio, and photo files.
  c. Moviemaker: an application that offers the ability to create and edit videos.
  d. Chatterpix: an application that makes anything talk. You can take or use a photo, draw and make a mouth and it will talk, recording the voice. Then, you will be able to share it through e-mail, social media. This application is great for the kids to create their own stories, scripts, or comic lines.
  e. Facetalker: an application that allows you to put words into a picture so that it seems as if your character or friend talks back to you. You can then share the video in class.
  f. Tellagami: an application that allows you to make your own visual character. Your character will be able to speak and show emotions. You are also allowed to create the setting. After you design your character, you can make a story and record your voice for up to thirty seconds.

We recommend that when using the resources mentioned above, educators take into the account the immigration trajectories of their own students (see chapter 4). Among the children's books that can be read in a classroom with bilingual learners that will facilitate the narration of the students' own stories or family stories are *My Name Is Jorge: On Both Sides of the River* (Medina, 1999); *Un mundo nuevo* (Figueredo, 1999); *My Diary from Here to There/Mi diario de aquí hasta allá* (Pérez, 2013); and *Nana's Big Surprise/Nana, ¡Qué sorpresa!* (Pérez, 2007). These books relate the experiences of young children facing family relocation, in some cases from one country to another, or from one place to another. The books also touch on overcoming obstacles and on how a child can cope with the loss of a relative or a friend and the feeling of homesickness or nostalgia.

Social Media: Blogging and YouTube

The widespread use of social media facilitates communication among family members and friends, allowing users to send and share messages, photographs, and videos. Educators of bilingual learners need to tap into what the students know and are familiar at home, such as social media. This section focuses on the potential use of social media to support bilingual learners.

Social media is defined as websites and technological applications used to communicate within a network of a group of friends. What is novel is that users can actively create messages, share their input, or post the information they want. At the same time, social media users are able to follow participants inside or outside their networks. However, we realize that schools limit the kinds of social media available to students during the school day, so you may not be able to use all the different kinds of social media available, depending on your school's restrictions. (Perhaps, for example, you can obtain district permission to use YouTube afterschool in an informal learning club.) Here we focus on blogging and YouTube. Because these practices require multiple modes of literacy, students are engaged in developing linguistic and academic skills that are critical to the process of becoming bilingual (Flores, Vásquez, & Clark, 2014).

"Blogging" has been defined in a variety of ways. With no one true definition, a "blog" can be defined as an online journal entry, an electronic discussion forum, or even a personal website. It includes features such as comments, posts, or links that create interactions with the reader. Blogging, then, is the creation of and maintenance of a blog.

Blogging is an online activity that provides students with an opportunity to build their confidence as authors as they practice their writing skills (Gunelius, n.d.). Blogging allows students to practice the grammatical forms and literary devices needed in school. Students are able to negotiate writing in a safe environment where risk-taking opens the door to a better understanding of purpose, audience, and voice. Blogging provides a model of a variety of writing structures, and within classroom blogs, teachers are able to guide the writing process and individualize it for each student (Gunelius, n.d.).

Kidblog is blogging platform that can be accessed as an application on an electronic device. Kidblog is a virtual space that is safe and secure and only accessible to an online blogging community created by the teacher. Teachers also have the ability to control posts and comments, ensuring a safe community for student writers. Kidblog is a kid-friendly application in which students engage in authentic writing experiences. Using it, teachers can take students through the stages of writing and provide feedback. Kidblog is not restricted to any one language variety, and it allows the student to write in the language of their choice. According to the Kidblog website (http://kidblog .org/home/), Kidblog is designed to accomplish a number of tasks that provide for a variety of authentic writing experiences.

- Book Club is a way to get students reading, writing, and responding to Latino literature. Students can include reviews of Latino books and record reactions through personal stories.
- Science Notebooks helps students develop and practice their science understanding, while also enhancing communication.
- Global Pen Pals motivates students to write by expanding their audience beyond the classroom.
- Digital Portfolio is an ideal way to demonstrate learning growth through pictures, video, writing, and more.

A very popular form of social media that students are exposed to at home is YouTube. It allows users to post their own videos and share them with known and unknown users. YouTube users can create their own channel, post their own videos, and select and post videos they like. Teachers and librarians can use YouTube to share presentations, videos, movies, songs, and video clips with students. Teachers and librarians can create their own channel that only they and their students can access and share.

Teachers can use YouTube for teaching procedural texts during reading and writing activities, particularly targeting how-to-do-informational and nonfiction text skills along with reading and writing activities for the same genre. For example, there are children's books that expose children to healthy eating habits while respecting family culinary traditions (see part V).

- *Adelita and the Veggie Cousins/Adelita y las primas verduritas* (Diane Gonzáles Bertrand, 2011)
- *A Day Without Sugar/Un día sin azúcar* (Anda, 2012)
- *Alicia's Fruity Drinks/Las aguas frescas de Alicia* (Ruiz-Flores, 2012)

Teachers can ask each student to share his or her family recipe, allowing the student to provide a written procedural text or recipe. Upon that, the student can demonstrate all the steps in their classroom's YouTube channel.

One of the areas in which young Latino students are struggling is reading comprehension, particularly in making inferences and predictions. Poetry presents a greater difficulty for bilingual students because of the vocabulary and figurative language involved. Teachers can have students perform poems as well as *dichos* then video record these and upload them to the classroom YouTube channel. Some of the books that can bridge family oral tradition and literary genre studies are:

- *Cool Salsa: Bilingual Poems of Growing Up Latino in the United States* (Carlson & Hijuelos, 2013),
- *Red Hot Salsa: Bilingual Poems of Being Young and Latino in the United States* (Carlson & Hijuelos, 2005),
- *Canta, rana, canta/Sing, Froggie, Sing* (Flores, 2013), and
- *¡Qué cosas dice mi abuela!/Things My Grandmother Says!* (Galan, 2013).

Digital literacies combined with traditional literacies like children's literature, poetry, and storytelling can open up new spaces for students, empowering them to actively engage in classroom and academic discussions because they know their teachers and peers will value their contributions.

CONCLUSIONS

This chapter drew from a multiliteracies framework to explore how educators can include digital literacies in any setting. Moving beyond reductive definitions of literacy as reading and writing allowed us to present a variety of literacy practices mediated by new technologies for bilingual students. Among these are digital storytelling, blogging, and various social media. We incorporated rich multicultural literature that educators can use to develop their students' literacies/biliteracies. Additionally, we demonstrated how teachers can include and blend traditional parts of their curriculum with technology in ways that are culturally relevant to Latino bilingual students.

Our discussion of these literacies highlights the need for educators to be aware of new technologies and how they can be used for instructional purposes. Educators need to recognize that Latino children and their families may use technology on a daily basis. For the generation of digital natives (Prensky, 2001), technology and its tools are "second nature" (p. 4) and almost like an extension of their own body. If educators are able to tap into their students' digital expertise for classroom instruction, they will be working toward closing the technology divide and thus will "ensure that all students benefit from learning in ways that allow them to participate fully in the public, community, and economic life" (NLG, 2000, p. 9). Our educational system and society benefit tremendously when Latino bilingual students are afforded opportunities to express and display their full intelligence, talent, and knowledge in their schools, communities, and, consequently, the future.

REFERENCES

Adams, C. (2009). Digital storytelling. *Instructor, 119*(3), 35.

Ancona, G. (1997). *Mayeros: A Yucatec Maya family*. New York, NY: Lothrop, Lee & Shepard Books.

Anda, D. (2012). *A day without sugar/Un día sin azúcar*. Houston, TX: Arte Público Press.

Brown, M. (2009). *Side by side: The story of Dolores Huerta and César Chávez/Lado a lado: La historia de Dolores Huerta y César Chávez*. New York, NY: HarperCollins.

Brown, M. (2011a). *Marisol McDonald doesn't match/Marisol McDonald no combina*. New York, NY: Lee & Low Books.

Brown, S. T. (2011b). *Enrique Esparza and the Battle of the Alamo*. Minneapolis, MN: Millbrook Press.

Carlson, L. M., & Hijuelos, O. (2005). *Red hot salsa: Bilingual poems of being young and Latino in the United States*. New York, NY: Henry Holt and Company.

———. (2013). *Cool salsa: Bilingual poems of growing up Latino in the United States*. New York, NY: Henry Holt and Company.

Coiro, J. K., Lankshear, M. C., & Leu, D. J. (Eds.) (2008). *Handbook of research on new literacies*. Mahwah, NJ: Lawrence Erlbaum Associates.

Ek, L. D., García, A. S., Garza, A. (2014). Latino children: Constructing identities, voices, linguistic, and cultural understandings. In E. R. Clark, B. B. Flores, & O. A. Vasquez (Eds.), *Generating transworld pedagogy: Reimagining La Clase Mágica* (129–42). Lanham, MD: Lexington Books.

Facer, K., & Furlong, R. (2001). Beyond the myth of the "cyberkid": Young people at the margins of the information revolution. *Journal of Youth Studies, 4*(4), 451–69.

Figueredo, D. H. (1999). *Un mundo nuevo*. New York, NY: Lee & Low Books.

Flores, B. B., Vásquez, O. A., & Clark, E. R. (2014). *Generating transworld pedagogy: Reimagining La Clase Mágica*. Lanham, MD: Lexington Books.

Flores, C. D. (2013). *Canta, rana, canta/Sing, froggie, sing*. Houston, TX: Piñata Books.

Galan, A. (2013). *¡Qué cosas dice mi abuela!/Things my grandmother says!* New York, NY: Scholastic.

Gallego, M. A., & Hollingsworth, S. (Eds.) (2000). *What counts as literacy? Challenging the school standard*. New York, NY: Teachers College Press.

García, O. (2009). *Bilingual education in the 21st century: A global perspective.* Malden, MA: Wiley-Blackwell.

Gonzáles Bertrand, D. (2011). *Adelita and the veggie cousins/Adelita y las primas verduritas.* Houston, TX: Arte Público Press.

González, B. R. (2014). *The boy made of lightning.* Retrieved from https://itunes .apple.com/us/book/the-boy-made-of-lightning/id693813095?mt=11.

Gunelius, S. What is a blog for beginning bloggers? Retrieved March 2015 from http://weblogs.about.com/od/startingablog/p/WhatIsABlog.htm.

Hagood, M. C., Leander, K. M., Luke, C., Mackey, M., & Nixon, H. (2003). Media and online literacy studies. *Reading Research Quarterly, 38*(3), 386–413.

Heath, S. B. (1983). *Ways with words: Language, life and work in communities and classrooms.* Cambridge: Cambridge University Press.

Holloway, S. L., & Valentine, G. (2003). *Cyberkids: Children in the information age.* London: Routledge Falmer.

Knobel, M., & Lankshear, C. (Eds.) (2007). *A new literacies sampler.* New York, NY: Peter Lang.

Lam, W. S. E., & Rosario-Ramos, E. (2009) Multilingual literacies in transnational digitally mediated contexts: An exploratory study of immigrant teens in the United States. *Language and Education, 23*(2), 171–90.

Lewis, C., & Fabos, B. (2005). Instant messaging, literacies, and social identities. *Reading Research Quarterly, 40*(4), 470–501.

Lewis, T. P. (1971). *Hill of fire.* New York, NY: HarperCollins.

Luke, A. (1994). *The social construction of literacy in the primary school.* Melbourne, Australia: Macmillan.

McCormack, C. M. (2009). *The fiesta dress: A quinceañera tale.* Tarrytown, NY: Two Lions.

Medina, J. (1999). *My name is Jorge: On both sides of the river. Poems in English and Spanish.* Honesdale, PA: Wordsong/Boyds Mills Press.

Moll, L. C., Sáez, R., & Dworin, J. (2001). Exploring biliteracy: Two student case examples of writing as social practice. *Elementary School Journal, 101*(4), 435–49.

Mulder, M. (2009). *After peaches.* Victoria, Canada: Orca Book Publishers.

Naidoo, J. C. (2011). Children's books to promote multiple literacies in classrooms and libraries. In J. C. Naidoo (Ed.), *Celebrating* cuentos*: Promoting Latino children's literature and literacy in classrooms and libraries.* Santa Barbara, CA: ABC-CLIO.

New London Group. (1996). A pedagogy of multiliteracies: Designing social futures. *Harvard Educational Review, 66*(1), 60–92.

———. (2000). A pedagogy of multiliteracies: Designing social futures. In B. Cope & M. Kalantzis (Eds.), *Multiliteracies: Literacy learning and the design of social futures* (pp. 9–38). London, UK: Routledge.

Palfrey, J., & Gasser, U. (2008). *Born digital: Understanding the first generation of digital natives.* New York, NY: Basic Books Group.

Pérez, A. I. (2007). *Nana's big surprise/Nana, ¡Qué sorpresa!.* New York, NY: Children's Book Press.

———. (2013). *My diary from here to there/Mi diario de aquí hasta allá.* New York, NY: Children's Book Press.

Prensky, M. (2001). Digital natives, digital immigrants. *On the horizon, 9*(5).

Reyes, I. (2006). Exploring connections between emergent biliteracy and bilingualism. *Journal of Early Childhood Literacy, 6*(3), 267–92.

Reyes, I., & Azuara, P. (2008). Emergent biliteracy in young Mexican immigrant children. *Reading Research Quarterly, 43*(4), 374–98.

Riojas-Cortez, M., Flores, B. B., Smith, H. L., & Clark, E. R. (2003). *Cuéntame un cuento* [Tell me a story]: Bridging family literacy traditions with school literacy. *Language Arts, 81*(1), 62–71.

Ruiz- Flores, L. (2012). *Alicia's fruity drinks/Las aguas frescas de Alicia.* Houston, TX: Arte Público Press.

Sánchez, C., Plata, V., Grosso, L., & Leird, B. (2010). Encouraging Spanish-speaking families' involvement through *dichos. Journal of Latinos and Education, 9*(3), 239–48.

Sánchez, P., & Salazar, M. (2012). Transnational computer use in urban Latino immigrant communities: Implications for schooling. *Urban Education, 47*(1), 90–16.

Shelby-Caffey, C., Úbéda, E., & Jenkins, B. (2014). Digital storytelling revisited. *Reading Teacher, 68*(3), 191–99. doi:10.1002/trtr.1273.

Skinner, E., & Hagood, M. C. (2008). Developing literate identities with English language learners through digital storytelling. *Reading Matrix, 8*(2). Retrieved May 15, 2015, from www.readingmatrix.com/articles/skinner_hagood/article.pdf.

Street, B. (2001). The new literacy studies. In E. Cushman, E. R. Kintgen, B. M. Kroll, & M. Rose (Eds.), *Literacy: A critical sourcebook* (pp. 430–42). Boston, MA: Bedford/St. Martin's.

Tafolla, C., & Tenayuca, S. (2008). *That's not fair! Emma Tenayuca's struggle for justice/¡No es justo! La lucha de Emma Tenayuca por la justicia.* San Antonio, TX: Wings Press.

Tonatiuh, D. (2013). *Pancho rabbit and the coyote: A migrant's tale.* New York, NY: Abrams Books for Young Readers.

———. (2014). *Separate is never equal: Sylvia Mendez and her family's fight for desegregation.* New York, NY: Abrams Books for Young Readers.

Vásquez, O. A., & Durán, R. (2000). La Clase Mágica and Club Proteo: Multiple literacies in new community institutions. In M. Gallego & S. Hollingsworth (Eds.), *What counts as literacy: Challenging the school standard* (pp. 173–89). New York, NY: Teachers College Press.

Verdugo, D. R., & Belmonte, I. A. (2007). Using digital stories to improve listening comprehension with Spanish young learners of English. *Language Learning & Technology, 11*(1), 87–101.

Villarreal, J. A. (1989). *Pocho* (3rd ed.). New York, NY: Anchor Books.

Yang, Y. T. C., & Wu, W. C. I. (2012). Digital storytelling for enhancing student academic achievement, critical thinking, and learning motivation: A year-long experimental study. *Computers & Education, 59*(2), 339–52.

Zentella, A. C. (1997). *Growing up bilingual: Puerto Rican children in New York.* Oxford, UK: Blackwell Publishers.

DISCUSSION QUESTIONS

1. How can children's home knowledge be transformed into literacies that are validated in the classroom and other settings?
2. What about this chapter challenges you to think about your own role as a teacher of bilingual learners or as a librarian who works with bilingual children?
3. We recommend that educators integrate technology into reading and language arts lessons. How are students using and accessing different types of technology at home? (You may want to initiate a dialogue with your students to learn about their interest in and ability to access different types of technology.)
4. Are you comfortable using the latest technology? Discuss with a colleague how you plan on balancing the time needed for teaching and for learning how to apply new technologies that support instruction.
5. In fostering the development of bilingual learners, what type of digital literacies do you foresee students using inside and outside their classrooms?
6. How can educators model the proper way to use technology for recent immigrants or newcomer students who may be lacking prior exposure to technology?
7. How can teachers and librarians involve parents and community members in the process of developing children's bilingualism and biliteracy?
8. In the event that some students' households may have an absence of printed texts (books, newspapers, magazines), how can educators, with the help of technology, integrate the children's and their family's stories into the curriculum?

ACTIVITIES

A. ThingLink: With ThingLink, students can annotate photographs or video with notes or embedded media links. Students can share ThingLink images in social media channels and blogs.
B. Comic Life: This application transforms story ideas into comic strips. Students can create a story using the script editor, add images or video, and use the application's tools to edit pictures or backgrounds.
C. Puppet Pals HD: With this application, students can pick out actors and backgrounds, drag them to the digital stage, and record movements and audio to play back. A variety of popular-culture characters or characters in personal photos can be downloaded and edited.

D. Animoto: Animoto is a cloud-based, video-creation service that produces videos from photos, video clips, and music.
E. VoiceThread: Students can use VoiceThread to connect and communicate with digital media (videos, presentation slides, images, documents). VoiceThread allows students to create discussions that engage participants at a level where standard, flat-text communication is limited.
F. GoAnimate: GoAnimate has video templates that students can use to make a video quickly and easily. GoAnimate can also be used to create personal e-cards.
G. Storybird: With this application students can create art-inspired picture books, stories, and poetry. Students can also read and comment on each other's work.
H. Explain Everything: A unique whiteboard and screen casting tool to import media, animate images, annotate videos, photographs, or documents, and record and play them.
I. Little Bird Tales: An application students can use to create reports, journals, creative writings, podcasts, commercials, history timelines, science experiments, drawings, and eBooks.

PROFESSIONAL READINGS

Black, R. W. (2007). Digital design: English language learners and reader reviews in online fiction. In M. Knobel & C. Lankshear (Eds.), *A new literacies sampler.* New York, NY: Peter Lang Publishing.

Lam, W. S. E. (2009). Multiliteracies on instant messaging in negotiating local, translocal, and transnational affiliations: A case of an adolescent immigrant. *Reading Research Quarterly, 44*(4), 377–97.

Machado-Casas, M., Sánchez, P., & Ek, L. D. (2014). The digital literacy practices of Latina/o immigrant parents in an afterschool technology partnership. *Multicultural Education Journal, 21*(3/4), 28–33.

Miller, L. Podcast: Lisa Miller on digital storytelling. Retrieved from www.sten house.com/html/lmillerpodcast.htm.

Naidoo, J. C. (Ed.). (2011). *Celebrating cuentos: Promoting Latino children's literature and literacy in classrooms and libraries.* Santa Barbara, CA: ABC-CLIO.

Prieto, L., Arreguin-Anderson, M., Yuen, T. T, Ek, L. D., Garcia, A., Machado-Casas, M., Sánchez, P. (2015). A sociocultural approach to mobile learning in La Clase Mágica, an afterschool technology club: Four case studies. *Proceedings of the International Mobile Learning Festival 2015: Mobile learning, MOOCs and 21st century learning,* May 22–23, 2015, Hong Kong.

Chapter Twelve

Latino Children's Literature in Picture Book Format

Miriam Martinez, Nancy L. Roser, Angie Zapata, and Erin Greeter

Yes, high-quality Latino children's literature is a roaring fire lighting people's path.

—Yuyi Morales (Naidoo, 2011, p. ix)

INTRODUCTION

For celebrated Latino children's picture book author/illustrator Yuyi Morales and others, picture books can reach through and beyond the boundaries of cultures and languages. Well-selected picture books deserve a central place in classrooms for their potential to engage children in aesthetic and literary reading (Rosenblatt, 1995) that fosters critical thinking, stretches visual understandings, and elicits cultural connections (Zapata, 2013).

Latino children's picture books are a literary form that speaks to cultural experiences through written and visual texts. By experiencing, connecting, inspecting, questioning, noticing, and naming details of the print and illustration together, children can explore the relationship between the two. As readers of Latino-specific literature, children can infer events in the story in English and/or Spanish, notice and interpret cultural motifs, or speculate on the meanings conveyed by the authors and illustrators in their use of aesthetic elements and literary bilingualism (Rudin, 1996).

In the slow but steady increase of fine Latino children's picture books found in libraries, classrooms, and homes, it is important for readers to understand the fullness of this literature's potential and promise as texts with literary and aesthetic appeal and cultural significance. This chapter aims to provide insights into the literary and aesthetic possibilities of Latino children's picture books by focusing on the unique features of these innovative texts.

THEORETICAL FRAMEWORK

Few researchers have explored the kinds of thinking that Latino children engage in as they read and respond to picture books reflecting their own culture and language. Martínez-Roldán and López-Robertson (2000) examined the responses of first-grade bilingual students who shared their thinking about Latino children's picture books during literature circles. The children's responses indicated they were: (1) making connections to life experiences, (2) looking at illustrations to validate their thinking, and (3) expressing opinions about issues of racial and language discrimination and gender inequity experienced by the characters. The researchers concluded that because the children were able to see their lives and language reflected in the picture books, they reached new understandings of text, of self and others, and of the world in which they lived.

Researchers have also found that when Latino children transact with picture books reflecting their worlds, they are able to draw on their own ways of knowing (Heath, 1983) and funds of knowledge (Moll & Greenberg, 1990) to construct meaning. Martínez-Roldán (2003) explored children's responses to Latino literature picture books in a bilingual second-grade classroom. Focusing closely on the role personal narratives played in one seven-year-old girl's participation in the literature circles, she found that the child often told personal stories connected to the lives, languages, and families represented in stories. It was through the sharing of her own stories that the child was able to construct meaning by drawing on personal experiences to mediate her understandings.

In a series of teacher researcher studies, López-Roberston (2004b; 2012a; 2012b) explored the mediational role personal storytelling plays in bilingual children's meaning-making. López-Roberston guided the children in *pláticas literarias* (literature discussions), helping them use their cultural traditions of storytelling to make connections with their lives and families and to events they had experienced either directly or indirectly. The children frequently shared their own stories as they worked to gain insight into characters' motivations, emotions, and experiences. In particular, López-Roberston found that the children were able to empathize with characters who faced challenging realities similar to their own experiences, including loss, separation from family, and experiences with the border patrol. The personal connections the children made led to a shared understanding of the issues raised by the books. These findings suggest that sharing personal stories serves young children as a means of engaging in meaningful discussions of Latino literature picture books.

Researchers have also found that young readers can inquire into and reflect on sociopolitical issues related to race, gender, language, and power in the presence of Latino children's picture books when those books present issues that are of relevance and concern to their own lives and communities. Expanding on her previous work in facilitating inquiry around Latino literature picture books, López-Robertson (2004a; 2010) investigated the critical talk and responses to text of second-grade bilingual students as they interpreted and questioned issues that were personally significant to them. The children in these studies demonstrated that they could think through sociopolitical messages alluded to in story worlds and in their own lives and take up critical and moral positions about what they would do in response to the injustices experienced by characters. Through discussion the children collaboratively reflected on the experiences of characters and drew conclusions about the possibilities for creating social change. These studies offer insight into the potential of Latino children's picture books as vehicles by which children can develop critical consciousness and nuanced understandings of relevant social issues.

Picture books about Latinos not only offer relevant content for children to explore, they also serve as pathways for understanding through all of their aesthetic features. Researchers have just begun to examine the potential of Latino children's picture books. For example, Zapata, Valdez-Gainer, and Haworth (2015) examined the multilingual and multimodal composition resources appropriated by third-grade students during a study of Latino children's picture books. In this teacher inquiry study, the researchers designed a five-week study centered on students' responses to the ways in which Latino authors and illustrators shape their texts. Carefully planned instruction and discussion enabled the students to develop an awareness of the visual and literary devices in Latino children's picture books that were later imported and remixed in the crafting of their own picture books. The findings revealed that deep involvement in the study of Latino children picture books as a literary genre and format positioned children to employ their Latino heritage assets as picture book makers.

These studies contribute to the small but growing body of research on children's responses to Latino representation in picture books. The findings suggest that Latino children's literature, in the context of teachers' thoughtful mediation, has the potential to evoke students' lives, languages, and everyday realities as resources for reading.

PRAXIS: APPLICATION OF THEORY

The Picture Book Format

Bringing high quality Latino children's picture books into the classroom or library promotes opportunities for children to create meaning and connect—both culturally and linguistically. To better understand the power of Latino children's picture books to evoke meaningful responses, we focus on the format itself—that is, the distinctive affordances of picture books that make them particularly powerful vehicles for eliciting children's thinking and responses. We introduce below some of the picture book features that help children inhabit the world of the story and become more aware of and more attuned to the multiple clues to the meanings of a text (in addition to words and illustrations). We then examine how these features support children's quests for meaning in culturally relevant picture books.

Affordances of the Picture Book Format

The picture book's distinctiveness is most often associated with its visual components and the "congruency" (Schwarcz, 1982, p. 15) between those visual components and the verbal text (Marantz, 1977; Schwarcz & Schwarcz, 1991). Sipe (2008) contends that the picture book is different from the illustrated text in that illustrations in a picture book are essential to making sense of the story. Rather than describing the relationship of words and pictures as a congruency, Sipe (1998b) suggests that text and illustrations relate synergistically, each contributing to a whole that is more complex than the effect of its components alone.

Even so, young readers and children learning a second language attend closely to illustration (rather than print) especially in unfamiliar picture books—viewing illustration as both pleasing and informing (Martínez-Roldán & Newcomer, 2011). The illustrations in well-crafted picture books that represent authentic cultural experiences of children serve not only to support understanding, but also to move readers into and through the story world.

Yuyi Morales's *Niño Wrestles the World* (Morales, 2013) is a Latino children's picture book that represents a playfully rendered, but culturally authentic, leisure time athletic competition. Animating the world of *lucha libre*, Mexican wrestling, the book's authentic and fluid use of English and Spanish, as well as distinctive picture book format, can support children's sense-making with stories. *Niño* is a "superhero" child who envisions himself as a *luchador*, a world-champion wrestling competitor. Arrayed in mask and cape, he conveys a bravado that children love to imagine and project as they take on and pulverize their own fearsome adversaries. Morales's text represents a complete and complex design in that nearly every element from front cover to back has been created to contribute to the storyline and story themes. The book invites,

> Come and play within a story world of hero and conquered—with you in the role of the luchador hero . . . and the conquered? Well, you as hero will both recognize your opponents, and triumph over them (because they are just too fun scary to win).

Peritext

The illustrators of picture books and their designers often make use of every component of the book to add meaning to the story, including the book's peritext. "Peritext" means "around" the text—with the prefix, "peri," from the Greek and meaning "surrounding" or "enclosing." In a picture book, anything besides the print can be labeled the peritext (Sipe, 1998a). This includes the covers (front and back), the endpapers, the copyright page, the title page, and any other features that lie outside the text but can be designed to contribute to the story. That is, these features (surrounding the text) can set the stage for the story, foreshadow the events, or allow for the story to begin prior to the first opening (or spread). Further, stories sometimes even conclude on the endpapers or back cover of a book.

Cover

The cover is the first peritextual feature that most young readers see (unless it is the book's spine). A century ago, most book covers could offer children only the choice of color and font to give clues to the story inside. But on the twenty-first-century front cover of *Niño Wrestles the World*, Yuyi Morales introduces Niño, the main character, prominently centered in a heroic stance, and wearing the bright red mask of a *luchador*. Behind Niño, the rays of a yellow spotlight brighten the page. The image of Niño is also framed by an arc of small, red stars shadowed in light blue and a textured orange banner highlighting his name in a large, bold font. The font used reflects a poster-art style that frequently announces community performances, circuses, and matches to convey the excitement. Above this announcement, the border reads, "Yuyi Morales presents!" proclaiming to the audience that the picture book maker is sharing an exhibition of talent. The back cover offers a closing salute—a final star-burst celebrating the hero as he performs his style of flying/tumbling maneuvers around the book's edges. The cover of this picture book clearly launches the story as an event, so much so that young reader Isaac, a fan of the book, asks his mother to "announce" his entrance as *luchador*, *El Tigre* [The Tiger].

Endpapers

Traditionally, endpapers have been the means by which the stitched "signatures" of pages are attached to the book's covers. Endpapers are as functional as a book's cover, and, like covers, they have offered another space for interpreting and foreshadowing (or even beginning) a story, or providing a visual epilogue at a story's end. *Niño's* endpapers feature an array of trading-card-style illustrations of the competitors within the book, including *Cabeza Olmeca* [Olmec Head] and *La Momia* [The Mummy] of Guanajuato. Each card features an image of Niño's competitors and intriguing "facts" (e.g., *La Momia* was "dug up from his tomb at Santa Paula cemetery; he has been chasing people since 1865"). The cards tantalize with hints of the challenges Niño is soon to face. On the final endpapers, the triumphant Niño has his own collector card as do his little sisters, Niño's final competitors who are "twice as terrible, double the diapers!" The text on the trader cards is in a decorative font to be sampled, inspected, or even overlooked by readers eager to get to the story's first page. But a teacher/librarian reader (or a second-time child reader) will note and slow for this display of dramatis personae, or pause at the closing endpapers for the final bow.

Title Page

Traditionally, the title page (even in a picture book) offered *only* the title and the names of the author and illustrator. The title page might also include the publisher's name and location. Sometimes, even teachers/librarians reading aloud can overlook the title page, often not realizing its full potential as part of the larger narrative. Reading through a book's title page can convey to children that books are created objects and full of conscious decisions. More and more, illustrators and book designers have begun to make use of the title page as an additional space to preview the events to come. Title pages can also function to establish an opening shot (the setting) or launch the story. In *Niño*, the title page is filled with puffy clouds, a bright blue sky, and a stylized sun; bursts of bold color announce *lucha* moves and classes of competition (e.g., *Máscara vs. Cabellera*). Niño is no longer central in the image. Rather, the page cannot contain his energy. Only his mask and uplifted eyes are visible on the full spread bleed, as Niño gazes at his name written in a large, circus-style font. The hero appears to revel in the contest to come.

Copyright Page

A typical copyright page offers an array of publication information including the classification of the text, its unique number among books (its ISBN), its edition and printing, and sometimes a brief précis and mention of the illustrator's media choices. The copyright page in *Niño* appears immediately following the final page of text. Here the page serves two additional purposes: to present an author's note with additional information about *lucha libre*, and to offer a visual epilogue. Through an illustration of Niño giving his tiny sisters (and final opponents) a scooter ride, the story of imaginative role play continues and leaves readers to infer the matches that will follow. Spotlight beams and stars still attend the hero: his is an ideal world of play.

Page Turns

Caldecott-winning illustrator Eric Rohmann (2012) tells his audiences about the careful attention creators of picture books must give to deciding on the placement of page turns in each story. The critical nature of the page turn, as the breaks in the text that allow for rising action and tension, serve to advance or to slow the story. Rohmann also describes the tension between text and illustration, noting that while an illustration begs the reader to slow and examine details, the text pulls the readers forward. Others have described this push-pull as the "drama of the turning page" (Bader, 1976, p. 1), the building and release of tension. In *Niño Wrestles the World*, Morales propels the reader through the use of such authoring and design elements as ellipses (signaling that the action continues); the use of an off-stage voice rendered in a speech balloon—the speaker (perhaps) to be revealed with a page turn; and "breaking the fourth wall"—that is, indicating the narrator's awareness of a reader. Morales's narration addresses the reader directly, asking, "What's a *niño* to do?" The implicit assumption is that the question may be answered if the reader turns the page. Further, there is the forward motion of the illustration itself when action moves up and across the spread. One such instance of forward motion can be found on the page that shows Niño's scooter almost exiting the recto (right-hand side) of the spread. Finally, there is the frozen moment of "Oh, no," a plot point at which Niño knows more than the reader. Something is amiss, he alerts them, using exclamation and gesture (twelfth opening), and may only be resolved by a page turn.

Design Elements

Illustrators use a variety of design elements with the potential to engage the reader in the story world, and invite him or her to make deeper sense of things. These elements include color choice and shifts in color, as well as font choices and purposeful changes in font. In Latino children's picture books, the diverse aspects of the visual displays can intersect to convey Latino-specific experiences.

Color   Color is a particularly expressive visual element (Itten, 1974) and is used by illustrators in a variety of ways, such as for establishing mood and conveying character emotions and personality traits (Kiefer, 1995; Moebius, 1986; Nodelman, 1988). Color has different meaning across cultures, but it is often interpreted similarly by members of a given community. Latino illustrators bring memories of colors to life in their stories as an expression of their heritage. Morales's story is filled with holly reds, canary greens, hot pinks, turquoise blues, and electric purples—brilliant and lively colors reminiscent of traditional Mexican folk art, or *artesanía*, as interpreted in Morales's other picture books.

Color Shifts   Illustrators also use *shifts* in color to develop stories in various ways. For example, they can signal emotional changes, character revelation, a sudden turn of events, or even movement from reality into an imagined world. An important change occurs in *Niño Wrestles the World* when Niño changes from dealing with his imagined opponents to meeting his real-world challenges, *las hermanitas* [the little sisters]. When the sisters awaken from their nap and look for their brother, Niño's imagined world shifts from an all-white background to a background suffused with multiple tones of pink, still ablaze in spotlights. The background color-shift may signal that one kind of play has come to an end and another is about to begin. Soon Niño is wrestling with the newest *rudas* ["tough guys"]—*las hermanitas*.

Font Choices and Shifts   In the picture book format, font choices and shifts typically play a far greater role in signaling meanings than in chapter books. For example, the comic book style of sound words blast from the pages of *Niño Wrestles the World*. It could be that Morales uses brightly colored fonts to help readers interpret sounds and emotions. Hand-lettered text gives voice to the grunts, groans, and laughter of the *luchadores*, while speech balloons in English and Spanish are rendered in selected fonts for different characters. Further, Morales's lively story is enhanced through fonts that do not adhere to horizontal lines; for example, the ticks and tocks surround the clock as Niño's speech follows the movement of a character in action.

In effect, through her masterful use of visual elements and cultural referents, Morales reveals the energy and vibrancy of a young Mexican American boy's imaginative world. It is not surprising that in the story, the four-year-old reader Joaquín readily steps into Niño's story world and announces during his play, "I'm the new *cabeza*. The new *cabeza olmeca* has laser eyes." Together, the varied font designs, visuals, and cultural references work to advance and bring Niño's energy to life.

Culturally Specific Language and Culturally Relevant Content

In the previous section, we explored tools and devices used by illustrators in the creation of culturally authentic picture books—those that portray worlds that many Latino children recognize as their own. Cultural authenticity can also be reflected in the linguistic diversity and content of picture books, and it can contribute to powerful portrayals of strong bilingual characters, landscapes, and themes (Fox & Short, 2009).

Language

Language is an integral part of identity, and the inclusion of Spanish in picture books can achieve cultural specificity when done artfully. Authors and illustrators of Latino children's picture books often infuse Spanish throughout the narrative in order to establish intimacy between family members in a scene or to establish and develop a character's history. Monica Brown (2013) does this in her Pura Belpré Award–winning book *Tito Puente: Mambo King/Rey del Mambo*. This picture book explores the contributions of Puerto Rican musician Tito Puente to the Latino jazz explosion. All textual elements appear in both English and Spanish, including the text of the story as well as the author note at the end of the book. Author/illustrator Carmen Lomas Garza's *Family Picture: Cuadros de familia* (1990) and *In My Family: En mi familia* (1996) feature double-page spreads that offer paintings on the recto depicting memories of Garza's childhood in Kingsville, Texas. The scenes represent everyday memories (e.g., a scene of her grandfather cleaning *nopalitos* (cactus), a family gathering to make *empanadas* (turnovers), as well as memories of special occasions (e.g., a birthday barbecue complete with a *piñata*, a trip to the *feria* [fair]). The text appears on the verso of the double-page spread in both English and Spanish. Some authors of Latino children's picture books also write fluidly in both languages instead of presenting them as separate texts. These authors write primarily in English and selectively infuse Spanish words and phrases throughout their texts. Authors sometimes introduce a word or phrase in Spanish and immediately follow it with an English translation, as Pat Mora does in *A Birthday Basket for Tía* (1992): "Today is special day. Today is my great-aunt's ninetieth birthday. . . . Ninety years old. *¡Noventa años!*" Others, like Pam Muñoz Ryan, introduce Spanish words and phrases in italics but do not translate them. In her picture book titled *Mice and Beans* (2001), Ryan surrounds her selective use of Spanish with English to provide such a rich verbal context that translation would likely be unnecessary, even for a monolingual English reader.

Thursday, Rosa María simmered the beans. She searched for her favorite wooden spoon, the one she always used to cook *frijoles*, but she couldn't find it.

"*No importa*," she said. "The beans will taste just as good if I use another spoon."

Still other books include Spanish without translation but provide a pictorial context that visually depicts the meaning of the words. In the award-winning concept book *Green Is a Chile Pepper: A Book of Colors* (2014), author Roseanne Greenfield Thong uses the Spanish word "*platos*" in the verse she creates for the color orange:

> Orange are the marigolds
> On Day of the Dead.
> Orange are the *platos*
> For special bread.

John Parra's accompanying illustration depicts family members presenting *pan de muertos* [Day of the Dead bread] carried on orange plates to a cart filled with *calaveras* [skeletons] playing musical instruments. The presence and integration of Spanish in bilingual picture books sends the message that children's language and cultural practices are valued.

Content

High quality Latino children's picture books present content with which Latino children can connect, which in turn creates a basis for children's meaning-making. This content is conveyed through both the visual and verbal texts of picture books. The content of some books depicts the everyday worlds of Latino children, and children readily step into these worlds. Others address broader experiences and sociopolitical issues often encountered by Latino families.

Picture Books Depicting the Worlds of Children

Many picture books about Latinos capture the nuances of daily life accurately, reflecting "attitudes, values and beliefs of members of the group portrayed" (Temple, Martinez, & Yokota, 2015, p. 91). Books that feature the everyday worlds of Latino children allow them to see themselves in books as well as important elements of their culture. In *Dear Primo: A Letter to My Cousin* (Tonatiuh, 2010), two cousins—one living in Mexico and one in the U.S.—exchange a series of letters. Through text and illustrations, readers come to understand the ways in which the lives of the boys converge (and diverge). Both boys love sports, but one plays soccer and the other plays basketball. Both enjoy various games (beyond sports), but the cousin in Mexico plays with *trompos* [tops] and *canicas* [marbles] while the cousin in the U.S.

plays jump rope and video games. Illustrations in the style of the Mixtecs add cultural details about life in both countries.

In *What Can You Do with a Paleta?* (2009), author Carmen Tafolla invites the reader into a barrio where the *paleta* [popsicle] wagon with its "tinkly bell" and "treasure of icy *paletas*" entices children. In response to the question posed by the book's title, the author proposes a myriad of possibilities for using a *paleta*. Tafolla creates an equally memorable world in *What Can You Do with a Rebozo?* (2008) as characters drape a *rebozo* over chairs to create a secret tunnel and turn a *rebozo* into the cape of a superhero. Details of this nature not only add texture to the story but also make the story more authentic and, hence, more believable.

Picture Books That Explore Issues

Rather than depicting the daily lives of Latino children, some picture books address significant contemporary and historical issues. *Pancho Rabbit and the Coyote: A Migrant's Tale* (Tonatiuh, 2013) is an animal fantasy that explores the exploitation that Central American and Mexican migrants often face as they seek safe passage to the U.S. While Tonatiuh's story explores the individual cost of such exploitation, the author's note at the back of the book delves deeper into some of the complicated issues surrounding immigration— why individuals leave their homelands, the contributions of immigrants to the economy of the U.S., and the need for comprehensive immigration reform.

¡Sí, se puede!/Yes, We Can! (Cohn, 2005), a bilingual picture book set against the 2000 janitors' strike in Los Angeles, tells the story of Carlitos, whose mother joins in the strike in an effort to ensure that she and other janitors earn a living wage. Wanting to support his mother's efforts, Carlos and his classmates join the strike with Carlitos, carrying a sign that reads, "I love my Mama. She is a janitor!" This Jane Addams Peace Award book has the potential to spark important conversations about issues of social justice and ways that children may become engaged in efforts to bring about social change (see chapters 4, 8, and 13 for further discussion).

Picture Books Are Not Limited to Fiction

There is also nonfiction that addresses the experiences of Latinos. *Separate Is Never Equal* (Tonatiuh, 2014) is one such work in picture book format. Tonatiuh's book focuses on a historical fight for school desegregation that culminated seven years before the Brown vs. the Board of Education ruling in which the U.S. Supreme Court declared separate educational facilities to be unconstitutional. *Separate Is Never Equal* documents the experiences of Sylvia Mendez and her family in their fight for the desegregation of California schools in 1944.

Sylvia and her brothers, U.S. citizens fluent in English, were denied enrollment in a school in Westminster, California, because they were Latinos. In response, Sylvia's father launched a long and hard-fought battle that culminated in a law that said "all children in California were allowed to go to school together, regardless of race, ethnicity, or language." Picture books such as this one can be vehicles through which all children, not just those of Latino heritage, can learn about a history that too often is omitted from the textbooks used in schools.

Picture book biographies also offer opportunities for exploring the cultural, social, and political contributions of Latinos. Excellent picture book biographies make cultural icons like Péle, Gabriel García Márquez, Diego Rivera, and Frida Kahlo relevant to new generations. In crafting *Viva Frida* (2014), a 2015 Caldecott Honor book, Yuyi Morales combined mixed-media artwork and simple two- and three-word sentences in English and Spanish to capture the vision and creative process of Frida Kahlo. In *Tomás and the Library Lady* (2000), Pat Mora tells of a summer in the childhood of Tomás Rivera, the man who grew up to be chancellor of the University of California at Riverside. While Tomás's parents worked in the fields of Iowa, a librarian took Tomás under her wing, sharing the world of children's books with this son of migrant workers and igniting what was to become Rivera's driving passion for learning and education.

There are also picture book biographies that tell compelling stories of Latino activists who worked to address social injustices in their communities. In *Side by Side/Lado a lado* (2010), Monica Brown features the experiences of two well-known activists, César Chávez and Dolores Huerta, who worked for the rights of Latino farm workers in California. Also, in *That's Not Fair!/¡No es justo!* (2008), Carmen Tafolla and Sharyll Tenayuca tell the story of Emma Tenayuca, an earlier and less-well-known Mexican American activist who organized workers in the 1930s to fight against low wages and unfair working conditions in pecan-shelling factories in San Antonio, Texas. Through biographies such as these, children gain a deeper understanding of the important contributions Latinos have made in the fight for social justice, and in turn children may come to realize that they too can make a difference in the world.

CONCLUSION

Ensuring that we get picture books about Latinos into the hands of children is essential. Books reflecting everyday Latino lives and languages can serve as mirrors for young Latino readers and windows for readers seeking to experience worlds different from their own. Because picture books have both visual and verbal text, the format has particular potential to animate cultural landscapes more fully. Research has shown us that when children read and discuss fiction connected to their own experiences, they more readily enter into story worlds, connect with characters and problems found in those story worlds, and reflect more deeply on the themes and messages shaping narratives. Similarly, nonfiction that explores topics and issues relevant to Latino children's experiences has the potential to motivate children's wide reading, foster critical thinking, and grow insights into histories that may be different from their own.

The values of Latino children's picture books are undeniable. Yet far too few picture books about Latinos are available. The Cooperative Children's Book Center (CCBC) has tracked diversity in children's books for twenty-five years (2014). For most of that time, books by and about people of color for young readers have been too few in number (see chapter 1). Recently the CCBC has found promising changes—at least for books by and about African Americans and Asian/Pacific Americans. Even so, the number of Latino books for children published each year has plateaued (Gilmore, 2015). The call put forth by the grassroots movement We Need Diverse Books (Flood, 2014), Walter Dean Myers (2014) and his son Christopher Meyers (2014), and Pat Mora (*Día de los niños/Día de los libros*) and similar initiatives must be heeded by publishers, educators, parents, and all who read with children to ensure that picture books about Latinos are placed in the hands of children.

REFERENCES

Bader, B. (1976). *American picture books: From Noah's ark to the beast within.* New York, NY: Macmillan.

Brown, M., & Cepeda, J. (2010). *Side by side/Lado a lado: The story of Dolores Huerta and César Chávez/La historia de Dolores Huerta y César Chávez.* New York, NY: Rayo/HarperCollins.

Brown, M., & López, R. (2013). *Tito Puente: Mambo king/Rey del mambo.* New York, NY: Rayo/HarperCollins.

Cohn, D., & Delgado, F. (2005). *¡Sí, se puede!/Yes, we can!* El Paso, TX: Cinco Puntos Press.

Cooperative Children's Book Center in Wisconsin. (2014). Retrieved from https://ccbc.education.wisc.edu/.

Flood, A. (2014, May 1). "We need more diverse books": Calls for more representative writing for children. *Guardian.* Retrieved from www.theguardian.com/books/2014/may/01/we-need-diverse-books-campaign-children.

Fox, D. L., & Short, K. G. (2009). Exploring the "critical" in critical content analysis of children's literature. In K. M. Leander, D. W. Rowe, D. K. Dickinson, M. K. Hundley, R. T. Jiminez, & V. J. Risko (Eds.), *58th Yearbook of the National Reading Conference* (pp. 129–43). Oak Creek, WI: NRC.

Garza, C. L. (1990). *Family pictures: Cuadros de familia.* San Francisco, CA: Children's Book Press/Libros Para Niños.

———. (1996). *In my family/En mi familia.* San Francisco, CA: Children's Book Press/Libros Para Niños.

Gilmore, N. (2015). CCBC stats show children's books shifting toward diversity. *Publishers Weekly.* Retrieved May 27, 2015, from www.publishersweekly .com/pw/by-topic/childrens/childrens-industry-news/article/65628-ccbc-stats -show-children-s-books-shifting-toward-diversity.html?utm_source=Publishers +Weekly&utm_campaign=3fe1bfc9e6-UA-15906914-1&utm_medium=email &utm_term=0_0bb2959cbb-3fe1bfc9e6-304534865.

Heath, S. B. (1983). *Ways with words: Language, life, and work in communities and classrooms.* Cambridge: Cambridge University Press.

Huerta, M. E. S., Gainer, J., Battle, J., & Morales, Y. (2010). Profiles and perspectives: Finding voice, defining self, an interview with Yuyi Morales. *Language Arts, 87*(4), 296–307.

Itten, J. (1974). *The art of color: The subjective experience and the objective rationale of color.* New York: NY: Wiley.

Kiefer, B. Z. (1995). *The potential of picturebooks: From visual literacy to aesthetic understanding.* Englewood Cliff, NJ: Merrill.

López-Robertson, J. (2004a). Crossing consciousness: A literature discussion exploring *Friends from the Other Side. Colombian Applied Linguistics, 6,* 58–76.

———. (2004b). Making sense of literature through story: Young Latinas using stories as meaning-making devices during literature discussions. Unpublished dissertation. University of Arizona.

———. (2010). "Lo agarraron y lo echaron pa'tras": Discussing critical social issues with young Latinas/Discutiendo críticas y temas sociales con niñas Latinas. *Colombian Applied Linguistics Journal, 12*(2), 43–54.

———. (2012a). "Esta página me recordó": Young Latinas using personal life stories as tools for meaning-making. *Journal of the National Association for Bilingual Education, 35*(2), 217–33.

———. (2012b). "Oigan, tengo un cuento": Crossing "la frontera" of life and books. *Language Arts, 90*(1), 30–43.

Marantz, K. (1977). The picturebook as art object: A call for balanced reviewing. *Wilson Library Bulletin, 52*(2), 148–51.

Martínez-Roldán, C. M. (2003). Building worlds and identities: A case study of the role of narratives in bilingual literature discussions. *Research in the Teaching of English, 37,* 491–526.

Martínez-Roldán, C. M., & López-Robertson, J. (2000). Initiating literature circles in a first-grade bilingual classroom. *Reading Teacher, 53,* 270–81.

Martínez-Roldán, C. M., & Newcomer, S. (2011). Reading between the pictures: Immigrant students' interpretations of "The arrival." *Language Arts,* 188–97.

Moebius, W. (1986). Introduction to picture book codes. *Word and Image, 2,* 141–51.

Moll, L. C., & Greenberg, J. B. (1990). Creating zones of possibilities: Combining social contexts for instruction. In L. C. Moll (Ed.), *Vygotsky and education: Instruc-*

tional implications and applications of sociohistorical psychology (pp. 319–48). New York, NY: Cambridge University Press.

Mora, P. (1997). *Tomás and the library lady.* (R. Colón, Illus.). New York, NY: Knopf.

Mora, P., & Lang, C. (1992). *A birthday basket for Tía.* New York, NY: Macmillan.

Morales, Y. (2013). *Niño wrestles the world.* New York, NY: Roaring Brook Press.

Morales, Y., & O'Meara, T. (2014). *Viva Frida.* New York, NY: Roaring Brook Press.

Myers, C. (2014, March 16). The apartheid of children's literature. *New York Times,* p. SR1.

Myers, W. D. (2014, March 16). Where are the people of color in children's picture-books? *New York Times,* p. SR1.

Naidoo, J. C. (2011). Celebrating *cuentos:* Promoting Latino children's literature and literacy in classrooms and libraries. Santa Barbara, CA: Greenwood Publishing Group.

Nodelman, P. (1988). *Words about pictures: The narrative art of children's picture books.* Athens, GA: University of Georgia Press.

Rohmann, E. (2012). "Crafting the Art for *Oh, No!*" Presentation at the University of Texas at San Antonio, San Antonio, TX, December 5, 2012.

Rosenblatt, L. M. (1995). *Literature as exploration* (5th ed.). New York, NY: Modern Language Association of America.

Rudin, E. (1996). *Tender accents of sound: Spanish in the Chicano novel in English.* Tempe, AZ: Bilingual Press.

Ryan, P. M., & Cepeda, J. (2001). *Mice and beans.* New York, NY: Scholastic.

Schwarcz, J. H. (1982). *Ways of the illustrator: Visual communication in children's literature.* Chicago, IL: American Library Association.

Schwarcz, J., & Schwarcz, C. (1991). *The picture book comes of age.* Chicago, IL: American Library Association.

Sipe, L. R. (1998a). Learning the language of picture books. *Journal of Children's Literature, 24*(2), 66–75.

———. (1998b). How picture books work: A semiotically framed theory of picture-text relationships. *Children's Literature in Education, 29,* 97–108.

———. (2008). Learning from illustrations in picturebooks. In N. Frey & D. Fisher (Eds.), *Teaching visual literacy: Using comic books, graphic novels, anime, cartoons, and more to develop comprehension and thinking skills* (pp. 131–48). Thousand Oaks, CA: Corwin Press.

Tafolla, C., & Cordova, A. (2008). *What can you do with a rebozo?* Berkeley, CA: Tricycle Press.

Tafolla, C., & Morales, M. (2009). *What can you do with a paleta?* Berkeley, CA: Tricycle Press.

Tafolla, C., Tenayuca, S., & Ybáñez, T. (2008). *That's not fair! Emma Tenayuca's struggle for justice/¡No es justo! La lucha de Emma Tenayuca por la justicia.* San Antonio, TX: Wings Press.

Temple, C., Martinez, M., & Yokota, J. (2015). *Children's books in children's hands* (5th ed.). Boston, MA: Pearson.

Thong, R. G., & Parra, J. (2014). *Green is a chile pepper: A book of colors.* San Francisco, CA: Chronicle Books.

Tonatiuh, D. (2010). *Dear primo: A letter to my cousin.* New York, NY: Abrams Books for Young Readers.

———. (2013). *Pancho rabbit and the coyote: A migrant's tale.* New York, NY: Abrams Books for Young Readers.

———. (2014). *Separate is never equal.* New York, NY: Abrams Books for Young Readers.

Zapata, A. (2013). Examining the multimodal and multilingual composition resources of young Latino picturebook makers. In P. J. Dunstan, L. B. Gambrell, S. K. Fullerton, V. R. Gillis, K. Headley, & P. M. Stecker (Eds.), *62nd Yearbook of the Literacy Research Association* (pp. 76–93). Alamonte Springs, FL: Literary Research Association.

Zapata, A., Valdez-Gainer, N., & Haworth, C. (2015). Enacting multilingual and multimodal composition: Making bilingual picturebooks in the elementary classroom. *Language Arts Journal, 92*(5), 343–58.

DISCUSSION QUESTIONS

1. How is the Latino children's picture book a unique format?
2. When reading Latino children's picture books, what aspects of the visual and written displays can be folded into the narrative?
3. How do authors' and illustrators' use of English and Spanish advance the narrative? Develop characters? Establish a setting?
4. In what ways can color and shifts in font enhance picture books?
5. What other features/content/genres not discussed in this chapter do you notice in Latino children's picture books? Traditional tales? Bilingual poetry?
6. What kinds of sociopolitical messages and themes can be explored in Latino children's picture books?

ACTIVITIES

A. Bilingual picture book study: Identify and share Latino literature picture books such as *Niño Wrestles the World* that use this format to its fullest potential as ideal touchstone texts to invite explorations of how image and print can function together to tell a story. Focus children's attention on the ways illustrations and written language come together to tell a culturally specific story that can make for rich and critical conversations and support students' understandings of ways their own and others' lives and languages can be portrayed visually and in print.

B. Author and illustrator study: Invite children to learn about the motivations and histories of Latino picture book authors and illustrators. This can excite children to uncover the ways these artists fold who they are into their stories, literary and aesthetic styles, and characters. Often sociopolitical activism and a deep desire to make hidden histories accessible to all motivate Latino picture book makers to publish their books. Uncovering these motivations and styles with children can help children uncover their ways of "doing and being" a picture book maker in order to perform their own lives, languages, and passions.

C. Language study: As our classrooms become increasingly multilingual, time dedicated to appreciating and understanding different ways with words becomes more and more important. Reading and responding to picture books that reflect fluid language use as artful and purposeful can open children to the linguistic difference in their own and others' lives as resources for writing. Sharing these books can be guided by questions such as, How do the authors write with different languages? What does using more than one language do for the story?

D. Biography study: Many fine Latino children picture books are focused on the lives and contributions of both well-known and unfamiliar figures in Latino history. Thoughtful integration of Latino biographies in picture book format can be enacted across diverse units of study in the classroom. Historical inquiries and learning about inventors and artists are occasions to integrate Latino biography—beyond Hispanic heritage month.

PROFESSIONAL READINGS

Bang, M. (2000). *Picture this: How pictures work.* San Francisco, CA: Chronicle Books.

Chappell, S., & Faltis, C. (2007). Spanglish, bilingualism, culture and identity in Latino children's literature. *Children's Literature in Education, 38*(4), 253–62.

DeNicolo, C. P., & Franquiz, M. E. (2006). "Do I have to say it?": Critical Encounters with Multicultural Children's Literature. *Language Arts, 84*(2), 157–70.

Feathers, K. M., & Arya, P. (2012). The role of illustrations during children's reading. *Journal of Children's Literature, 38*(1), 36–43.

Fox, D. L., & Short, K. G. (2003). *Stories matter: The complexity of cultural authenticity in children's literature.* Urbana, IL: National Council of Teachers of English.

Johnson, D. (2009). ¡Léanos en español, por favor! Bilingual children's literature as a bridge to another language and culture. *Journal of Children's Literature, 35*(2), 42–49.

Madura, S. (1995). The line and texture of aesthetic response: Primary children study authors and illustrators. *The Reading Teacher, 49*(2), 110–18.

Naidoo, J. C. (2011). *Celebrating cuentos: Promoting Latino children's literature and literacy in classrooms and libraries.* Santa Barbara, CA: Libraries Unlimited.

Nathenson-Mejía, S., & Escamilla, K. (2003). Connecting with Latino children: Bridging cultural gaps with children's literature. *Bilingual Research Journal, 27*(1), 101–16.

Parsons, L. T. (2006). Visualizing worlds from words on a page. *Language Arts, 83*(6), 492–500.

Sipe, L. R. (2001). Picturebooks as aesthetic objects. *Literacy Teaching and Learning, 6*(1), 23–42.

Soto Huerta, M. E., Gainer, J., & Battle, J. (2010). Finding voice, defining self: An interview with Yuyi Morales. *Language Arts, 87*(4), 296–307.

Zapata, A., Valdez-Gainer, N., & Haworth, C. (2015). Enacting multilingual and multimodal composition: Making bilingual picturebooks in the elementary classroom. *Language Arts Journal, 92*(5), 343–58.

Chapter Thirteen

Técnica Con/Safos: Visual Iconography in Latino Picture Books as a Tool for Cultural Affirmation

Lettycia Terrones

INTRODUCTION

An examination of the visual elements in picture books becomes essential to understanding how the overall narrative experience of the story works. In discussing the uniqueness of the picture book as an art form, celebrated children's book author and illustrator David Wiesner (2012) calls attention to how the visual language of the picture book ushers the child into the world of the story through "a visual language that is rich and multileveled, sophisticated in its workings despite its often deceptively simple appearance" (n.p.). The quality of picture books is measured against how well the written and visual elements work together to create a unified story, or "aesthetic whole" (Horning, 1997, p. 90). Because the visual elements in picture books complement the textual narrative, it becomes important to evaluate how images are presented and how they interplay with the text, and to question the intentionality of the artistic choice behind the image (see chapter 12). This exercise is of particular importance in evaluating cultural relevance in picture books that aim to mirror the real-world experiences of children of color and affirm to them a sense of self-worth and value. Rudine Sims Bishop (2003) reminds us how the transmission of cultural values and morals, and the healing aspects of storytelling, can occur through children's literature that is representative of children of color. She writes, "When a group has been marginalized and oppressed, the cultural functions of story can take on even greater significance because storytelling can be seen as a means to counter the effects of that marginalization and oppression on children" (Bishop, 2003, p.

25). Similarly, Alma Flor Ada (2003) notes the transformative power Latino children's literature can have in influencing a child's understanding for moral decision-making by providing examples for how to deal with "life situations" (p. 10). The issue is the disparity of Latino children's literature available for young readers to provide these life representations and also the type of visual images chosen to carry out and complete a unified narrative message that can impart to a child the ability to make sense of his or her world.

This chapter is interested in exploring how the visual language specific to the Latino experience as articulated in picture books, and how specific Chicano art aesthetics and iconography in picture books serve to affirm messages of inclusivity and social equity, and to in turn cultivate self-efficacy and beliefs of cultural/self-worth among children. The chapter explores the following questions: (1) How do specific cultural/visual tropes in picture books work alongside textual narratives to mirror real-world experiences and representation of Latino children as navigators and social brokers? (2) How do picture book illustrators intentionally employ Chicano art aesthetics as visual language tools to affirm messages of cultural wealth found in the narrative? (3) How do opportunities for critical literacy practices open up in reading Latino picture books with an eye toward addressing the visual messages of cultural wealth imparted by Chicano art iconography? A content analysis of contemporary Latino picture books will offer approaches to these questions.

Before delving into the questions shaping this chapter, a note on the term "Chicano" is needed in order to both establish the scope/criteria for selecting the picture book sample, and also to emphasize the social justice imperative underlying the intent of this chapter. As educators, we are reminded that the pedagogical act/performance is not a neutral one. In fact, how we choose to teach is reflective of our pedagogical ethic (Freire, 2000; Hooks, 1994). In constructing democratic multicultural classrooms, critical pedagogy challenges us to create teaching spaces "where everyone feels a responsibility to contribute" (Hooks, 1994, p. 39). The potential for this space is possible if we "teach in a manner that respects and cares for the souls of our students" (Hooks, 1994, p. 13). Thus, the following discussion of the term "Chicano" and how this term speaks to the picture book selected for content analysis is informed by Hook's pedagogical imperative.

THEORETICAL FRAMEWORKS

A Definition of Chicano Art Aesthetics

The word "Chicano" became a term of empowerment emerging from the Chicano civil rights movement of the 1960s. Among its social justice demands were an end to discrimination and exploitation. The movement inspired the rise of Mexican American youth activism that challenged racist institutional structures and demanded equality in education. The term "Chicano," formerly a pejorative racial slur used against Mexican Americans, became reappropriated as a term of cultural empowerment and politicized ethnic identity. Several scholarly works on Chicano art articulate the organic connection between the Chicano art production and the political/social protest crucible from which it emerged (Chavoya & González, 2011; González, Fox, & Noriega, 2008; Griswold del Castillo, McKenna, & Yarbro-Bejarano, 1991; Jackson, 2009; Keller, 2002; Pérez, 2007; Vargas, 2010). Furthermore, the term "Chicano," and in turn Chicano art production, extends beyond strict notions of racial and national identity as having roots in Mexico. In his work *Chicana and Chicano Art: ProtestArte*, Carlos Francisco Jackson (2009) articulates this point while providing a framework for the elements at play in Chicano art aesthetics:

> To identify a community or its artistic and cultural production as Chicano solely because it is connected to the Mexican American experience is problematic because the Mexican American community in the United States is composed of a complex *mestizaje*, or racial and cultural mixture. . . . Defining Chicano cultural production instead on the basis of how the activity of art making relates to the ideas of the Chicano movement, "equality, self-determination, human rights, and social justice," offers the potential to transcend the negative ideas that have often perpetuated social inequality and injustice. . . . Through Chicano art we see the experience of those people most often invisible in society—the poor and disposed—highlighted and venerated. We see women breaking down a historically oppressive patriarchal culture, we see farmworkers and service workers celebrated as heroes, and we see examples of family unity and solidarity with international social movements. Chicano art also provides the best representation of the physical and metaphorical experience of living on the border. (pp. 2–3)

Thus, the term "Chicano," and in this treatment, the art production of "Chicanos," is charged with the same imperatives that lay at the heart of critical pedagogy and the practices of critical literacy via storytelling that affirms cultural wealth and efficacy. I have decided to use a Chicano cultural lens to review the textual and visual narratives of the pictures books selected for this chapter. The affinity between the elements of a social-justice-oriented Chicano art aesthetics and the principles of transformative education serve as a framework for teaching multicultural literature, and in particular Latino children's literature (Ada, 2003). The content analysis of Latino picture books will draw connections between the Chicano art aesthetics present in picture books and how the messages they impart via their image-making help "students understand their role as members of communities—their family, their classrooms, their school, their neighborhood—[thereby increasing] their sense of belonging . . . and share in the liberating experience of being able to construct a better world" (Ada, 2003, p. 6). The content analysis of picture books to follow will list specific artistic tropes at the heart of Chicano art aesthetics, providing a lens to analyze how visual narratives affirm and sing the beauty of what it means and what it looks like to be Chicano. The terms "Mexican American" and "Latino" do not necessarily evoke the social justice origins and imperatives that the term "Chicano" connotes (see chapters 1 and 3).

Community Cultural Wealth

Studies of the stereotyped images of Mexican Americans in picture books abound (Barrera & Garza de Cortés, 1997; Chappell & Faltis, 2007; Naidoo, 2010; Nilsson, 2005). Naidoo's survey of the literature on the representations of Latino cultures in children's picture books notes the stereotypical categories typically befalling picture books, where "four themes are observable in the literature: holidays, migrants, immigrants, and food" (p. 66). This disservice in representation is articulated in Motoko Rich's (2012) article for the *New York Times* regarding the disparity of Latino children's literature. Rich interviewed Kimberly Blake, a third-grade teacher at a predominately Latino school in Philadelphia, who "struggles to find books about Latino children beyond the stereotypical storylines involving 'migrant workers' or 'special holidays'" (p. 3). Given the history of racial stereotypes in Latino children's literature, any discussion of the quantity (or lack) of multicultural children's literature must include an analysis of the visual representations found in picture books. Moreover, the manner in which visual representations in picture books authentically capture the experiences of Latino children becomes complicated when read against a rubric of cultural wealth versus a discourse of deficit.

Yosso's (2005) theoretical concept of community cultural wealth offers a counterpoint that challenges established cultural capital theory that operates from a deficit perspective. Yosso instead posits that communities have unique forms of cultural capital expressed through "an array of knowledge, skills, abilities and contacts," that allow people to resist historical/social/institutional forms of oppression (Yosso, p. 77). Community cultural wealth builds upon critical race theory (CRT), a critical theory framework that examines how race and racism impact social discourse and intuitions. Communities of color have six types of cultural capital that work in concert. These types are (1) aspirational, (2) navigational, (3) social, (4) linguistic, (5) familial, and (6) resistant capital. Yosso (2005) explains,

For example, as noted above, aspirational capital is the ability to hold onto hope in the face of structured inequality and often without the means to make such dreams a reality. Yet, aspirations are developed within social and familial contexts, often through linguistic storytelling and advice (*consejos*) that offer special navigational goals to challenge (resist) oppressive conditions. Therefore, aspirational capital overlaps with each of the other forms of capital, social, familial, navigational, linguistic and resistant. (p. 77)

Using the community cultural wealth lens, the critic is invited to determine if the visuals found are affirmative or perpetuate cultural stereotypes. Picture books employing visual language to impart messages affirming the cultural capital can serve as counter-stories that actively resist cultural stereotypes. The use of CRT as a means of counter-storytelling can challenge dominant, racist cultural stereotypes and assumptions by telling the stories of marginalized and oppressed people (Delgado & Stefancic, 2012). An effective CRT lens can inform current research in multicultural literature challenging dominant cultural stereotypes found in narrative storylines (Chaudhir & Teale, 2013; Hughes-Hassell, 2013). A content analysis of Latino picture books is offered to demonstrate how cultural visual tropes in picture books work alongside textual narratives for meaning-making, to mirror real-world experiences and the representation of Latino children as navigators and social brokers.

PRAXIS: APPLICATION OF THEORY

Capturing Common Experiences

Artist Robert Casilla's opening illustration in *Let's Salsa/Bailemos Salsa* (2013) accurately captures a common scene found in many Mexican American working-class neighborhoods. The protagonist, Estela, a school-age Latina, is peeking into the Zumba class at her local community recreation center where she attends an afterschool program. There she sees "Doña Rosa, Doña María and several neighbors shaking their hips to the fast rhythm . . . sweating and puffing [but with] wide smiles on their faces" (Ruiz-Flores, 2013). The juxtaposition of the giggling Estela and the *Doñas* (a title of respect given to elder women) is a wonderful invitation into this story that centers on Estela's efforts to improve her mother's health. *Let's Salsa/Bailemos Salsa* takes on a common theme found in Latino children's literature: food. Refreshingly, this theme is explored in the context of nutritional health to bring positive solutions to both family and community. Estela's curiosity in watching the *Doñas* is born out of a childhood delight. In telling her mother about seeing the neighborhood *mujeres* exercise, Estela remarks in glee, "It's pretty funny." However, a seed of aspiration for improving her mother's health is also planted in Estela. As she continues watching the *mujeres* dancing and reaping the benefits of exercise, she begins to want the same for her mother, and she suggests, "Why don't you join *Doña* Maria and *Doña* Rosa at those dancing classes?" Here Ruiz-Flores's text and Casilla's illustrations work together to demonstrate how a community manifests social assets toward health and well-being. The community space which allows this encounter to happen, and which consequently moves Estela to act on her aspiration to improve her mother's health, exemplifies Yosso's (2005) definition of social capital as being the "networks of people and community resources [where] social contacts [provide] instrumental and emotional support" (p. 79). Casilla's illustrations capture how the community's expression of social capital affects Estela's consciousness. The illustrations depict Estela in the act of observation and reflection, both in her community space as well as in her family home. The reader can see when Estela makes the connection that the *Doñas* are just like her mom. The community knowledge that the *Doñas* impart to Estela becomes something she can share with her mother. In this way, the text and narrative work together to communicate how Estela is an integral part of her community network, a resource herself, with the capacity to participate in the spreading of social capital.

The story's plot offers a conflict and resolution that further exemplify a community cultural wealth model. Estela successfully convinces her mother to join the women's salsa exercise class, and she also joins in on the fun. Soon after, the director of the community center enforces a rule preventing children from participating in the class. And so, Estela is banned. The next day in school, Estela's teacher, depicted by Casilla as a woman of color, writes the word "petition" on the chalkboard and begins a discussion of women's suffrage. When examined from a community cultural wealth lens, this becomes an important juncture in the story's narrative. The author's choice to specifically reference women's struggle for the right to vote serves to buttress the narrative's previous device that uses women as actors of community social capital. The teacher, in the role of institutional voice, sets the stage for Estela to ask, "What is a petition?" Both the text and the visual illustration work in harmony to communicate a message of resistance. Supported by the adults in her community, as well as her parents, Estela organizes a petition to create a salsa class for kids, and she is successful in her efforts. She is recognized even by the mayor, who agrees that "an afterschool program for the young people, especially an exercise program that is fun and healthy, is good for the community." Estela is surrounded with adults who help her navigate institutional structures to effect positive change in her neighborhood. Both the text and illustration work together to impart this message.

Harkening to acts of *huelga* (strike), the story points to an essential ingredient of the Chicano experience. Casilla's illustration of Estela's petition in front of the supermarket brings to mind images of the United Farm Workers grape boycotts that took place in front of grocery stores in many Mexican American *barrios*.

Let's Salas/Bailemos Salsa (2013) exemplifies the symbioses in community cultural wealth assets—aspirational, familial, social, navigational, resistant capitals—working together to support and inform how children too are important agents in their community. By presenting the hero of this story as a young Latina, the author and illustrator send a message that children have the capacity for using their community cultural wealth as a resource. In this way, *Let's Salsa* offers a primary source for carrying forth acts of resistant capital, that is, "knowledges and skills fostered through oppositional behavior that challenges inequality" (Yosso, 2005, p. 80).

Horning (1997) reminds us that a unique feature of the picture book aesthetic is found in the experience that happens when picture books are read aloud to children. The act of sharing *Let's Salsa* in a read-aloud offers educators opportunities for "maintaining and passing on the multiple dimensions of community cultural wealth" as a way to engage in acts of resistant capital (Yosso, 2005, p. 80). In her discussion of Latino children's literature, Ada (2003) argues for the role of constructivist transformative education in the multicultural classroom, where students are viewed as creators of knowledge and given spaces to bring "to the classroom a wealth of knowledge and experiences" (p. 6). Ada posits that the act of reading *Let's Salsa* is a critical literacy practice that applies the community cultural wealth model.

Depicting Protest Art

Two recent works by the award-winning author and illustrator Duncan Tonatiuh also present the type of picture book narrative that lends itself to critical literacy practices as well as offers examples of resilient resistance in both the textual and visual narrative. Tonatiuh's *Separate Is Never Equal: Sylvia Mendez and Her Family's Fight for Desegregation* (2014) and *Pancho Rabbit and the Coyote: A Migrant's Tale* (2013) present a characteristic theme of Latino art as a "purveyor of cultural and political awareness" (Vargas, 2010, p. 18). George Vargas discusses how communicating a social message held prominence in the artworks of Chicanos in the 1960s. Often influenced by pre-Columbian art as well as the civil rights movements of that time, Chicano artists strove to create "a people's art that would carry messages not only of a growing Chicano political movement but also of a larger liberation movement lead by people of all colors" (Vargas, p. 18). This protest art served to instruct and impart cultural values characteristic of Chicanos, and it gave voice to the marginalized by articulating struggles for justice. The theme of art as vehicle for social justice is present in both Tonatiuh's works. *Separate Is Never Equal* deals with the 1946 school desegregation case *Mendez v. Westminster School District*, preceding *Brown v. Board of Education of Topeka*, which ended the unconstitutional practice of segregating Mexican American students in California schools. Tonatiuh's text and illustration trace the events leading up to the case, including the Mendez family's appeals to local and county school district superintendents who denied equal educational access to the Mendez children and other Mexican American students (see chapters 3 and 4).

Tonatiuh depicts protagonist Sylvia Mendez's moment of racial self-awareness in a two-page spread that shows young Sylvia examining herself against her two lighter-skinned cousins, who are able to pass as white. "Sylvia looked at her cousins. They had light skin and long auburn hair, and their last name was Vidaurri—their father was Mexican of French descent. Then she looked at her bare arms. She wondered, 'Is it because we have brown skin and thick black hair and our last name is Mendez?'" (Tonatiuh, 2014, p. 10). The scene depicts the complicated manifestation of racism as comprised of "micro and macro components . . . institutional and individual forms . . . conscious and unconscious elements [and their] cumulative impact on both the individual and the group" (Solórzano, 1997, p. 6). Sylvia's self-awareness as a target of racism and its microaggressions is connected to her understanding that her skin color and ethnic background are what determine her access to education. Tonatiuh's signature style of illustrating his characters using Mixteca-codices-inspired visual tropes serves to reinforce the moment of Sylvia's complex racial awareness, or double-consciousness. She is an American girl, and a Mexican girl. Daniel Solorzano (1997) notes how intelligence, personality, and physical appearance are used as racial stereotypes to justify segregation, low academic expectations, remediated curriculum, and expectations of menial labor roles. Racial stereotyping by Orange County school districts and their administrators is depicted in the courtroom scenes found in *Separate Is Never Equal* with dialogue recorded in the court transcripts (Tonatiuh, 2014, p. 39). When asked to justify why Mexican American students are segregated from their white counterparts, Mr. Kent, district superintendent declares, "For their social behavior. They need to learn cleanliness of mind, manner, and dress. They are not learning that at home. They have problems with lice, impetigo, and tuberculosis. They have generally dirty hands, face, neck, and ears" (Tonatiuh, 2014, p. 26). The Mendez family's persistence and resilience in seeking justice against sheer racism—communicated best by this scene—is emphasized by several page spreads that illustrate the family organizing within their community, carrying petitions, and talking with other families to build support for the cause. The illustrations communicate how the Mendezes' struggle is not only an individual struggle for justice, but rather one impacting their community (see chapter 14). Later illustrated spreads depict national civil rights organizations, such as the National Association for the Advancement of Colored People and the Japanese American Citizens League, in solidarity with the struggle to end school segregation, thus supporting Mrs. Mendez's remark, "Cuando la causa es justa, los demás te siguen" (Tonatiuh, p. 33).

Viewed through a community cultural wealth theoretical lens, *Separate Is Never Equal* exemplifies a story where aspiration for a better future via educational opportunities is fought with resiliency using social and navigational assets born from the protagonists' community resources. The linguistic assets theorized in the community cultural wealth model then become possible in a critical literacy classroom where learning outcomes include "focusing on sociopolitical issues, and taking action [to] promote social justice" (van Sluys, Lewison, & Flint, 2006, p. 198). In the concluding author's note, Tonatiuh expresses his hope that his book will help children learn about the important place this case has in U.S. history and the struggle for civil rights. Moreover, Tonatiuh hopes that children "will see themselves reflected in Sylvia's story and realize that their voices are valuable and that they too can make meaningful contributions to this country" (Tonatiuh, 2014, p. 36). It is a hope that is articulated in Solórzano's (1997) call to action that teacher education discourse, and in turn, the pedagogical practices emergent from this discourse, examine the roots and effects of racial stereotyping in order to counteract it.

Corridos and Borderlands Stories

Duncan Tonatiuh provides an example of a critical literacy practice afforded by transformative educational pedagogies that create spaces for students to share their cultural knowledge. On his website, Tonatiuh links to a video created by Caroline Sweet's (2013) students at Metz Elementary School in Austin, Texas, in response to their reading of *Pancho Rabbit* (2013). Read by the children, the video is a multivoice poem that describes their personal and family experiences of journeying across borders to reach the U.S. (see chapter 4). Their stories are very similar to what Tonatiuh captures in his powerful fable *Pancho Rabbit and the Coyote*, which uses animal characters to unfold a very human and quintessential migrant's story. The story opens, "One spring the rains did not come and the crops could not grow. So *Papá* Rabbit, *Señor* Rooster, *Señor* Ram, and other animals from the *rancho* set out north to find work in the great carrot and lettuce fields. There they could earn money for their families" (Tonatiuh, 2013). The scene is complemented by illustrations showing *nopales* in the background, a *casa de adobe*, and the Rabbit family holding hands and watching the *Señores* of the *rancho* start their trek north. Tonatiuh's artistic style, inspired by the visual aesthetic of Mixtec codices, shows the characters with distinctive indigenous designs. This scene shows how this migration continues to be accurate today just as it has been for centuries. It is akin to the homeland journey of Aztlán that forms a central part of Chicano identity (Gaspar de Alba, 2004). Tonatiuh accurately depicts common experiences faced by migrants crossing from Mexico into the U.S.

When Pancho Rabbit sets out on his own to find his father who has failed to return to the *rancho* as planned, he encounters Coyote, who offers to accompany Pancho on his journey north and show him the way, but at steep price. The term "coyote" in Spanish vernacular is used to describe a person who smuggles or helps people cross the Mexican–U.S. border. Castro (2000), in writing about the term "coyote" in Chicano folklore, notes the ambiguous role held by this trickster figure who serves a necessary function yet "profit[s] tremendously from poor people's dreams and ambitions" (p. 78). The narrative unfolds concisely with adherence to a traditional plot structure showing an economical exposition, rising, climax, falling action, and resolution. We see Pancho Rabbit negotiate with Coyote, who offers to get him closer to his father, but only if he gets something in return. In this case, Pancho Rabbit has to trade the food he has packed for his trip north. Tonatiuh's visual depictions of border crossing atop trains and through rivers, including treacherous encounters with rattlesnakes guarding the tunnels leading north and the deathly thirsts of the vast deserts, are all presented with accuracy yet appropriate for a child's eye. Tonatiuh humanizes the harrowing migration journey both through illustration and the literacy device of fable, which instructs through its communication of moral values (Lerer, 2008; Bottigheimer, 2004). This allows children to enter into the story with compassion for the protagonist's desire to do whatever it takes to reunite his family. The climax is resolved with *Señor* Rabbit coming to his son's rescue and returning home to the *rancho*. The fable in children's literature is commonly used to serve as an instructional, didactic tool, and it has been a typical mainstay of classroom instruction. Aided by this literary format, the themes explored in *Pancho Rabbit and the Coyote* become important in a critical literacy classroom.

The story's narrative pacing, in both text and illustrations, is reminiscent of the Mexican tradition of *corridos*, which are folksongs or narrative ballads told in a straightforward manner as vehicles for oral history.

For many Mexicans and Chicanos, the corridor has long served as one of the most important forms of oral history and storytelling. [*Corridos* have] been a vital means of documenting social and political changes, and passing knowledge from one generation to the next. (Jackson, 2009, p. 33)

From an artistic point of view, the influence of *corridos* on Chicano art is manifold. Mexican *corridos*, most famously illustrated by lithographer José Guadalupe Posada, were usually accompanied by broadside illustrations (Berdecio & Appelbaum, 1972) containing song lyrics and providing a visual component to communicate the story's moral. These productions were intended for the common folk and were written in a language understood by all segments of society (Jackson, 2009; Castro, 2000). In the language of critical theory, *corridos* are vehicles for counter-storytelling, narrating stories seldom told, stories from the margin, or borderlands. *Pancho Rabbit and the Coyote* falls into this tradition precisely because of its positionality as a children's story. Tonatiuh (2013) writes in his author's note at the conclusion,

We seldom see the dangerous journey immigrants go through to reach the U.S. and the longing that their families feel for them back at home. It is my desire that *Pancho Rabbit and the Coyote: A Migrant's Tale* captures some of that sentiment . . . the human emotion and side of the story.

Medina and Martínez-Roldán (2010) describe critical literacy approaches used in literature discussion circles in the classroom that open spaces for children to interpret and engage in readings that deal with notions of borderland spaces (see chapters 6, 8, and 14). To mount their argument, the authors use Anzaldúa's theoretical framework of borderlands—geographical, physical, linguistic, psychological, imaginative, gendered, and social—where identity is forged through a *mezcla* of the lived experiences brought forth from these transformational spaces (Medina & Martínez-Roldán, 2010; Anzaldúa, 1987). Medina and Martínez-Roldán (2010) recommend that children's literature, culturally specific *literatura fronteriza*, should engage students as co-creators in interpreting stories by sharing how they personally connect with the literature.

We perceive the spaces created in literature discussions as locations where children bring their "cultural intuition" as they construct narratives and interpret aspects of their identities and social movements as strengths and not deficits. . . . Through their responses, the students are co-constructing stories . . . which [reflect] on the past and collectively [redefine] the present. (p. 261)

Pancho Rabbit and the Coyote exemplifies how culturally authentic borderland stories can be used to tap into the linguistic assets children can bring to the story, serving as modes of cultural affirmation and resilient resistance to the marginalization of migration stories. Anzaldúa (2009) reminds us how in the act of storytelling, the dance between author and reader, "there are certain things that the author sets up for the reader, but the reader is, to some degree, a co-author" (p. 190). The multivoice poem created by the Metz Elementary School students uses their lived experiences to demonstrate how children bring experiential knowledge to co-create and become agents in meaning-making and identity construction. The multivoice poem captures the argument posited by Medina and Martínez-Roldán (2010):

> Culturally specific Latino literature should hold a special place in the class-room, and libraries for that matter, because it mediates not only students' rep-resentation of past and present experiences. . . . [It has the] potential to engage students in rewriting and co-authoring those stories through their own personal narratives. In doing so, possibilities are created for the children to position themselves as children with agency, children who reinvent themselves through narratives and borderlands in literature discussion. (p. 270)

Pancho Rabbit and the Coyote resonates especially now as the U.S. is seeing a historic and unprecedented rise in the number of unaccompanied mi-grant children. A report by the Center for Gender & Refugee Studies (2014) states that an estimated sixty thousand unaccompanied children entered the U.S. in fiscal year 2014. Certainly *Pancho Rabbit and the Coyote* is a story that affects more than just people who have the experiential knowledge of this migrant journey. It is a story important to all of us. Moreover, it is a *mezcla* of political art aesthetics and *the corrido* narrative style that imparts a moral transmitting cultural knowledge. Also, it serves as crucible for children to become co-creators and agents by opening up a space for discussions and the sharing of experiences.

Domesticana Rasquache and Barrio Art

Carmen Lomas Garza's Illustrations

The picture books of Carmen Lomas Garza similarly work as transmitters of Mexican American cultural knowledge. Her two seminal works in children's literature, *Family Pictures/Cuadros de familia* (1990) and *In My Family/ En mi familia* (1996) invite the reader to "eat at the table" (Woodson, 2003) of her experience as a Chicana from Kingsville, Texas. Using *monito*-style paintings (Mesa-Bains, 1999) and *papel picado*, Garza brings to life everyday family experiences in what Bishop (2007) calls "slice-of-life" visual images or *cuadros* paired with textual descriptions of various culturally specific fam-ily acts. These include *tamaladas, quinceañeras*, neighborhood cake walks, *bailes*, star gazing, hanging out in grandma's *cuarto*, and special events like visiting the apparition of the *Virgen de Guadalupe* in the neighborhood. The life experiences represented in Garza's illustrations accurately capture a Mex-ican American sensibility and way of life. Garza's art embodies a Chicano art aesthetic at once familial and political, both in the act of bringing voice to her experience as a Chicana and in her choice of artistic mediums with which she creates her artworks. In speaking about her art and what inspires her, Garza explains, "Your environment is you. . . . If you deny your environment then you deny your existence. When I was young and sketching my family at the very beginning, that was Chicano art!" (cited in Vargas, 2010, p. 40). Pérez (2007) refers to the restorative and "community-sustaining psychological and political effects" of Garza's folk art (p. 104). In fact, Garza (1996) names this restorative act.

> Every time I paint, it serves a purpose—to bring about pride in our Mexican American culture. When I was growing up, a lot of us were punished for speaking Spanish. We were punished for being who we were, and we were made to feel ashamed of our culture. That was very wrong. My art is a way of healing these wounds, like the *sávila* plant (aloe vera) heals burns and scrapes when applied by a living parent or grandparent.

The restorative acts brought forth by Garza's art production exemplify what Delgado Bernal (2001) refers to as pedagogies of the home, that is, "the communication, practices and learning that occur in the home and community, [which] serve as a cultural knowledge base offering strategies for resistance" (p. 624). Pérez draws this connection between Garza's artworks as demonstrations of pedagogies of the home when she writes, "[Garza's] *monito* paintings are nonetheless a balm reminding us of the pleasures of loving familial relations and traditions against the dehumanizing assumptions and projections about Mexican American culture and values" (p. 106). How pedagogies of the home become healing practices as well as modes of resistance is informed by what Mesa-Bains (1999) calls, in her analysis of Chicano art aesthetics and production, a *Domesticana Rasquache* sensibility, or theoretical framework. She writes,

> Related to the creative functioning of the domestic shared space is the ongoing practice of healing skills. Special herbs, talismans, religious imagery, and photos of historic faith healers are essential to this cultural tradition. Young women learn from older women such practices as *limpias* with burned herbs and the application of homeopathic cures. (p. 157)

Garza's *cuadro*, titled *Healer/Curandera*, in *In My Family/En mi familia* (1996), brings to life this very tradition of folk healing in the Chicano community. The scene captures Doña Maria, a *curandera*, performing a *limpia* or cleansing/healing ritual on Garza's little sister, Mary Jane, a rebellious pre-teen. Garza's text informs the reader of the tools of the *curandera*'s trade: the *ruda* plant used for the ceremony, *copal* incense, and the prayers said. Garza explains, "Besides being a healer, the *curandera* was also a counselor. She helped my mother and my sister communicate. I think that's why my sister got better." The visual text is abundant in cultural references that illuminate a Latino worldview, full of the community cultural wealth assets articulated by Yosso (2005). The illustration shows Mary Jane at the center of her grandmother's bedroom, with Carmen in her role as big sister, her mother and her little brother watching as Doña Maria sweeps the leaves of the *ruda* plant over Mary Jane, coaxing the incense smoke from the *copal* into the ceremonial space. Above her grandmother's bed there is an *altar con veladora* on the wall with a portrait of *La Virgen de San Juan de los Lagos* overlooking the scene. A crucifix on the facing wall, a cozy fringed peach bedspread or *colcha*, a framed formal portrait of a family elder, and the many *manteles tejidos* that dot the room accurately bring to life a woman-centered transfer of cultural knowledge, a pedagogy of the home. The act of transmitting epistemological knowledge between two generations is captured by and serves witness in the scene Garza paints. Mesa-Bains (1999) lists these very objects we see in Garza's *Curandera* in her positing of *Domesticana* aesthetics where familial objects and home decorations work semiotically to communicate through tangible objects the cultural value of passing on family history, spiritual beliefs, and personal experiences. In writing about pedagogies of the home, Delgado Bernal (2001) elaborates, "Chicana feminist pedagogies are partially shaped by collective experiences and community memory. . . . This knowledge that is passed from one generation to the next—often by mothers and other female family members—can help us survive in everyday life by providing an understanding of certain situations and explanations about why things happen under certain conditions" (pp. 624–25). Clearly, linguistic assets in the form of prayers and *consejos*, as well as familial assets, demonstrated through intergenerational participants, and the social assets of enlisting the help of the community *curandera* to restore family harmony, all point to a family cultural production that affirms resiliency.

Garza's rendering of this intimate, woman-centered family moment is furthermore strongly rooted in a *rasquache* Chicano art aesthetic. Ybarra-Frausto (1991) defines this uniquely Chicano aesthetic and Chicano feminist epistemology: "Rasquachismo is rooted in Chicano structures of thinking, feeling, and aesthetic choice. It is one form of a Chicano vernacular, the verbal-visual codes we use to speak to each other among ourselves" (p. 155). Rasquachismo employs a *los de abajo* (underdog) community resource and imaginative approach/attitude to create, construct, and problem solve using what is at hand. Mesa-Bains (1999) explains,

> In rasquachismo, one has a stance that is both defiant and inventive. Aesthetic expression comes from discards, fragments, even recycled everyday materials such as tires, broken plates, plastic containers, which are recombined with elaborate and bold display in yard shrines (*capillas*) domestic decor (*altares*),

and even embellishments of the car. In its broadest sense it is a combination of resistant and resilient attitudes devised to allow the Chicano to survive and persevere with a sense of dignity. The capacity to hold life together with bits of string, old coffee cans, and broken mirrors in a dazzling gesture of aesthetic bravado is at the heart of rasquachismo. (pp. 157–58)

In order to extend the concept of *rasquachismo*, an examination of other works is needed for resourcefulness is seen in all marginalized communities, and it can be said that the legacy of repurposing materials is important (Gonzaléz & Clark, 2015).

Susan Guevara's Illustrations

The art aesthetics present in the illustrations for Susan Middleton Elya's *Little Roja Riding Hood* and Gary Soto's *Chato* series reflect the layering of multiple objects that are representative of differing Latino cultural productions. The opening spread in *Little Roja Riding Hood*—a contemporary retelling of "Little Red Riding Hood"—opens a window into a female-centered home. The text, using code-switching, invites the reader in: "There once was a *niña* who lived near the woods. She liked to wear colorful *capas* with hoods" (Elya, 2014). Visually, Domesticana Rasquache is captured by an illustrated spread showing Little Roja prancing in front of a Mexican tin mirror, swishing her leopard-print red cape, with her Southwest *botas* in mid-*tapatio* step. There are books piled on the floor, and Roja's cat is atop her Mexican mini *silla*. In the background, we see her mother in hot pink and wearing a *rosario*, busily cooking while watching a telenovela on a television that sits on the kitchen counter next to her nail polish remover and manicure set. The spread is framed by three tiny, blind mice wearing *gafas oscuras* [sunglasses]. Guevara's choice to include the available reference points is to tweak and make her own cultural production. We see how this cultural sensibility is intergenerational and transmitted through women, as in the scene where *Lobo*, disguised as Little Roja, enters *Abuela*'s home. The visual narrative here challenges stereotypes on different levels. For instance, Lobo wears a *calavera* chain and a tough-guy bandana, yet he dons Little Rojas's sassy-fem cheetah-print cape. The readers' eye then moves towards Abuela, who is in bed typing away on her laptop when Lobo tricks his way into her room. This peek into Abuela's world disrupts the typical positionality and gender roles ascribed to Mexican American grandmothers (and grandmothers in general) as docile and meek. We see instead an active, empowered *abuelita* engaged in the creative act of writing, and we see the balled up papers of her manuscript strewn across her bed, which is decorated with a Mexican *colcha bordada*. Guevara's *abuela* looks like she would easily fit in the milieu of Chicana *mujeres escritoras* with her turquoise jewelry, multiple ear piercings, chic *trenzas*, rosary necklace, and peace-sign pajamas. Her books are piled in various places of her bedroom, which is decorated by a very prominent and colorful figurine of the Catholic saint *San Judas Tadeo*, easily one of the most beloved saints in Mexican culture. Guevara's artistic style favoring an aesthetic of layering multiple objects representative of Latino cultural productions is evident in the collision of colors, strewn objects, *santos*, flamboyant clothing, remixed canonical fairytale tropes, and empowered gender roles.

Barrio Art

The unabashed stance and artistic attitude of Guevara illustrations is harmonious with her visual renderings of the barrio in Gary Soto's *Chato* series, particularly in her artwork for *Chato and the Party Animals* (2000). Ybarra-Frausto (1991) locates the barrio as a rasquache cultural production, writing,

> The visual distinctiveness of the barrio unites the improvisational attitude of making do with what's at hand to a traditional and highly evolved decorative sense. In the barrio, the environment is shaped and articulated in ways that express the community's sense of itself, the aesthetic display projecting a sort of visual biculturalism. . . . Traditional items like religious shrines . . . [mix with] objects from mass culture. (p. 157)

Guevara's many spreads in *Chato and the Party Animals* depicting the working-class Mexican American neighborhood of Boyle Heights in East Los Angeles, California, visually speaks to *rasquachismo*. Her work references barrio art, an important aesthetic trope found in Chicano art where "the unique cultural forms and life-styles of the barrio, or urban community, became sources of inspiration and affirmation" (Griswold del Castillo, McKenna, & Yarbro-Bejarano, 1991, p. 256). Guevara's work pays respect to this barrio aesthetic by making specific reference to Boyle Heights and the iconic Chicano mural artwork created by the people of this neighborhood. The reader is treated to an abundant visual narrative that layers the many cultural productions of this neighborhood. These include the historic Estrada Court Murals that emerged from the Chicano arts movement of the 1970s; some East LA street paintings of *La Virgen de Guadalupe*; a troop of *mariachis* in front of *Farmacia Ramirez*; and Evergreen Cemetery, which sits next to *El Mercadito*, a marketplace. Guevara's illustrations are harmonious with Chicano artist Roberto Gutiérrez's paintings of East Los Angeles that champion a barrio aesthetic with abundantly layered sights and sounds of life in Boyle Heights (*Papel Chicano*, 2007, p. 38). In writing about the artistic process undergone in creating the illustrations for *Chato and the Party Animals*, Guevara (2003) notes how her visits to East LA allowed her to localize the images she chose to portray in her work. Her visits "helped [her] to record the detail of the neighborhoods, the slouch of a vendor, the bounce of a child, the duty of a mother" (p. 56). One effect that emerges from the localization of specific neighborhood detail is that it creates a visual language that is identifiable to an insider. A child from East LA would have her experiences of walking and living within these specific sights and sounds reaffirmed and reflected in Guevara's visual narrative. The effect of this visual exchange as a living experience recalls what Chicano artist Judith F. Baca (2005) theorizes in her articulation of how murals function: "A mural is not an easel painting made large. A mural is a work of art created in relatedness. . . . Murals build common. . . . Murals sing gospel from our streets and preach to us about who we can be, what we fear, and what we can aspire" (p. 155). Baca brings attention to the moral imperative found in the production of murals and in what they capture through their illustration. She argues how murals open spaces for telling of specific stories yet are inclusive and wide enough to encompass the experience of many as opposed to the few, or those privileged to have their stories told regularly through a dominant discourse (Baca, 2005). Similarly, Guevara's artistic choices in her representation of specific barrio geographies open a space for uniquely Chicano stories that have a capacity for changing the dominate discourse of children's literature which sees very little diversity in its production. Guevara represents East LA as a living, breathing cultural space communicating the common ground of children who often do not see their lives reflected in texts that socialize and contribute to their sense of self (Collier, 2000; Quiroa, 2010). This mirror is at once reflective, affirming the value of a Chicano experience, and an act of resilience in its addition of this experience to the space of children's literature.

Con Safos Técnica

The editors of the influential 'zine/street periodical *Con Safos: Reflections of Life in the Barrio* (1968), which emerged at the start of the Chicano movement, articulate the importance of barrio-derived artistic and literary expressions.

In the introduction to the first two issues of *Con Safos*, editor-in-chief Arturo Flores (1968) writes,

> The cause of Con Safos, if we must have a cause, has no ideology. It is rather an attempt at expressing the entire spectrum of feelings that are the soul of the barrio. . . . Con Safos magazine is a part of . . . an aesthetic outgrowth which is ultimately the soul of the [Chicano] movement. . . . Con Safos symbolizes [the] beginning of a Chicano literary genre, a definition of the Chicano identity, and an assertion of the moral and aesthetic values of the barrio experience.

The vision set forth by *Con Safos* captures at once the ingredients that come together in a Chicano art aesthetic born from the experiences of people's lives in the barrio and their cultural productions as necessarily political in their resilient acts of voicing experience that is often underrepresented and thereby instructional to both insider and outsider. The spectrum metaphor reinforces a Chicano *rasquache* sensibility in that everything is useable in the creative act. In the vernacular of Caló, and in Chicano graffiti, the term "*con safos,*" is written as a symbol in abbreviated form as "C/S" and is used as a charm or verbal amulet signifying protection from harm or defacement, so that "whatever touches this returns to you" (Castro, 2000, p. 70; Polkinhorn, Velasoco, & Lambert, 2005). *Con safos* is an amalgamation of the aesthetic ingredients that make up Chicano cultural productions. Figuratively, evoking con safos as the literary mirror afforded by culturally relevant picture books becomes a resilient critical practice, or *técnica*, for both reflecting and bouncing back the life experience for Latino children. This has the potential to reflect both the lives of children it authentically represents and affirm the value of their culture, while also serving to connect children to experiences they have not lived themselves but with which they can find commonality.

> We see our lives mapped in the lives of characters and plots and this serves as a reaffirmation of who we are. We also admit that through Latino literature we are able to discover the worlds and lives of other *hermanos y hermanas* (brothers and sisters) who we do not know. We may not know what it means to move around and live the life of migrant farm workers and we are grateful to those writers who make those realities visible through their stories. (Medina & Martínez-Roldán, 2011, p. 270)

Thus the possibilities for what can be reflected and returned/shared through a *con safos* practice can have positive potential for engaging us in critical discussions. Moreover, the cultural experiences and representations shared in a *con safos* practice are unabashedly and confidently declarative.

This *con safos técnica* is clearly an expression of the resilient capital central to Chicano identity. Yuyi Morales's picture book *Niño Wrestles the World* (2013) captures this *con safos* practice in the blending of textual narrative and illustration choices. Morales showcases some of the most iconic and recognizable characters in Mexican folklore—from *La Llorona* to *Las Momias de Guanajato* and even *El Chamuco* himself—to bring to life the story of Niño, a boy *luchador* whose bravery, wit, and playful nature help him conquer even the most frightful of childhood anxieties represented in these cultural figures. Morales's narrative panache draws the reader in both textually and visually by engaging the reader as a participant through her expressive interjections such as *ajúa* and *recórcholis*, which are classic exclamations. Visually, Morales represents of Niño playing a strategic game of *canicas* (marbles) against his scary opponent; tempting the devil with a popsicle; and contending with his twin *hermanitas* who give him a run for his money with their *lucha libre* skills. These are the very ingredients found in the diverse soup of Latino culture. Morales's stylistic presentation of the total narrative—text and illustrations—is unapologetic in presenting this cultural story. In this affirmation of culture, a sense of love and value for what makes one uniquely Chicano and what gives one a Chicano sensibility is also communicated through the narrative. Vargas (2010) theorizes, "When Chicano artists emphasize social production of art, they become cultural workers as well as artists, speaking from the heart and soul of their communities" (p. 10). The picture book *Niño Wrestles the World* exemplifies how children can contribute their knowledge of similar cultural experiences and also learn of others' experiences. This reflective mirror lifts the demoralizing curtain (erasure) brought on by a dearth of available and culturally responsive Latino children's literature.

CONCLUSION

Culturally responsive picture books interplay with and contribute to narrative elements to authentically reflect the lives of Latino children as navigators and social brokers. The use of specific aesthetic elements and visual tropes, in turn, serves as an instructional device that illustrates how Latino children are holders of valuable cultural capital and assets born of their unique cultural/ historical space. Pedagogical imperatives urge educators to serve as facilitators of storytelling and discussion spaces that promote participatory critical literacy practices among all children in order to affirm and cultivate an awareness and appreciation of communities' cultural wealth. That is, the myriad of Latino children's life experiences are valuable cultural productions that can share equally important spaces among the diverse cultural experiences of all children, despite ethnicity.

REFERENCES

Ada, A. F. (2003). *A magical encounter: Latino children's literature in the classroom*. Boston, MA: Allyn & Bacon.

Anzaldúa, G. (1987). *Borderlands/La frontera: The new mestiza*. San Francisco, CA: Spinsters/Aunt Lute.

Anzaldúa, G., & Keating, A. (2009). *The Gloria Anzaldúa reader*. Durham, NC: Duke University Press.

Baca, J. F. (2005). The human story at the intersection of ethics, aesthetics and social justice. *Journal of Moral Education, 34*(2), 153–69. doi:10.1080/300572405001 37029.

Barrera, R. B., & Garza de Cortes, O. (1997). Mexican American children's literature in the 1990s: Toward authenticity. In V. J. Harris (Ed.), *Using multiethnic literature in the K–8 classroom* (pp. 129–54). Norwood, MA: Christopher-Gordon Publishers.

Berdecio, R., & Appelbaum, S. (1972). *Posada's popular Mexican prints: 273 cuts by José Guadalupe Posada.* New York, NY: Dover Publications.

Bishop, R. S. (2003). Reframing the debate about cultural authenticity. In D. L. Fox & K. G. Short (Eds.), *Stories matter: The complexity of cultural authenticity in children's literature* (pp. 25–37). Urbana, IL: National Council of Teachers of English.

———. (2007). *Free within ourselves: The development of African American children's literature.* Portsmouth, NH: Heineman.

Bottigheimer, R. B. (2004). Fairy tales and fables. In P. S. Fass (Ed.), *Encyclopedia of children and childhood: In history and society* (pp. 337–39). New York, NY: Macmillan Reference.

Castro, R. (2000). *Dictionary of Chicano folklore.* Santa Barbara, CA: ABC-CLIO.

Center for Gender and Refugee Studies & Kids in Need Defense (2014). Treacherous journey: Child migrants navigating the U.S. immigration system. Retrieved from www.uchastings.edu/centers/cgrs-docs/treacherous_journey_cgrs_kind_report.pdf.

Chappell, S., & Faltis, C. (2007). Spanglish, bilingualism, culture and identity in Latino children's literature. *Children's Literature in Education, 38*(4), 253–62. doi:10.1007/s10583-006-9035-z.

Chaudhir, A., & Teale, William H. (2013). Stories of multiracial experience in literature for children, ages 9–14. *Children's Literature in Education, 44,* 359–76. doi:10.1007/s10583-013-9196-5.

Chavoya, C. O., & González, R. (2011). *ASCO: Elite of the obscure, A retrospective, 1972–1987.* Ostfildern, Germany: Hatje Cantz.

Collier, M. D. (2000). Through the looking glass: Harnessing the power of African American children's literature. *Journal of Negro Education, 69*(3), 235–42. doi:10.2307/2696234.

Delgado Bernal, D. (2001). Learning and living pedagogies of the home: The mestiza consciousness of Chicana students. *Qualitative Studies in Education, 14*(5), 623–39. doi:10.1080/0958390110059838.

Delgado, R., & Stefancic, J. (2012). *Critical race theory: An introduction.* New York, NY: New York University Press.

Elya, S., & Guevara, S. (2014). Little *roja* riding hood. New York, NY: G. P. Putnam's Sons.

Flores, A. (Ed.). (1968). *Con Safos: Reflections of life in the barrio.* Los Angeles, CA: Con Safos.

Freire, P. (2000). Pedagogy of the oppressed. New York, NY: Continuum.

Garza, C. L. (1990). *Family pictures.* San Francisco, CA: Children's Book Press.

———. (1996). *In my family.* San Francisco, CA: Children's Book Press.

Gaspar de Alba, A. (2004). There's no place like Aztlán: Embodied aesthetics in Chicana Art. *CR: The New Centennial Review*, *4*(2), 103–40. doi:10.1353/ncr.2005.0007.

Gonzaléz, D. A., & Clark, E. R. (2015). Proceedings from the *III Congreso Internacional de Historia, Arte y Literatura en el Cine en Español y Portugués*. June 24–26, 2015, Salamanca, Spain.

González, R., Fox, H. N., & Noriega, C. A. (2008). Phantom sightings: Art after the Chicano movement. Berkeley, CA: University of California Press.

Griswold del Castillo, McKenna, R., & Yarbro-Bejarano, T. (Eds.). (1991). *Chicano art: Resistance and affirmation, 1965–1985*. Los Angeles, CA: UCLA Wight Art Gallery.

Guevara, S. (2003). Authentic enough: Am I? Are you? Interpreting culture for children's literature. In D. L. Fox & K. G. Short (Eds.), *Stories matter: The complexity of cultural authenticity in children's literature* (pp. 50–60). Urbana, IL: National Council of Teachers of English.

Hooks, B. (1994). *Teaching to transgress: Education as the practice of freedom*. New York, NY: Routledge.

Horning, K. T. (1997). *From cover to cover: Evaluating and reviewing children's books*. New York, NY: HarperCollins.

Hughes-Hassell, S. (2013). Multicultural young adult literature as a form of counter-storytelling. *Library Quarterly*, *83*(3), 212–28. doi:10.1086/670696.

Jackson, C. (2009). *Chicana and Chicano art: ProtestArte*. Tucson, AZ: University of Arizona Press.

Keller, G. D. (2002). *Contemporary Chicana and Chicano art: Artists, works, culture, and education*. Tempe, AZ: Bilingual Press/Editorial Bilingüe.

Lerer, S. (2008). *Children's literature: A reader's history from Aesop to Harry Potter*. Chicago, IL: University of Chicago Press.

Medina, C. L., & Martínez-Roldán, C. (2010). Culturally relevant literature pedagogies: Latino students reading in the borderlands. In J.C. Naidoo (Ed.), *Celebrating cuentos: Promoting Latino children's literature and literacy in classrooms and libraries* (pp. 259–72). Santa Barbara, CA: Libraries Unlimited.

Mesa-Bains, A. (1999). "Domesticana": The sensibility of Chicana *rasquache*. *Aztlán*, *24*(2), 157–67.

Morales, Y. (2013). *Niño wrestles the world*. New York, NY: Roaring Brook Press.

Naidoo, J. C. (2010). Reviewing the representation of Latino cultures in U.S. children's literature. In J. C. Naidoo (Ed.), *Celebrating cuentos: Promoting Latino children's literature and literacy in classrooms and libraries* (pp. 59–78). Santa Barbara, CA: Libraries Unlimited.

Nilsson, N. L. (2005). How does Hispanic portrayal in children's books measure up after 40 years? The answer is "It depends." *Reading Teacher*, *58*(6), 534–48. doi:10.1598/RT.58.6.4.

Pérez, L. (2007). *Chicana Art: The politics of spiritual and aesthetic altarities*. Durham, NC: Duke University Press.

Polkinhorn, H., Velasco, A., & Lambert, M. (2005). *El libro de Caló: The dictionary of Chicano slang*. Moorpark, CA: Floricanto Press.

Quiroa, R. (2010). *Bailando ante el espejo*: Responses to culturally familiar themes in picture books. In J. C. Naidoo (Ed.), *Celebrating cuentos: Promoting Latino children's literature and literacy in classrooms and libraries* (pp. 227–38). Santa Barbara, CA: Libraries Unlimited.

Rich, M. (2012, December 4). For young Latino readers, an image is missing. *New York Times*. Retrieved from www.nytimes.com/2012/12/05/education/young-latino-students-dont-see-themselves-in-books.html.

Ruiz-Flores, L., & Casilla, R. (2013). *Let's salsa/Bailemos salsa*. Houston, TX: Piñata Books.

Solórzano, D. G. (1997). Images and words that wound: Critical race theory, racial stereotyping, and teacher education. *Teacher Education Quarterly*, *24*(3), 5–19. Retrieved from www.teqjournal.org/.

Soto, G., & Guevara, S. (2000). *Chato and the party animals*. New York, NY: Putnam.

Sweet, C. (2013, October 25). Our journeys: A multivoice poem by Ms. Sweet's 4th graders. Retrieved from http://youtu.be/aM6oQEVRyDc.

Tonatiuh, D. (2013). *Pancho rabbit and the coyote: A migrant's tale*. New York, NY: Abrams Books for Young Readers.

———. (2014). Separate is never equal: Sylvia Mendez and her family's fight for desegregation. New York, NY: Abrams Books for Young Readers.

Van Sluys, K., Lewison, M., & Flint, A. S. (2006). Researching critical literacy: A critical study of analysis of classroom discourse. *Journal of Literacy Research*, *38*(2), 197–233. doi: 10.1207/s15548430jlr3802_4.

Vargas, G. (2010). *Contemporary Chican@ art: Color & culture for a new America*. Austin, TX: University of Texas Press.

Wiesner, D. (2012). Forward. In L. S. Marcus (Ed.), *Show me a story! Why picture books matter, Conversations with 21 of the world's most celebrated illustrators*. Somerville, MA: Candlewick Press.

Woodson, J. (2003). Who can tell my story? In D. L. Fox & K. G. Short (Eds.), *Stories matter: The complexity of cultural authenticity in children's literature* (pp. 41–45). Urbana, IL: National Council of Teachers of English.

Ybarra-Frausto, T. (1991). *Rasquachismo*: A Chicano sensibility. In R. Griswold del Castillo, R. McKenna, & Y. Yarbro-Bejarano (Eds.), *Chicano art: Resistance and affirmation, 1965–1985* (pp. 155–62). Los Angeles, CA: UCLA Wight Art Gallery.

Yosso, T. J. (2005). Whose culture has capital? A critical race theory discussion of community cultural wealth. *Race Ethnicity and Education*, *8*(1), 69–91. doi: 10.1080/136133205200034106.

DISCUSSION QUESTIONS

1. How can identifying visual evidence of community cultural wealth capital help children strengthen self-efficacy?

2. Does the author's/illustrator's intentionality in including culturally responsive cultural wealth through the narrative and/or visual imagery enhance opportunities for critical literacy practices?
3. How can teachers advocate for community resource spaces, such as a public library, to encourage story time spaces to engage in critical literacy practices?
4. How does the sharing and reading of Latino picture books that depict community cultural wealth capital benefit all children?

ACTIVITIES

A. Find textual evidence (narrative and/or visual) that demonstrates one or more aspects of community cultural wealth capital.
B. Create student video diaries to share family *cuentos* and/or book responses to Chicano picture books.
C. Watch the student-created documentary *Surrounded by Art: The Murals of City Terrace*. Lead a student discussion on how aspects of Chicano murals show up in the picture books of Duncan Tonatiuh, Susan Guevara, and Yuyi Morales.
D. Have students take a photograph of their home life (their kitchen, their pet, their parents, their neighbors, etc.). Help students describe their photo in terms of community cultural wealth capital.
E. The Mexican and Chicano oral tradition of *corridos* is used to tell a story and to pass along information. Have students create their own *corrido* about a current event.

Chapter Fourteen

Latino Children's Multicultural Literature and Literacy Practices as Social Imagination: Becoming a Culturally Efficacious Educator

Belinda Bustos Flores, Ellen Riojas Clark, and Howard L. Smith

INTRODUCTION

Our world is changing in many ways, but most evident is the diversity that abounds in our communities. In our first chapter, we provide evidence of this demographic shift; however, we contend that the Latinization of the U.S. is not novel. If we truly examine the history of the Americas, it is important to acknowledge that prior to European settlements, the indigenous peoples/ first nations were scattered across the Americas with five hundred to one thousand different languages spoken and bilingualism common among the people (Baker, 2011). Moreover, nearly one hundred years before English settlements (e.g., James Fort, circa 1604, later known as Jamestown, 1619), there were early Spanish settlements in the current states of Florida (e.g., San Augustine, 1565), and later, the regions now known as Texas, Colorado, New Mexico, and California were being settled by the Spanish as the original colonies were being established. Hence, the Latinization began long ago, but our history has often been disregarded, hidden, and considered unofficial knowledge (Apple, 1993, 2014). We are treated as colonized people (see chapter 8).

In the case of Latinos, as *mestizos*, our literacy practices are an intersection of the old and the new world. This *mestizaje* experience, the result of European and indigenous blood, has been further influenced through contact with other European groups. According to Clark and Flores (2014), our cultural literacy is an intersection of language, culture, and thought. Each of us has had different cultural and literacy experiences in becoming bicultural/ bilingual individuals. These experiences contribute to our worldviews and our knowledge, assisting us in navigating the world, supporting our interactions with others, and aiding us to encounter cultural, economic, historical, social boundaries. Essentially, our cultural literacy allows for meaning-making. Unfortunately, in the case of Latinos, and other minority groups, our cultural literacy has often been and continues to be negated. Our voices need to be heard, and we must not be silenced.

THEORETICAL LENS AND REVIEW
OF LITERATURE: *TESTIMONIOS*

Hence, we use *testimonios*, as narratives, to share our cultural literacy experiences and to demonstrate our counter-resistance to deficit thinking (Valencia, 1997, 2010), official knowledge (Apple, 1993, 2014), and subtractive schooling experiences (Valenzuela, 1999). In contrast to the "traditional narrative, life stories, or autobiography, *testimonio* calls for collective action through the voicing of personal struggles situated within larger sociopolitical contexts that transcend time, place, and location" (DeNicolo & González, 2015, p. 112; see chapter 7). Our *testimonios* serve as our theoretical lens in which we weave in our epistemologies and anchor our review of literature.

Belinda Bustos Flores's *Testimonio*

As a child, I was raised in a bilingual/bicultural home environment; I was also fortunate to have my grandmother live next door, who had been a *normalista* (normal school teacher), and I would spend my days with her. Mamá Julia was a storyteller and I enjoyed hearing her *cuentos*. It was much later in life that I realized that my Mamá Julia's stories were drawn from traditional *cuentos infantiles* as well as from *Grimm's Fairy Tales* and the *Arabian Nights*. Mamá Julia taught me to read and write in Spanish well before I entered first grade. I remember vividly her teaching me the letters and the *sílabas*: *ba, be, bi, bo, bu*, etc., and then forming words, followed by reading sentences, *Mi mamá me ama a mí*. In first grade, I was able to transfer these literacy skills as I began to read in English.

I also recall one day when Mamá Julia's returned from visiting *familia* in Nuevo Laredo, México; she brought me a *cuaderno* [work book] with a beautiful cover picture of *La imagen de la alegoría de La Patria*—a *mestizo* women majestically holding the Mexican Flag drawn by Jorge González Camarena (1962). At the time (circa 1966), it must have been illegal to bring any Mexican/Spanish books to the U.S. So my Mamá Julia told me that I could not tell anyone that she had *cruzar contrabando ilegalmente*, especially since these books promoted a unified Mexican ideology. Even when I was a young child, she would have me read from adult books including medical reference books, religious and bible texts, as well as newspapers and *caricaturas* [cartoons]. I enjoyed these enriching literacy experiences, which definitely allowed me to embrace my bicultural/bilingual identity. Yet, in reflection, *caricaturas* like *El Negrito Memín Pinguín*, a very popular Latin America cartoon, were rather racist in their depiction of the characters. I would contend that my grandmother was not racist, but rather that she had not critically considered the racist overtures of such depictions. My point here is that while indeed my Mamá Julia added to my literacy and cultural capital (Delgado-Bernal, 2001), she also inadvertently exposed me, as a child, to inappropriate literature. As educators, it is vital that we have the knowledge and skills to critically select literature that is authentic and culturally appropriate (see chapters 2 and 6) and also to guide families in their selection of appropriate texts.

Unequivocally, the funds of knowledge (González, Moll, & Tenery, 1995) afforded to me as a child as well as my cultural and linguistic capital (Delgado-Bernal, 2001) supported my academic success in school. However, once in school, I never read a book depicting my family's stories and *aventuras*, only those of Dick and Jane and, of course, Spot running in a luscious green yard. Dick and Jane never ran in the *monte* [woods] or *rancho* to pick wild berries or gather *nopales* with their Mamá Julia. They never had a *piñata* to celebrate birthdays. They never made *tamales* with their *familia*.

When I was in third grade, my parents bought an encyclopedia set with a series of children's books. I remember reading and rereading these stories as well as the reference books. While I was voracious reader with a much worn-out library card, I did not know that Latino literature existed other than the oral stories told to me by Mamá Julia or the stories *en mis cuadernos* about *Hernán Cortez y la Conquista; Benito Juárez y el Grito; La Revolución Mexicana con sus Adelitas, Pancho Villa, Emiliano Zapata;* and *Los niños héroes del Castillo Chapultepec,* among others. Needless to say, Mamá Julia's *cuentos* and *mis cuadernos* allowed me to see multiple realities, provoked my social imagination, and ignited my passion for reading and learning.

Unfortunately, I was not exposed to Latino/Chicano literature until in 1978 when I, as a bilingual teacher candidate, read Tomás Rivera's (1971) epic novella, *Y no se lo tragó la tierra.* Perhaps, I was also fortunate that when he arrived in San Antonio to work at the University of Texas at San Antonio, he and his family were my neighbors and I was able to have some stimulating conversations with him. Also, my husband broadened my cultural literacy; he would read and share (and continues to do so to this day) his favorite various Spanish literary greats beginning with Cervantes and Lope de Vega as well as other acclaimed Latin American writers such as Fuentes, Borges, Sor Juana Inés de la Cruz, Vargas Llosa, Paz, and Gabriela Mistral, as well as his favorite Chicano celebrated writers: Tomás Rivera, Rudolfo Anaya, *y otros revolucionarios.*

My schooling experiences reflect the assimilation process promulgated in the U.S. as a means to Americanize individuals, while dismissing the language and culture of my family (Valenzuela, 1999). Even when I was a teacher candidate, it was only in bilingual education courses that my bilingualism and biculturalism were affirmed.

My bilingual education preparation validated the importance of affirming children's identities, culture, and language. My *conocimientos* (e.g., beliefs, bicultural/bilingual identity, funds of knowledge, linguistic and cultural capital) allowed me to anchor my teaching practices. Researchers support the notion that bilingual teacher candidates are well grounded in their *creencias* [beliefs] (Flores, Ek, & Sánchez, 2011) and *conocimientos* (Saldaña & Mendez-Negrete, 2014). However, when I began teaching in 1980, the only Spanish children's books I could find were those I purchased across the border. While nicely written and illustrated, these books did not reflect the U.S.–Latino experience. As a parent, while I was proud that my daughter could name various children's authors, I was bothered that she was not exposed to Latino children's literature. It was through concerted efforts that as a family we would attend readings by Carmen Tafolla and Pat Mora along with other literacy experiences such as Shakespeare at the Park, Cervantes's plays at San Jose Mission, or *El Cucuy* Walks at the Guadalupe Theater in San Antonio. I am proud to note that my daughter, now a speech pathologist, has a wonderful library of Latino children's literature that she uses in speech therapy for vocabulary and language development, alliteration, articulation, etc., and she is an avid reader of multicultural adult literature. I share these experiences to demonstrate the importance of *concientización* (Freire, 1990) that educators must have to engage in critical praxis. We must interrogate the premise of only teaching the standards and counter the pressure to teach to the test. As Green (1995) notes,

> Now, with so many traditional narratives being rejected or disrupted, with so many new and contesting versions of what our common world should be, we cannot assume that there is any longer a consensus about what *is* valuable and useful and what ought to be taught, despite all the official definitions of necessary outcomes and desired goals. (p. 3)

Upon reflection, it is no wonder I became a bilingual education teacher and later a teacher educator and researcher. Just as literature can transform your world, I have always been driven to ensure that children have the opportunity to see themselves in all aspects of the learning setting. Indeed, Latino children's multicultural literature can serve this purpose as evident throughout this book.

Ellen Riojas Clark's *Testimonio*

My experience is so different from that of Belinda Flores, but it may be more reflective of the majority of us born in the U.S. of Spanish-speaking heritages. All I read and knew as a small child and as a primary and secondary student was traditional literature in English. My mother, a voracious reader and lover of "good literature" [her term], developed in her children a love of reading and books. Books and magazines abounded in our home. An early memory of when I was about three or four was the neighborhood excitement when we received a big wooden box in the mail. Everyone groaned when my parents opened the box with great care to reveal a complete set of the *Book of Knowledge* and I remember all of us running off. A few stayed behind to listen as my mom began to read. This became a daily event and a lasting memory: to listen to my mother reading stories, poetry, fables, etc. Our imaginations soared as we listened to stories from throughout the world. Upon reflection, we never heard a story from any country in Central or South America, or even México. Though I know my mother could read as well as speak Spanish, it was not encouraged at home, for my parents wanted us to fit into our white neighborhood and schools. She always said we would learn correct Spanish when we got older. So we continued to read, to go to the library with our red wagon and pile it high with books that we devoured when we got home: Nancy Drew, Laura Ingalls Wilder, etc. Though I read Willa Cather as a child, I never associated her themes with me as she described New Mexico settings. So never, never, did I read about me in those many books I read. In an unpublished essay I write,

> I was born different—I was always different, that is, I saw myself as different. . . .
> I was brown in a community of white, quiet where everyone spoke, a reader instead of a contender. . . . Called many things: bookworm, poor little thing, scaredy cat, blind as a bat, shy, weird, whatever the word was for nerd, and on and on.

Anzaldúa reiterates,

> I am visible—see this Indian face—yet I am invisible. I both blind them with my beak nose and am their blind spot. But I exist, we exist. They like to think I have melted in the pot. But I haven't, we haven't. (1987, p. 108)

What a provocative statement to read, it hit me in my most inner being. *This Bridge Called My Back: Writings by Radical Women of Color* was the first book with Gloria Anzaldúa's (1981) works that I read, and it changed my

world. To finally be exposed to ideas and to analysis that dealt with my experiences and thoughts was groundbreaking for me. Never before had I read
work like this revolutionary collection of essays, letters, and poems. To be
exposed to the thoughts and conflicts associated with the painful process of
struggle, denial, acceptance, revitalization, and validation of self was world
shattering for me. To not only read someone's counter-analysis of society's
view of me, but also to see it as a valid, theoretical framework and a philoso-
phy, was radical. It required more of me than just a blanket assumption of
her views; it meant that I had to review my socialization not just within the
institutionalization of my family practices but from the white northside community I grew up in, the schools I attended, my white friends, my English,
my Methodist church, and my life until then. I remember how perplexed my
father was when my younger brother chastised him with "Why don't we live
on the Westside?" My poor father who had never lived on the Westside (the
Mexican American side of town) did not understand my brother's dilemma;
in retrospective, my brother was speaking about his own ethnic identity, his
lack of Spanish, his sense of understanding himself in the complexity of the
borderlands that existed in trying to integrate into both ethnic groups. I, on
the other hand, was fortunate to read and be provoked by Gloria's words and
thoughts. The awakening of my inner self, my social imagination, to be able
to work toward understanding and changing those borders created an internal
psychological change.

> The struggle is inner: Chicano, indio, American Indian, mojado, mexicano,
> immigrant Latino, Anglo in power, working class Anglo, Black, Asian—our
> psyches resemble the bordertowns and are populated by the same people. The
> struggle has always been inner, and is played out in outer terrains. Awareness
> of our situation must come before inner changes, which in turn come before
> changes in society. Nothing happens in the "real" world unless it first happens
> in the images in our heads. (Anzaldúa, 1987, p. 87)

To understand that my sociocultural worlds were shifting and my inner being
was strengthening and that I had to know who I was in order to be productive
was the beginning of a conscious approach to my own empowerment and to
that of social justice. It was not happening just to my brother or me but to a
whole community that was now undergoing a cultural, linguistic, and ethnic
self-acceptance to understanding Anzaldúa's (1987) statement that "ethnic
identity is twin skin to linguistic identity" (p. 113).

My first exposure to Chicano literature had been in the early 1970s at Trin-
ity University. It was fascinating literature. Yes, it was great, but all by men:
Jose Antonio Villarreal, Oscar Acosta, Raymond Barrio, Rudy Anaya, Al-

urista, Sabine Ulibarrí, and Rudy Gonzáles. They described some of my experiences but not my thoughts, nor my social imagination. I don't remember
readings by women except for some occasional poems in *Quinto Sol*. But then
in the 1980s, women exploded on the literary scene, and among them a short,
dark, woman, Gloria Anzaldúa, a woman from Texas, like me, born in the
Rio Grande Valley of south Texas in 1942, a year younger than me. Unlike
me, she grew up speaking and being in Spanish and English, in a combination
of two languages, two cultures, two histories, aware and sure of her twoness.
She crossed over and back again many times and this, I think opened her to
the dynamics of crossings and creating pathways. These situational contexts
coupled with her descriptions and reflections formed a valid framework for
the revolutionary work she articulated that has continued to impact and challenge the premises for our thinking and actions. Based on Antonio Machado's
work, Anzaldúa (1981) posits, *"Caminante, no hay puentes, se hace puentes
al andar* [Voyager, there are no bridges, one builds them as one walks]."

It was those initial works that stirred me into rethinking who I was in the
worlds that I lived in. The magnitude of her writings continues to reshape my
work and my worlds. To quote Anzaldúa (1997),

> At some point, on our way to a new consciousness, we will have to leave the
> opposite bank, the split between the two mortal combatants somehow healed so
> that we are on both shores at once and, at once, see through serpent and eagle
> eyes. Or perhaps we will decide to disengage from the dominant culture, write
> it off all together as a lost cause, and cross the border into a wholly new and
> separate territory. Or we might go another route. The possibilities are numerous
> once we decide to act and not react. (p. 101)

We had to "create new categories for those of us left out or pushed out of
the existing ones," as Gloria (1990, p. 26) so eloquently articulates. We had
to take into account all those exogenous factors such as space, history, gender, politics, and culture that existed in our time of being. These sociocultural
contexts differ for us all based on where we grew up, when we grew up, and
how we grew up. To think that it is not just an either/or perspective but that
it is a totally new *mestiza* way of thinking, an in-depth look, a beyond view
of our selves was not only innovative but also radical—it was that of social
justice.

These explorations have led my colleague Belinda Flores and me to examine the development of identity as the basis for positive teacher efficacy
with bicultural/bilingual students. In our work we have expressed the need for
teachers to understand that the sociocultural, historical, and political context
acts as a mediator for their students' identities. We deem it important that

individuals should have a sense of equality based on equity rights and that ethnic identity leading to ethnic solidarity is the conduit for social esteem and equity. We feel that this goes beyond self-reflection but to the development of social imagination that can lead to a sense of social justice. It requires an examination of one's social, cultural, ethnic, linguistic, and economic positioning in society. Again, we draw on Anzaldúa (1987),

> I am an act of kneading, of uniting and joining that not only has produced both a creature of darkness and a creature of light, but also a creature that questions the definitions of light and dark and gives them new meanings. (p. 306)

In our work, we use the means of exploration leading to cultural identity as a way of seeing and understanding self and others, and the basis for this is Gloria's framework. Exploration starts us on the road to not only understanding others and their identities, but also to looking within to expand our perspectives in articulating our own cultural identity. We want educators to use their own cultural and ethnic identity as a medium to constructing empathy and promoting social justice in their classrooms. We, like Gloria (1987), feel that the transformation of self is power. "I want the freedom to carve and chisel my own face, to staunch the bleeding with ashes, to fashion my own gods out of my entrails" (p. 615). So I will continue in Gloria's (1981) revolutionary legacy because I am the woman that as "I change myself, I change the world" (p. 208).

Now, I understand that we have to draw strength from our past and our cultural histories and recognize that these beliefs and values are central to who we are. So my work in cultural literacy is to present the values of friendship and a positive, culturally rich portrayal of Latino families, language, and cultures in whatever work I do. I think that more than any academic writing, my work on the PBS series *Maya and Miguel* (2005–2007) represents a concrete application of culture and language, weaving these seamlessly into the storylines and characters' practices and behaviors. Based on feedback, I know this series has had an impact on children's self-awareness.

As a woman determined to share my *conocimientos*, I have written Latino literature book reviews for the general public, which have also generated great interest, provoked intellectual challenge and discussion, and most importantly, increased interest in reading in San Antonio and beyond. These reviews range from novels to artistic, cultural, historical, political, literary, linguistic treaties written for the general public by many noted Latino authors. These critical reviews model the application of a new process for conducting critical reviews and discussion through a culturally diverse lens in a dialogical style. Now, on a national scale, I continue these book reviews and author interviews with children on books by Latinos. In a recent book review with elementary school students Izel and Azucena Piñeda (2015), sisters, on *Separate Is Not Equal* by Duncan Tonatiuh, Izel reflects,

> segregation! It shows how we fought for the right to be together with other races, and how we had perseverance! It changed the way schools are today and how Mexicans are viewed through society (p. 14).

These are the cultural literacy experiences that continue to drive my spirit.

Howard L. Smith's *Testimonio*

From my earliest days I remember books and other reading materials in my home. The paperboy dropped off the morning and the evening newspapers. The coffee table held *The Crises* and *Ebony* magazines. Behind the glass doors of the bookcase in the living room and the secretary in the dining room, three generations of family members had stored their college and professional texts. The Spanish-English dictionary that my great-aunt had used for her college studies in the 1920s, I later used for my own. The family Bible had its own little table by the front door. There were sheets of piano music with lyrics in the piano bench as well as a multivolume set of "hymns and sacred music" in its bright red letter binding perched on the upright spinet piano that my mother and her cousins had played in their youth.

My mother purchased storybooks for me, as did other relatives for Christmas and other special occasions. I do not remember much from those "Golden Books" or tales from the Disney franchise. What did stay in my mind were the oral traditions (Ajayi & Fabarebo, 2009; Foley, 1998) like the Biblical stories my mom would tell me from memory—"Jonah and the Whale" was my favorite—and *Aesop's Fables*.

While I clearly remember countless things to read in my house, I do not recall anyone actually reading at length in my house—at least not for pleasure. My family—my mother, grandparents, many uncles, aunts, and cousins—had attended college, but I would describe them more as "task readers" and not "pleasure readers." They wrote shopping lists, reviewed utility bills, read the sports pages, or the annual Christmas card. Rosenblatt (1986) proposed that some acts of reading were for the senses, emotions, and imagination (aesthetic). While at the other end, she argued, we find efferent reading experiences—those that center more on the information the reader takes away with them. I was a legitimate peripheral witness to literacy activities (Lave & Wenger, 1991; Safran, 2010), but my family model was efferent reading.

In school, reading was little more than word call and the synthetic stories from the Jack and Janet basal reading series (McKee, 1966). Even though the public schools I attended were predominantly African American, I do not recall any books in the libraries that featured people that looked or lived like me. In tenth grade, when I told my uncle that we were to write a book report on a novel of our choice, he gave me *Manchild in the Promised Land* (Brown, 1965). While the autobiography was a vicarious adventure story about a young African American male, it still was not my story. It was not until my doctoral program that I was actually introduced to children's literature that featured people of parallel cultures (Bishop, 2012).

One of my professors had written a grant specifically to infuse diversity into the teacher education college curriculum. I was hired as a graduate assistant, and one of my primary tasks was to locate, review, and purchase authentic children's literature. I found catalogs and began to order children's stories by Brian Pinkney, Nikki Grimes, Jacqueline Woodson, Christopher Paul Curtis, and so many more. Then I learned of the great Latino children's books penned by Bobbi Salinas, Carmen Tafolla, Gary Soto, and many other gifted writers. I learned that children from almost any culture could find themselves in a book. Reading is not only a fact-finding process. It can also be a "self-finding" process, an aspect that has helped me as an educator.

In these *testimonios*, we note the power of multicultural literature to affirm identity, expand worldviews, assist with border crossings, and negotiate meaning. While each of us is bilingual and bicultural, we have our unique literacy experiences. Our families played a critical role in our literacy experiences. Each of us benefited from these experiences even though the schooling process negated the essence of our very being. We must not forget that formal education is a representation of power (Darder, 2011). Often, the official knowledge held premium within a classroom is sanctioned as a means of control (Foucault, 1980; Green, 1995). Throughout history, we have observed that limiting access to knowledge creates vulnerability and produces the conditions for subjugation, manipulation, and utter destruction (Foucault, 1980; Freire, 1990).

It appears unthinkable that children can be denied the very essence of who they are, but, in fact, this happens to this day. Therefore, as educators we must recognize the cultural literacy and multiliteracies that children possess and that these knowledges must be incorporated into our praxis. In addition to guiding families in selecting appropriate literature, our role is also to provide opportunities for children to expand their knowledge through the exposure of Latino multicultural and other literature and experiences. As educators, "we also have our imagination: the capacity to invent visions of what should be and what might be in our deficient society, on the streets where we live, and in our schools" (Green, 1995, p. 5). In doing so, we provide children with the space to release their social imagination (Green, 1995).

PRAXIS: APPLICATION OF THEORY

In the following section, we extend the role of the educator in grounding and extending Latino children's multicultural literature in the learning setting. We cannot underemphasize the importance of educators becoming culturally efficacious; that is, they must have a firm identity and *concientización*, with positive beliefs in which they believe that they can make a difference in children's lives and be able to engage in critical/culturally responsive practices (Flores, Clark, Claeys, & Villarreal, 2007; Flores, Vasquez, & Clark, 2014; see chapter 1).

Several researchers concur that teachers must have the capacity to engage in critical culturally responsive pedagogies in order to ensure equity and social justice (Brindley & Laframboise, 2002; Escamilla & Nathenson-Mejía, 2003; Flores, Sheets, & Clark, 2011). Specifically, Escamilla and Nathenson-Mejía (2003) suggest that Latino children's literature can be a "powerful tool" (p. 240) of social justice. Educators can use it to enhance their compassion, heighten their understanding and capacity to deal with controversial issues, increase their knowledge of the lives of Latino students, and augment their capacity to connect with their Latino students. After the study, Escamilla and Nathenson-Mejía (2003) observed that teachers used the Latino children's literature bibliography to order books for their classrooms and school libraries. As an educator, you have the power to select the literature that will meet the needs of the children and that will relate to their lives in authentic ways.

In addition to being critically/culturally responsive, and in pursuit of social justice, it is also important that teachers be linguistically responsive (Lucas, Villegas, & Freedson-González, 2008). Even if you are not a bilingual education teacher, you can use Latino children's literature to enhance your linguistic and children's capacity. Latino children's literature can be used to validate children's identity, scaffold content, facilitate the use of the native language, create a non-threatening language environment, and authentically assess language and conceptual development.

Similar to Clark, Flores, and Vásquez (2014), we see learning as *crecimiento* (development) grounded in Engeström's (2001) notion of expansive learning. "Expansive learning is an inherently multi-voiced process of debate, negotiation and orchestration" (Engeström & Sannino, 2010, p. 5). Using this notion of expansive learning, learners' knowledges are supported and scaffolded through interaction with others, text, and other tools. Utilizing the snail shell cyclical contours in a graphic as symbolic of *crecimiento*, Clark, Flores, and Vásquez (2014) suggest, "As learners encounter others along their cyclical path, their sphere of knowledge widens and deepens" (p.

215). We also suggest that learners' social imagination is released with these enriching experiences. Hence, in the subsequent paragraphs, we provide suggestions as to how to extend literacy practices beyond the storytelling listening/reading experience. As opposed to the drudgery of filling in the blank or bubbling in the response, these literacy practices can also serve as tools to authentically assess children's understandings, interpretations, and meaning-making.

Critical Book Reviews

Book reviews are a creative way for children to express their thoughts about children's multicultural literature. Clark (2013, 2014, 2015) has several examples of book reviews in which she engages children in critical dialogue through reflection, prompting questions about the characters, storyline, and illustrations (see professional readings at the end of this chapter for a complete listing). In a review, Clark and Davis (2013) write about Duncan Tonatiuh's *Pancho Rabbit and the Coyote*. The importance of having children voice their thoughts about children's literature is evident in Melony's reflection that "it is written for us, so we should say if we like it or not" (p. 13). In another review (Davis & Clark, 2015), Melony interviews Duncan Tonatiuh about his inspirations and illustrations. These types of authentic experiences do much to expand the child's knowledges.

In reviewing *Side by Side: The Story of Dolores Huerta and César Chávez/ Lado a lado: La historia de Dolores Huerta y César Chávez*, Clark and twin sisters Lina and Paola Casas (2014) engage in dialogue about the book. Their identity and cultural pride is evident in these reflections.

> Lina: I like that he was brave like a hero, better than Superman! Because he (César Chávez) is a real person. I like that he was proud and brown, that he spoke Spanish, and he loved being Mexican. He loved his family—and did not like to see them sad. He did not like to hear his mom cry. He did not like it when they [people] treated them bad. (p. 21)

> Paola: . . . It is a really good book to learn about our heroes like us—who are Latinos who fought for us so we could have rights. We need to read this book in our classrooms. I also like to see Dolores Huerta as she is showing courage by taking all that he did and she is now fighting for it. I like that! I want to be a leader and fight for their rights. (p. 14)

As in this example, Latino children's literature can serve to heighten children's awareness of historical and social issues, while enhancing the meaning-making capacity of such issues. In the book review of *Separate Is Never*

Equal: Sylvia Mendez and Her Family's Fight for Desegregation by sisters, Izel Piñeda, Azucena Piñeda, and Clark (2015),

> Izel: I liked that they keep fighting for what is right, even when they've been told multiple times that change can't happen. And in the end, they do win and she even makes friends with the people at her new school. (p. 13)

> Azucena: They [Latino children] should know about this because they should know that Sylvia worked hard to get herself into that school that didn't want her. They should also know that what Sylvia Mendez did is something that has helped people who are white be friends with people who are Mexican because they can be in the same school. We learn about Martin Luther King, Jr., every year; we should learn about Sylvia Mendez. (p. 14)

Literature Circles

Literature circles, as opposed to round-robin reading, can be used to explore controversial issues, encourage dialogue, and empower children in their own learning (see chapter 8). According to DeNicolo and Fránquiz (2006), literature circles invite children "to use their life experiences as linguistic and cultural tools for personal understanding and for bringing about understanding in others" (p. 163). In the case of bilingual learners, this type of experience provides opportunities to read, speak, and listen in a more authentic manner.

Role-Playing and Pretend Play

Another example is role-playing, dramatic, or pretend play, as opposed to question-and-answer routines, that can be used a tool to augment the literacy experience (see chapter 6). This type of play brings "stories to life," while supporting children's literacy development (Rowe, 2007 p. 37). After listening to or reading a story, encouraging bilingual learners to role-play different book characters allows them to use language in authentic ways, engages them in creativity and social imagination, and also reveals their understanding of the plot of the story.

Readers' Theater

Similar to role-playing, readers' theater is an activity children may also enjoy. Readers' theater engages children in oral storytelling through performance. Corcoran and Davis (2005) found readers' theater a useful tool to assist students with learning disabilities. Specifically, they found that readers' theater increased children's interest in reading, their confidence, and their fluency.

While many educators believe that readers' theater is only appropriate for English proficient children, Liu (2000) demonstrates that this technique can be successfully adapted for all students.

The Arts and Aesthetic Activities

Yet, another example of enhancing the literacy experience is art and aesthetic activities (McDonald & Fisher, 2006). Through the arts, children are expressing their interpretations of text through symbols that make sense to them. Regardless of children's linguistic capacity, allowing children to draw, paint, create posters, and use apps like Kidblog, Scribblify, and Storykit can help them express their ideas, engage in creativity, and demonstrate their understanding of the story.

Digital Stories

Digital stories can also be used to extend the literacy experience (see chapter 11). After listening to or reading a book, children can create digital stories in which they retell the story from their experiences or from another perspective. This technique has been successfully used with bilingual learners (Ek, García, & Garza, 2014). Again, children's creativity and social imagination are enhanced when they are the producers of knowledge rather than the consumers of knowledge.

Testimonios

Testimonios can also be used as a pedagogical tool (DeNicolo & González, 2015; see chapter 7). Children can document their bilingual/biliteracy experiences in the home, school, and community. Bilingual learners can reflect on the benefits of these literacy experiences for their identity, bilingualism, and biculturalism. They can be encouraged to reflect on schooling experiences in which they have felt that their bilingualism/biculturalism has not been valued. Engaging children in such a critical activity will be empowering and affirming.

CONCLUSION

In sum, all children need space to create and imagine. Using Latino children's multicultural literature that is relevant to the lives of Latinos allows children to feel connected to the world and expand their cultural literacy. Multiliteracies, such as storytelling, picture books, illustrated books, and digital literacies provoke children's social imagination. Allowing children to express their thoughts through book reviews, role-playing, art, writing stories, *testimonies*, etc., enhances those opportunities to engage in social imagination.

Our modern world requires thinkers who can navigate in an ever-changing world. As educators, we create the conditions for social justice through transworld pedagogy, which situates the learning experiences as *crecimiento* rather than alienation, domination, and subordination (see chapter 1). In countering assimilation, we ensure that Latino children have equal opportunity to learn. As an educator (teacher, librarian, curriculum developer, etc.), you demonstrate your power through the authentic Latino literature you select and the literacy practices in which you engage children as transworld citizens. These critical practices support Latino children's identity development, build on their knowledge, and enrich their lives.

To expand your social imagination as an educator, it is important to engage in dialogue with knowledgeable others, challenge yourself, and expand your literacy experiences. Reading Latino children's multicultural literature from a critical perspective can assist you in achieving this goal. Notably, becoming a culturally efficacious educator and engaging in transworld pedagogy are not checklists that you simply check-off; these are dynamic processes that require your full commitment, embodiment, and action. Friere (1990) calls on us to transform the world, so rather than standing at the precipice of change or denying that our world is transforming, become the educator whose praxis allow children's dreams to become realities, inspires the imagination, and expands their *conocimientos*.

REFERENCES

Ajayi, G., & Fabarebo, S. I. (2009). *Oral traditions in black and African culture.* Lagos, Nigeria: Concept for Centre for Black and African Arts and Civilization.

Anzaldúa, G. E. (1981). *El mundo zurdo*: The vision. In C. Moraga & G. E. Anzaldúa (Eds.), *This bridge called my back: Writings by radical women of color* (pp. 195–96). New York, NY: Kitchen Table: Women of Color Press.

———. (1981). *La prieta.* In C. Moraga & G. E. Anzaldúa (Eds.), *This bridge called my back: Writings by radical women of color* (pp. 198–209). New York, NY: Kitchen Table: Women of Color Press.

———. (1987). *Borderlands: The new mestiza = la frontera.* San Francisco, CA: Spinsters/Aunt Lute Foundation Books.

———. (1990). *Making face, making soul:* Haciendo caras. *Creative and critical perspectives by feminists of color.* San Francisco, CA: Aunt Lute Foundation Books.

———. (1997). *La conciencia de la mestiza*: Toward a new consciousness. In A. M. García (Ed.), *Chicana feminist thought: The basic historical writings* (pp. 270–74). New York, NY: Routledge.

Apple, M. W. (1993). What post-modernists forget: Cultural capital and official knowledge. *Curriculum Studies, 1*(3), 301–16.

———. (2014). *Official knowledge: Democratic education in a conservative age*. New York, NY: Routledge.

Baker, C. (2011). *Foundations of bilingual education and bilingualism*. Philadelphia, PA: Multilingual Matters.

Bishop, R. S. (2012). Reflections on the development of African American children's literature. *Journal of Children's Literature, 38*(2), 5–13.

Brindley, R., & Laframboise, K. L. (2002). The need to do more: Promoting multiple perspectives in preservice teacher education through children's literature. *Teaching and Teacher Education, 18*, 405–19.

Brown, C. (1965). *Manchild in the promised land*. New York, NY: MacMillan.

Camerena, J. G. (1962). *La imagen de la alegoría de la patria*. Retrieved May 15, 2015, from https://gerardomorah.wordpress.com/2008/06/23/alegoria-a-la-patria-portada-del-antiguo-libro-de-texto/.

Clark, E. R., Casas L., & Casas, P. (2014, January–March). Review of "Side by side/ Lado a lado: The story of Dolores Huerta and César Chávez/La historia de Dolores Huerta y César Chávez, by M. Brown & J. Cepeda." *NABE Perspectives, 36*(1), 21.

Clark, E. R., & Davis, M. (2013, January–February). Review of "Pancho rabbit and the coyote: A migrant's tale, by Duncan Tonatiuh." *NABE Perspectives, 35*(1), 13.

Clark, E. R., & Flores, B. B. (2014) The metamorphosis of teacher identity: An intersection of ethnic consciousness, self-conceptualization, and belief systems. In P. Jenlink (Ed.), *Teacher identity and struggle for recognition: Meeting the challenges of a diverse society* (pp. 3–14). Lanham, MD: Rowman & Littlefield.

Clark, E. R., Flores, B. B., & Vásquez, O. A. (2014). Iluminadas a través de cosmovisión: A new age of enlightenment for pedagogía transmundial. In B. B. Flores, O. A. Vásquez, & E. R. Clark (Eds.), *Generating transworld pedagogy: Reimagining La Clase Mágica* (pp. 209–19). Lanham, MD: Lexington Books.

Clark, E. R., Piñeda, A., & Piñeda, I. (2015 , January–March). Review of "Separate is never equal: Sylvia Mendez and her family's fight for desegregation." *NABE Perspectives, 15*, 16.

Corcoran, C. A., & Davis, A. D. (2005). A study of the effects of readers' theater on second- and third-grade special education students' fluency growth. *Reading Improvement, 42*(2), 105.

Darder, A. (2011). *Culture and power in the classroom: A critical foundation for the education of bicultural students*. Boulder, CO: Paradigm Press.

Davis, M., & Clark, E. R. (2015, January–March). Interview with prize-winning author Duncan Tonatiuh. *NABE Perspectives, 37*(1), 15–16.

Delgado Bernal, D. (2001). Learning and living pedagogies of the home. The *mestiza* consciousness of Chicana students. *International Journal of Qualitative Studies in Education, 14*(5), 623–39.

DeNicolo, C. P., & Fránquiz, M. E. (2006). "Do I have to say it?" Critical encounters with multicultural children's literature. *Language Arts, Special Issue: Multilingual and Multicultural. Changing the Ways We Teach, 84*(2), 57–170.

DeNicolo, C. P., & González, M. (2015). *Testimoniando en Nepantla*: Using testimonio as a pedagogical tool for exploring embodied literacies and bilingualism. *JoLLE@UGA: Journal of Language and Literacy, 2*(1), 109–26.

Ek, L. D, García, A., & Garza, A. (2014). Latino children: Constructing identities, voices, and linguistic and cultural understandings. In B. B. Flores, O. A. Vásquez, & E. R. Clark (Eds.), *Generating transworld pedagogy: Reimagining La Clase Mágica* (pp. 129–42). Lanham, MD: Lexington Books.

Engeström, Y. (2001). Expansive learning at work: Toward an activity theoretical reconceptualization. *Journal of Education and Work, 14*(1), 133–56.

Engeström, Y., & Sannino, A. (2010). Studies of expansive learning: Foundations, findings and future challenges. *Educational Research Review, 5*(1), 1–24. doi:10.1016.j.edurev.2009.12.002.

Escamilla, K., & Nathenson-Mejía, S. (2003). Preparing culturally responsive teachers: Using Latino children's literature in teacher education. *Equity & Excellence in Education, Special Issue: Partnering for Equity, 36*(3), 238–48, doi:10.1080/714044331.

Flores, B. B., Clark, E. R., Claeys, L., & Villarreal, A. (2007). Academy for teacher excellence: Recruiting, preparing, and retaining Latino teachers though learning communities. *Teacher Education Quarterly, 34*(4), 53–69.

Flores, B. B., Ek, L., & Sánchez, P. (2011). Bilingual education candidate ideology: *Descubriendo sus motivos y creencias*. In B. B. Flores, R. H. Sheets, & E. R Clark (Eds.), *Teacher preparation for bilingual student populations: Educar para transformar* (pp. 40–58). New York, NY: Routledge.

Flores, B. B., Sheets, R. S., & Clark, E. R. (2011). *Teacher preparation for bilingual student populations: Educar para transformar.* New York, NY: Routledge.

Flores, B. B., Vásquez, O. A., & Clark, E. R. (2014). *Generating transworld pedagogy: Reimagining La Clase Mágica.* Lanham, MD: Lexington Books.

Foley, J. M. (1998). *Teaching oral traditions.* New York, NY: Modern Language Association.

Foucault, M. (1980). *Power/knowledge: Selected interviews and other writings 1972–1977.* (C. Gordon, Ed. and Trans.). New York, NY: Pantheon.

Freire, P. (1990). *Pedagogy of the oppressed.* New York, NY: Continuum Press.

González, N., Moll, L., & Tenery, M. (1995). Funds of knowledge for teaching in Latino households. *Urban Education, 29*(4), 443–70.

Greene, M. (1995). *Releasing the imagination: Essays on education, the arts, and social change.* San Francisco, CA: Jossey-Bass.

Lave, J., & Wenger, E. (1991). *Situated learning: Legitimate peripheral participation.* New York, NY: Cambridge University Press.

Liu, J. (2000). The power of readers' theater: From reading to writing. *ELT Journal, 54*(4), 354–61.

Lucas, T., Villegas, A. M., & Freedson-González, M. (2008). Linguistically responsive teacher education: Preparing classroom teachers to teach English language learners. *Journal of Teacher Education, 59*(4), 361. doi:10.1177/0022487108322110.

McDonald, N. L., & Fisher, D. (2006). *Teaching literacy through the arts*. New York, NY: Guilford Press.

McKee, G. P. (1966). *Tip and Mitten*. New York, NY: Houghton Mifflin.

Rivera, T. (1971). *Y no se lo tragó la tierra/And the earth did not devour him*. (H. Rios, Trans.). Berkeley, CA: Quinto Sol.

Rosenblatt, L. M. (1986). The aesthetic transaction. *Journal of Aesthetic Education, 20*(4), 122–28.

Rowe, D. (2007). Bringing books to life: The role of book-related dramatic play in young children's literacy learning. In K. Roskos & J. Christie (Eds.), *Play and literacy in early childhood: Research from multiple perspectives* (pp. 37–63). Mahwah, NJ: Lawrence Erlbaum Associates.

Safran, L. (2010). Legitimate peripheral participation and home education. *Teaching and Teacher Education, 26*(1), 107–12. doi:10.1016/j.tate.2009.06.002.

Saldaña, L., & Méndez-Negrete, J. (2014). Bilingual preservice teachers *conocimientos*: Shifting and evolving consciousness. In P. Jenlink (Ed.), *Teacher identity and the struggle for recognition: Meeting the challenge of a diverse society* (pp. 228–44). Lanham, MD: Rowman & Littlefield.

Valencia, R. R. (Ed.). (1997). *The evolution of deficit thinking: Educational thought and practice*. London, UK: Falmer Press.

———. (2010). *Dismantling contemporary deficit thinking*. New York, NY: Routledge.

Valenzuela, A. (1999). *Subtractive schooling: U.S.–Mexican youth and the politics of caring*. Albany, NY: State University of New York Press.

DISCUSSION QUESTIONS:

1. What do the authors mean when they state, "As an educator, you have the power to select the literature that will meet the needs of the children and that will relate to their lives in authentic ways"?

2. Pretend you are being interviewed for a position as a teacher; respond to the following questions: (1) Why is it important to use authentic Latino children's multicultural literature? (2) What is your role in creating an environment that promotes social justice?

3. As a teacher, how will you use Latino children's multicultural literature in your classroom?

4. What were some tools mentioned in this chapter to enhance the literacy experience? In addition to these ideas presented, discuss other ideas to augment the literacy experience.

5. What are some literacy experiences that you, as a teacher, will use to enhance your cultural and linguistic competence and efficacy?

ACTIVITIES

A. Develop your personal *testimonio*: Reflect on your literacy experiences and how they have impacted your beliefs, view of the world, and your own literacy and learning.
B. Read two to three books from the appendix; reflect on these books and identify how these books helped you to expand your cultural and linguistic competence.
C. Select one of the books mentioned in this chapter or in the appendix; read the book to a group of children. Enhance the literacy experience using one of the tools mentioned in the chapter. Write a two- to three-page reflection on this experience.
D. Examine the following apps: Kidblog, Scribblify, Storykit; for each app, identify how you could use it to enhance the literacy experience; also identify the strengths and limitations of each app.
E. Look for other apps that can be used for children to create stories and/or to augment the literacy experience.
F. Create a rubric that you can use to assess children's language, conceptual, and cultural development to extend the literacy experience.

PROFESSIONAL READINGS

Anti-Defamation League curricular guide to Duncan Tonatiuh's newest book, *Separate Is Never Equal*. Retrieved from www.adl.org/assets/pdf/education-outreach/book-of-the-month-separate-is-never-equal.pdf.

Clark, E. R., Casas L., & Casas, P. (2014 , January–March). Review of "Side by side: The story of Dolores Huerta and César Chávez/Lado a lado: La historia de Dolores Huerta y César Chávez by M. Brown & J. Cepeda." *NABE Perspectives, 36*(1), 21.

Clark, E. R., & Davis, M. (2013 , January–February). Review of "Pancho rabbit and the coyote: A migrant's tale, by Duncan Tonatiuh." *NABE Perspectives, 35*(1), 13.

Clark, E. R., Piñeda, A., & Piñeda, I. (2015 , January–March). Review of "Separate is never equal: Sylvia Mendez and her family's fight for desegregation." *NABE Perspectives, 15*, 16.

Davis, M., & Clark, E. R. (2015, January–March). Interview with prize-winning author Duncan Tonatiuh. *NABE Perspectives, 37*(1), 15–16.

Delgado Bernal, D. (2001). Learning and living pedagogies of the home: The *mestiza* consciousness of Chicana students. *International Journal of Qualitative Studies in Education, 14*(5), 623–39. Retrieved May 16, 2013, from http://dx.doi.org/10.1080/09518390110059838.

DeNicolo, C. P., & Franquiz, M. E. (2006). "Do I have to say it?" Critical encounters with multicultural children's literature. *Language Arts, Special Issue: Multilingual and Multicultural. Changing the Ways We Teach, 84*(2), 157–70.

Duncan Tonatiuh's blog is full of information that would be useful for teachers and students: www.duncantonatiuh.com/.

Duran, R. P. (2015). Review of "Generating transworld pedagogy: Reimagining La Clase Mágica. B. B. Flores, O. A. Vásquez, & E. R. Clark (Eds.). *International Journal of Extended Research, 2*(2), 143–46.

Ek, L. D, García, A., & Garza, A. (2014). Latino children: Constructing identities, voices, and linguistic and cultural understandings. In B. B. Flores, O. A. Vásquez, & E. R. Clark (Eds.), *Generating transworld pedagogy: Reimagining La Clase Mágica* (pp. 129–42). Lanham, MD: Rowman & Littlefield.

Prieto, L., & Villenas, S. A. (2012). Pedagogies from nepantla: *Testimonio*, Chicana/ Latina feminisms and teacher education classrooms. *Equity & Excellence in Education, 45*(3), 411–29.

Torres-Guzman, M. E. (2014, January–March). Review of "Generating transworld pedagogy: Reimagining La Clase Mágica." B. B. Flores, O. A. Vásquez, & E. R. Clark (Eds.). *NABE Perspectives, 36*(1), 17.

Part V

UNA FUENTE DE RECURSOS: DIMENSIONS OF CULTURAL HERITAGE AND LITERACY

Figure 15.1.

I saw one child go from a sad little girl who could barely hold her head up, to a little girl who could not stop smiling and beaming, after she was asked to read aloud from one of my books and chose to read the Spanish version. Her mother cried. If bilingual/multicultural literature can save even one little girl (or boy)—then its importance is monumental.

—Carolyn Dee Flores, November 4, 2014

Chapter Fifteen

Realizing and Capitalizing on Our Cultural Literary Heritage: The Big Brown Elephant in the Room

Oralia Garza de Cortés

El nombre mío que he perdido,
¿dónde vive, dónde prospera?
Nombre de infancia, gota de leche,
rama de mirto tan ligera.

—Gabriela Mistral

INTRODUCTION

For the past forty-five years, educators, librarians, and parents have articulated, voiced, and insisted on the need for Latino children to be represented and included in the canon we know as American Children's Literature. Well-established children's literature awards such as The Américas Award, The Pura Belpré Award, and The Tomás Rivera Mexican American Children's Book Award (see chapter 2) have paved the way for the recognition of quality children's literature, serving as pre-selection tools over the past twenty years, offering teachers, librarians, and parents recommended material with which to select and share great literature. Compelling literature such as Pam Muñoz Ryan's rags-to-riches story *Esperanza Rising* (2002) and Julia Alvarez's *Return to Sender* (2009) have given and continue to give Latino children and all children much needed culturally relevant stories to help them make sense of the world they live in, thus giving voice to their humanity. What Latino audience is not endeared by *Señor Calavera* (2003), Yuyi Morales's snippy yet beloved character who although representing impending death is himself lured to all the fun to be had at Grandma Beetle's smashing birthday parties, derailing the inevitable as he keeps coming back each year for yet more fun and adventure? Sweepstakes winner-take-all of the three aforementioned awards, Yuyi Morales is today a Caldecott Honor Illustrator Award winner for *Viva Frida* (2014) and a success story, particularly given that Morales discovered the world of children's picture books in English for the first time as a young immigrant mother. Yet for all of her accomplishments, full access to Morales's titles continues to remain problematic in that her major works remain unpublished in Spanish, inaccessible to the very audiences who stand to gain so much from her brilliant work. Eleven years after its original publication, *Just a Minute: A Trickster Tale and Counting Book* (Morales, 2003) is available in English only, and at that, only in its original hardback edition. A paperback edition of Morales's story that could serve to mitigate economic issues of affordability and accessibility for family-friendly literacy programs, home libraries, or simply for a child's own individual reading pleasure has yet to be produced.

THEORETICAL FRAMEWORK

Dearth in Publishing

The Cooperative Children's Book Center (CCBC), a university-based non-circulating library, book examination, and teacher education resource center at the University of Madison-Wisconsin has kept statistics on the number of books published by people of color in the United States since 1994. In 2002, the CCBC began differentiating between those books published specifically by and those published about Latinos. Of the approximately 3,150 books examined by the center that year, books authored by Latinos numbered a meager forty-eight, or 1.5 percent of all books examined. While the numbers have fluctuated from year to year, in 2014 that number had increased by a mere eleven to bring the total number of books published by Latino authors to fifty-nine, or 1.7 percent, a 0.02 percent increase since 2002 (see chapter 1). Regrettably, these figures speak volumes about the publishing industry's failure to pay attention to the demographic changes that predicted the browning of the U.S. and the explosive 39 percent growth of the Latino population of children in the first decade of the twenty-first century (Horner, 1996). These dismal publishing figures demonstrate that the number of published Latino authors has not even begun to keep pace with the increased growth of the Latino population of children (Ryan, 2013). The figures also ask the question of just who is writing for Latinos, if not Latinos themselves, and it raises other important questions about authenticity and representation (Hehrlich, 2015). Fifty years ago, Nancy Larrick, one of the first to write about the lack of literature for African American children, decried in her seminal article the "all white world of children's books" (Larrick, 1965). The statistics still give pause.

Many factors may account for the current state of publishing. Industry publishers, squeezed between an economic recession and a continuously tight economy and diminished library budgets, have also faced major technological changes including a demand for electronic, digital-driven products like e-books. With large corporate takeovers continuing to drive the bottom line, publishers are hard-pressed to produce material about a subject matter that touches on unfamiliar (to them) territory that falls outside the norm of their own comfort zones. The result is a huge market potential in the hands of publishers stuck in old ways of doing things and clueless on how best to diversify their company staff and ramp up production and marketing schedules so as to be more responsive to the needs of a changing U.S. If large businesses and corporations figure out the economic potential of a vibrant Latino market, surely Latino-savvy book industry marketing managers can be sought to help the industry figure out how best to carve out and create new avenues for the production, marketing, and distribution of these much-needed books (see chapter 1). If done properly, their contribution to the culture of literacy would surely make a difference in children's reading experiences, creating much-needed changes to the industry and ultimately to Latino children's educational success.

Added to this dynamic is an overt climate of hate over language rights in the form of English-only laws and the equally contentious nature of an anti-immigrant debate soured by a broken immigration system. As a result, well-intentioned U.S. publishers like Abrams, for example, are disinclined to issue Spanish editions for books like Duncan Tonatiuh's *Pancho Rabbit and the Coyote* (2013) that could help the very students the story was intended to reach. Relevant stories with important social themes like immigration help all students to better understand the dire circumstances that many children and families find themselves in. Pancho Rabbit and Señor Coyote aid students in developing much-needed empathy for the plight of immigrants, poor people, and the "other." Toniatuh's multiple-award-winning *Separate Is Never Equal: Sylvia Mendes and the Struggle for Equal Education* (2014), an important civil rights story about the education of Mexican American children in the U.S. during the Jim Crow era is another title that deserves a wider readership and should be made available through its own Spanish edition (see chapter 4).

In the interim, what are we to do when clearly the number of books published in any given year does not match up to the diverse needs of Latino students? According to Professor Melanie Kloss, "Classroom teachers should actively seek out titles that get it right. Children are more likely to read and value the importance of reading when they can see and connect to characters that are like them" (Kloss, 2015). But Pat Enciso, professor and a member of the Tomás Rivera Mexican American Children's Book Award selection committee, sees it differently. She notes that what is available is "not finding its way into classrooms" (Rich, 2012). Publishers would do well to revisit their inventory and reprint those titles that they did get right and employ new and better marketing strategies to promote and develop plans to disseminate these materials and make these titles more accessible to children.

Diversity Partners in the Struggle

Latinos, however, are not alone in demanding more literature that represents the multiplicities of cultures and experiences of Latinos in the U.S. Shortly before his death, Walter D. Myers (2014) rattled the book publishing industry in an article titled "Where are the People of Color in Children's Books?" This was a simple question in response to industry statistics that only ninety-three books published in 2013 were actually authored by blacks. In a companion opinion piece, his son Christopher Myers (2014) was even bolder, calling the lack of publishing plain and simply, apartheid. His most profound insight, however, was calling for a new paradigm that offers children a map of the imagination that allows for "a more expansive landscape upon which to dream" (Myers, C., 2014).

The organization We Need Diverse Books, founded in 2014, is a mixed group of authors, illustrators, and other book professionals calling for change in the book publishing industry so that it better "reflects and honors the lives of all young people" (We Need Diverse Books, 2014, p. 3). Already they have begun to make inroads. In an effort to diversify the face of editorial boardrooms, they have called for the establishment of scholarships and publishing intern positions. A successful event during the BookCon 2014 conference held in New York City marked their debut as an organization that will not go away. The We Need Diverse Books leadership reorganized a panel that previously lacked ethnic and gender representation and included a line-up of mostly white male authors (Querechi, 2014). Another organization, Latinas4Latino Literature, an online community of Latina moms debuted in 2013, shortly after a *New York Times* article brought to light the lack of literature for Latino children (Rich, 2012). Their online presence has helped to bring further attention to the notable lack of publishing of Latino literature, and it has promoted currently published books about Latinos.

Lee & Low Books is a giant in the field of multicultural children's publications. They played a critical role in acquiring the landmark Children's Book

Press collection, retaining it as its own imprint at Lee & Low Books. In essence, they found a vibrant home for the continued distribution of some of the most beautiful earlier Latino Children's literature as envisioned by the press's founding publisher Harriet Rohmer. Most notably, Jason Low (2015) is leading a major challenge by insisting that mainstream publishers take an initial baseline diversity survey that can help the industry to begin taking small steps that can lead to change in the industry (Low, 2015).

Changes are also evident in the approach that the traditional book review journals have recently taken to reviewing children's books with unique Latino cultural content. Children's book review editor Vicky Smith at *Kirkus Review* has taken concerted steps to find professional book reviewers with more in-depth knowledge and insight into Latino culture. At *School Library Journal*, senior editor Shelly Diaz (2013) has enhanced the diversity conversation with respect to Latino books through her careful analysis and insight. She collaborates with REFORMA, a national organization of committed, knowledgeable librarians who have paved the way for the establishment of the Pura Belpré Award.

PRAXIS: APPLICATION OF THEORY

But to look for books for Latino children published only in the U.S. and only in English is to offer today's Latino students access to only half of their literary heritage. A wealth of beautiful literature for children *en Español* exists beyond our borders. The literature from the Spanish-speaking world completes the full spectrum of the literature for the biliterate child published by obscure names like Ekaré, Fondo de Cultura Económica, and Media Vaca, just to name a random few publishing houses from Venezuela, Mexico, and Spain. These are but a sampling of the many outstanding children's publishing houses that year after year continue to publish quality Spanish language children's literature. Many of these Spanish language children's publishing houses attend the Bologna Book Fair held yearly in Bologna, Italy, where the absolutely best books are featured, honored, bought, and sold. Those purchased titles are then produced and distributed en masse. Large Spanish publishers like SM or Alfaguara may have global publishing headquarters in Spain, but they are also in Buenos Aires, Bogota, Mexico City, San Juan, and Santiago de Chile. Some, like Grupo Editorial Norma and Grupo Editorial Panamericana, are based in Latin America with offices and book distribution throughout the Americas. Children exposed to the vast array of children's books produced in Latin America and Spain are privileged because in essence, by reading books in Spanish from other countries, they enter the realm of international children's literature. Access to this full spectrum of books in Spanish privileges the reader through exposure to even broader perspectives and worldviews. Such a diverse collection provides access to global literature that few U.S. children can really claim.

The global world of Spanish language literature also holds much potential for the recognition and inclusion of U.S. Latino authors like Tonatiuh and Morales, whose appealing stories deserve a broader, much wider international readership. As of this writing, these particular authors are little known in Mexican or Latin American children's publishing circles, writing from that in-between space known to the Nahuas as *Nepantla* (Anzaldúa & Keating, 2013), where authors and illustrators operate much like prophets in their own land. Both Tonatiuh and Morales are currently living in Mexico, a choice made possible by virtue of their ability to navigate their worlds through their dual citizenship. Educational professionals, then, would do well to find other avenues and resources for the wealth of material available to children and should continue to venture out beyond their own borders to find the quality material missing from the classroom, school, and public libraries. Teachers and librarians must continue in the "beat the bushes" tradition of finding this fine literature, scouring the book halls of international book fairs like the Feria Internacional del Libro (FIL), held in Guadalajara, Mexico, the last weekend in November of each year. To enter the huge fair is to be dazzled by the amazing wealth and size of Spanish publishing in full display, with *novedades,* or new titles, featured prominently. Now in its twenty-ninth year, FIL, also known as the Guadalajara Book Fair, attracts publishers and book aficionados from throughout the world. In 2014, twenty thousand professionals from throughout the world attended this important book fair where 1,900 publishers and forty-four countries were represented, making it the largest Spanish language book fair in the world. It is at FIL where one can mine the gems critical to children's literacy development.

At FIL 2014, an exciting Chilean children's publisher, Editorial Amanuta, debuted an amazing collection of four never-before-published titles authored by Gabriela Mistrál. With measured poetic prose embedded in the cultural landscape of her native Chile, Mistrál, Latin America's foremost Nobel Prize winner in literature, retells four classic fairy tales, *La Cenicienta* (Mistral, 2013), *La Bella Durmiente del bosque* (Mistral, 2013), *Blanca Nieve en la casa de los enanos* (Mistral, 2013), and *Caperucita Roja* (Mistral, 2013), thus making this priceless literature available to a new, twenty-first-century generation of young Spanish language readers. All four titles in the series received an Honorable Mention for the New Horizons Award at the prestigious 2014 Bologna Book Fair. The International Children's Digital Library located in Munich, Germany, named *Caperucita Roja* (2013) to the prestigious White

Raven List in 2013. Exposing bilingual learners to the absolute best of Spanish language children's literature exposes them to the most authentic source for their own literacy and cultural development.

No Translation. No Transliteration.
No Language Lost to Translation.

The introduction of poetic, authentic text for children serves to strengthen and enrich a child's early literary experience with words, word play, and poetry, accelerating a child's learning into that pathway to an even further enriched language learning pattern. All Spanish-speaking children, U.S. Latino children included, deserve to know the giants of Spanish literature who also wrote for children as well as the popular contemporary writers writing for children today. Children deserve to know the writings of literary giants like Mistral and Lorca, as do they deserve to know the literature of the Colombian poet Rafael Pombo, the beloved Cuban writer José Martí, and the Hans Christian Andersen Award Medalist Ana María Machado from Brazil, whose many works are also available in Spanish. They also need to know the body of literature from Mexico that includes such writers as María Barranda, Emilio Carbajillo, Pascuala Corona, Francisco Hinojosa, and Margarita Robleda.

Other Venues: Lea-LA and LA Librería

Another new venue for examining this valuable literature is Lea-LA, a Spanish language book fair sponsored by the University of Guadalajara Foundation, the same sponsor of the Guadalajara Book Fair. Now in its fourth year, this now biennial book fair takes place in May in Los Angeles. The book fair brings choice children's authors from Mexico and provides many opportunities for audiences to interact with the authors. In 2014, the devaluation of the peso kept many children's publishers from attending. However, LA Librería, an exciting new Spanish children's bookstore in Los Angeles started by two mothers with children in a local public school's dual-language program, was able to represent many of these children's publishers at Lea-LA in 2014. The LA Librería bookstore offers excellent, quality book choices made available to those outside the Los Angeles area via their online bookstore. Schools and public libraries have at their disposal the excellent books and services offered by Spanish language distributors such as Bilingual Publications, Cinco Puntos Books, and Lectorum.

Books in Spanish published in their original country of origin are also recognized and nourished by the International Board of Books for Young People (IBBY, 2014), an international organization dedicated to peace through literature. With chapters in many Latin American countries, IBBY's local children's literacy experts review and select the best books from their country for consideration for the prestigious Hans Christian Andersen Award (IBBY, 2014). This organization is significant because local professionals decide which of their authors and illustrators best represent their country and launch these authors and/or illustrators and their works onto a world stage. Their publications are easily accessible online and can serve as essential tools in the book selection process.

CONCLUSION

With such a wealth of resources, school librarians, teachers, and parents need not feel helpless in their quest to find the needed resources. Bilingual children in the U.S. deserve the absolute best of children's literature that both reflects their cultural experience and allows them to see themselves represented in this literature. Additionally, bilingual children deserve access to that vast world of beautiful stories and poems in Spanish that is their mother tongue, their birthright, and literary heritage. It is our obligation as concerned professionals to provide them with that literature that can only serve to propel them into an exciting world that holds much promise for their educational success as well-read readers and world citizens.

REFERENCES

Alvarez, J. (2009). *Return to sender.* New York, NY: Knopf Books for Young Children.

Anzaldúa, G., & Keating, A. (2013). *This bridge we call home: Radical visions for transformation.* New York, NY: Routledge.

Diaz, S. (2013). Librarians sound off: Not a lack of Latino lit for kids but a lack of awareness. *School Library Journal.* Retrieved from www.slj.com/2013/01/collection-development/librarians-sound-off-not-a-lack-of-latino-lit-for-kids-but-a-lack-of-awareness/#.

Hehrlich, H. (2015). The diversity gap in children's publishing. Retrieved from blog.leeandlow.com/2015/03/05/the-diversity-gap-in.

Horner, L. L. (Ed.). (1997). *Hispanic Americans: A statistical sourcebook.* Palo Alto, CA: Information Publications.

International Board of Books for Young People. (2014). Retrieved from www.ibby.org/about.0.html.

Kloss, M. (2015). *White, white and read all over: Lack of diversity in children's books continues.* DeKalb, IL: Northern Illinois University. Retrieved June 2, 2015, from www.newsroom.niu.edu/2015/06/02/white-white-and-read-all-over.

Larrick, N. (1965). The all-white world of children's books. Saturday Review. Retrieved May 29, 2015, from www.unz.org/Pub/SaturdayRev-1965sep11-00063.

Low, J. (2015). Why we're asking publishers to join our diversity baseline survey. Retrieved from http://blog.leeandlow.com/category/diversity-102/.

Mistral, G., & Ballestelleros, C. (2013). *Blanca nieve en la casa de los enanos*. Santiago de Chile. Editorial Amanuta.

Mistral, G., & Cardemil, C. (2013). *La bella durmiente del bosque*. Santiago de Chile. Editorial Amanuta.

Mistral, G., & Ojeda, B. (2013). *La cenicienta*. Santiago de Chile. Editorial Amanuta.

Mistral, G., & Valdivia, P. (2013). *Caperucita roja*. Santiago de Chile. Editorial Amanuta.

Morales, Y. (2003). *Just a minute: A trickster tale and counting book*. San Francisco, CA: Chronicle Books.

———. (2014). *Viva Frida*. New York, NY: Roaring Brook Press.

Myers, C. (2014). The apartheid of children's literature. *New York Times*. Retrieved May 1, 2015, from www.nytimes.com/2014/03/16/opinion/sunday/the-apartheid-of-childrens-literature.html?_r=0.

Myers, W. D. (2014, March 15). Where are the people of color in children's books? *New York Times* Sunday Review, Opinion.

Querechi, B. (2014). WeNeedDiverseBooks campaign comes to inaugural BookCon. Code switch: Frontiers of race, culture and identity. National Public Radio. Retrieved June 03, 2015, from www.npr.org/sections/codeswitch/2014/06/02/318098926/-weneeddiv.

Rich, M. (2012). For young Latino readers, an image is missing. Retrieved June 10, 2015, from www.nytimes.com/2012/12/05/education/young-latino-students-dont-see-themselves-in-books.html.

Ryan, C. (2013). Language use in the United States: 2011. American community survey reports. U.S. Census Bureau.

Ryan, P. M. (2002). *Esperanza rising*. New York, NY: Scholastic.

School Library Journal, www.slj.com/2013/01/collection-development/librarians-sound-off-not-a-lack-of-latino-lit-for-kids-but-a-lack-of-awareness/.

Tonatiuh, D. (2013). *Pancho Rabbit and the Coyote*. New York, NY: Abrams.

———. (2014). *Separate is never equal: Sylvia Mendez and her family's fight for desegregation*. New York, NY: Abrams.

We Need Diverse Books (2014). Annual Report. Retrieved from weneeddiversebooks.org/annualreport2014/.

Chapter Sixteen

Cultural Dignity: Personal Foundations, Present Realities, and Vision of Future Productions

Daniel Alejandro González

Making lists of places I've been—
Did I leave someone better off?
Did I do something worthwhile?

—Margarita D. González, Skopje, Macedonia, 1999

Exercises of remembering and directed questioning helped my mother, Margarita D. González, to reflect on her travels, her life, and her legacy. To practice these, she often wrote about personal and cultural subjects that were meaningful to her life. Some writings were in the form of children's stories or fables. She would give these as gifts to family and friends whom she thought would appreciate a message that would speak to their particular situation and reality. Most of the themes she wrote about were personal in nature and involved identity, gender, cultural heritage, overall sense of well-being, and spirituality. Many stories prompted the reader to capitalize on family history and ethnicity by turning them into useful resources. She seldom thought of looking for these types of books at commercial bookstores. She felt the need to communicate these special messages through an original text. The books that she would want to buy for these occasions did not exist or were not readily available for purchase. She was creating her own space where she could contribute to society from a position of dignity as an individual and cultural person.

The practices of remembering and reflecting on these questions were also something she urged of me. For one of life's fundamental lessons, she once gave me a book titled *Everything I Know about Losing a Parent.* I opened it and found that every single page was completely blank. Somehow, the book was insightful and actually helpful for me. From this book, I understood that my mother wanted me to know something important and that there was no existing text that would relay the messages and values that she wanted to share. I understood that she wanted what was best for me. I understood that she herself did not know how to completely articulate her ideas and advice on every subject. So this blank book was a call for me to fill it with my own findings and my own words. At the prompting of this seemingly empty book and from her other writings and modeling, I began this practice of reflection for myself, a practice she had honed and that had become a way of life for her.

In my own experiences there always seemed to be an interesting place or event available if I could just find the right angle to see it, to access it, to experience it. It was a priority for me to keep myself open for connections and possibilities. My life and educational opportunities took me to faraway places like New Zealand, Egypt, Slovenia, and China. These exposed me to the many shared experiences and connections among people, revealing the abundance and power of languages and cultural heritages. Through the varied voices of parents, grandparents, and other oral and literary vehicles, each community and country was expressing its own history, present situation, vision for growth, and a living cultural dignity. These travels always included bookstore visits and countless conversations about what were the essential stories of a country, a region, a city, a town, a community, a particular group of people, or the person sharing time with me. I was curious to know what the base foundation was for the region and the people I met. In order to contribute and give back to the people and places I encountered, I was compelled to learn as much as I could about who they were, where they've been, and where they wanted to go.

Since South Texas and my hometown of San Antonio has stories and cultural legends like the *Cucuy*, *Chupacabras*, and the school bus tragedy at the railroad tracks, I wanted to know what stories other people had and I wanted to share ours with them. This curiosity led me to books on fantastical places with confusing and magical characters like *Crazy Harman* from Turkmenistan and the Egyptian mythology tale of *Rhodopis*, which is the earliest known variant of Cinderella. There were fascinating Maori folktales like the *Golden Kowhai* that felt similar to stories of *Pachamama*, *La princesa Ixbucane*, *Popol Vuh*, and elements from the biblical book of Genesis. I was also fascinated to read the beautiful and spiritual sensations and exploration of life in Neruda's writings. However, the most important accounts for understanding the places and people that I met were not always written fables or existing communal tales, but rather personal stories that people wanted to share. I was once told a fascinating oral history account set high in the Caucasus Mountains of the Republic of Georgia, near Armenia and Turkey, about competitions between two men slashing at each other with small makeshift blades while buried to their waists in snow. While sport and competition are familiar concepts, this story gave me images of rural activities that were not common in my life.

To continue learning and contribute to my extended community, I have ongoing conversations with colleagues regarding concepts for new projects, analysis, and writing. They share ideas and lenses concerning research on applied arts, gender roles, sexuality, identity formation, migration, and immigration. They are also exploring fascinating ideas to include spirituality in educational settings through arts and creative practices. These discussions and the work of the larger research community provoke more curiosity and thoughts of new angles for exploration that are fundamental to our community's vitality, sustained cultural dignity, self-determination, and overall freedom. In addition to traditional research, my future projects and collaborations will involve historical narratives, retelling community stories, and biographical portraits in the form of films and books for children and families. Through the ethnographic film series on Latino visual artists, I also will continue the exploration of learning and identity within communities of practice.

Being involved in this volume has been a wonderful entry into new ways to practice pedagogies of unity by focusing on and accessing the wealth of knowledge and resources within our communities. This has illuminated the importance and value of a viable and applied cultural dignity, and created a transparent sense of urgency for research efforts. This is an urgency not of time exactly, but of direction to what students need from themselves, from us as educators, from our community, and from our institutions.

> We are guilty of many errors and many faults, but our worst crime is abandoning the children, neglecting the fountain of life. Many of the things we need can wait. The child cannot. Right now is the time his bones are being formed, his blood is being made, and his senses are being developed. To him we cannot answer "Tomorrow," his name is "Today."
>
> —Gabriela Mistral

UNA FUENTE DE RECURSOS:
A LITERARY GUIDE FOR PARENTS,
EDUCATORS, AND CHILDREN

An Introductory List of Latino Children's Books

Daniel Alejandro González and Amanda A. Hernández

This guide introduces children's books with a Latino perspective. It should be used as a starting point since it is not all-inclusive. Up-to-date references can be accessed through the book's website at https://www.facebook.com/Theirworlds.

Latino authors and illustrators comprise the majority of the list. We have included other authors and some from Mexico whose work speaks to Latino themes. In some instances we included Latino illustrators who have penned their own stories or created the art for writers who are not Latino. They were included to honor their work and contribution to children's literature. In addition, it is important to note that translation is an art and pivotal to the integrity of many texts. This list does not have translators listed, not out of disrespect for their wonderful transformative work but out of practicality.

There are four types of books included in these lists.

1. Books in English, without Spanish translation.
2. Books with separate English and Spanish versions.
3. Bilingual books, with both versions in the same volume.
4. Books in Spanish, without English translation.

Alma Flor Ada

Gathering the sun: An alphabet in Spanish and English. Ill. by S. Silva. (2001). New York, NY: HarperCollins.

I love Saturdays y domingos. Ill. E. Savadier. (2004). New York, NY: Aladdin Paperbacks.
Island Treasures. Growing up in Cuba. Ill. A. Martorell and E. Rodríguez. (2015). New York, NY: Atheneum Books for Young Readers.
The lizard and the sun/La lagartija y el sol: A folktale in English and Spanish. Ill. F. Dávalos. (1997). New York, NY: Doubleday.
Me encantan los Saturdays y los domingos. Ill. E. Savadier. (2004). Miami, FL: Alfaguara. SantillanaUSA.
Me llamo María Isabel. Ill. K. D. Thompson. (1996). New York, NY: Atheneum Books for Young Readers.
Me llamo María Isabel. Ill. by K. D. Thompson. (1993). New York, NY: Aladdin Paperbacks/Libros Colibri.
My name is María Isabel. Ill. by K. D. Thompson. (1993). New York, NY; Toronto, Canada: Atheneum.
with I. Campoy (eds.). *Yes! We are Latinos!* Ill. by D. Diaz. (2013). Watertown, MA: Charlesbridge.
with I. Campoy. *¡Pío Peep! Traditional Spanish nursery rhymes.* Ill. by V. Escrivá. (2003). New York, NY: Harper Collins.
with G. M. Zubizarreta. *Dancing home.* (2013). New York, NY: Atheneum Books for Young Readers.
with G. M. Zubizarreta. *Love, Amalia.* (2012). New York, NY: Atheneum Books for Young Readers.

Marjorie Agosín

I lived on Butterfly Hill. Ill. L.White. (2014). New York, NY: Atheneum Books for Young Readers.

Francisco Alarcón

Angels ride bikes and other fall poems/Los Ángeles andan en bicicletas y otros poemas de otoño. Ill. by M.C. González. (1999). San Francisco, CA: Children's Book Press Imprint.
Animal Poems of the Iguazú/Animalario del Iguazú. (2013). Ill. by M.C. González. San Francisco, CA: Children's Book Press.
From the bellybutton of the moon and other summer poems/Del ombligo de la luna y otros poemas de verano. Ill. by M. C. González. (1998). San Francisco, CA: Children's Book Press.
Iguanas in the snow: And other winter poems/Iguanas en la nieve: Y otros poemas de invierno. (2001). Ill. by M. C. González. San Francisco, CA: Children's Book Press.
Laughing tomatoes and other spring poems/Jitomates risueños y otros poemas de primavera. Ill. by M. C. González. (1997). San Francisco, CA: Children's Book Press.

Julia Alvarez

Before we were free. (2004). New York, NY: Dell Laurel-Leaf.
Devolver al remitente. (2010). New York, NY: Yearling.
A gift of gracias: The legend of Altagracia. Ill. B. Vida. (2005). New York NY: Knopf Book for Young Readers.
How the García girls lost their accents. (2010). Chapel Hill, NC: Algonquin Books of Chapel Hill.
How Tía Lola came to (visit) stay. (2010). New York, NY: Random House Children's Book.
How Tía Lola ended up starting over. (2009). New York, NY: Alfred A. Knopf.
How Tía Lola learned to teach. (2009). New York, NY: Alfred A. Knopf.
How Tía Lola saved the summer. (2004). New York, NY: Dell Laurel-Leaf.
Las huellas secretas. Ill. F. Negrín. (2002). New York, NY: Dragonfly Books.
El mejor regalo del mundo: La leyenda del La Vieja Belén/The best gift of all: The legend of la Vieja Belén. (2009). Miami, FL: Santillana USA Publishing.
Return to sender. (2009). New York, NY: Alfred A. Knopf.
The secret footprints. Ill. F. Negrín (2002). New York, NY: Dragonfly Books.

Rudolfo Anaya

Elegy on the death of César Chávez. (2005). El Paso, TX: Cinco Puntos Press.
The Farolitos of Christmas. Ill. by E. Gonzáles. (1995). New York, NY: Hyperion Books for Children.
Roadrunner's dance. Ill. by D. Diaz. (2000). New York NY: Hyperion Books for Children.

Gloria Anzaldúa

Friends from the other side/Amigos del otro lado. Ill. by C. Mendéz. (1993). San Francisco, CA: Children's Book Press.
Prietita and the Ghost Woman. Ill. by M. C. González. (2001). San Francisco, CA: Childrens Book Press.

Jorge Argueta

Arroz con leche: Un poema para cocinar/Rice pudding: A cooking poem. Ill. By F. Vilela. (2010). Toronto, Canada: Groundwood Books.
Guacamole: Un poema para cocinar/A cooking poem (bilingual cooking poems). Ill. by M. Sada. (2012). Toronto, Canada: Groundwood Books.
A movie in my pillow/Una película en mi almohada. Ill. by E. Gómez. (2001). San Francisco, CA: Children's Book Press.
Salsa: Un poema para cocinar/A cooking poem. Ill. by D. Tonatiuh. (2015). Toronto, Canada: Groundwood Books.

Sopa de frijoles: Un poema para cocinar/Bean soup (bilingual cooking poems). Ill. by Rafael Yockteng. (2009). Toronto, Canada: Groundwood Books.

Talking with Mother Earth/Hablando con Madre Tierra. Ill. by L. A. Pérez. (2006). Toronto: Groundwood Books.

Xochitl and the Flowers/Xóchitl, la niña de las flores. Ill. by C. Angel. (2003). San Francisco, CA: Children's Book Press.

El Zipitio. Ill. G. Calderón. (2008). Toronto, Canada: Groundwood Books.

Zipitio. Ill. G. Calderón. (2008). Toronto, Canada: Groundwood Books.

Carmen T. Bernier-Grand

Alicia Alonso: Prima ballerina. Ill. by Raúl Colón. (2011). Tarrytown, NY: Marshall Cavendish Children.

César: Sí, se puede!/Yes, we can! Ill. by D. Diaz. (2004). New York,NY: Marshall Cavendish.

Diego: Bigger than life. Ill. by D. Diaz. (2009). New York: Marshall Cavendish Children.

Frida: Viva la vida/Long live life. (2007). New York, NY: Marshall Cavendish Children/Marshall Cavendish Corp.

Picasso: I the king, Yo el rey. Ill. by D. Díaz. (2012). Las Vegas, NV: Amazon Children's Books.

Diane Gonzáles Bertrand

The empanadas that abuela made/Las empanadas que hacía la abuela. Ill. by A. Pardo DeLange. (2003). Houston, TX: Piñata Books.

Family, familia. Ill. by P. Rodriguez Howard. (1999). Houston, TX: Arte Público Press.

The last doll/La última muñeca. Ill. by A. Accardo. (2000). Houston, TX: Piñata Books.

The party for Papá Luis. Ill. by A. Galindo. (2010). Houston, TX: Piñata Books.

Sip, slurp, soup, soup/Caldo, caldo, caldo. Ill. by A. P.Delange. (2008). Houston, TX: Piñata Books for Children.

Sofia and the purple dress. Ill. by Lisa Fields. (2012). Houston, TX: Pinata Books.

Trino's choice. (1999). Houston, TX: Arte Público Press.

Monica Brown

Butterflies on Carmen Street/Mariposas en la calle Carmen. Ill. by April Ward. (2007). Houston: Piñata Books/Arte Público Press.

Chavela and the magic bubble. Ill. by M. Morales. (2010). New York, NY: Clarion Books.

Clara and the curandera. Ill. by T. Muraida. (2011). Houston, TX: Piñata Books/ Arte Público Press.

Marisol McDonald and the clash bash/Marisol McDonald y la fiesta sin igual. Ill. by S. Palacios. (2013). New York, NY: Lee & Low Books.

Marisol McDonald doesn't match/Marisol McDonald no combina. Ill. by S. Palacios. (2013). San Francisco, CA: Children's Book Press.

Me llamo Gabriela/My name is Gabriela. Ill. by J. Parra. (2005). Flagstaff, AZ: Luna Rising.

Pablo Neruda: Poet of the people. Ill. by J. Paschkis. (2011). New York, NY: Henry Holt.

Side by side: The story of Dolores Huerta and César Chávez/Lado a lado: La historia de Dolores Huerta y César Chávez. Ill. by J. Cepeda. (2010). New York, NY: Rayo/HarperCollins.

Tito Puente: Mambo king/Rey del mambo. Ill. by R. Lopez. (2013). New York, NY: Rayo/HarperCollins.

Waiting for the biblioburro. Ill. by J. Parra. (2011). Berkeley, CA: Tricycle Press.

F. Isabel Campoy

Poesía eres tú. Antología poética. Ill. by Marcela Calderón. (2015). Doral, FL: Santillana USA.

Rosa Raposa. Ill. by J. Aruego and A. Dewey. (2002). San Diego, CA: Gulliver Books, Harcourt Inc.

with A. F. Ada. *Cuentos que contaban nuestras abuelas: Cuentos populares Hispánicos.* Ill. by F. Dávalos, V. Escrivá, S. Guevara, L. Torres. (2006). New York, NY: Atheneum.

with A. F. Ada. *Tales our abuelitas told.* Ill. by F. Dávalos, V. Escrivá, S. Guevara, and L. Torres. (2006). New York, NY: Atheneum Books for Young Readers.

with T. Howell. *Maybe something beautiful. How art transformed a neighborhood.* Ill. by R. López. (2016). New York, NY: Houghton Mifflin Harcourt.

Viola Canales

The tequila worm. (2005). New York, NY: Wendy Lamb Books.

Amelia Lau Carling

Alfombras de aserrín. (2005). Toronto, Canada: Groundwood Books.
La tienda de Mamá y Papá. (2003). Toronto, Canada: Groundwood Books.
Mama and Papa have a store. (1998). Toronto, Canada: Groundwood Books.
Sawdust carpets. (2005). Toronto, Canada: Groundwood Books.

Julia Mercedes Castillo

Emilio. (1999). Houston, TX: Arte Público Press.

Angela Cervantes

Gaby, lost and found. (2013). New York, NY: Scholastic.

Sandra Cisneros

Hairs/Pelitos. Ill. by T. Ybañez. (1994). New York, NY: Knopf.

Diana Cohn

¡Sí, se puede!/Yes, we can! Ill. by F. Delgado. (2005). El Paso, TX: Cinco Puntos Press.

Lucha Corpi

Where fireflies dance/Ahí donde bailan las luciénagas. Ill. M. Reisberg. (1997). San Francisco, CA: Children's Book Press.

Barbara Cruz

Triumphs and struggles for Latino civil rights. From Many Cultures, One History Series. (2008). Berkeley Heights, NJ: Enslow Publishers.

Felipe Dávalos (Illustrator)

El rey colibrí. Una leyenda guatemalteca. By A. Palacios. (1993). Mahwah, NJ: Troll.
Heart of the gaguar. By M. Talbert. (1992). New York, NY: Simon & Schuster.
Home at last. By S. Middleton Elya. (2002). New York, NY: Lee & Low.

Lulú Delacre

Salsa stories. (2012). New York, NY: Scholastic Press.
Vejigante masquerader. (1993). New York, NY: Scholastic Press.

David Diaz (Illustrator)

De colores/Bright with colors. (2008). New York, NY: Marshall Cavendish.
Feliz Navidad. (2004). New York City, NY: Scholastic, Inc.
Going Home. By E. Bunting. (2013). Columbus, OH: Zaner-Bloser.
Me, Frida: Frida Kahlo in San Francisco. By Amy Novesky. (2010). New York, NY: Abrams Books for Young Readers.
Smoky night. By. Eve Bunting. (1999). San Diego, CA: Harcourt Brace.

Wilma unlimited: How Wilma Rudolph became the world's fastest woman. By K. Krull. (2000). San Diego, CA: Harcourt.

Myra L. Dole

Drum, Chavi, drum! Ill. by Tonel. (2003). San Francisco, CA: Children's Book Press.

Margarita Engle

Drum dream girl: How one girl's courage changed music. Ill. by R. López. (2015). New York, NY: Houghton Mifflin Harcourt.

Enchanted air: Two cultures, two wings: A memoir. (2015). New York, NY: Antheneum Books for Young Readers.

The firefly letters: A suffragette's journey to Cuba. (2010). New York, NY: Henry Holt.

Hurricane dancers: The first Caribbean pirate shipwreck. (2011). New York, NY: Henry Holt.

The lightning dreamer: Cuba's greatest abolitionist. (2013). New York, NY: Houghton Mifflin Harcourt.

Mountain dog. Ill. by O. Ivanov & A. Ivanov. (2013). New York, NY: Henry Holt.

The poet slave of Cuba: A biography of Juan Francisco Manzano. Ill. by S. Qualls. (2006). New York, NY: Henry Holt.

Silver people: Voices from the Panama Canal. (2014). New York, NY: Houghton Mifflin Harcourt.

The sky painter: Louis Fuertes, bird artist. Ill. by A. Bereghici. (2015). New York, NY: Two Lions.

The surrender tree: Poems of Cuba's struggle for freedom. (2008). New York, NY: Henry Holt.

Carmen Lomas Garza

Family pictures: Cuadros de familia. (1990). San Francisco, CA: Children's Book Press.

In my family/En mi familia. (1996). San Francisco, CA: Children's Book Press.

Magic windows/Ventanas magicas. (1999). San Francisco, CA: Children's Book Press

Xavier Garza

Creepy creatures and other cucuys. (2004). Houston, TX: Piñata Books.

The great and mighty nikko. (2015). El Paso, TX: Cinco Puntos Press.

Lucha libre: The man in the silver mask: A bilingual cuento. (2005). El Paso, TX: Cinco Puntos Press.

Maximilian & the bingo rematch: A lucha libre sequel. (2013). El Paso, TX: Cinco Puntos Press.
Maximilian & the mystery of the guardian angel: A bilingual lucha libre thriller. (2011). El Paso, TX: Cinco Puntos Press.

Judy Goldman (Mexican Author)

Whiskers, tales & Wings: Animal folk tales of Mexico. Ill. by F. V. Broeck. (2013). Watertown, MA: Charlesbridge.

Lucía González

The bossy gallito/El gallo de bodas. Ill. by L. Delacre. (1999). New York, NY: Scholastic.
The storyteller's candle/La velita de los cuentos. Ill. by L. Delacre. (2013). New York, NY: Lee & Low Books.

Rigoberto González

Antonio's card. Ill. by C. C. Alvarez González. (2005). San Francisco, CA: Children's Book Press.

Gilbert Hernandez

Marble season. (2013). New York, NY: Drawn & Quarterly.

Juan Felipe Herrera

Calling the doves/El canto de las palomas. Ill. by E. Simmons. (1995). San Francisco, CA: Children's Book Press.
Laughing out loud, I fly: Poems in English and Spanish. Ill. by K. Barbour. (1998). New York, NY: Harper Collins Publishers.
Portraits of Hispanic American heroes. Ill. by R. Colón. (2014). New York, NY: Dial Books for Young Readers.
Super cilantro girl. Ill. by H. Robledo. (2003). San Francisco, CA: Children's Book Press.
The upside down boy/El niño de cabeza. Ill. by E. Gómez. (2000). San Francisco, CA: Children's Book Press.

Francisco Jiménez

Breaking through. (2002). Boston, MA: Houghton Mifflin.

Cajas de carton: Relatos de la vida peregrina de un niño campesino. (2002). New York, NY: Houghton Mifflin.
The circuit: Stories from the life of a migrant child. (1997). New York, NY: Scholastic, Inc.
La mariposa. Ill. by S. Silva. (2000). Boston, MA: Houghton Mifflin.
Mas alla de mi. (2009). Boston, MA: Houghton Mifflin.
Reaching out. (2008). Boston, MA: Houghton Mifflin.
Senderos fronterizos. (2002). New York, NY: Houghton Mifflin.

Laura Lacámara

Floating on Mama's song. Ill. Y. Morales. (2010). New York, NY: HarperCollins.

René Colato Laínez

From north to south/Del norte al sur. Ill. by J. Cepeda. (2010). San Francisco, CA: Children's Book Press.
I am René, the boy/Yo soy René, el niño. (2005). Houston, TX: Arte Público Press.
¡Juguemos al fútbol!/Let's play fútbal and football! (2013). Doral, FL: Alfaguara Santillana USA.
My shoes and I. Ill. by F. Vanden Broeck. (2010). Honesdale, PA: Boyds Mill Press.
Playing lotería: El juego de lotería. Ill. by Jill Arena. (2005). Flagstaff, AZ: Rising Moon Books.
René has two last names/René tiene dos apellidos. Ill. by F. G. Ramírez. (2009). Houston, TX: Piñata Books.
Señor Pancho had a rancho. Ill. by E. Smith. (2013). New York, NY: Holiday House.
The Tooth Fairy meets El Ratón Pérez. Ill. by T. Lintern. (2010). Berkeley, CA: Tricycle Press.
Waiting for Papá/Esperando a Papá. Ill. by A. Accardo. (2004). Houston, TX: Piñata Books.

Antonio Hernandez Madrigal

The eagle and the rainbow: Timeless tales from Mexico. Ill. by T. DePaola. (2010). Golden, CO: Fulcrum Publishing.

Sonia Manzano

The revolution of Evelyn Serrano. (2012). New York, NY: Scholastic.

Victor Martinez

Parrot in the oven: Mi vida. (1996). New York, NY: HarperCollins Publishers.

José Manuel Mateo

Migrant. Ill. by J. Martínez Pedro. (2014). New York, NY: Abrams, English Edition.
Migrar. Ill. by J. Martínez Pedro. (2011). Mexico City, Mexico: Ediciones Tecolote.

Jane Medina

My name is Jorge: On both sides of the river. (1999). Honesdale, PA: Wordsong/
Boyds Mills Press.

Nicholasa Mohr

Felita. (1979). New York, NY: Dial Press.
Going home. (1999). New York, NY: Puffin Books.

Víctor Montejo

Blanca Flor: A mayan princess/Una princesa maya. Ill. R. Yockteng. (2005). Toronto, Canada: Groundwood Books.
Popol Vuj: A sacred book of the Maya/Libro sagrado de los Mayas. Ill. L. Garay.
(1999). Toronto, Canada: Groundwood Books.

Pat Mora

The beautiful lady. Our lady of Guadalupe. S. Johnson & L. Fancher. (2012). New
York, NY: Knopf.
A birthday basket for Tía. Ill. by C. Lang. (1992). New York, NY: Macmillan.
Doña Flor: A tall tale about a giant woman with a great big heart. Ill. by R. Colón.
(2005). New York, NY: Knopf.
I pledge allegiance. Ill. L. Martinez. (2014). New York, NY: Knopf.
La noche que se cayó la luna: Mito Maya. Ill. Domi. (2009). Toronto, Canada:
Groundwood Books.
A library for Juana: The story of Sor Juana Inés. Ill. by B.Vidal. (2014). New York,
NY: Alfred A. Knopf.
The night the moon felt. A Mayan myth. Ill. Domi. (2009). Toronto, Canada: Ground-
wood Books.
The rainbow tulip. Ill. by E. Sayles. (2003). New York, NY: Puffin Books.
Tomás and the library lady/Tomás y la señora de la biblioteca. Ill. by R. Colón.
(1997). New York, NY: Knopf.

Yuyi Morales

Harvesting hope: The story of César Chávez. By K. Krull. (2003). San Diego, CA:
Harcourt.

Los gatos black en Halloween. (2006). New York, NY: Henry Holt and Company.
Just in case: A trickster tale and Spanish alphabet book. (2008). New York, NY: Roaring Brook Press.
My abuelita. By T. Johnston. Photographed by T. O'Meara. (2009). Orlando, FL: Harcourt Children's Books.
Niño wrestles the world. (2013). New York, NY: Roaring Brook Press.
Viva Frida. Photographed by T. O'Meara. (2014). New York, NY: Roaring Brook Press.

Sonia Nazario

Enrique's journey. (2013). New York, NY: Delacorte Press.

Amada Irma Pérez

My diary from here to there/Mi diario de aquí hasta allá. Ill. by M. C. González. (2002). San Francisco, CA: Children's Book Press.
My very own room/Mi propio cuartito. Ill. by M. C. González. (2000). San Francisco, CA: Children's Book Press.
Nana's big surprise. Ill. by M. C. González. (2007). San Francisco, CA: Children's Book Press.

Juan Carlos Quesadas

Jennifer y Luis en: César Chávez & la máquina del tiempo. Ill. by Bef. (2014). Los Angeles, CA: La Librería.

Margarita Robleda (Mexican Author)

Maria, Una niña Latina en los Estados Unidos. Ill. by D. Ramirez. (2005). Miami, FL: Santillana USA.
Paco un niño en los Estados Unidos. Ill. by D. Rodríguez. (2005). Miami, FL: Santillana, USA.

Luis J. Rodriguez

América is her name. (1997). Willimantic, CT: Curbstone Press.

Pam Muñoz Ryan

Becoming Naomi León. (2004). New York, NY: Scholastic Press.
The dreamer. (2010). New York, NY: Scholastic Press.
Esperanza rising. (2000). New York, NY: Scholastic Press.

Mice and beans. Ill. by J. Cepeda. (2001). New York, NY: Scholastic.
El soñador. Ill by P. Sis. (2010). New York, NY: Scholastic.

Gary Soto

Baseball in April. (2000). New York, NY: HMH Books for Young Readers.
Buried onions. (2006). New York, NY: HMH Books for Young Readers.
Chato's kitchen. Ill. by S. Guevara. (1997). New York, NY: Puffin Books.
Chato y los amigos pachangueros. Ill. by S. Guevara. (2004). New York, NY: Puffin Books.
If the shoe fits. Ill. by T. Widener. (2002). New York, NY: Putnam Juvenile.
¡Qué montón de tamales! Ill. by E. Martínez. (1998). New York, NY: PaperStar.
The skirt. (1997). New York, NY: Yearling.
Too many tamales! Ill. by E. Martínez. (1996). New York, NY: Puffin Books.

Carmen Tafolla

That's not fair! Emma Tenayuca's struggle for justice/¡No es justo!: La lucha de Emma Tenayuca por la justicia. Ill. by T. Ybánez. (2008). San Antonio, TX: Wings Press.
What Can You Do with a paleta? Ill. by M. Morales. (2009). Berkeley, CA: Tricycle Press.
What Can You Do with a rebozo? Ill. by A. Córdova. (2008). Berkeley, CA: Tricycle Press.

Roseanne Thong

Green is a chile pepper: A book of colors. Ill. by J. Parra. (2014). San Francisco, CA: Chronicle Books.

Duncan Tonatiuh

Dear primo: A letter to my cousin. (2010). New York, NY: Abrams Books for Young Readers.
Diego Rivera: His world and ours. (2011). New York, NY: Abrams.
Pancho Rabbit and the coyote: A migrant's tale. (2013). New York, NY: Abrams Books for Young Readers.
Separate is never equal: Sylvia Mendez and her family's fight for desegregation. (2014). New York, NY: Abrams Books for Young Readers.

Leyla Torres

Liliana's grandmothers. (1998). New York, NY: Farrar, Straus, and Giroux.

Subway sparrow/Gorrión del metro. (1993). New York, NY: Farrar, Straus, and Giroux.

Eric Velásquez

Grandma's gift. (2013). New York, NY: Walker Publications.
Grandma's records. (2004). New York, NY: Walker Publications.
Los discos de mi abuela. Trans. by E. De La Vega. (2006). New York, NY: Lectorum Publications.
El regalo de mi abuela. (2013). New York, NY: Lectorum Publications.

Angel Vigil

The corn woman, and other stories and legends from the Hispanic southwest/La mujer de maíz: Y otros cuentos y leyendas del suroeste. (1994). Englewood, CO: Libraries Unlimited.

An Introductory List of Books in Spanish for Children

Oralia Garza de Cortés and
Daniel Alejandro González

Alonso, F. (2011). *El hombrecillo de papel*. Ill. U. Wensell. Leon Everest.

Arciniegas, T. (1991). *Los casibandidos que casi roban el sol y otras historias.* Mexico D.F., Mexico: Fondo de Cultura Económica.

Baranda, M. (2012). *Diente de león*. Ill. I. R. Esquivel. Mexico D.F., Mexico: Ediciones el Naranjo.

Bencastro, M. (2004) *Viaje a la tierra del abuelo*. Houston, TX: Piñata Books/Arte Público Press.

Carballido, E., & Cardemil, C. (1998). *Los zapatos de fierro*. Mexico D.F., Mexico: Fondo de Cultura Economica.

Carroll, L. (2015). *Alicia en el país de las maravillas*. Spain: Editorial Lumen.

Castañeda, O. (1994). *El tapiz de abuela*. New York, NY: Children's Book Press.

Castillo, J. M. (1999). *Emilio*. Houston, TX: Arte Público Press.

Corona, P. (2003). *Baulito de cuentos contados*. Tlalnepantla, Mexico: Grupo Editorial Norma.

———. (1991). *El pozo de los ratones y otros cuentos al calor del fogón*. Ill. B. Dorantes. Mexico D.F., Mexico: Fondo de Cultura Económica.

Darío, R. (2014). *El canto errante*. [*Adaptado para niños*]. Santiago de Chile, Chile: Editorial Amanuta.

———. (1979). *Margarita*. Ill. M. Doppert. Caracas, Venezuela: Ediciones Ekaré.

de la Colina, J. (2008). *El mayor nacimiento del mundo y sus alrededores*. Ill. M. Viard. Mexico D.F., Mexico: CIDCLI.

Freire de Matos, I. (2004). *El pececito mágico*. Ill. W. Torres. Guaynabo, Puerto Rico: Alfaguara Santillana.

González de Leon, U. (1982). *Las tres manzanas de naranja*. Ill. C. Pellicer López. Mexico D.F., Mexico: CIDCLI.

Hinojosa, F. (2000). *A golpe de calcetín.* Ill. Rafael Barajas "El Fisgón." Mexico D.F., Mexico: Fondo de Cultura Económica.

———. (2000). *A golpe de calcetín.* Ill. Rafael Barajas "El Fisgón." Mexico D.F., Mexico: Fondo de Cultura Económica.

———. (1992). *La peór señora del mundo.* Ill. R. Barajas "El Fisgón." Mexico D.F., Mexico: Fondo de Cultural Económica.

Krull, K. (2004). *Cosechando esperanza: La historia de César Chávez.* Ill. Y. Morales. Boston, MA: HMH Books for Young Readers.

Kurusa. (2007). *La calle es libre.* Ill. M. Doppert. Caracas, Venezuela: Ekaré.

Lázaro, G. (2009). *Federico García Lorca.* New York, NY: Lectorum Publications.

———. (2004). *El flamboyan amarillo.* Ill. L. Delacre. New York, NY: Lectorum Publications.

———. (2006). *Julia.* Ill. P. Marichal. New York, NY: Lectorum Publications.

———. (2001). *¡Ya llegan los Reyes Magos!* Ill. M. Fuenmayor. New York, NY: Lectorum Publications.

Lee, C. (2002). *Mandaderos de la lluvia: Y otros poemas de América Latina/Messengers of rain: And other poems of Latin America.* Berkeley, CA: Groundwood Books.

Machado, A. M. (2003). *De carta en carta.* Ill. I. Basulto. Mexico D.F., Mexico: Santillana.

———. (1994). *Niña bonita.* Ill. R. Faría. Caracas, Venezuela: Editorial Ekaré.

———. (2012). *Un pajarito me contó.* Ill. F. Masai. Mexico D.F., Mexico: Fondo de Cultura Económica.

Martí, J. (2013). *La Niña de Guatemala.* Santiago de Chile, Chile: Editorial Amanuense.

———. (1997). *Los Zapaticos de Rosa.* Ill. L. Delacre. New York, NY: Lectorum Publications.

Menchú, R. (2006). *LiM'in, Una niña de Chimel.* Doral, FL: Santillana USA.

———. (2003). *El vaso de miel.* Madrid, Spain: Alfaguara.

Mistral, G. (2014). *Blanca nieve en la casa de los enanos.* Ill. C. Ballestelleros. Santiago de Chile, Chile: Editorial Amanuta.

———. (2013). *Caperucita roja.* Ill. P. Valdivia. Santiago de Chile, Chile: Editorial Amanuta.

———. (2013). *La bella durmiente del bosque.* Ill. C. Cardemil. Santiago de Chile, Chile: Editorial Amanuta.

———. (2013). *La cenicienta.* Ill. B. Ojeda. Santiago de Chile, Chile: Editorial Amanuta.

Nazoa, A. (1995). *La fábula de la avispa ahogada.* Ill. V. Sempére. Caracas, Venezuela: Ediciones Ekaré.

———. (1995). *La fábula de la ratita presumida.* Caracas, Venezuela: Ediciones Ekaré.

Núñez, A. (2006). *Y la luna siempre es una.* Ill. A. Castellanos Mexico D.F., Mexico: CIDCLI.

Pombo, R. (1996). *Cuentos pintados y morales.* Bogotá, Colombia: Editorial Panamericana.

Quiroga, H. (2000). *Cuentos de la selva y otros relatos*. Madrid, Spain: Editorial Alianza.

Ramírez, A. (2004). *Napi.* Ill. Domi. Toronto, Canada: Groundwood Books.

———. (2006). *Napí funda un pueblo/Napí Makes a Village*. Ill. Domi. Toronto, Canada: Groundwood Books.

———. (2006). *Napí va a la montaña*. Ill. Domi. Toronto, Canada: Groundwood Books.

Rondon, J. (1994). *El sapo distraído*. Ill. M. Cabrera. Caracas, Venezuela: Ediciones Ekaré.

Schimel, L. (2010). *¡Vamos a ver a Papá!* New York, NY: Lectorum Publications.

Sendak, M. (2014). *La cocina de noche*. Pontevedra, Spain: Kalandraka Editora.

———. (1996). *Donde viven los monstrous*. St. Louis, MO: Turtleback Books.

Tan, S. (2007). *Emigrantes*. Albolote, Spain: Barbara Fiore Editora.

Unger. D. (2012). *La casita*. Mexico D.F., Mexico: CIDCLI.

Uribe, V. (2006). *Doña Piñones*. Ill. F. Krahn. Caracas, Venezuela: Ediciones Ekaré.

Winter, J. (2009). *Sonia Sotomayor: La juez que creció en el Bronx*. Ill. E. Rodriguez. New York, NY: Atheneum Books for Young Readers.

Online Resources

Daniel Alejandro González and
Amanda A. Hernández

Selected sites offering critical information and perspectives, children's and young adult literature awards with a multicultural focus, organizational information, websites, and articles.

Academy for Teacher Excellence (ATE): https://ate.utsa.edu. "Located at the University of Texas at San Antonio, [ATE] is grounded in the College of Education and Human Development's "Culturally Efficacious Teacher" model.

American Library Association: www.ala.org. "ALA is the oldest and largest library association in the world, providing association information, news, events, and advocacy resources for members, librarians, and library users."

Américas Award: http://claspprograms.org/americasaward. Award established in 1993 by CLASP, the Consortium of Latin American Studies Program, which annually recognizes up to two quality titles that focus on Latin America, the Caribbean, or Latinos in the U.S. Also includes a commended list of titles for classroom use.

Colorín Colorado: http://www.colorincolorado.org. The premier national website serving educators and families of English language learners in grades pre-K–12.

Cooperative Children's Book Center (CCBC): http://ccbc.education.wisc.edu/books/pcstats.asp. "Statistics Gathered by the Cooperative Children's Book Center School of Education, University of Wisconsin–Madison."

Feria Internacional del Libro (FIL): www.fil.com.mx. Attracting over 20,000 professionals, 1,900 publishers, and a huge attendance from over 44 countries, FIL is the largest Spanish language book fair in the world. The event is held yearly in Guadalajara, Mexico, on the last weekend in November.

La Librería: www.la-libreria.net. An outstanding bookstore devoted to making books in Spanish available to families. Their choice book selections are also available for purchase online.

Latinas 4 Latino Lit: http://latinas4latinolit.org. An organization of social-media-savvy Latina moms devoted to promoting Latino books for children. Their online blog provides book resources and projects like an online summer reading program as well as hands-on projects that help extend the reading experience.

Latino Children Literature Conferences: www.latinochildlitconf.org. "National conference celebrating Latino children's and young adult literature and literacy. Conference is for anyone interested in Latino literacy, literature, and education and promotes sharing of strategies to address informational, cultural, recreational, and traditional literacy needs of Latino children and young adults."

Lea—LA Los Angeles Spanish Language Book Fair: http://en.lea-la.com. Biennial Spanish language book fair held in Los Angeles during spring each biennium.

Multicultural Literature for Latino Children: Their Words, Their Worlds: https://www.facebook.com/Theirworlds. Page has information including recommended readings, notices about new Latino children book titles, recent awards, notices about upcoming conferences, presentations, curriculum, and activities.

Pura Belpré Award: www.ala.org/alsc/awardsgrants/bookmedia/belpremedal. A premier Latino children's book award that annually honors Latino authors and illustrators for books that best portray the Latino experience in a book for children ages 0–14. The award is cosponsored by REFORMA and the Association of Library Services for Children, a division of the American Library Association.

REFORMA: www.reforma.org. National organization of librarians devoted to serving the library and information needs of Latino and Spanish-speaking communities throughout the U.S. REFORMA is a cosponsor of the Pura Belpré Award.

Tomás Rivera Mexican American Children's Literature Award: www.riverabookaward.org. Sponsored by Texas State University, San Marcos, Texas, this annual award honors works by authors and illustrators who produce works specifically about the Mexican American experience in children's literature.

Top Latino Children's Books: http://mamiverse.com/top-latino-childrens-books-60054. "Supplemental list of Latino children's books for parents who want to read books that celebrate and reflect a multitude of cultures."

We Need Diverse Books: www.weneeddiversebooks.org. "A grassroots organization of children's book lovers that advocates essential changes in the publishing industry to produce and promote literature that reflects and honors the lives of all young people."

Linked Articles

Celic, C., & Seltzer, K. (2012–2013). Translanguaging. CUNY-NYSIEB. Retrieved August 27, 2014, from www.nysieb.ws.gc.cuny.edu/files/2013/03/Trans languaging-Guide-March-2013.pdf.

Chilton, M. (2015). Malorie-Blackman-deserves-our-support. www.telegraph.co.uk/culture/books/children_sbookreviews/11055696/Malorie-Blackman-deserves-our -support.html.

Higgins, J. J. (2002). "Multicultural children's literature: Creating and applying an evaluation tool in response to the needs of urban educators." New Horizons for Learning, www.newhorizons.org/strategies/multicultural/higgins.htm.

Hurtado, V. (2015). "Lunchtime author Google hangout with author/illustrator Duncan Tonatiuh." http://latinas4latinolit.org/author/viviana-hurtado.

Hurtado, V. (2014). "Open letter to the *New York Times*: Latino children's authors & illustrators have earned a place on the year-end list." http://latinas4latinolit.org/?s= latino+children+authors+earned+a+place.

Kirch, C. (2014). "More than a hashtag: We Need Diverse Books moves forward." www.publishersweekly.com/pw/bytopic/childrens/childrens-industry-news/ article/63508-more-than-a-hashtag-we-need-diverse-books-moves-forward.

Latinas for Latino Literature. (2014). "Remarkable Latino children's books of 2014." www.nbcnews.com/news/latino/latinas-latino-lit-remarkable-childrens-books -2014-n248846.

Naidoo, J. (2010). "Celebrating diverse Latino cultures, literature, and literacy everyday." www.ala.org/alsc/sites/ala.org.alsc/files/content/confevents/institute/ institutehandouts/Diversity%20Handout.pdf.

O'Hara, M. (2014). "Poverty and class: the latest themes to enter the US banned-books debate" www.theguardian.com/society/2014/oct/21/us-adds-poverty-to-dangerous -readinglists?utm_source=Publishers+Weekly&utm_campaign=d00463bdbe -UA-15906914-1&utm_medium=email&utm_term=0_0bb2959cbb-d00463bdbe -304534865.

Rich, M. (2012). "For young Latino readers, an image is missing." http://www .nytimes.com/2012/12/05/education/young-latino-students-dont-see-themselves -in-books.html?_r=0.

Rosario, V. P. & Cao, V. (2015). "The CUNY-NYSIEB guide to translanguaging in Latino/aliterature." Latino_Literature_Guide_-_01-28-15_-_Final-libre.pdf.

Schaffer, J. (2014). "17 writers on the importance of reading: Never trust anyone who has not brought a book with them." www.buzzfeed.com/jenniferschaffer/

literature-is-freedom?utm_source=Publishers+Weekly&utm_campaign=7f7b8a
8956-UA-15906914-1&utm_medium=email&utm_term=0_0bb2959cbb-7f7b8a
8956-304534865.

Seltzer, S. (2015). "We need diverse books: Can children's authors end publishing industry prejudice—and change the way America reads?" http://flavorwire
.com/502081/we-need-diverse-books-can-childrens-authors-end-publishing
-industry-prejudice-and-change-the-way-america-reads.

Index

Ada, Alma Flor: *I Love Saturdays y domingos,* 36, 91, 114; Latino children's literature, lack of, 30; moral decision-making, influence of literature, 242; *My Name is María Isabel,* 81, 95, 131; *Nacer bailando,* 156; poem, *ix;* on transformative education, 148, 247

African American children's literature, 9, 30, 31, 34, 104–05, 274, 289

Alvarez, Julia, 6, 55–56, 76, 155, 287

Américas Award, 34, 48, 109

Antonio's Card (González), 93, 135

Anzaldúa, Gloria, 77, 251, 269–72

apps, 213, 215, 220–21, 278, 283

Argueta, Jorge, 88

Asociación Internacional de Literatura Infantil en Español y Portugués, *xv–xvi*

aspirational capital, 244–45, 247

authenticity in children's literature: acceleration of learning, aiding in, 293; believability, enhancing, 233; checklist, 46; co-construction of authentic books, 106–07; cultural affirmation, 148, 251; cultural authenticity, 35, 37, 38, 39, 72, 74, 77, 130, 231; cultural consciousness, 26; diversity, promoting, 160; everyday situations, featuring, 96; *familismo* as a consideration, 38; identity and self-esteem, impacting, 105, 122, 149; importance and benefits of, 103, 118, 127, 282; Latino contributions, validating, 25; picture books and, 31, 226, 231, 258, 259 prior knowledge, making connections to, 104; in social studies education, 147, 150; Spanish word choices, 47, 58, 108, 138; Tomás Rivera Award, honoring, 34; transworld pedagogy, as part of, 86. *See also* selection of texts

Baca, Judith, 257

barrio art, 256–57

Belpré, Pura, *xv, xvi,* 34–35. *See also* Pura Belpré Awards

Bernal, Delgado, 171–72, 253, 254

biases in school curriculums, 145–46, 147, 149, 191

bibliotherapy, 73, 77–78

About the Contributors

Alma Flor Ada, PhD, born in Camagüey, Cuba, could be considered the most prolific and recognized bilingual children's writer of all time. Her awards are numerous: NCSS/CBC Notable Children's Trade Book in the Field of Social Studies; American Booksellers "Pick of the List"; Parent's Honor Choice Book; Aesop Accolade from the American Folklore Association; Simon Wiesenthal Museum of Tolerance Award; Parenting Magazines Gold Medal; Marta Salotti Gold Medal; California PTA Yearly Award; Latina Writers' Award; José Martí World Award; San Francisco Public Library Laureate; Purá Belpré Gold Medal; and many more.

María Guadalupe Arreguín-Anderson, PhD, is an assistant professor of early childhood and elementary education at the University of Texas at San Antonio. Her work illuminates the intricacies of cultural and linguistic factors that influence minority students' access to education in early childhood and elementary bilingual settings, specifically in the area of science education.

Ysaaca Axelrod, EdD, is an assistant professor in teacher education and curriculum studies at the University of Massachusetts, Amherst. She received her EdD from Teachers College at Columbia University. Previously she was a kindergarten teacher in the Bay Area in California. Her research interests include the language and literacy development of young children, particularly emergent bilinguals; the intersections between identity, language ideologies; and language development and ethnographic research in the classroom. Dr.

Axelrod has published in major early childhood journals such as *Young Children*; *Journal of Early Childhood Literacy*; *Contemporary Issues in Early Childhood*; and *Early Childhood Education Journal*.

Raquel Cataldo, MA, is a first-year doctoral student at the University of Texas at San Antonio. Her focus is early childhood education and literacy. She has a master's degree in curriculum and instruction from National Louis University. Raquel spent twenty-eight years in grades 1–12, with the majority of her years working in elementary schools serving both monolingual and bilingual students.

Joe Cepeda is the award-winning illustrator of more than twenty books for children written by Toni Morrison, Pam Munoz Ryan, Monica Brown, and René Colato Laínez, among others, while continuing to create images for magazines and other publications. He is president of the Society of Illustrators of Los Angeles.

Sandra Cisneros is the author of two highly celebrated novels, a story collection, two books of poetry, and, most recently, *Have You Seen Marie?* and *A House of My Own*. She is the recipient of numerous awards, including National Endowment for the Arts fellowships; the Lannan Literary Award; the American Book Award; the Thomas Wolfe Prize; and a MacArthur Fellowship. Her work has been translated into more than twenty languages. Cisneros is the founder of the Alfredo Cisneros Del Moral and Macondo Foundations, which serve creative writers. Her first children's book was *Pelitos/Hair* and she is currently working on another one featuring her dog.

Ellen Riojas Clark, PhD, is professor emerita of bicultural-bilingual studies at the University of Texas at San Antonio. Her research examines self-concept, teacher identity, ethnic identity, efficacy, and Latino cultural studies.

Oralia Garza de Cortés, MA, is an assistant professor at St. Edwards University and a bibliographer, writer, and librarian. She has served as President of REFORMA, affiliate of the American Library Association (ALA). Cortés cofounded the ALA Pura Belpré Award, honoring the best in Latino writing and illustration for children, and the Children and Young Adult Services Committee of REFORMA. Oralia was the first Latina children's librarian elected to serve on the 2000 Caldecott Committee and the first Latina elected (1995) to serve on the Board of Directors of ALSC, the Children's Division of the Association of Library Services for Children.

Christina Passos DiNicolo, PhD, is an assistant professor of bilingual and ESL education at the University of Illinois at Urbana-Champaign. Her research examines the relationship between sociopolitical contexts and implementation of bilingual education programs, and the nature of student learning and literacy development within bilingual programs.

Lucila D. Ek, PhD, is an associate visiting professor in the Department of Education, Culture and Society at the University of Utah. Her research focuses on language, literacy, and identity of students of color, particularly Latinos, as well as bilingual teacher education. She has published in *Anthropology and Education Quarterly*; *Equity and Excellence in Education*; *Bilingual Research Journal*; and the *High School Journal*.

Belinda Bustos Flores, PhD, is a professor and chair of bicultural-bilingual studies at the University of Texas at San Antonio. Her research focuses on teacher development including self-concept, ethnic identity, efficacy, beliefs, teacher recruitment/retention, high stakes testing, and family cultural knowledge. Flores is founder of the Academy for Teacher Excellence.

Carolyn Dee Flores has illustrated four books for children: *Sing, Froggie, Sing/Canta, rana, canta*; *Dale, dale, dale*; *Una fiesta de números/A Fiesta of Numbers*; and *Daughters of Two Nations*. Her original artwork may be found in the Mazza Museum of International Art and at the Arne Nixon Center for the Study of Children's Literature. A newcomer to the field, she has received numerous awards, including Skipping Stones Award for Excellence in Multicultural Literature; Tejas Star Reading List; Tomas Rivera Award Finalist; 20 Most Remarkable Books; Best 20 Latino Books; National Picture Book Champion; and Arte Público Author of the Month.

Xavier Garza is an author, artist, and storyteller who has written and illustrated numerous books. His work has received such awards as the Tejas Star Book Award; the Pura Belpre Honor Book Award; the Libros de las Americas Honor book Award; and the Texas Institute of Letters Children's Book Award.

Cristina Gillanders, PhD, is an associate professor of early childhood education at the School of Education and Human Development at the University of Colorado, Denver. Her research focuses on Latino emergent literacy; bilingualism; early childhood teaching practices for Latino dual-language learners; early-childhood teachers' professional development; and minority parents' beliefs and practices. She has published in major journals such as *Young Children*; *Journal of Early Childhood Literacy*; *Early Childhood Education Journal*; *Early Childhood Research Quarterly*; and *The Reading Teacher*. She authored the book *Aprendizaje de la lectura y escritura en los años prescolares: Manual para el docente.*

Daniel Alejandro Gonzaléz, MA, is a researcher and ethnographic filmmaker from San Antonio, Texas. His research examines identity formation in bicultural settings and inclusion and organizational structures in educational settings and communities in low-income areas. He has consulted and collaborated with numerous organizations including public school districts; NASA; and Avance Inc. Films from the series he produces with Dr. Ellen Riojas Clark, The Artist Speaks, have been presented locally at academic conferences and film festivals, as well as in the UK and Spain.

Maya Cristina González is an artist, author, and educator who has illustrated over twenty award-winning multicultural children's books, and written four children's books. She has a small independent press and online school where she teaches the art of creating children's books. She lives and works in San Francisco.

Erin Greeter, MA, is a doctoral candidate at the University of Texas at Austin, and a former elementary bilingual teacher. She is completing her doctorate in language and literacy with a focus on the meaning-making processes of bilingual children learning through drama.

Myriam Jimena Guerra, MA, is a doctoral candidate in the Culture, Literacy, and Language Program in the Department of Bicultural-Bilingual Studies at the University of Texas at San Antonio. She has worked for fifteen years in the educational setting, working with bilingual and English language learners and mentoring bilingual educators as well. Currently, she is in her second year as a language support teacher at a Title I bilingual school. Jimena was born and raised in Colombia and graduated from La Pontificia Universidad Javeriana in Bogotá, Colombia, with a degree in social communication and journalism.

Amanda A. Hernández is a graduate student at the University of Texas at San Antonio in the Bicultural Bilingual Program with a focus on the representation of Mexican American children's literature. She has twenty years of experience teaching bilingual education students and in working in public and educational library settings. Her graduate research focuses on critical analysis and the ethnic representations in children's literature.

Mary Esther Soto Huerta, PhD, is an associate professor of culture, literacy, and language at Texas State University and she teaches graduate and undergraduate courses in the bilingual bicultural/ESL teacher preparation program. Her peer-reviewed research focuses on biliteracy; the sociocultural development of language; and literacy development in multilingual settings. Dr. Huerta's multiple publications include *Reaching Out to Latino Families of English Language Learners*, and she has served as a member of the steering committee of the Tomas Rivera Mexican American Children's Book Award for five years.

Maria Teresa (Maite) Landa, MA, is a doctoral student in the Culture, Literacy and Language Program in the Department of Bicultural-Bilingual Studies at the University of Texas at San Antonio. Her research interests include biethnic identity formation and children's literature. Maria Landa's current project is a children's book she is writing in collaboration with her two pre-teen daughters.

Carlos A. LópezLeiva, PhD, is an assistant professor in the Department of Language, Literacy, and Sociocultural Studies at the University of New Mexico. His research interests are in the social construction of culturally and linguistically diverse learners; the social dimension of teaching, learning, and doing mathematics in different educational environments and integrated with other fields; identity development of Latinos and/or Hispanics as bilingual doers of mathematics; mathematization processes; critical pedagogy; and practitioner and participatory action research.

Miriam Martinez, PhD, is a professor of literacy in the Department of Interdisciplinary Learning and Teaching at the University of Texas at San Antonio, where she teaches classes in reading and children's literature. She is a coeditor of the *Journal of Children's Literature*. Her research interests focus on children's literary understanding and on textual factors that shape literary understanding.

Pat Mora writes, presents, and promotes creativity, inclusivity, and bookjoy. Among her many children's books are *The Beautiful Lady: Our Lady of Guadalupe*; *Yum! ¡Mmm! ¡Qué Rico!*; and *Doña Flor: A Tall Tale about a Giant Woman with a Great Big Heart*. She has received an ALA Notable listing, the Pura Belpré Author Honor Award, and the Golden Kite Award from the Society of Children's Book. Among her other honors are honorary membership in the American Library Association, and a Civitella Ranieri Fellowship in Umbria, Italy.

Jamie Campbell Naidoo, PhD, is an endowed associate professor at the University of Alabama School of Library and Information Studies and a former elementary-school librarian. His primary areas of teaching and research include the representations of diverse cultures in youth (children's and young adult) literature and library services to diverse children and their families. He is active in the Association for Library Service to Children (ALSC) and REFORMA, an affiliate of the American Library Association dedicated to serving Latino and Spanish-speaking populations. Jamie has published several books and articles related to underserved populations with children's literature and media.

Lindsey Olivares is a freelance illustrator and visual artist. In 2009 she received her BFA in computer animation from the Ringling School of Art and Design, where she was a Presidential Scholar. After graduation, she began work at PDI Dreamworks as a visual development artist. Lindsey has worked with Disney, Dreamworks, and others. She was nominated for her work on *Madagascar 3* in 2012 and received the Siggraph Award for her short film, *Anchored*, in 2009. Lindsey was invited to the Nemo Academy in Florence, Italy, to hold a visual development workshop in 2012.

Ruth E. Quiroa, PhD, is an associate professor of reading and language at National Louis University and a former kindergarten and bilingual (Spanish/English) second-grade teacher. Her university teaching focuses on literature for youth, pre-service literacy methods, and language and literacy for both monolingual and bilingual students (ESL/bilingual). Ruth is actively engaged with teachers in Chicago's western suburbs, and with local, national, and international professional literacy and library organizations. Her research concentrates on the impact of multicultural literature on teachers' instructional practices; trends and issues in Latino-themed youth literature; and wordless picture books.

Mari Riojas-Cortez, PhD, is chair and professor of early childhood education in the Department of Interdisciplinary Learning and Teaching at the University of Texas at San Antonio. Her research focuses on Latino family engagement and children's play in school settings, particularly for bilingual children. Dr. Cortez has published in major journals including *Young Children*; *International Journal of Early Childhood*; *Early Childhood Education Journal*; *Advances in Early Education and Day Care*; and *Journal of Early Childhood Teacher Education*; and she has coauthored *Parents as Partners in Education: Families and Schools Working Together*. She is the editor for the *Dimensions of Early Childhood* journal.

Nancy Roser is a professor of language and literacy studies, the Flawn Professor of Early Childhood, and a distinguished teaching professor at the University of Texas at Austin. She teaches undergraduate elementary reading and language arts as well as classes in children's literature. Her research interests include the close inspection of children's book conversations in classrooms.

José Ruiz-Escalante, EdD, has retired as a professor of bilingual education from the University of Texas at Pan American in McAllen, Texas. He has taught courses dealing with bilingual education and cultural diversity in schools as well as in society. Dr. Ruiz-Escalante obtained his doctorate of education from the University of Washington in Seattle, and a master of education in bilingual multicultural education and his bachelor of arts in political science and Latin American Studies from the University of Arizona in Tucson.

Patricia Sánchez, PhD, is an associate professor in the Department of Bicultural-Bilingual Studies at the University of Texas at San Antonio. Her research examines issues related to globalization, transnationalism, Latino immigrant students and families, and teacher preparation. Dr. Sánchez has published in such journals as *Urban Review*; *Linguistics and Education*; and the *International Multilingual Research Journal*. She has coauthored a book on educational policy and immigrant students as well as a bilingual children's book on transnational Latino families called *Recuerdo mis raíces y vivo mis tradiciones/Remembering My Roots and Living My Traditions* (2004).

Sonia N. Sánchez is a PhD candidate in the Culture, Literacy, and Language Program in the Department of Bicultural and Bilingual Studies at the University of Texas at San Antonio. She obtained a BS in bilingual education from Boston University, and she received her MA in bicultural-bilingual studies from the University of Texas at San Antonio. Sonia has served as a bilingual teacher and a Texas Title I Priority Schools grant manager, and she is currently a school improvement facilitator.

Howard L. Smith, PhD, is an associate professor in the Department of Bicultural Bilingual Studies at the University of Texas at San Antonio. Dr. Smith conducts research and publishes in the areas of biliteracy, family literacy, and multiculturalism. He collaborated on the reading series titled *Lectura Scott-Foresman*, and his forthcoming volume, *ELLs in Texas, What Teachers Need to Know*, is coauthored with John Seidlitz and Monica Lara.

Yoo Kyung Sung, PhD, is an assistant professor at the University of New Mexico teaching children's literature courses. Her studies center on analysis of cultural representations in picture books and ideology in early literacy. She serves on committees for the IRA Global Society Book Award; Worlds of Words; the Asahi Award; and the Literature Inquiry Project at the University of New Mexico. She also serves as board member of the U.S. Board on Books for Young People, and she is an editorial member of the *Journal of Children's Literature*.

Carmen Tafolla, PhD, is an associate professor of practice in transformative literature at the University of Texas at San Antonio. Her published works have received numerous honors, including the 2010 Americas Award; the Charlotte Zolotow Art of Peace Award; five International Latino Book Awards; two Tomas Rivera Book Awards; two ALA Notable Books listings; a Top Ten Books for Babies listing; and recognition by the National Association of Chicana and Chicano Studies. In 2012, San Antonio mayor Julian Castro named her the first poet laureate for the city, and she is now the 2015 Texas state poet laureate.

Lettycia Terrones, MLIS, serves as education librarian at the Pollak Library at California State University, Fullerton. Her research interests are in Chicano children's literature and critical literacy. Lettycia is an American Library Association Spectrum Scholar and a member of REFORMA.

Duncan Tonatiuh is an award-winning author and illustrator who has received several Tomás Rivera Mexican American children's book awards; an Americas Award Commended Title; a Notable Book for a Global Society listing; and many Pura Belpré Awards. He graduated from Parsons The New School for Design and from Eugene Lang College in New York City in 2008. His work is inspired by Ancient Mexican art, particularly that of the Mixtec codex. His aim is to create images that honor the past but that address contemporary issues that affect people of Mexican origin on both sides of the border.

Angie Zapata, PhD, is an assistant professor of literacy education at the University of Missouri. Her current research focuses on multimodal and multilingual composition and how diverse literature for children and youth can support language and literacy learning in all classroom settings.

CPSIA information can be obtained at www.ICGtesting.com
Printed in the USA
BVOW02*1656221115

427501BV00004B/7/P